MARRIAGE AND FATHERHOOD IN THE NAZI SS

From 1931 to 1945, leaders of the SS, a paramilitary group under the Nazi party, sought to transform their organization into a racially elite family community that would serve as the Third Reich's new aristocracy. They utilized the science of eugenics to convince SS men to marry suitable wives and have many children.

Marriage and Fatherhood in the Nazi SS, by Amy Carney, is the first book to significantly assess the role of SS men as husbands and fathers during the Third Reich. The family community, and the place of men in this community, started with one simple order issued by SS leader Heinrich Himmler. He and other SS leaders continued to develop the family community throughout the 1930s, and not even the Second World War deterred them from pursuing their racial ambitions.

Carney's insight into the eugenic-based measures used to encourage SS men to marry and to establish families sheds new light on the responsibilities these men had not only as soldiers, but as husbands and fathers as well.

(German and European Studies)

AMY CARNEY is an associate professor in the Department of History at Penn State Behrend.

German and European Studies
General Editor: Jennifer J. Jenkins

AMY CARNEY

Marriage and Fatherhood in the Nazi SS

UNIVERSITY OF TORONTO PRESS
Toronto Buffalo London

© University of Toronto Press 2018
Toronto Buffalo London
utorontopress.com

ISBN 978-1-4875-0258-4 (cloth) ISBN 978-1-4875-2204-9 (paper)

(German and European Studies)

Library and Archives Canada Cataloguing in Publication

Carney, Amy Beth, author
Marriage and fatherhood in the Nazi SS / Amy Carney.

(German and European studies ; 30)
Includes bibliographical references and index.
ISBN 978-1-4875-0258-4 (cloth). ISBN 978-1-4875-2204-9 (paper)

1. Family policy – Germany – History – 20th century.   2. Fatherhood –
Germany – History – 20th century.   3. Marriage – Germany – History –
20th century.   4. Nationalsozialistische Deutsche Arbeiter-Partei.
Schutzstaffel.   I. Title.   II. Series: German and European studies ; 30

HQ625.C37 2018   306.850943   C2018-900083-X

University of Toronto Press acknowledges the financial assistance to its publishing
program of the Canada Council for the Arts and the Ontario Arts Council, an agency
of the Government of Ontario.

Canada Council   Conseil des Arts
for the Arts   du Canada

ONTARIO ARTS COUNCIL
CONSEIL DES ARTS DE L'ONTARIO
an Ontario government agency
un organisme du gouvernement de l'Ontario

Funded by the   Financé par le
Government gouvernement
of Canada   du Canada

Canadä

Contents

Illustrations

Acknowledgments

I owe a debt of gratitude to a number of people who supported me throughout my doctoral program and early in my professional career. They provided me with critical insight, offered valuable advice, and posed insightful questions that guided me as I completed first my dissertation and now this book. I am grateful for the continuing support and mentorship of Nathan Stoltzfus. I am also appreciative of the guidance that I received from my dissertation committee: Matt Childs, Fritz Davis, Jonathan Grant, Robert Gellately, and Birgit Maier-Katkin. Many friends and colleagues have helped me along the way with research, writing, and editing, but I am especially indebted to Patrick Barr-Melej, Tim Bernshausen, Wolfgang Bialas, Jeff Bloodworth, Daria Bocciarelli, John Champagne, Aaron Gillette, Christopher Griffin, Wayne Harden, Victoria Hightower, Melissa Kravetz, Glenn Kumhera, Stephanie Laffer, André Mineau, Bradley Nichols, Ryan Perks, Richard Ratzlaff, Mara Taylor, Annette Timm, and Richard Weikart.

Over the years, I received assistance from many archivists, librarians, and staff at the following archives: the Bundesarchiv in Berlin, the Bundesarchiv in Freiburg, the Institut für Zeitgeschichte in Munich, the International Tracing Service in Bad Arolsen, the Landesarchiv Nordrhein-Westfalen/Düsseldorf, the Max Planck Gesellschaft Archiv in Berlin, the Staatsarchiv Darmstadt, the Staatsarchiv Ludwigsburg, the Staatsarchiv Marburg, the United States Holocaust Memorial Museum in Washington, DC, and the United States National Archives at College Park. I am also indebted to the library personnel at Florida State University and Pennsylvania State University for their help.

I would also like to express my thanks to the School of Humanities and Social Sciences at Penn State Behrend for an endowment grant, as well as the Institute for the Arts and Humanities at Pennsylvania State University for an individual faculty grant.

Finally, I could not have completed this project without the love and encouragement of my parents, John and Phyllis Carney.

Portions of this research were previously published: a chapter in *Racial Science in Hitler's New Europe, 1938–1945*, edited by Anton Weiss-Wendt and Rory Yeomans and published by the University of Nebraska Press, and a chapter in *Ideologie und Moral im Nationalsozialismus*, edited by Wolfgang Bialas and Lothar Fritze, published in German by Vandenhoeck and Rupecht and in English by Cambridge Scholars Publishing.

MARRIAGE AND FATHERHOOD IN THE NAZI SS

Introduction

"If you, my dear Annie, have this letter in your hands, I am no more."[1] With these words, SS-Obersturmbannführer Hermann S. began his final letter to his wife. Writing during the Second World War, Hermann said he hoped he had died fighting to give their children a better life, and he implored his wife to focus on them because they would be "your solace for the future and also your strength." Hermann also left final words for his children. "The time will come where you will very much miss your father," he wrote. "Both of you and your mother must resolutely hold together." He then addressed his oldest child Roland, telling him to "always learn diligently if you want to get ahead in life and [that] whoever wants to command must first learn to obey." Hermann urged his son to pay attention to his mother's guidance: "believe me, if I had listened to my mother's advice so many times, I would have been saved from some disappointment." He added that Roland could do anything he wanted in life because he and his fellow soldiers were now fighting to secure his future. At the same time, Hermann noted that his son would still have to work hard, and he urged him to stay an honest and decent person and to remain true to his comrades. Finally, he informed his son that his experiences would serve him well later in life as he sought to find a wife, though he advised Roland to look for a woman with a suitable hereditary disposition.

For his little girl Ute, he had fewer words, although they seemed no less heartfelt. Hermann professed that while she could not remember him as well as her mother or brother, the two of them did have some special time together during his last furlough from the front. As he would not be there for her as she grew up, Hermann counseled Ute to listen to her mother, especially when it came to learning how to be a mother herself. Then, towards the end of his letter, Hermann returned to his wife. He did not want her to be a "grieving widow," but instead "a German woman who has lost much, but [who] protects her children as my legacy." Beyond caring for their children, he also beseeched Annie to be proud of him because he had fallen not only for the Führer and Germany, but for her future, too. He ended by thanking his wife for her love and stating that while they had only had a short time together, "it was a wonderful time ... it would have become even more wonderful, but it shall not be."

In June 1943, *Das Schwarze Korps*, the newspaper of the Schutzstaffel ("Protection Echelon," or SS), reprinted Hermann's letter. It was neither the first nor the last time the paper published such a testimonial. But printing this letter was about more than just relaying one man's words to his family. The editors chose his letter because of the larger messages it conveyed. They wanted readers to identify with Hermann not only because he had died a heroic death for his country, but also because of the meaning he attributed to his life through his children. His sacrifice for them demonstrated that the family was the centre of life, the germ cell (*Keimzelle*) from which all things – the SS, the Nazi Party, and the German Reich – were built. Hermann's letter confirmed that the father, whether at home or at the front, was an active and important participant in this community. A man had a vital role to play in his family while he was alive, but, as Hermann's letter proved, even in death he lived on through his children. The victory in the cradle, as seen through his children's survival, was meant to complement the military victory for which Hermann and his comrades fought. Above all, the letter showed that being a father – both biologically through passing on one's genetic lineage and physically through raising one's children – was important. For the SS, fatherhood and the creation of a family represented essential ideals.

The Allies who stood in judgment over Nazi Germany more than two years later understood the significance of these ideals. They discerned that SS families like Hermann's had occupied a specific place in the Third Reich. Warren Farr, the assistant trial counsel for the United States, summed up this position one month into the Nuremberg Trial: "The SS was to be the living embodiment of the Nazi doctrine of the superiority of the Nordic blood – the carrying into effect of the Nazi conception of a master race."[2] With these words, he succinctly acknowledged that the once formidable SS had been an elite organization from its inception. Farr, along with his fellow prosecutors, returned to this elitism throughout the trial, showing how "the SS was the very essence of Nazism."[3] They likewise confirmed the organization's characterization as Nazi Germany's "new aristocracy."[4]

The purpose of this book is to examine how the SS established itself as such an elite. Men like Hermann were at the core of this burgeoning racial aristocracy, but they were not alone; their wives and children played a vital role, too. Each family contributed to the development of the SS as a unique community in the Third Reich, in particular a family community (*Sippengemeinschaft*). That community was indeed as Farr described it: a living embodiment of the Nazi doctrine of a master race. My objective is to evaluate this family community and to assess its place in the evolution of the SS. Also, though each family member belonged equally to the family community, I particularly want to analyse the role of SS men as husbands and fathers.

The notion of the SS as an elite family community was not evident from its foundation; rather, its self-perception, along with its ambitions, changed throughout its existence. The SS began modestly with the formation of the Stabswache in the spring of 1923. It was replaced later that year by the Stosstrupp Adolf Hitler. This unit was dissolved as a consequence of Hitler's November 1923 putsch, for which he was sentenced to a short term in prison. After his release in early 1925, he reconstructed the Nazi Party, a process that included the creation of a new unit personally dedicated to him. By May 1925, the nucleus of what would evolve into the SS had been formed.[5]

From its origins, SS leaders defined their group as a small but elite organization on which the Führer could rely, although its tasks hardly differed from those assigned to the larger Sturmabteilung ("Storm Troopers," or SA), the party's political soldiers.[6] The guidelines for the SA, compared with those of the SS, indicate that the latter's small size and self-proclaimed elite status were the only factors distinguishing the two groups. Further differentiation only began after Hitler appointed Heinrich Himmler Reichsführer-SS, or leader of the SS, on 20 January 1929.[7] When Hitler promoted him, there was nothing to suggest that Himmler would radically reshape the elite ideal of the SS, especially because the organization was subordinate to the SA. Yet through his personality, views, and goals, Himmler restructured the organization over the next decade and a half. His bureaucratic abilities enhanced the position of the SS, first within the party and later within the state.

Due to the loyal service of its members, Hitler established the SS as an independent branch of the party following the June 1934 purge of the SA, known as the Night of the Long Knives. This freedom aided the organization's meteoric growth. Himmler had free reign to set whatever standards he desired for admission into the SS. Earlier criteria had focused on good health and a robust physique, but this was soon superseded by prospective members' racial health. This new emphasis stemmed from Himmler's contention that race, and with it blood, formed the core of a healthy *Volk*; only a person who descended from a superior racial lineage would have the hereditary credentials to join. To Himmler, SS men represented the prime carriers of Nordic blood, and through their dedication to National Socialism and its ideals, especially its racial ideals, they would establish an elite community.

Himmler remained steadfast in his convictions about race. But his obsession with racial purity, not to mention physical fitness, was not without irony. Unlike many of his subordinates, the Reichsführer himself was a stark contradiction to these ideals, with his flabby physique and poor eyesight just two of his more obvious shortcomings – deficiencies that contemporaries noticed.[8] Yet while some people questioned the elitist ideals of the SS, other people readily accepted them. The exclusivity of the SS made it appealing. By the end of 1931, the organization had recruited almost 15,000 members; a year and a half later, over 100,000 men had joined. The organization continued to grow over the next decade, reaching almost 800,000 members by the summer of 1944.[9] These men served in an ever-increasing number of offices and units, each of which had a specific purpose based on the escalating ambitions of Himmler and other SS officers. But Himmler was not interested in creating an organization focused solely on service to the Nazi state in the present. Rather, he wanted to establish a community that would perpetually lead Hitler's Thousand Year Reich.

In particular, Himmler envisioned creating a family community to which not only SS men, but also their wives, children, and future descendants had the potential to belong. Unlike past communities built on commonalities such as class, ethnicity, history, language, and/or religion, the one that Himmler sought to construct was based on something far more immutable: heredity. Although traits such as blond hair and blue eyes were valued, the more important aspect of a person's heredity was proving that he belonged to the Nordic race. Since the late nineteenth century, both popular and scientific literature had proclaimed that the Nordic race represented the apex of civilization, and Himmler used this racial ideology when fostering his family community.

The use of inclusion and exclusion to define a community or nation has a long history.[10] However, Himmler's ambition was about more than including a minority and excluding the majority. The use of biology to delineate the family community was the cornerstone of a much larger effort to reconceptualize the purpose and value of the family. With this greater end, the family community can be conceived of as an "imagined community," one with political, social, cultural, and economic dimensions.[11] It was a limited community designed to accept people whose heritage was racially pure. Through the family community, the SS sought to build camaraderie among its members and their families. Any factor that might have divided them, including religion, regional identity, or socio-economic status, was to be overcome through unity based on the common possession of Nordic blood.

Having the appropriate racial lineage was only the first step, as it meant that each man and his wife were qualified to serve the SS and the Third Reich in the present. However, admission into the family community also meant accepting other requirements. Every couple was primed to have children with the right racial credentials; these offspring would be the first of many generations that would ensure the longevity of the SS and the Reich. Without enough racially pure children, a long-lasting Nazi state could not exist. Therefore, while the SS family community represented one imagined community, so did the Third Reich. It aimed to become a "racial state," specifically a national community (*Volksgemeinschaft*).[12] This conception of a nation was not simply to be built from on high through party and government directives, but through the interaction of the state with its people.[13] And if National Socialist Germany was to become this racial state, then the SS was to be its racial elite – its members would be the vanguard that would set standards first for itself, and then for the nation.

This book examines the place of the SS family community in the organization's attempt to transform itself into a racial aristocracy. The foundation of my analysis is an in-depth examination of the marriage and family policies whose purpose was to encourage each man to wed a racially suitable wife and to have hereditarily healthy children. I demonstrate that these policies did not remain static, but rather they shifted to meet the ever-evolving needs of the SS. While Himmler and other SS leaders remained committed to building the family community, they repeatedly adapted to the circumstances at hand and modified their policies accordingly.

But this book is not just about policy. I have included case studies that provide insight into how individual men and women responded to policies that intruded into nearly every facet of their personal lives.

These accounts show that the attempt to build the family community was not simply a one-way conduit from above to below, but rather a negotiated process that constantly evolved. The interaction between SS leaders and SS men (or their wives) fostered a dialogue that established a relationship between ideology and practice.

This commitment of the SS to enhancing the racial quality of its members and to unifying them into a select community was bolstered through the actions of the Nazi state, which was dedicated to promoting the racial well-being of the German population. But while the prominence of racial ideals in Nazi Germany complemented the work of the SS, the state was not the sole source of legitimacy. The idea of promoting the well-being of a nation and its people by regulating its biological heritage had existed for decades in the form of a then respected scientific discipline known as eugenics. Founded in the late nineteenth century by British scientist Francis Galton, eugenics sought to use scientific and medical knowledge to enrich the heredity of a population by improving the health of each generation. It quickly gained a sizeable international following.

Early German eugenicists focused more on the effects of class than race. They defined "superior" and "inferior" individuals based on their productivity and achievements, which reflected their own upper- and middle-class bias. Eugenicists were additionally concerned with social and demographic problems due to Germany's late, and rapid, industrialization and urbanization. As many of them were physicians, and therefore saw themselves as the custodians of the nation's health, they saw in eugenics a means of redemption. This is not to suggest that all doctors advocated eugenics, but many did.[14] Eugenics represented a solution through which they could shape the biological heritage of the nation by encouraging the "superior" elements of the population to have child-rich (kinderreich) families of at least four children. At the same time, they could limit the reproduction of anyone whom they deemed "inferior" while making sure those people received adequate medical care.[15]

Apprehension among medical and scientific professionals about the health and well-being of the population intensified during the First World War. German eugenicists worried about the war's dysgenic effects, in particular the consequences of millions of wartime deaths, which stripped the country not only of its youngest and most fit men, but their potential offspring as well. Eugenicists attempted to persuade the imperial government to enact reforms to prevent further degeneration.

They suggested that the government should provide economic privileges to large families, abolish impediments preventing soldiers from marrying early, and persuade brides and grooms to exchange health certificates. Despite this encouragement, the Wilhelmine government did not pass one eugenics-related law.[16]

Germany's defeat in 1918 did little to alter the goals of the eugenics movement. Its proponents continued to participate in scientific research and to publish their results. One notable post-war publication was written by legal scholar Karl Binding and psychiatrist Alfred Hoche; they proposed allowing both suicide and euthanasia for individuals deemed unworthy of life.[17] However, among these publications, none was as influential as *Human Heredity and Racial Hygiene*.[18] Written by botanist and physician Erwin Baur, anthropologist Eugen Fischer, and physician Fritz Lenz, this book became the standard text on heredity and eugenics. Additional works by them and other scientists contributed to the diffusion of eugenics. By the late 1920s, eugenics was viewed as a legitimate science worthy of study, discussion, and implementation. Eugenic ideas had also permeated popular culture and influenced how people viewed heredity.

Though the Weimar government initially paid little attention to these developments, it started to respond to eugenicists' calls to take action by the mid-1920s. Vacillation by the government contributed to the founding of the Kaiser Wilhelm Institute for Anthropology, Human Heredity, and Eugenics (or KWI-A) in Berlin in September 1927.[19] Eugen Fischer, its first director, set the institute's agenda, claiming that its research would investigate human races and their differences. The results of this research would culminate in measures that, if implemented, would improve the hereditary health of the people. Fischer filled positions in the KWI-A with colleagues whose work complemented this agenda; among them were his co-authors Baur and Lenz, biologist Hermann Muckermann, and geneticist Otmar von Verschuer.[20]

One of the institute's tasks was the dissemination of scientific knowledge via a series of courses on eugenics and genetics. The primary recipients of these seminars were medical and welfare officials.[21] The classes allowed KWI-A scientists to spread their ideas on eugenics while establishing a strong relationship with government officials, a relationship that continued under the National Socialist government. This was not a direct relationship in which one side explicitly did as the other wanted; nor did it mean that all German eugenicists completely backed the Nazi government, or that the ideas of the Nazi Party were founded solely on the work of these eugenicists. However, the two sides clearly interacted with one another. In doing so, the KWI-A, through the domestic and international reputation of its scientists, conferred legitimacy on Nazi policies, while the government supported the institute's work.[22] In addition, the relationship between the KWI-A and the Nazi state extended to party organizations – notably the SS.

Himmler was among the people who saw value in eugenics, and his decision to establish the family community was based on his selective adherence to this science. Starting at the end of 1931, eugenic-based regulations were used to investigate the heritage of anyone seeking to join the SS and to determine if he or she had the hereditary and racial credentials to belong to its family community. This investigative process was managed through one of the organization's major offices, the Race and Settlement Main Office (Rasse- und Siedlungshauptamt, or RuSHA). The requisite steps of this process were continuously publicized. Therefore, the men who joined the SS and the women who married them were aware of the admission criteria and the expectations that would be placed on their future families. The majority of them submitted to this scrutiny when it came to getting married. However, once admitted to the SS elite, they failed to live up to Himmler's expectations by not having enough children. The victory in the cradle, and with it the creation of the *Sippengemeinschaft*, remained incomplete.

When analysing documents in an attempt to reconstruct the development of the family community, it immediately becomes evident that the ideology used to promote the creation of life was also used to justify its destruction.[23] This dichotomy is important to acknowledge. Only by investigating all facets of SS and Nazi ideology can historians attempt to explain how and why events unfolded as they did. Yet penetrating the mindset of the people who created, disseminated, and adhered to this ideology is challenging. In his biography of Reinhard Heydrich, Robert Gerwarth addresses this issue; he additionally posits that historians have a responsibility to examine and contextualize the past rather than judge it. Contextualization is also at the core of Ian Kershaw's biography of Hitler.[24] The social and political contexts of Hitler's decisions are crucial to understanding his actions and their impact. Generational and institutional contexts are equally significant in deciphering the motives and actions of other Nazis, as seen in Michael Wildt's collective biography of leaders in the Reich Security Main Office.[25] Jutta Mühlenberg provides a similar analysis of the female auxiliary corps of the Waffen-SS.[26] With the SS family community, scientific context is crucial as it was founded on the selective use of eugenics. Also central were social, economic, and educational factors, as well as the balance that individual men and their wives maintained between ideology and personal desires.

Besides context, the need to empathize with SS men and their wives presents another challenge. If I want to explain their motives and actions, then I need to attempt to perceive specific orders and the situations in which they were formulated as these individuals might have. This is a formidable but essential task, one that historians, including Kershaw and Christopher Browning, have addressed.[27] So, too, has Gerwarth with his concept of "cold empathy." He reconstructs Heydrich's life and assesses his place in the history of the Third Reich by allowing his subject's words and deeds to speak for themselves.[28] The best way to explore the connection between SS racial ideology and the family community, and ultimately to evaluate their importance, is to allow SS leaders and members to speak for themselves. This necessitates evaluating the commands and guidelines issued by officials as well as the documentation produced by the men and women affected by this process. Admittedly, there is more official than personal documentation, but the existing records demonstrate that a discourse existed among many people throughout the SS hierarchy.

The majority of the documents utilized for this book come from the Bundesarchiv in Berlin. Himmler's files, along with those of several SS offices, notably RuSHA, form the core. I also found sources in state and private archives. Of particular importance was the Staatsarchiv in Marburg, which contains files for the SS regional unit Oberabschnitt Fulda-Werra. Two books published about twenty years ago, the first a biography of the leader of Oberabschnitt Fulda-Werra and the second an examination of what married life entailed for SS wives, relied on this archive, but otherwise Marburg has been underutilized.[29] Its documents were crucial in determining how local units responded to the policies ordered by Himmler and managed by RuSHA. Marburg also has a small collection of personnel files. Many case studies originated in these files and were then supplemented with documentation from the Berlin Document Center.[30]

Another resource is the recently opened International Tracing Service in Bad Arolsen. This private archive has files on the Lebensborn program. These documents contain information about medical and welfare issues as well data about marriage and baptism ceremonies that correspond with resources on SS ceremonies found in other archives. Finally,

Das Schwarze Korps, the aforementioned SS newspaper, is an invaluable source. Two books have reviewed its history and significance. The earlier one, *The Voice of the SS*, mentions marriage and family within the context of race propaganda and racial ideology.[31] By contrast, I analyse how the family was a recurrent theme in *Das Schwarze Korps*, thus showing how the family community was a core part of the organization's identity. I have used these sources to construct a narrative that assesses how the *Sippengemeinschaft* found a balance between ideology and practice, and the ways in which reality consistently tempered what the SS could achieve.

The attempt to shape the SS into a racial elite is significant for several reasons, as this book tries to show. First, it contributes to our understanding of eugenics and the biological sciences in the Third Reich. The family community was not solely based on Himmler's romanticized whims; rather, he employed the eugenic measures that best suited his needs. This implementation was the largest and most sustained effort to apply eugenics in a "positive" manner – that is, to increase the size and improve the quality of the population. Most literature on eugenics and Nazi Germany only briefly mentions this relationship between science and the SS. The majority of works focus on eugenics in Britain, Germany, and the United States; the articles and books that explore German eugenics cover the Wilhelmine, Weimar, and Nazi periods. They often show continuity among these periods, demonstrating that Nazi racial thought had its origins in earlier periods.[32]

Just as Nazi racial ideology had earlier origins, so, too, did SS racial ideology. Furthermore, the SS interacted with the KWI-A: this scientific body provided just as much legitimacy for SS racial policies as it did Nazi ones. The racial ideology of the SS, and subsequently its family community, could not have been founded without earlier eugenic work and later interaction with prominent German eugenicists. As Robert Proctor shows, these scientists were neither apolitical nor passive, and many leading professionals in a variety of fields willingly participated in the construction of Nazi racial ideology.[33] As I show in this book, that participation was equally true for the SS. Scientists and physicians provided the SS with the means to enable its officials to become the arbiters of racial and hereditary health.

This attempt to build the family community based on the racial and hereditary worthiness of its members was tantamount to biological determinism. Such efforts proclaimed that a person's genetic lineage was the only thing to consider when determining his worth, and that the environment played no role in shaping his life.[34] While accepted by many scientists, this extreme emphasis on biology was nonetheless censured at the time, most famously by Julian Huxley and Alfred Haddon. They derided the Nazis' attempt to produce citizens who would be "as blond as Hitler."[35] This derision aside, biological determinism permeated SS racial ideology – indeed, the entire family community was based on it.

But while examining the relationship between science and the SS, and specifically the connection between eugenics and the family community, is one of this book's contributions, another is demonstrating the place and significance of the family community in the SS, as well as emphasizing that men had a meaningful role in this community as fathers. By exploring the contours of fatherhood and the family community, my objective is to provide a more nuanced understanding of the SS. Earlier scholars initially sought to ascertain the origins of the SS and to interpret its purpose and character.[36] Their work is insightful but limited in that it presents the SS as a monolithic criminal organization under Himmler's complete control. Later scholarship, starting with the work of Robert Lewis Koehl, has challenged this assessment. Koehl shows that the SS was not a monolith with a never-changing purpose, but rather an order that constantly adapted itself to meet the needs of the party and the Reich. He also underscores the importance of recognizing what the SS wanted to be as well as what it actually became.[37]

Koehl's evaluation of the SS is relevant when assessing the family community: just as the organization was not static, neither was this community. The guidelines that defined its parameters shifted throughout the existence of the SS. In addition, while Himmler shaped the development of the family community, the contributions of others – SS leaders, RuSHA officials, and individual men and women – were equally significant. By examining the evolution of the family community, this book provides a stronger understanding of what that community was supposed to be (particularly what Himmler wanted it to be) and what it actually was based on how officials implemented orders and policies as well as how SS men and their wives responded to official edicts and ideology.

Beyond the literature on the SS as an organization, other researchers have explored its constituent offices. These works show the breadth of activity undertaken by the SS and again prove that it was not a monolithic organization with a set and unvarying purpose, but rather a vast enterprise with a range of different objectives. Among the sources that focus on a limited segment of the SS, of particular importance is the literature on the Race and Settlement Main Office. James Weingartner wrote the first in-depth analysis of RuSHA.[38] In it he provides an overview of the office's history, its purpose, and the contributions of its first chief, Richard Walther Darré. More recently, Isabel Heinemann has written about the work of RuSHA's racial experts.[39] She examines the nature of their tasks, especially the radicalization of RuSHA's policies following Darré's departure and the start of the war.

This book builds on Weingartner's and Heinemann's efforts. I, too, explore the history of this office. RuSHA began with the sole function of inspecting marriage applications. However, as the SS grew and its purpose evolved, RuSHA assumed greater responsibilities. Among other functions, it served as the primary authority on racial and family policies. While the family community was not the only component of these policies, it was a core element. Thus, I assess how the family community – both its ideal and its reality – was an integral part of the development of RuSHA.

The establishment of the family community was likewise a significant part of the identity of the SS as an elite organization, as can be seen in the works of Herbert Ziegler and Manfred Wolfson.[40] They do emphasize the SS as a burgeoning aristocracy, and they examine the contours of this aristocracy; Ziegler, moreover, delves briefly into Himmler's attempt to manage reproductive decisions. Both scholars also analyse the composition of the SS leadership. Their analyses provide crucial information, as the personal backgrounds of SS men shaped their mentality towards establishing families. Yet the elite ideal was about more than just leaders or even men. The family community included wives and children, and it is not possible to discuss the SS as a racial aristocracy without incorporating them into this narrative. By including the entire family, this book demonstrates that the family community should not be at the periphery of scholarship about the SS. Rather, because it was crucial to the organization's self-identify as an elite racial order, the family community must be a focal point when discerning the ideals, ambitions, and actions that shaped the trajectory of the SS.

This book makes two additional contributions, one of which is engagement with works on sexual politics. One prevalent theme in the literature on sex is deviance. Part of how the Nazi state defined acceptable sexual behaviour was through the proscription of everything it deemed objectionable. Himmler was particularly obsessive when it came to prosecuting what he believed was abnormal behaviour, especially, as Geoffrey Giles examines, homosexuality.[41] A second theme in the literature on sex focuses on procreation. The Nazi government sought to regulate the sexual lives of the people, establishing with whom it was and was not acceptable to have sexual relations. This regulation was based on perceptions of race. Sex was not only acceptable, but in fact encouraged, when both partners had the right racial lineage. George Mosse appraises how the Nazi state tried to direct the sexuality of the *Volk*.[42] He focuses on masculinity under fascist rule as well as the emphasis on home life and family as a means to shape sexual morality. Stefan Maiwald and Gerd Mischler present a similar analysis, claiming that all decisions were based on the perception that sex was nothing more than a means of reproduction.[43]

There is some truth to this perspective. Sex was a tool for creating the family community; bluntly put, this community could not exist if SS men did not have sex with their wives with the intention of conceiving children. Himmler expected that his men would obey any command he issued, and when it came to family life, he counted on them to persuade their wives to adhere to this goal. Obedience was part of his definition of the SS, and so it is important to understand the means through which he tried to influence members' sexual behaviour by reconceptualizing the purpose and value of sex. To this end, I seek to discern a regulated discourse on sex, most notably a discourse on marriage as the anchor of this regulated sexuality.[44] Sex became the focal point around which life could be most efficiently managed, thus leading to a constant discourse about marriage and reproduction.

Although regulation and discourse were central features in establishing the family community, sex was never just about restriction and oppression. It was also, as Dagmar Herzog shows, about pleasure and freedom.[45] She argues that the Nazis have been misrepresented as sexually repressive. Instead, the regime redefined appropriate sexual behaviour, and part of this redefinition was acknowledging the value of sex for pleasure. Personal satisfaction coexisted with newly delineated public mores in Nazi society, a perspective that other research confirms.[46] Therefore, while I focus on the biological function of sex, I am in no way trying to undermine Herzog's argument.

The final contribution this book makes is supplementing the research on family life in Germany. Interest in Nazi family policies existed concurrently with the Third Reich, with most analyses highlighting the role of women.[47] Later research also emphasizes women's roles as wives and mothers.[48] Numerous works contribute to a greater understanding of family life and the place of women in German society, and they illustrate why the Nazi state valued large and hereditarily healthy families. Nonetheless, the majority of this literature ignores men as participants in family life. This is partly the result of the regime's ideals and policies, which underscored the responsibility of women for the establishment of a home and family. Yet it was the exclusion of men from the secondary literature that originally prompted me to ponder what the role of the father was in the Nazi family. My attempt to answer that question led me to the SS family community, although my interest in fatherhood did not diminish – hence my decision to emphasize paternal involvement in the narrative.

As I show in this book, Himmler tasked each SS man with the responsibility of fathering a racially healthy family; that duty was repeatedly emphasized in commands, rhetoric, and policy. However, as other documents illustrate, biological duty was only one facet of fatherhood. While women always remained at the centre of family life, men were expected to assume some parental responsibilities. Therefore, I contend that determining the place of an SS man as a husband and a father is an important aspect of the family community, one that augments existing research on the family in the Third Reich.

This insight into fathers and family life also provides a stronger context for family studies produced in and/or about the post-war era. Bertram Schaffner and David Rodnick independently conducted interviews in the American occupation zone and wrote studies about the cultural patterns and attitudes in the German family.[49] They both address the father as an authority figure. Schaffner depicts the father as a disciplinarian who had to maintain his authority and who preferred respect and gratitude from his children rather than love. Rodnick presents a much softer image of men who lavished their children with affection. According to this view, there was nothing unmanly about fatherly attention; a man found no shame in holding his baby or playing with his children. The image of the SS father, especially as presented in *Das Schwarze Korps*, reveals a father figure akin to the one depicted by Rodnick.

This common image was not the only continuity in post-war Germany. With a sizeable portion of the adult male population dead or imprisoned, there was a crisis in masculinity that prompted the divided nation to redefine the concept of patriarchy.[50] Patriarchal power shifted as the two Germanys sought to create new national identities, and this resulted in adjustments in family dynamics.[51] One area where we see this is the role of widows. Katharina Tumpek-Kjellmark examines the social meaning of widowhood in West Germany, and even delves into the place of SS widows.[52] The family unit and the father's place in it were also redefined, as Till van Rahden shows.[53] He argues that the formation of democracy in West Germany occurred simultaneously with alterations to family life and paternal authority. New methods of child rearing and a more egalitarian perspective on gender were necessary for a democratic polity to succeed. Yet while these changes were being made, one idea remained from the earlier era – that of viewing the family as the biological germ cell of the nation. Despite all of the changes in post-war Germany, the idea of the family as the central unit around which everything else could be built remained the same. During the National Socialist era, SS men and their families had been the mainstay of this idea. As the racial elite, they were poised to set the standard for family life that other members of the *Volk* could emulate.

That standard began with the foundational order of the family community: the 1931 engagement and marriage command; chapter 1 reviews the creation of this order and its evolution until the start of the Second World War. Chapter 2 examines family policy during the same period, while chapters 3 and 4 assess how marriage and family policies, respectively, shifted as a result of the war. Chapter 5 delves into how SS officials used education, ceremonies, and welfare initiatives to generate a sense of belonging among family members. Finally, as SS families did not meet the quantitative standard of four children, chapter 6 evaluates possible explanations for this failure. Collectively, these chapters illustrate the significance of the family community as a biological and a cultural construct, one that was central in establishing and promoting the SS as the racial aristocracy of the Third Reich.

Chapter One

The Engagement and Marriage Command

With the longevity of the SS in mind, Himmler appropriated the eugenic ideas that best suited his needs, and on 31 December 1931, he created his most significant eugenic order: the engagement and marriage command. It served as the basis for securing the continuation of the SS as an elite order by requiring every man to obtain permission to marry. The command also contributed to the organization's growth and systemic bureaucratization. The Race and Settlement Main Office was founded to process marriage applications and to ensure the racial suitability of each man and his prospective bride. This chapter will explore the creation and implementation of this bureaucratic procedure and its enforcement until the Second World War. No detail in the process of getting married was insignificant to SS leaders. Whether a man joined the SS as a full-time, salaried member, or as a part-time, unpaid one, he was expected to comply with each requirement as stipulated by Himmler and RuSHA. As will be seen, most men had no difficulty completing the requirements and receiving permission to wed in a relatively timely manner. But complications did occur – both for the men and with the approval process. Resolving individual dilemmas, along with modifying policies to address new issues, became standard practice as the engagement and marriage order evolved from a single, relatively straightforward command into an increasingly complex process.

The requirement of formal approval for marriage was – as with many ideas adopted by the Nazis – not unprecedented. Prior to 1918, army and navy officers needed the Kaiser's permission to marry. Financial and social criteria were used to guarantee that each marriage would not bring disrepute to the officer's corps and that the couple could live in a manner befitting an officer.[1] Eugenicists also called for the implementation of marital guidelines. Social and financial factors did influence their work, yet these men argued for their ideas based on their supposed scientific merit. For example, Wilhelm Schallmayer wanted the state to issue health passports to gather data on the population so that it could assist in regulating marriages, while Fritz Lenz stated that maintaining marriage and family was a prerequisite for all population politics (*Bevölkerungspolitik*).[2] Alfred Ploetz not only promoted the link between eugenics and marriage, but sought to regulate the decisions of a segment of the population. The German Society for Racial Hygiene, founded by Ploetz in 1905, implemented a marriage pledge. Its members, who came from the well-educated upper and middle classes, agreed to submit to a medical examination before marrying; anyone who failed the examination was to promise to refrain from marrying and having children.[3] This agreement was notable, but its impact was limited due to the organization's small size.

By contrast, Himmler was the first person to apply "positive" eugenic measures to a large and select group. His December 1931 order established in ten short points that every SS man who wanted to marry would have to obtain the Reichsführer's personal authorization (see appendix A).[4] As the primary goals of these unions were the conservation of good blood and the formation of healthy Nordic families (*Sippe*), he would approve or deny a request based solely on racial and hereditary health criteria. If Himmler rejected an application and the SS member still wanted to wed the unsuitable woman, he would be dismissed from the organization, although he was given the opportunity to resign. While Himmler had the final say, he created a Race Office (Rassenamt) to process each application as well as to maintain the Family Book of the SS, which was to contain the names of each couple that had received permission to marry. When processing this material, the Reichsführer and Race Office officials would be bound to secrecy. In the final point of the engagement and marriage command, Himmler commented that the SS had taken an important step toward securing its racial health; mockery or scorn by others should not influence the organization's future course because, as he put it, "the future belongs to us!"

The engagement and marriage command brought to fruition decades of eugenics proposals. At the time the order was signed, the SS had only 15,000 men, but within two years that number had expanded to over 200,000, and that number continued to grow for more than a decade (see appendix B). The future might not have completely "belonged" to the SS, but the organization undoubtedly played a significant role in shaping the course of the Third Reich. In addition, although the engagement and marriage command was an order, membership in the SS during the 1930s remained voluntary. Anyone who did not support the policy could have chosen to leave (though, as will be shown later, very few men opted out for this reason).

The command did not go unnoticed by the scientific community. Fritz Lenz, for example, had already praised Hitler in 1931 as the first statesman who sought to place eugenics at the centre of politics.[5] In 1932 Lenz published "An attempt at racial hygienic guidance of marriage selection" in *Archive for Race and Societal Biology*, a prominent scientific journal dedicated to eugenics. In this article, he informed the scientific community about the decision of the SS to use the principles of racial hygiene to guide its members. He reprinted Himmler's order and commented briefly on its content. In short, Lenz called the command "a very meritorious attempt."[6] He noted that while some might raise various misgivings about the state regulating marriages, such objections could not be aimed at a voluntary organization. Ultimately, Lenz claimed, the success of this command depended not only on the standards to which SS members were held, but also on the fate of the National Socialist movement.

Lenz's article gave scientific credibility to Himmler's command. His endorsement may have meant very little to the average SS man, but – like the order itself – it represented a crucial shift in the identity of the SS, from an organization committed to serving and protecting the Führer to an elite corps that in many ways influenced the development of Nazi Germany. The engagement and marriage command and the public praise it garnered also helped differentiate the SS from the brawling street fighters of the SA. That differentiation served to accentuate an ever-widening gap between the two. This did not mean that the SS relinquished crude violence, as seen with the Night of the Long Knives and the bestial behaviour of SS guards towards concentration camp inmates.[7] But it did mean that brutal and oftentimes calculated sadism did not alone define the SS; rather, the ideal of a Nordic, blood-based family community equally shaped the organization's trajectory.

Himmler had an active role in the implementation of his command, but he did not oversee the daily affairs of the Race Office. Rather, he appointed SS-Standartenführer Richard Walther Darré its head.[8] Darré was hardly a random choice. He had most likely met Himmler in the mid-1920s, when both had belonged to the Artamanen League. Begun in 1924, the approximately two-thousand-member league was composed of agrarian romantics who wanted to see the German people return to the countryside. The association believed the government needed to aid this migration and to encourage the development of a strong peasantry. Some of its members belonged to the Nazi Party, and when the league dissolved in 1930, many of them joined the SS. Himmler and Darré also crossed paths due to their agricultural work. Prior to his appointment as Reichsführer, Himmler, trying to encourage rural residents to vote for the Nazi Party, had campaigned for the party in the mid-1920s, while Darré worked for the department of agriculture. In 1930, the Nazi Party recruited him to serve as the leader of its agrarian movement.[9]

In addition to this work, Darré wrote articles and books throughout the 1920s and early 1930s. Reflecting his university education in farming, most of these works focused on animal and plant breeding. His most well-known publications combined this knowledge of farming with his reflections on the Nordic race: *The Peasantry as the Life Source of the Nordic Race* and *A New Aristocracy from Blood and Soil*. In these books, Darré glorified both the peasant way of life and the Nordic race – and in fact, he connected the two by claiming that the basis of Nordic racial superiority was the people's close ties to the soil. Just as it had in the past, claimed Darré, the future German elite would emerge from this Nordic agrarian stock. Darré was not the first person to argue for the connection between blood (*Blut*) and soil (*Boden*), but he did popularize the concepts.[10]

Himmler undoubtedly found Darré's interpretation of the blood and soil ideology appealing, partially because of his own university education in agriculture and his background as a chicken farmer, but especially because it buttressed his perspective regarding the superiority of the Nordic race.[11] Following his entrance into the SS in 1931, Darré's potential influence over Himmler's thinking on racial matters and the connection between the peasantry and a blood-based aristocracy most likely increased. This influence apparently did not extend to the development of the engagement and marriage command, as Darré claimed after the war that he was surprised when Himmler told him of his intentions less than two weeks before the command was created. Even if the order was unexpected, as the leader of the Race Office, Darré had some measure of control over its implementation, and he quickly came to believe that regulating marriages was the office's "most important" task.[12]

However, as was typical of every SS office during the 1930s, the Race Office grew beyond its original purpose, to the point where reviewing engagement and marriage applications was soon only one of its tasks. To reflect its additional responsibilities, Himmler changed the name of the office in June 1932 to the Race and Settlement Office (Rasse- und Siedlungsamt). It was one of the first three independent offices in the SS.[13] Divided into seven departments, the office was now responsible for ideological training, selecting new members, overseeing family welfare, and maintaining close relations between the SS and the peasantry. The office also supplied educational leaders, race advisers, and farm consultants to serve in the regional SS divisions, known as Oberabschnitt, all the way down to local units, the Sturm (see appendix D).[14]

On 14 January 1935, Himmler elevated the Race and Settlement Office, along with the other two SS offices, to a main office (*Hauptamt*), a designation they would eventually share with nine other branches. The tasks assigned to the renamed Race and Settlement Main Office (RuSHA) remained the same, although its departments were reorganized several more times in an attempt to manage its duties efficiently.[15] The constant expansion and restructuring of RuSHA was not an anomaly among SS main offices. The longer the SS existed, the larger and more complicated the bureaucracy of each main office became. This growing complexity was reflected in many of Himmler's orders, especially as he habitually amended his directives.

The engagement and marriage command represented one of the orders that became more complicated with each passing year. The first addendum was issued in February 1932. It indicated that SS men who had proposed to their fiancées prior to 8 January – the day the engagement and marriage order was officially announced – did not need to apply for authorization. This decree allowed for exemptions because an existing engagement was a legal act that the SS command should not disrupt. However, any SS man who intended to become engaged after 8 January had to report his intention along with his fiancée's information at least three months in advance.[16] Again, because Himmler and his staff regarded an engagement as a legal act, they wanted to have enough time to evaluate the prospective bride and determine if she were suitable to become a member of the burgeoning SS community. While Himmler sought to alter his men's perceptions of marriage and family, this addendum shows that he did not want to alienate them. Requiring an engaged man to choose between the SS and his fiancée could have resulted in the loss of a valuable man of Nordic blood as well as that man's potential offspring at a time when the SS was still relatively small. Moreover, emphasizing legality further accentuated the divide between the SS and the SA. The SS came increasingly to represent a seemingly respectable side of National Socialism, especially when compared with the rabble-rousing storm troopers.[17]

Beyond the issue of legality, Himmler released orders that re-emphasized other elements of the engagement and marriage process. In March 1936, for example, he issued a decree reminding men that they needed to submit "complete records" to the Race and Settlement Main Office "at least three months before the intended engagement." As if this wording did not emphasize his point clearly enough, Himmler commented three times that all paperwork must be submitted "in a timely manner." RuSHA needed this time to process the application and ensure that each intended marriage would fulfil the goal of fostering "hereditarily healthy ... Nordic" families.[18] Just over a year later, another command connected the applicants' physical health with the engagement and marriage order. In this 1937 decree, Himmler indicated that he wanted each SS man under the age of fifty to have earned the appropriate sports badge for his age; without it, this man could not obtain authorization to wed.[19]

Himmler applied similar criteria to women; future SS brides born in 1920 or later had to prove they had earned a Reich sports badge.[20] As of November 1936, women were also required to attend a course offered by the Reich Mother's Service that familiarized them with their responsibilities as wives and mothers. The need for such education existed because, according to Himmler, too many marriages had failed because women were unacquainted with their domestic responsibilities. The mother's education course would remedy this problem, and RuSHA would not grant authorization to wed unless a woman provided certification that she had completed the class.[21]

The regulations shifted again with another supplementary decree issued in March 1939. Similar to the one issued in February 1932, this order indicated that any SS applicant, man, or officer who had married prior to 31 December 1935, but who "did not yet belong to the SS before this time can be waived from obtaining additional marriage authorization."[22] This decree built upon earlier decisions that allowed men who had wed prior to the December 1931 command to follow the same procedure; it appeared to be applicable to men who already belonged to the SS, as well as those who joined later.[23] These men and their wives nonetheless had to submit the required records to RuSHA, the completion of which had no bearing on the legitimacy of an already-existing marriage. However, their hereditary health was still examined for any faults that could affect their future children, especially if they later sought to join the family community as a member or a spouse.

If these orders had represented the only additions to the engagement and marriage command, the procedure would have been relatively straightforward, and the approval (or denial) of an application would have taken little time. However, the reality was more complicated than these supplementary commands suggest. Besides clarifying who did and did not need to apply for permission, indicating where they needed to submit an application, and demanding proof of physical fitness, Himmler also circulated decrees that laid out the exact process each couple needed to follow. It was this process that underscored the increasing bureaucratization in RuSHA. This complexity furthermore demonstrated that the formation of a family represented more than just a personal decision. Instead, it was the first of many times when an SS man was expected to comply willingly with the Reichsführer's interference in his familial choices.

The marriage process began when a man requested the appropriate forms. Originally, he obtained them from his unit, which had acquired them through official service channels, but by early 1936, a petitioner could order the forms directly from RuSHA.[24] In making this request, he had to submit his mailing address, date of birth, SS number, rank, and unit. He likewise had to include the address and date of birth of his future bride; the address, rank, and unit of his immediate SS superior; the address of the SS doctor(s) who would examine him and his bride; and the addresses of two guarantors who belonged to the party and could vouch for his fiancée and her family. The SS man also had to indicate in this original petition to RuSHA that he had notified his immediate superior of his request.

For someone employed full-time by the SS, as well as anyone serving in its early infantry unit, the Verfügungstruppe, additional regulations existed. A full-time employee could not request the forms unless he was at least twenty-five years old and included a statement outlining his assets and debts. For a member of the Verfügungstruppe, the regulations were slightly more complicated. A commissioned officer had to have at least obtained the rank of SS-Obersturmführer before he could marry; for a non-commissioned officer, it was SS-Oberscharführer (see appendix C). An enlisted man could not request authorization until he reached age twenty-five, although unlike other full-time members, once he reached that age, there were no further requirements.[25]

After an SS man received the paperwork, both he and his future wife were responsible for completing four forms: a race and settlement questionnaire (*RuS-Fragebogen*), a genealogical tree (*Ahnentafel*), a hereditary health form (*Erbgesundheitsbogen*), and a medical examination form (*Ärztlicher Untersuchungsbogen*). He also had to submit a statement summarizing his finances, as well as answer a basic questionnaire about his future bride – if she were related to him by birth or marriage, how long he had known her, if she were fond of children, her spending habits, and her commitment to National Socialism. He also had to specify whether he believed his fiancée would make a suitable wife for an SS member.[26] By providing these answers, a man had the opportunity to give RuSHA a positive first impression of the woman he wanted to marry. RuSHA officials, however, did not rely solely upon his assessment; an SS man had to obtain a written report from his immediate superior as well. Himmler preferred to have each officer meet with the couple in an informal setting in order to form a personal impression of them.[27]

RuSHA officials used the information collected from the four other forms to decide whether a prospective couple met the conditions to belong to the family community. The race and settlement questionnaire dealt with background information. Although both man and woman needed to fill out a copy, most questions were directed at the SS man. Among the particulars requested were details of his service in the SS and, if applicable, in the party and the SA. He had to indicate any prior employment in a military or police unit and any honours he may have received from that service. He then had to list his profession, specify where he lived, and denote his marital status as single, widowed, or divorced; if it were the last, he had to include the ruling that confirmed the dissolution of his previous marriage.[28]

Since, as of mid-1933, the Nazi state offered financial assistance to married couples, the race and settlement questionnaire also required the man to acknowledge if he had applied for the state marriage loan. For those who had, so long as their medical examination had been conducted within the past six months, RuSHA would forward the medical records necessary to submit a loan application to the relevant state health department.[29] On an even more personal level, a man had to submit a picture of himself and a one-page personal and professional vita (*Lebenslauf*). He also had to provide basic facts about his parents and grandparents, including their names, ages, any illnesses they survived, and, if dead, the cause of death. Lastly, an SS man signed and dated the questionnaire. With this signature, he avowed that his statements were, to the best of his knowledge, truthful, and he acknowledged that falsehoods would lead to his expulsion from the SS.

The purpose of the next form, a genealogical tree, was to prove one's Aryan descent. Enlisted men and non-commissioned officers had to confirm their ancestry back to 1800, commissioned officers to 1750.[30] For the women, the boundaries were the same; if a woman wanted to marry a commissioned officer, she, too, had to trace her ancestors back to 1750. The form did not explain the use of the term "Aryan." It was originally interchangeable with the word "Nordic," but by the early twentieth century Nordic had become the main term for people who possessed the appropriate racial characteristics; it was more accepted by the scientific community, and even the Nazi government preferred "Nordic" or "German-blooded" in official documentation. However, "Aryan" was still used in two contexts: in popular speech (thus leading to the misconception that the term was widely used), and in reference to people of so-called non-Aryan descent (i.e., as a synonym for being Jewish, as most prominently codified in the Nuremberg Laws).[31] This second use of the term was used in the SS to complete one's genealogical tree and prove oneself free of Jewish ancestry. Otherwise, "Nordic" was used far more frequently in SS documents.

The genealogical tree also did not specify why the specific genealogical time frame had been chosen. But setting the boundaries at 1800 and 1750 was not a random choice. During the French Revolution and the Napoleonic era, new laws had been proclaimed in the French Empire as well as in independent but militarily defeated kingdoms, including Prussia and Austria. These laws emancipated the Jews and allowed them to integrate with the Christian population. Following the defeat of Napoleon in 1815, each German state determined the legal status of its Jews; some revoked emancipation while others expanded religious freedoms. Full emancipation in the German states (minus Austria) remained incomplete until the unification of the Second Reich in 1871.[32]

The shifting legal status of the Jews prompted Himmler to set chronological boundaries to ensure that Jewish blood did not taint his organization. To prove himself free of Jewish blood, an SS member (and his future wife) had to verify – most often through church records – the births, baptisms, and marriages of his (and her) ancestors. Himmler eventually wanted to require background checks as far back as the end of the Thirty Years' War in 1648. He suggested that this year represented the farthest back he could mandate because many earlier church records no longer existed.[33] For those applicants who could trace their lineage back to the mid-seventeenth century or earlier, and who subsequently found a Jewish ancestor, RuSHA had to send their records to Himmler. Surprisingly, Himmler told RuSHA that he was apt to allow these men and women to remain in the SS, but in each case, he reserved the right to decide.[34]

While RuSHA did not provide the relevant historic details, it did provide SS men and potential brides with instructions on how to fill out the genealogical chart. A man had to include the full name of each of his ancestors, their date and place of birth, date and place of death, religion, occupation, and date and place of marriage. The chart provided space for an SS man to include the relevant details for his mother's and his father's families for six generations. If an SS man found the instructions included with the chart inadequate, he could have referred to a guidebook written by Erhard Lange, a RuSHA official in the Office for Family Affairs (Sippenamt).[35] Available as of late 1936, individual SS men could have purchased this booklet, although all units were required to have a copy to ensure that men did not refer to other publications not approved by the SS.[36]

The SS man and his potential wife did not complete the final two forms: the hereditary health form and the medical examination form. Instead, they had to undergo a physical examination, at which point the doctors evaluating them filled out these forms. As of May 1937, Himmler required that these doctors belong to the SS, and he refused to acknowledge any examination conducted by a non-SS doctor unless RuSHA had given the applicant permission.[37] He justified his strictness because of the significance of hereditary health to the family community. Himmler wanted "every SS member to establish a racially valuable, healthy, German family," and the physician's examination produced "a clear picture of the appearance, the health, and the hereditary value of the SS member and his future bride."[38]

This decision may have been influenced by a financial factor. On several occasions prior to this May 1937 order, officials had remarked that if a physician belonged to the SS, then the examination would not cost the potential bride or groom anything.[39] They never clarified whether SS doctors provided the examination for free or if the SS reimbursed them for their services. In either case, it would have been financially beneficial for a couple to choose an SS doctor, and it would not have been difficult for an SS man and his future bride to meet this demand. By this time, according to Robert Proctor, not only did approximately half the doctors in the country belong to the Nazi Party, but the number of doctors represented in the SS was seven times that of the average employed male.[40] By contrast, as of April 1936, non-SS couples seeking medical exams as part of the loan process had to pay for these visits. Even with the costs covered by each couple, many doctors were inundated with requests for such examinations.[41]

In this May 1937 order, Himmler did not restrict himself to commenting on who should conduct the examination. Despite his lack of medical training or expertise, he advised doctors on how to do their jobs. Among the instructions he gave, Himmler noted that an examination for the engagement and marriage application absolved the physician of doctor-patient confidentiality; in other words, while Himmler and RuSHA officials were, as stated in the December 1931 order, bound to secrecy, the doctors had to reveal every detail. Himmler then reminded the physicians to proceed carefully, to double-check all statements, and to remain tactful when examining women, especially when reviewing gynecological issues and determining, through vaginal examinations, their childbearing ability.[42]

Based on this examination, a physician completed the paperwork.[43] The hereditary health form required some general personal information about the patient, but it focused primarily on the patient's family medical history. During their conversation, a doctor had to discern the health of not only his patient's mother and father, but of his grandparents, aunts, uncles, cousins, and siblings; if the patient had any children, the doctor had to compile information on them, too. In the course of this discussion, the doctor had to learn if his patient or any of his relatives suffered from a wide range of medical and social problems.

The medical examination form recorded the results of the physical. While the doctor specifically assessed the childbearing abilities of the woman, he otherwise completed the same examination for an SS man and his future bride. He marked off the physical characteristics of his patient, commenting on the health of their teeth, eyes, lungs, heart, and reflexes. Finally, he pronounced whether he had any misgivings regarding the patient's future genetic and reproductive capabilities. Once he had completed both forms, the doctor sealed them and then either gave them to his patient or mailed them to RuSHA; in either case, he had to include his medical credentials.[44]

When making a decision, RuSHA used the information from all of the forms, but these last two documents were especially significant. The officials who filled them out were experts who could best determine the racial worth of each individual, and were thus able to judge the potential contribution of each potential spouse to the SS. Part of this expertise was gained in medical school, as by the 1930s both genetics and eugenics had become standard fields in medical coursework. However, SS doctors also received supplemental education on racial hygiene, and it was most likely for this reason that Himmler insisted his men and their future brides go to these doctors rather than their non-SS-affiliated colleagues.

SS doctors obtained guidance from their medical peers in the organization. Dr. Ernst Robert Grawitz, the chief medical officer of the SS, issued a document outlining the tasks of SS doctors. He proclaimed that they were health leaders responsible for judging the hereditary well-being and genetic suitability of SS men and their fiancées, as well as influencing these couples to contribute to a positive population policy.[45] Reich Health Leader Dr. Leonardo Conti published a short guidebook for SS doctors. He explained the value of hereditary health and urged doctors to use their medical knowledge to foster the growth of the *Volk* because the end result of all medical policies was the creation and preservation of racially healthy, child-rich families.[46] Other supplemental education was disseminated at the institutional level. The SS had an officer's school for doctors in Alt Rehse.[47] It also had a medical academy, first located in Berlin, and then in Graz, where it was associated with the city's university.[48]

More important than the medical academy and its university connection was the relationship between the SS and the KWI-A. From the fall of 1934 until at least the spring of 1937, KWI-A officials offered courses on genetics and racial hygiene for SS doctors. Turning to the premier eugenics institute for medical education was an obvious choice, but it did not come without some controversy. Among the party and SS officials who did not look fondly on the KWI-A director, Eugen Fischer, was the head of RuSHA. Apparently, he had written reviews panning Darré's books, and Darré had not forgotten this slight. The two men had come to terms with one another somehow by late 1934; it was highly likely that Himmler reminded Darré that Fischer and his institute were a valuable resource, and that he compelled his RuSHA chief to accept this association.[49]

The KWI-A began its first course, which lasted nearly a year, on 1 October 1934. Together with the National Socialist Office for Racial Policy, RuSHA chose twenty-one doctors to participate, although Fischer did have some say in who could attend. While ostensibly designed for the benefit of the SS, the Reich Ministry of the Interior paid for this course.[50] The seminars that followed did not last as long, but took place over approximately one week each month and accommodated up to one hundred doctors. Such changes not only meant that more physicians could participate, but also that the doctors would not need an extended leave of absence from their medical or SS duties, as had been the case during the first course.[51] These later courses were not, according to Fischer's KWI-A activity report, held at the institute any longer, but at the Interior Ministry.[52]

In 1935 and again in 1936, Dr. Arthur Gütt, a ministry official and the chief of the SS Office for Population Politics and Hereditary Health Care, provided guidelines for the course.[53] He indicated that because of its brevity, participants were expected to have a basic knowledge of the most important hereditary rules. Gütt required them to review Dr. Hermann Siemens's book *Genetics, Race Hygiene, and Population Politics* in advance. Most of the people who taught the courses came from the SS or the KWI-A. Among the SS officials were Gütt, Conti, Grawitz, Falk Ruttke, Lothar Loeffler, and Bruno K. Schultz, while Fischer, Lenz, and Otmar von Verschuer belonged to the KWI-A. Other notable state officials who gave lectures were statistician Friedrich Burgdörfer and physician Walter Groß. From these instructors, participants learned about a range of medical, racial, and political topics, including hereditary health care, racial history, population politics, hereditary diseases, racial politics and ideology, the medical services of the SS, the meaning of genetic selection, the relationship between race and the law, and the role of the SS doctor in the National Socialist state.

The ongoing connection between the SS and the foremost eugenics experts in Germany benefited both sides. For the KWI-A, the relationship with the SS not only bolstered the institute's position, but also led to an almost yearly increase in funding.[54] Officials at the institute responded positively to the participation of SS doctors, as noted in a letter from Verschuer to Fischer.[55] After completing one of the courses, many physicians worked in some capacity for the KWI-A, with several of them serving as research assistants to Fischer, Lenz, and Verschuer.[56] For the SS, the involvement of KWI-A personnel further validated its policies. No greater legitimacy could be conferred on Himmler's racial ideology, and if his doctors were informed of the most current eugenics research, then it stood to reason that they represented the best arbiters when it came to evaluating the health and racial qualities of each SS man and his future bride.

Just as the SS provided support for medical officials, it likewise sought to help individual men navigate the engagement and marriage process. The organization published the *Order Bulletin*, which printed commands and reminders, including one informing men what paperwork they needed to submit.[57] Articles in *Das Schwarze Korps* also explained the purpose of the order. One noted that it represented the first selection law in the SS, while others elucidated why RuSHA required a family tree tracing lineage back to 1800 and why the wife of an SS man had to be racially healthy.[58] Additional articles defended the command by proclaiming that the Reichsführer had intervened in the private affairs of his men as a means to protect the German race. Promoting healthy marriages meant promoting healthy children, which in turn promoted a healthy *Volk*.[59]

Besides publications, RuSHA appointed race experts and training leaders in each Oberabschnitt to supervise racial education, although they could assist with engagement and marriage paperwork, too.[60] On a lower level, in August 1937 Himmler ordered the creation of a support agency in every Standarte (the third-largest division, two below the Oberabschnitt). Each agency had four employees responsible for matters concerning family care, as outlined by RuSHA: a leader, typically the officer in charge of the Standarte; a full-time adviser who processed the paperwork; a doctor who assisted with the relevant engagement and marriage forms and counseled couples about the importance of having numerous children; and a full-time clerk. Of these four people, RuSHA placed particular emphasis on the duties of the adviser, requiring that he be no less than thirty years old, married, and a father.[61] This emphasis on familial status related to the tasks handled by each support agency, which included proofreading engagement and marriage paperwork and promoting the formation of hereditarily healthy, child-rich families.[62] Throughout 1938 and into 1939, units submitted reports detailing the establishment of support agencies.[63] Before the start of the war, over fifty agencies had been created, with additional ones set up in the following years.[64]

Once an SS man and his future bride had submitted their paperwork, officials in RuSHA's Office for Family Affairs processed applications for enlisted men and non-commissioned officers. For commissioned officers, as well as any application where refusal was highly possible, Himmler reserved the right to make the decision.[65] This division demonstrated how he did not give autonomy to the people he had placed in charge of a main office, but instead routinely became involved in decision making. The chiefs of RuSHA were well aware of Himmler's proclivity to intervene. Otto Hofmann, the third person to serve in the position, commented in his post-war testimony: "I can tell you from my own personal experience ... that during a flight from Berlin to Lodz I observed how [Himmler] was looking through the engagement and marriage applications and later he said to me that this was almost a rest from his whole duties, this examination of the applications."[66] Himmler explained his involvement in a 1937 speech, proclaiming he examined "20 such requests daily because I want to remain familiar with the practice."[67] This constant familiarization allowed him to set standards for spousal selection, create precedence for future decisions, and signify that establishing a family was not a private matter. In the relevant cases, RuSHA forwarded the paperwork to him along with a letter, oftentimes marked "secret" to maintain the privacy required by the original command. When Himmler consented to a marriage, he wrote his initials and the date next to the words "yes" or "approved" in the margins of the letter from RuSHA.[68]

Whether Himmler or RuSHA reviewed an application, in both cases a RuSHA official filled in another form, the family dossier (*Sippenakte*). In this two-page record, the official recorded the most relevant information gleaned from the documents submitted by each couple. Once the official, or Himmler, had approved the application, a simple comment along the lines of "No essential misgivings" or "No objections" was entered into the family dossier. The official then wrote a letter to the SS man, informing him that RuSHA had authorized his marriage.[69] If any problems were found, temporary approval could not be given. Instead, the RuSHA official sent a letter to the SS man indicating where the deficiencies in his paperwork lie. One of the most common problems was with the genealogical tree. Typically, applicants had not provided enough ancestors to meet the target date of 1800 or 1750, had made a chronological error, or had not written in all of the information about each ancestor. The SS man (or his future bride) was asked to correct the problem and resubmit the relevant forms.[70]

Completing the necessary paperwork, however, did not necessarily result in approval. In scrutinizing each application, Himmler, along with officials in the Office for Family Affairs, found plenty of reasons to deny a request. This included association with Jews or Jewish organizations, as well as the conviction and incarceration of either the bride or one of her family members. Himmler insisted that such flawed individuals would not make suitable wives or in-laws for an SS man. He was also loathe to approve a marriage where the bride descended from a non-Germanic background.[71] A "non-Germanic" bride, such as a Czech or a Pole, would have been denied less for her nationality than for her supposed racial unsuitability. By contrast, a suitable "Germanic" bride would have been a German woman, a *Volksdeutsche* (an ethnic German living in another country), or a foreign national of Nordic blood (such as a Dane, Norwegian, or Swede).[72]

If either petitioner could not provide the required information about his or her family, RuSHA officials could not properly judge their hereditary health, which was itself grounds for rejecting an application.[73] So, too, was any inherited medical condition suffered by either petitioners' family members. If that condition was among those listed in the 1933 Law for the Prevention of Genetically Diseased Offspring, not only did RuSHA reject the application, but the SS man – if it were his family member – risked expulsion from the SS. Any man who had joined after 1933 was released not because he himself was hereditarily ill, but because his family lineage indicated that his future offspring could suffer from such conditions; if the man had joined prior to 1933, Himmler decided his fate. Another reason that justified the rejection of a marriage and expulsion from the SS was impotency. If the man were found to be impotent, he could not enter into a marriage because he would be depriving a healthy woman of the ability to have children. Furthermore, he would be released from the SS if he had joined after 1933 because he could not fulfil his obligation to have a child-rich family.[74]

Himmler and RuSHA officials also rejected applications if they found that a woman would not make an appropriate wife for an SS man and would therefore not be a suitable addition to the family community. For example, a woman could be deemed unsuitable if she did not conform to the organization's ideal physical standards. That proved to be the problem with the application of SS-Rottenführer Hans Sch. and Hedwig P., who submitted their paperwork in October 1935. In early December, Darré forwarded their application to Himmler. He rejected it primarily because Hedwig was too short (she was about 4 feet 8 inches), although apparently Hans's physique (about 5 feet 6 inches and 212 pounds) did not conform to SS standards either. In early January, RuSHA informed Hans of the decision and gave him two weeks to decide whether he wanted to break off his intended engagement or, in accordance with the December 1931 command, request a dismissal from the SS.[75]

His response was neither. In a letter to a fellow SS man, Hans claimed it was difficult for him to accept RuSHA's harsh decision. He declared

"that under no circumstances can I, as an SS man, decide to part volun-
tarily from the SS," and yet neither would he renounce his relationship
with Hedwig.[76] They had known one another since 1927 and had long
since established their intention to wed. Hans stated that he sought to
comply with the marriage regulations as soon as he had learned about
them. He had heard of people who, to his chagrin, had married without
permission, something that he did not want to do. Rather, he sought
support from officers in his unit and the higher divisions above it.

He received their support. The leader of the unit to which Hans
belonged, Standarte 33, wrote a letter to the next higher unit, Abschnitt
XI. He noted that Hans, who he deemed "body and soul an SS man,"
had belonged to the organization since February 1932.[77] The officer also
raised the fact that Hans had known Hedwig since 1927, and that those
serving with him knew he "did not want to break his word to her." With
his man placed in a precarious situation, the Standarte leader requested
that RuSHA re-examine the application; so, too, did the leader of
Abschnitt XI, SS-Brigadeführer Richard Hildebrandt – a future wartime
chief of RuSHA.[78] In a letter to the next higher unit, Oberabschnitt Rhein,
Hildebrandt claimed that since Hans had intended to marry Hedwig
prior to the 1931 order, he was not bound to the requirements stipulated in the command. However, he was an SS member with a very good
reputation who always sought to comply with all of the organization's
ideals and obligations, which had led him to apply for permission to
marry. Hildebrandt asserted that it spoke highly of Hans's character that
he intended to remain committed to his promise to wed Hedwig in spite
of the difficulties raised. As for his intended bride, Hildebrandt pointed
out that her stature aside, she otherwise met the racial requirements.

With these endorsements, RuSHA presented the application to Himmler a second time. He not only rejected it again, but ordered that Hans
be dismissed from the SS.[79] But this dismissal did not occur. Hans continued to request approval throughout 1936, leading RuSHA to present
his application to Himmler a third time. At this point, Himmler finally
approved the marriage in January 1937, commenting that the union
was "approved on the responsibility of the petitioner."[80] This conditional acceptance meant Hans and Hedwig could marry, but they were
not eligible to join the family community and would not be granted
permission to have their union entered into the SS family book – a book
that had not been created yet.[81]

This approach of approving a marriage by releasing it to the responsibility of the petitioner was one that Himmler employed periodically.

The situation tended to follow the pattern as seen in the Hans-Hedwig case: an application was rejected, a request was made for Himmler to reconsider his decision, and in many cases Himmler released the marriage after reviewing the documentation for a second (or even third or fourth) time. The groom's service, particularly if he had belonged to the SS prior to January 1933, tended to work in his favour. This was at least the case until the start of the Second World War, when the exigencies of the war necessitated greater flexibility.

Lack of physical stature was one issue that led to the re-evaluation of an application, but it was not the only reason a woman was rejected. The most common reason was age. Despite (or perhaps because of) the fact he had done so himself, Himmler did not want his men to marry older women on the grounds that few, if any, children could emerge from such a marriage. Himmler's wife Marga was seven years older, and they only had one child, a daughter named Gudrun, who was born in 1929.[82] However, just as Himmler did not want his men to marry women who could not provide them – and by extension the family community – with many hereditarily healthy children, he was none too pleased when a man put in the paperwork after the woman was pregnant. In October 1935, he directed RuSHA to submit all applications to him when the prospective bride was pregnant. He commented that he was likely to consent to such marriages if, and only if, the parents of the bride cared for their daughter until the wedding and the couple met every other requirement.[83]

Himmler had apparently approved more than a few requests on such grounds because in March 1936 he released an order covering pregnancy. In this command he lambasted SS men who had served in the organization for several years but who did not submit their paperwork prior to their prospective bride's eighth or ninth month of pregnancy. He furthermore reprimanded the officers above these men for not properly informing their troops of the significance of the engagement and marriage command. In the future, Himmler proclaimed, he would hold both the SS man and his superior officer responsible for this oversight.[84] While Himmler attributed this failure to a lack of knowledge, it is plausible that some men might have intentionally delayed submitting their paperwork. If a couple was concerned that Himmler or RuSHA might reject their application, waiting until the end of the pregnancy could have been a strategy to improve their odds of receiving permission to wed.

One final complication that emerged in the implementation of the engagement and marriage process involved SS members who had left the organization and then later sought readmission. Most often these men had left to complete their work for the Reich Labor Service, a duty required of all young men as of 1935 and women as of 1939. They often left to serve in the military as well, especially after the reintroduction of compulsory military service in March 1935. With the latter service, neither Himmler nor the military wanted the men concurrently serving in the SS – hence the need for them to resign. However, after completing one or both of these duties, many men sought readmission. Complications arose when their applications revealed that some of them had gotten married in the interim.

None of the available documentation suggests that any man married during his time away from the SS in a deliberate attempt to circumvent marriage regulations. Yet, as in the situation with pregnancies, some men might have viewed their temporary dissociation from the SS as an opportunity to marry without going through the formal approval process. As seen in a September 1935 order, this was not the case.[85] Any member who left to complete his duty for the Labor Service or the Wehrmacht still needed to obtain authorization from RuSHA. Those men who had married without permission could only rejoin if RuSHA gave belated approval. All SS members were to be informed about this ruling, and unit leaders had to remind those men who left temporarily of this obligation. The available records show that men were able to request reinstatement and apply for authorization concurrently. RuSHA worked with the SS Main Office, which was responsible for admission, to coordinate the readmission and approval processes.[86]

Having to focus on these intricate details and account for a myriad of updates and adjustments to the original command suggests that RuSHA officials had to dedicate an extensive amount of time to evaluating each application. By 1937, such intensive scrutiny led to a backlog. Himmler was not pleased to learn of this delay, and he expressed his displeasure to Darré in a letter from May of that year.[87] He indicated that he had recently met with Hitler, and they had spoken about the authorization process. According to Himmler, Hitler said he had the impression this process took an extremely long time, and he noted in a half-joking, half-serious tone that perhaps RuSHA's tardiness presented an obstacle to marriage. This discussion with the Führer prompted Himmler to inquire with the Office for Family Affairs, which notified him, to his "horror and astonishment," that there were over twenty thousand outstanding requests.[88] Himmler wanted to shorten the excessive amount of time that an SS man had to wait for a response from RuSHA, but he told Darré that his office would not receive any more funding to solve this problem. Otherwise, any solution to the backlog was acceptable to Himmler as he did not want his men faced with the decision of either marrying without permission and risking punishment, or waiting for approval and not marrying in a timely manner. He ended his letter by telling Darré not to allow this issue to anger him because they would find an appropriate solution.

For the most part, the extensive application process and the backlog resulting from it did not deter most SS men. By the mid- to late 1930s, approximately 1,700 to 2,000 requests were filed each month.[89] These applications demonstrated most men's willingness to accede to Himmler's orders and to wait, even for a prolonged period of time, for approval from RuSHA. A minority of these men, however, did not wish to comply, prompting Himmler to address the issue even before the backlog mounted. In March 1935, he released an order indicating that he had strongly censured an officer because, "contrary to the command known to all SS members," this officer had gotten engaged and had announced it in a newspaper prior to receiving approval. Himmler declared that in the future such a transgression would lead to expulsion.[90]

Less than three months later, Himmler issued a supplementary command that outlined a judicial procedure for SS members who got engaged or married without permission.[91] Contravention of the engagement and marriage command would be reported to the SS court in Munich. The court would hold a hearing, and all transgressions committed before 1 August 1935 would result in a reprimand for the offending member. Furthermore, the court would admonish his superior officer for neglecting his responsibility to inform the men under him about the proper procedures, as it appeared that part of the problem was that SS men were being incorrectly or incompletely informed about the regulations.[92] After 1 August, the court could dismiss anyone who knowingly disregarded the command, although for officers found guilty, it could propose both demotion and expulsion. To ensure that every member understood the severity of this judicial procedure, Himmler not only required every unit to announce this command once a month, but he also insisted that each unit had to record this monthly recitation in its service book. Each Oberabschnitt received instructions on the matter as well. They had to ensure that violations did not occur and to inform the men in their respective subunits that even attending the engagement or wedding celebration of an SS man who had not received permission was a punishable act.[93]

The results of these disciplinary measures are unclear. There is some documentation showing that disciplinary measures were initiated against SS men between 1935 and 1937.[94] However, this evidence is fragmentary, making it impossible to discern whether these men were punished, expelled, or granted belated permission for their marriages. Similarly, several subunits in Oberabschnitt Fulda-Werra filed reports in 1937 and 1938 that gave statistics for violations in twenty different categories.[95] Most, but not all, of these reports listed violations against the engagement and marriage command. Those numbers were typically among the smallest reported violations. Still, they do reveal that a few SS men disobeyed.

Slightly more can be ascertained from the annual statistical reports produced by the SS, which took into account the entire the organization. Based on numbers from 1937, the organization had 208,364 members. By the end of the year, 7,960 men had been discharged, mostly honourably and of their own volition.[96] Of that number, only 320 – about 4 per cent of the dismissals – related to the engagement and marriage command. In comparison, far more people resigned or were expelled for occupational reasons (40.3 per cent); health reasons (15.4 per cent); an assignment with the military (11.2 per cent); or a transfer to another branch of the party (7.5 per cent). The situation vis-à-vis the engagement and marriage command and dismissal improved in 1938. From a total of 238,159 members, 5,638 men were dismissed.[97] Only 83 (1.5 per cent) of the men who received an honourable discharge and 24 (0.43 per cent) of the men who received a dishonourable discharge left because of the engagement and marriage command.

Clearly, these numbers show that Himmler and the SS court allocated punishments for disobedience. They likewise indicate that men were allowed to receive honourable discharges based on their decision not to comply. However, these honourable discharges were not the only flexibility shown; in the same approximate time frame, Himmler demonstrated leniency towards his men, and he relaxed the regulations regarding violations. One example of clemency involved SS-Unterscharführer Eugen G. He had married in August 1935 without permission. According to official reports, Eugen knew the consequences of his actions. On the day he wed, he requested to be dismissed from the SS. Instead, his commanding officers sought to punish and expel him.[98] To this end, his records were passed up the chain of command, but instead, the decision was made in December 1935 to grant Eugen's request for dismissal.[99] Less than a year later, Eugen requested readmission. Based on certificates of good conduct and leadership, along with his service in the Wehrmacht, no objections to his request were raised. The only caveat was a request to demote him from Unterscharführer (the lowest rank for a non-commissioned officer) to Rottenführer (the highest enlisted rank).[100] It is unclear whether this demotion went through, but his readmission must have been granted by the end of 1936 because RuSHA finalized the belated approval of his marriage in December.[101]

A second example of clemency can be seen in the case of SS-Sturmbannführer Wilhelm H. According to his personnel and RuSHA files, he had requested the required paperwork, but he and his fiancée did not submit the documents prior to getting married in January 1935. The very act of requesting the forms proved that Wilhelm knew of the engagement and marriage command, yet he chose to disregard it and only sent in the forms after the fact. When the issue came to Himmler's attention in March 1936, he dismissed Wilhelm from the SS on the grounds that he expected his officers to set "a good example," and his inappropriate decision had proven that Wilhelm "did not possess the inner aptitude for a higher SS officer."[102]

The matter would have been concluded had the Oberabschnitt to which Wilhelm belonged not questioned Himmler's decision a month later. The head of Oberabschnitt Nordost wrote to Darré for clarification about Wilhelm's status because, according to Oberabschnitt records – which had been forwarded from RuSHA – Wilhelm had received belated permission for his marriage from Himmler in February 1936. The Oberabschnitt leader wanted Darré to clarify which of the contradictory orders, each endorsed by Himmler, he needed to relay to Wilhelm: the February one approving his already-existing marriage or the March one dismissing him from the SS. In the end, Himmler approved Wilhelm's marriage again in April. Furthermore, despite his earlier admonition about Wilhelm's character and suitability as an officer, Wilhelm eventually reached the rank of Brigadeführer, a rank four grades higher than when he had gotten married and one of the highest ranks in the SS.[103]

Beyond this specific case, Himmler sometimes mitigated the possibility of punishment. In late June 1937, he decreed that no further penalties would be imposed for violations of the engagement and marriage command. However, Himmler still wanted each man who did not comply with the order to be investigated and to have a file created so that, if he desired, penalties could be imposed later.[104] The chief of the SS court, SS-Gruppenführer Paul Scharfe, forwarded this order to RuSHA, the SS Main Office, and the Reich Security Main Office as well as to each Oberabschnitt. In November, Scharfe passed on an updated order. The Reichsführer still wanted all cases investigated, and he needed to know whether noncompliance was due to a man's carelessness or his difficulties procuring the necessary records. Regarding punishments, Himmler had no intention of creating new penal regulations until a support agency was established in each Oberabschnitt, which did not occur until 1938–39.[105]

Neither of the orders forwarded by Scharfe indicated why Himmler had changed his mind, but there are several possible reasons. First, Germany was preparing for war by this time, and Himmler could have wanted to increase the size of the SS before a conflict broke out. While the majority of men did not belong to the Verfügungstruppe, this branch did serve as the core of a potential fighting force. Himmler most likely understood that such a unit, if successfully employed, would improve his standing with Hitler, which in turn would strengthen his position in the party and the state. Second, as seen in the statistics from 1937 and 1938, those men who were dismissed either because they did not want to comply with the engagement and marriage command or because they had violated it outright represented a minority of those who left the organization. With so few transgressions, it might not have been worth the SS court's time and effort to prosecute these cases. Third, eliminating punishments might have encouraged others to stay in the SS and complete the paperwork when the time came to get married, thus positively reinforcing the original 1931 command. Retaining these men meant keeping as much good Nordic blood as possible in the SS, and as Nordic blood was believed to produce the best military and political leaders, this retention could have influenced the organization's future growth.

Beyond these possibilities, there is perhaps one other reason why Himmler relaxed the penalties. Statistics show that most men who got married complied with his command, but they highlight another problem: not all men got married, and the majority who did failed to do so in a timely manner. Young SS men and officers were not allowed to apply for authorization until age twenty-five; after this point, the organization's leadership wanted them to pursue the task of finding a wife aggressively and to get married by twenty-seven – an age corresponding with the average marriage age in the Reich. But this desired correlation between age and marital status did not come to fruition. According to statistics from 1936 and 1937, less than half of twenty-seven-year-old officers were married, and the average marriage age in the SS was five years above the Reich median.[106]

In general, marriage rates in the SS remained below 50 per cent. As of August 1936, 69.3 per cent of all members (enlisted men, non-commissioned officers, and commissioned officers) were single, 30.3 per cent were married, and 0.4 per cent were widowed or divorced. By September 1937, 54.4 per cent were single, 44.6 per cent were married, and 0.9 per cent were widowed or divorced. Finally, as of the end of 1938, 60.3 per cent were single, 39.1 per cent were married, and 0.6 per cent were widowed or divorced. However, SS statisticians did note in 1937 and 1938 that approximately half of the unmarried men were twenty-five years old or younger, and as such, were not expected to be married yet.[107]

Among the officers, the percentages were higher. In 1936, 74.1 per cent of officers – both those serving in full-time paid positions and those serving unpaid during nights and weekends – were married; in 1937, 76.7 per cent were married; and by the end of 1938, 77.3 per cent were married – a high point that was almost 4 per cent above the percentage of married men in the Reich. Nonetheless, Himmler commented in late 1938 that this higher SS number should not serve as an excuse for officers who were single to remain so because "the SS should be a germ cell [*Keimzelle*] of the German Volk."[108] This desire to see the SS become a model for the *Volk*, at least with regards to marriage, remained unfilled. When the marriage statistics were broken down by age, not even the oldest age group, containing all officers forty-one years and older, were married; over 5 per cent remained single.[109]

Various offices and departments produced marriage statistics during the mid- and late 1930s, all of which, as shown above, demonstrated the problem of convincing SS men to get married. However, those created by the SS Personnel Chancellery addressed the low marriage rates among officers by conveying the justifications that officers had reported when surveyed. Four explanations emerged: they were impeded by economic conditions; they had not finished their education and had no job; they lacked the time and opportunity to find a wife; and they had not met a suitable woman. The person who wrote the two statistical reports briefly scrutinized and rejected each explanation. Economic conditions could not be an impediment for two reasons: one, the economic situation in the country had improved since the end of the Weimar Republic, and two, anyone employed by the SS on a full-time basis received a salary. The second explanation was refuted for similar reasons, although the author did acknowledge that people who pursued an academic education usually married later in life.[110] The SS employed many men who had obtained a university education in a wide range of fields, and certain occupations were overrepresented in the SS. For example, professionals in the field of health care and hygiene represented 2 per cent of the population, but 3 per cent of SS members.[111] Again, as recognized by the author of the Personnel Chancellery's report, this overrepresentation of certain professions might have influenced the lower marriage rates among SS officers.

The third and fourth explanations were rejected with statistics. The report's author provided figures not just for officers, but also broke them down into two categories: full-time, salaried versus part-time, unsalaried. In a year-by-year analysis, a higher percentage of part-time, unsalaried officers were married. Based on these numbers, the author's combined rejection of the third and fourth reasons followed these lines: if a part-time officer could hold down a job, commit himself to the SS with unpaid service during nights and weekends, and still find time to get married, then a full-time officer who received his salary from the SS could not lack the time to meet and marry a suitable woman.[112]

This analysis highlights the fact that SS officials spent a great deal of time analysing the marital status of their men. The majority of their interest revolved around establishing marriages, but of course not all marriages lasted (as noted above, divorces were included in the statistics). In principle, Himmler did not oppose divorce.[113] He simply required that any enlisted man or non-com who ended his marriage submit a transcript of the court judgment to the SS Main Office; officers had to send their records to the SS Personnel Chancellery.[114] This information allowed the relevant offices to update a man's personnel file, as well as take his new status into account the next time statistics were generated. There were very few divorces, and so in comparison with the vast documentation about marriage, there is minimal information on divorce. This lack of information notwithstanding, it is still reasonable to presume that, barring any unfavourable report on a man's character or any concern over the racial suitability of his ex-wife, the end of his marriage would not have affected his status in the SS. He would have been encouraged to remarry and to have children if he had none from his first marriage.

All of these details illustrate the fact that the SS sought to micromanage every decision relating to getting married and to scrutinize its statistical outcome; no detail was too inconsequential. However, not everyone shared this perspective towards the end of the decade. By late 1937, Darré had begun to mistrust Himmler, and he grew increasingly worried about the future of the SS. Indeed, by early 1938 Darré began to wonder if he should give up his position as RuSHA chief "because the SS develops into a capitalist praetorian guard under Jesuit supreme command."[115] More concerned with the welfare of the peasantry than with crafting the SS into a master elite, Darré offered Himmler his resignation in February. Himmler refused it, and their relationship subsequently began to deteriorate. Their estrangement was probably evident to anyone working in the Berlin office of RuSHA, including George Ebrecht. During his tenure as the RuSHA staff officer in 1937 and 1938, Ebrecht saw how Himmler began to intervene more and more in RuSHA affairs. This interference resulted in Darré spending less time in the office, to the point where he withdrew almost completely from his responsibilities.[116] In September 1938, Himmler finally accepted Darré's resignation and appointed Günther Pancke as his replacement.[117] This change in leader did not alter RuSHA's purpose. While the office was initially founded to evaluate engagement and marriage applications, its responsibilities had greatly expanded by the end of the 1930s. This expansion was part of the overall growth of the SS, both in size and ambition.

The engagement and marriage process had likewise evolved since the original 1931 command. It had transformed into a far more complicated and time-consuming endeavor, not only for each couple, but also for the officials tasked with assisting them and ultimately determining who among them should and should not belong to the family community. But even with these changes, the intent of the engagement and marriage process remained the same: to serve as the first step in creating a self-sustaining elite order. Vetting SS men and their fiancées on racial and hereditary grounds had turned scientific rhetoric into practice by fostering eugenically sound marriages. With these unions in place, Himmler could construct additional policies to build on this marital foundation.

Chapter Two

Establishing SS Families

"[M]arriage cannot be an end in itself, but must serve the one higher goal, the increase and preservation of the species and the race."[1] Hitler dictated these words during his time in prison. Less than a decade later, Himmler sought to fulfil this objective, of which regulating marriages was only the first step. The next was encouraging men to start families, with the goal that every family would produce at least four racially healthy children. As this chapter will show, throughout the mid- to late 1930s, various measures were initiated to advance this ideal. Letters, speeches, and newspaper articles highlighted the merits of having children – legitimate and illegitimate, biological and adopted – while various stipends provided for the financial well-being of SS families. These measures were collectively designed to encourage every man to accept that having children represented a vital duty. They emphasized the value of healthy blood to each family and to the SS. Every child strengthened the family community, and in turn, this community had the potential to secure the future of the Reich by ensuring its longevity as a racial state.

Building a sustainable community meant continuing to adhere selectively to ideas outlined by eugenicists in the 1930s. Among these ideas was the notion that a two-child system – that is, an average of two children per marriage – could not sustain the population. Adherence to such a system would lead, according to statistician Friedrich Burgdörfer, to the extinction of the German people in approximately three centuries. He calculated that merely conserving the population would require a birth rate of 3.4 children per marriage, or 3.1 if illegitimate births were included.[2] Reversing this decline in the national birth rate was crucial because, as Burgdörfer suggested, "a Volk without youth would be a Volk without hope, a Volk without a future."[3] Many eugenicists concurred and called for hereditarily healthy families to have a large number of children, typically at least four.[4] But while insisting that the best elements of society produce high numbers of children, eugenicists did not specify how these people would achieve this goal.

Scientists wanted the government to construct policies that fostered the establishment of families. In particular, they wanted to see economic benefits extended to large and healthy families, and any measure that was advantageous to childless and child-poor couples curtailed. A state that did not care for its healthy families did not, in the words of pathologist Martin Staemmler, "have any moral right to continue to exist. It is no Volk state."[5] Eugenicists likewise wanted the government to ensure the security of the state from domestic and foreign threats, such as the impact of foreign races.[6] They contended that the government had to fight to preserve the biological heritage of its people, and in return the people had the responsibility to increase that heritage. This became a prominent leitmotif in the Nazi state, one that gave credence to the racial and population goals of the SS.

By the mid-1930s, SS men should have been aware of the connection between the ideas of eugenicists and the racial goals of their order. This was an explicit theme, for example, of the Week of the German Book. Orchestrated between 1935 and 1938 by the Reich Ministry for Public Enlightenment and Propaganda, this yearly program promoted the works of German authors.[7] Himmler required each SS unit to collect money from its members to purchase titles from a list of approved books. For every book a unit selected, it had to buy two copies – one for the unit's library and the other for a group such as the Hitler Youth or the League of German Girls.[8] Books by prominent Nazis were on the list, but more importantly, so were books by scientists and physicians, many of whom had promoted the racial ideals adopted by the SS. Among these authors were Ludwig Ferdinand Clauss, Hans F.K. Günther, Werner Jansen, and Martin Staemmler.[9] Staemmler's 1934 book *Racial Care in the Völkish State* would have most likely struck a chord with SS readers. In it, he praised the engagement and marriage command and lauded the examination process. He suggested that the stringent requirements would create awareness about racial and hereditary health among SS men, knowledge that could be implemented when they founded their own families.[10]

Beyond seeking to fulfil the ideals posited by eugenicists, SS family policies were designed to serve in conjunction with government and party organizations, including the Office for Racial Policy. Founded in May 1934 and headed by Walter Groß, this office designed most of the important racial policies, including the 1935 Nuremberg Laws. It also educated medical personnel, and its staff participated in the KWI-A courses for SS doctors. One of its departments was the Reich Association of the Child-Rich, which had the task of overcoming Germany's declining birth rate.[11] In essence, the Office for Racial Policy, and with it the Reich Association of the Child-Rich, performed a similar function in the Nazi state as RuSHA did in the SS. This parallel office reinforced the functions of RuSHA by normalizing racial population politics on a national level.

Reinforcement did not come without the potential for conflict. In April 1934 Himmler recognized that friction might occur between the SS and party or state offices when it came to training officials and issuing propaganda about racial matters. He therefore issued an order indicating that RuSHA was in charge of all SS racial affairs, and he directed RuSHA officials to report any problems with other organizations up the appropriate chain of command.[12] The potential for discord was compounded by the fact that Darré and Groß had differing opinions on racial matters: Darré focused on building up the Nordic race through the peasantry while Groß emphasized more negative actions, such as eliminating foreign races from Germany.[13] These opposing perspectives would have complicated working relations between these men and their respective organizations. But beyond this possible problem, there was also the potential for conflict over control of racial affairs and policy as other organizations and their leaders – including the National Socialist Doctor's League under Gerhard Wagner and the Expert Council for Population and Racial Policy under Arthur Gütt – attempted to wrest control of racial and health matters from the Office for Racial Policy.[14] Even with conflicting and overlapping areas of control, the interest in creating party and state bodies to regulate the racial health of the nation normalized what the SS sought to do in its own ranks by expanding the context in which these goals would be pursued.

Beyond these offices, the government passed measures to aid population growth. The most prominent was a financial act: the Law for the Promotion of Marriages, which was contained in the Law for the Reduction of Unemployment.[15] This marriage law, which went into effect in August 1933, created jobs for men by encouraging women to return to their domestic and maternal duties. To this end, if a woman left her job and subsequently married, her husband could apply for an interest-free loan of up to 1,000 Reichsmarks (RM). This loan was not a cash payment, but rather vouchers the couple could redeem at stores for household goods and furniture. A couple repaid the loan at a rate of 1 per cent per month; these payments would begin two months after they had received the vouchers. By the summer of 1938, the state had allocated almost a million loans.[16]

There were two caveats attached to the program. First, to qualify for a loan, each couple had to undergo a medical examination to establish their mental and physical health. Any signs of a defect – such as a genetic illness, as defined by the 1933 sterilization law – resulted in disqualification.[17] As of late 1935, these health standards also included racial suitability, as defined by the Nuremberg Laws.[18] The second caveat related to children. For each child a couple bore, the state canceled one-quarter of their loan. The population implications were obvious. The state did not want the loan repaid; it wanted each couple to have four children. And there was an increase in the number of children born, yet overall, the people's response was tepid. Of the nearly one million loans granted, only 840,000 children had been born, but most often these were first or second children, meaning that most loans were only partially canceled.[19] In addition, not all children counted, as *Das Schwarze Korps* pointed out in an article titled "Child = Child." The SS newspaper commended the loan, but at the same time objected to one element – the fact that a portion of it could only be deferred for a child born in wedlock. The author argued that the deferral should also apply to a couple who had a child and then later married because the purpose – although not the wording – of the law was to encourage the birth of healthy children. When the child was born was irrelevant; the point of the law was not to reprimand parents on moral grounds or to subject them to bourgeois morals.[20] This criticism aside, the marriage loan was the most important law the government passed with regards to promoting population growth in a positive manner. As with the establishment of the Office for Racial Policy, the loan normalized the regime's racial and population policies, and it demonstrated the high regard that it accorded hereditary health.

While designed to aid the growth of a healthy population, state measures were never as rigorous as those put forth by the SS. Although the organization's members could take advantage of government policies, their leader held them to a higher standard when it came to their families, and he created measures solely for them. In speeches and letters throughout the 1930s, Himmler sought to convince each SS man of his responsibility to preserve his racial heritage, especially because he viewed Nordic blood as a vital tool for the Führer to wield as he constructed his greater German Reich. "I am ideologically convinced," Himmler said in one speech, "that in the last analysis and in the long run, only good blood will bring about the highest achievements."[21] Yet, while he considered it self-evident that Nordic blood was the prime vehicle for the SS to become Germany's new aristocracy, Himmler understood that it would take time to inculcate his men with this perspective. "Permanent success" would only be achieved "if an inner reorientation takes place," one that would convince SS men that Germany's imminent decline would be prevented if they, the bearers of valuable Nordic blood, had enough children.[22]

In espousing this perspective, Himmler adopted the standpoint taken by Baur, Fischer, and Lenz in their seminal work, that the Nordic race was the leading element in Western culture. He took the task of finding and managing this blood seriously, commenting at one point in a speech to high-ranking SS officers that

> all good blood in the world is German blood, [and] what is not on the German side can only be our undoing. Therefore, it is each German with the best blood whom we take for Germany ... I really have the intent to get, to rob, and to steal the Germanic blood in the whole world where I can.[23]

As this comment demonstrates, Himmler, like German eugenicists, emphasized nature over nurture. This view was likewise in agreement with the views Hitler had laid out in *Mein Kampf*.[24] He had contended that an individual could not cater to his selfish whims when it came to the good of the *Volk*. If that individual were unhealthy, it was his responsibility to abstain from having children; conversely, if he were healthy, it would be "reprehensible" for him to deny the nation his progeny.[25] The fertility of the healthiest members of society had to be "consciously and systematically promoted," Hitler proclaimed, because the entire *Volk* would benefit from their offspring.[26]

Himmler promoted these notions as he attempted to reorient his men's views towards their paternal obligations. In a June 1935 letter to all SS officers, he wrote that "SS families must be child-rich families for all the future."[27] In a second letter from September of the following year, he reinforced the value of the prolific SS family by stating that "we have all fought for nothing if we do not add the victory of the birth of good blood to the political victory" of the Nazi Party.[28] The notion that a political victory was in vain without a victory in the cradle was one Himmler repeated several times throughout the 1930s, and a variation on this theme became important during the war.[29] Besides stressing the relationship between the two victories, Himmler noted in a September 1936 letter that "the question of many children is not the private concern of the individual, but is the duty towards his ancestors and our Volk."[30] By emphasizing these sentiments, Himmler indicated to his men that having children represented a greater ideal than merely establishing a family. These children represented the future of the *Volk* because they represented the people who would continue the legacy their fathers had built with the Führer.

Himmler wanted his men, especially his officers, to embrace the ideal of expanding the SS from an order of men to a community of families. However, for it to become, as Himmler stated in a November 1937 speech, "a new aristocracy that supplements itself again and again from the best sons and daughters of our Volk," the organization's members had to regard family affairs as a responsibility that was no less significant than any other obligation to the SS.[31] Yet encouraging his men to produce high-quality children was only the beginning for Himmler. He was not content simply telling them to be fruitful and multiply; that alone would not have fulfilled their biological duty. Quality – as defined by their ability to pass down their supposedly superior genetic material – was of only limited value unless it was combined with quantity.

Here again Himmler agreed with eugenicists. He contended that if at least three children emerged from every marriage, then Germany would have a positive birth rate, but he pointed out that this number did not reflect childless marriages and bachelors. Himmler therefore asserted that SS marriages had to carry the burden of compensating for those people who had not contributed to the *Volk*. This would mean that SS members would have to have four children, which Himmler defined as the "minimum child number of a good and healthy marriage."[32] The reason for four children was further clarified in a December 1938 memorandum produced by the SS Personnel Chancellery: the first two children replaced their own parents; the third substituted for a loss within the family; and the fourth made up for those Germans whom the government had deemed incompetent and unable to reproduce.[33]

The idea of SS men counteracting the reproductive inactivity of other Germans reinforced their fidelity to the Nazi Party and its leader, as loyalty had defined the organization since its participation in the quelling of the Stennes putsch in 1931.[34] The December 1938 memorandum re-emphasized this point: "The order of the SS is no community of sanc-timonious loafers, no death chamber of good genetic makeup, but it should become the life cell of the German Volk."[35] The memorandum set down a timeline in which it would be possible for a man and his wife to have the requisite number of children. The couple would have the first two years after they wed to themselves before they would be required to have their first child. After the birth of this child, they would be expected to have another child every three years. According to the memorandum, this plan would allow for an SS family to produce five children.[36] Through the successful discharge of this duty, "the sight of the SS uniform" would be associated with "a healthy flock of children" who represented the future of the Reich.[37]

It would take more than rhetoric, however, to encourage SS members to fulfil their paternal responsibilities. In his capacity as Reichsführer-SS, as well as in his position as chief of the German police (which he had held since 1936), Himmler initiated measures designed to influence the actions and behaviour of SS men. Some of these measures aided the cre-ation of large families, while others prohibited certain types of behav-iour. For the latter, he sought to control the social behaviour of SS men and police officers by prohibiting them from swing dancing while in uniform, abusing alcohol and subsequently misbehaving while under the influence, and using nicotine and cigarettes. The last prohibition was slightly ironic, given that some of the most prominent advertise-ments in the SS newspaper were for cigarettes, and at one point the SS itself had promoted cigarette sales.[38]

None of these prohibitions were as significant as the ones aimed at combatting abortion and homosexuality.[39] Himmler summarized his views on abortion in a June 1937 speech before the Expert Council for Population and Racial Policy, a government commission established by the Reich minister of the interior in 1933 on which Himmler and many eugenicists served. Himmler indicated that there were around 500,000 abortions in Germany every year, despite its proscription under para-graphs 219 and 220 of the penal code. Preventing them would help the nation in two ways, Himmler argued. First, if at least 20 per cent of aborted children were saved (even if they were illegitimate), their num-bers could decisively influence the future of Germany, especially when it came to increasing the number of men available for military service. Himmler argued that no commander would care if his soldiers were legitimate or not if they could alter the fate of Germany, or perhaps even the world.[40] The second reason related to the mothers. He was adamantly convinced that in many cases abortion caused sterility, leading not simply to the death of one child, but to "the killing of motherhood for a lifetime."[41]

Himmler was far more obsessive in his abhorrence of homosexuality, the elimination of which he pursued with greater fervour than any other Nazi leader. He suggested that homosexuality destroyed the state because "the homosexual is through and through a mentally sick human being."[42] Through his work as chief of police, Himmler claimed that there were between 1 and 2 million homosexuals in Germany. In 1937, he estimated that the country had a population of 67 to 68 million people, of whom approximately 20 million were sexually capable men over the age of sixteen. The presence of up to 2 million homosexuals represented an "epidemic" because they did not contribute to the growth of the *Volk*. Furthermore, when homosexuals were combined with the 2 million men who had fallen during the First World War, Germany faced, according to Himmler, a possible catastrophe when it came to sustaining its population. And for any homosexual who proclaimed that what he did in his personal life was of no concern to anyone else, Himmler offered a contrary view: their lack of reproduction was as grave a concern as any other reproductive matter because the presence or absence of children meant the life or death of the *Volk*.[43]

Portraying homosexuality as an "epidemic" had many ramifications. The term implied a disease, a characterization that many German and British physicians had used since the late nineteenth century. Homosexuality represented a malady from which an otherwise healthy *Volk* suffered.[44] As such, Himmler suggested, it was something that should be eliminated in order to save the *Volk*. To combat this blight on the population, Himmler ordered an investigation into homosexuals' mental constitutions. He even requested research about a possible connection between homosexuality and left-handedness, some of which was carried out by Eugen Fischer's institute.[45]

In October 1936, Himmler established the Reich Central Office for Combating Homosexuality and Abortion. A special department in the police, it was responsible for recording all reported cases of homosexuality and abortion.[46] In early 1937, Himmler devised a draconian disciplinary measure for homosexuality in the SS after he learned that there were approximately eight to ten cases of homosexuality per year in the organization (not to mention charges that SS men were molesting boys in the Hitler Youth).[47] After being publicly humiliated and discharged from the SS, a former member would be tried and sentenced by the court. Though homosexuality had been illegal in Germany since 1871, in 1935 the Nazi government broadened the definition of homosexuality, which allowed authorities to increase their prosecution to the point where evidence of physical contact between two men was not even necessary.[48] However, punishment by the state was not enough for Himmler. In addition to the court-assigned penalty, the Reichsführer declared that a former SS man would be sent to a concentration camp where he would be "shot while trying to escape."[49] Afterwards, the unit in which this individual had served would be informed of his crime and punishment. Through this process, Himmler demonstrated that he was not above using a humiliated, convicted, and executed corpse to make his point, again emphasizing that a man's decisions regarding his personal life were anything but private when it came to the health and well-being of the SS and the *Volk*.[50]

But prohibitions alone would not raise the birth rate; positive initiatives to encourage reproduction were also needed. One source of encouragement was *Das Schwarze Korps*, which frequently promoted the family. The importance of marriage lay in producing children, the newspaper claimed.[51] Other articles emphasized the same point by noting that a childless marriage could not contribute to the *Volk*.[52] The newspaper also advocated early marriage by reminding readers that the younger they got married, the higher the possibility that a couple would raise a child-rich family.[53] And, in agreement with eugenicists, *Das Schwarze Korps* promoted the idea that every fertile marriage needed to have four children.[54]

The newspaper used stories from its readers to reinforce this message. One case involved a recently married twenty-seven-year-old man.[55] He and his wife wished to have at least four children; after speaking with his friends, he learned that they, too, wanted large families. However, he and his friends realized that not only had all of them come from small families, but their parents and older relatives were against them having large families. This older generation was trying to convince their offspring that they were still young and that children would only disrupt their lives. The young man disagreed and proclaimed that it was the elders who needed to change their attitude.

Quantity was clearly crucial, yet *Das Schwarze Korps* recognized that quality was important, too.[56] Children were only valuable if they came from healthy members of the *Volk*; as the bearers of the best blood, the involvement of SS members was therefore essential. One article, "The Inner Security of the Reich," specifically noted that SS men were taught that "*the most precious good is the German child.*"[57] Other articles articulated a similar point.[58] The future of the German *Volk* depended on children; they were to be valued and families were to be supported. The newspaper took umbrage at any measures detrimental to the family, especially child-rich families, as seen in two articles from the summer of 1939. In the first, two child-rich fathers in Berlin were fined by the police when their children made too much noise, and in the second, a restaurant in Hanover was criticized for not being friendly to children in strollers.[59]

In a more positive manner, the newspaper periodically printed poems about the family; one of them began, "A Volk has no greater good / than its families."[60] What made these poems notable, beyond their lyrical adoration of the family, was the fact that *Das Schwarze Korps* printed the names of their authors – in contrast to the paper's policy of leaving most articles unsigned.[61] Providing names gave the impression that readers, rather than the editorial staff or regular contributors, wrote these poems. Also, most of the authors were men. The inclusion of the poems indicates that the newspaper's content about the family resonated so much with these readers – who were likely fathers – that they submitted a contribution.

Such content continually promoted the significance of the family to the *Volk* and the nation. Additional articles advocated active parenting. The mother had long since been viewed as the primary caregiver in the German family, and the newspaper sustained that perspective.[62] However, it also published articles emphasizing the father's essential role. Fatherhood was not limited to a biological contribution; fathers were expected to participate in rearing and educating their offspring. According to one article, "the most precious and happy goods in life are as follows: health, love, and children; man cannot buy these with money, they are gifts of heaven that we should gratefully and humbly accept."[63] Thus, one facet of fatherhood exemplified in the newspaper was men's reactions to the birth of their children. This provided a simple means of indicating how fathers should take pride in their ability to fulfil their racial responsibilities to the nation. For example, the newspaper reported the immeasurable satisfaction of Helmut L. as he attempted to compose the birth announcement for his sixth child. He wrestled to find the right words to express his ecstasy over his third son, and after realizing how his son would benefit the nation, he declared, "Germany shall live even if we must die!"[64] By including these words, the newspaper implied that every father should respond to his newborn with similar candour and excitement.

"Ist das ünmännlich?" *Das Schwarze Korps*, 10 August 1939, p. 13

Once the fathers had welcomed the babies into their families, they had other paternal responsibilities. Two articles discussed these duties. The first, "Is this unmanly?," illustrated day-to-day tasks and emphasized the acceptable actions that a father should undertake for his children. It stated plainly that a father should not take over the responsibilities of a mother, but it was permissible for a man to assist his wife with domestic duties. In doing so, he would lose nothing of his manliness or dignity, but would instead prove his position as "a genuine man and a proper husband."[65] The article contained five photographs demonstrating the acceptable care that any SS man or father should provide for his children. The first image depicted a father pushing a baby carriage while taking a stroll with his wife and son; the caption exclaimed, "This father does not fear appearing unmanly. He decreases the troubles of his wife."[66] The second photograph showed a family on an outing. The uniformed father carried his daughter. According to the caption, "The smallest of the family has become tired from a walk in the forest. Now should the mother … no, our SS comrade shows that he has no fear." The third snapshot revealed an SS man in uniform aiding a mother with her baby carriage, and beneath it the caption noted: "Uniform and baby carriage, both rescue the soldier." The last two pictures portrayed a man feeding a bottle to, and changing the diaper of, his baby. Once again, the caption encouraged these deeds: "Why shouldn't the father also provide for his child …? He thereby loses nothing of his masculinity, but he shows himself in such a way that his love for his wife and his child is not only lip service."

The second article, "Best Friends," focused on the time that a father should spend with his older children, especially his sons.[67] The authors recounted the fond memories they had with their own fathers, which included playing games and listening to their fathers speak about when they were young. The authors proclaimed that in this time together, the father ceased to be an authority figure and instead acted as a comrade who taught his sons the value of love, respect, and trust: "we believe today that something like camaraderie developed between us and our fathers in these hours."[68] They argued that every father had time for his children; if nothing else, he could spend time with them when on vacation. They also derided fathers who refused to be seen cavorting with their children as cowardly, suggesting, "Daddy, you are foolish!"[69] Nothing could replace the time a father spent with his children, and while acknowledging that the activities could be tiring, the authors proclaimed that the rewards were worthwhile.

As with the previous article, "Best Friends" reinforced its message with images. Each picture showed a father interacting with his son or sons – giving swimming lessons, constructing a fort, climbing a tree, and building a camp fire. These depictions furnished a persuasive argument with respect to the participation of a father in the daily upbringing of his children. They imparted a vision of an active father who cared for his family, and in this way made clear that fatherhood encompassed far more than biological responsibility, and that fatherly admiration and care were acceptable and admirable traits for men. In short, there was nothing unmanly in fatherly affection.

While newspaper articles highlighted the merits of family and fatherhood, they were not the only means to encourage reproduction. Another positive initiative was monetary allowances. Not only could SS men apply for the state marriage loan, but men employed full-time by the SS received more money if they were married; this variance in pay based on marital status most likely carried over from when the SS was a part of the SA.[70] For example, according to figures from 1936, a married SS man received 140 RM per month, whereas his unmarried counterpart received only 125 RM. For an Obergruppenführer – then the highest rank – this disparity was even greater. A married Obergruppenführer earned 1,350 RM per month while an unmarried one earned 100 RM less.[71] To receive this increased income, the married SS man had to submit his marriage certificate to the Administration Main Department, the precursor of the Economic and Administrative Main Office.[72] Pay differential was not limited to monthly salaries. On special occasions, such as the Nuremberg rallies, extra funds were allocated according to rank and marital status.[73]

A similar pattern existed for children. Throughout the 1930s, the government offered monetary allowances for families who had three or more children and whose yearly income was less than 8,000 RM.[74] Most full-time, salaried SS men would have been eligible for this assistance; only officers at the rank of Oberführer and above would have earned too much to qualify. Beyond government money, the SS granted additional funds based on the number of children. Salary regulations from 1935, 1936, and 1938 indicate that a man received an additional 20 RM per month for his first and second child, 30 RM for his third and fourth child, and 40 RM for his fifth and every subsequent child.[75] This money was granted for legitimate children as well as adopted children or stepchildren for whom an SS man had taken responsibility. In addition, he could receive money for an illegitimate child if his paternity had been verified and he had taken responsibility for the offspring.

These funds were allocated until a child reached the age of sixteen. They could be extended to twenty-one if the child were still in school or occupational training and did not have an independent income. Every time a new child was born or one became financially independent, the allowance was adjusted.[76] For instance, if an SS man welcomed a third child into his family, his monthly allowance would increase from 20 to 30 RM. While the Administrative Main Department kept records on how much child support an SS man received, the disbursement of money took place through the unit to which he belonged. Selected records from Oberabschnitt Rhein showed that these funds represented a very small portion of its budget – less than 3 per cent of the money it spent each month.[77]

Outside of these regulated amounts, additional funds were periodically made available. The most common time for extra money to be distributed was right before Christmas. In 1936 and 1937, units were granted permission to provide holiday funds to the men they employed full-time if they had the financial means.[78] Once again, married men received more money. The units were also allowed to provide a small bonus to men already receiving a stipend for their children from the SS. Because the payments were based on the funds available in each unit, some units had the means to give money to all full-time SS men, whereas others selectively distributed money based on its members' specific financial needs. During the 1938 holiday season, there was a special, one-time allowance given to all child-rich families.[79] An extra 25 RM was paid to families for their fourth, fifth, or sixth child, and an extra 100 RM was paid to families for their seventh and additional children. Special funds were still available in 1939, although by 1940 the SS had moved towards providing families with Yule candlesticks.[80]

Another source of funding was *Das Schwarze Korps*, which from its start in March 1935 was immediately successful.[81] Strong sales generated considerable revenue, most of which the party press, Eher Verlag, transferred to the SS. In early 1937, Himmler decreed that these extra funds were to be used to give 50 RM to every child-rich SS couple upon the birth of their sixth, seventh, or eighth child.[82] Later in the year, this stipend was extended to families who had their fourth or fifth child. Himmler ordered a similar distribution of funds in 1938, and later correspondence from various units and offices indicate that child-rich families continued to receive a stipend from the newspaper's revenue for the birth of their fourth, fifth, and subsequent child until late 1944.[83]

There are a couple of ways to put these salaries, stipends, and special grants into perspective when it comes to examining their potential impact on family size. Regarding salaries, one method is to compare the salaries of full-time SS men and officers with the wages earned by their contemporaries. The average weekly gross earnings for a German worker in 1936 was 34.39 RM, or 1,788.28 RM per year.[84] Among the highest paid professions were jobs involving book printing, with a wage of 50.49 RM per week, or 2,625.48 RM per year. At the bottom of the pay scale was the average wage for people employed in the baking industry, who earned 23.20 RM per week, or 1,206.40 RM per year. Based on these numbers, it is reasonable to presume that, accounting for both skilled and unskilled labour, the average, full-time German worker earned between 1,200 and 2,600 RM in 1936.[85]

In comparison, the lowest paid full-time SS member, an unmarried recruit, earned 125 RM per month, or 1,500 RM per year.[86] If a man had fulfilled the organization's ideal of joining the SS and advancing in rank – as outlined in a 1935 service guide – he would hold this entry-level position for approximately a year and a half.[87] Once he became an SS man, he would have the opportunity to ascend to the enlisted, non-commissioned, and commissioned officer ranks, which would allow him to earn more money. To make more than what the average German worker earned per year (1,788.28 RM), this unmarried SS man would have had to become a Rottenführer, which was the highest enlisted grade and came with a pay rate in 1936 of 160 RM per month, or 1,920 RM per year. For him to earn more than the highest non-SS wage earner, at 2,600 RM per year, he would have had to achieve three promotions to the non-commissioned officer rank of Oberscharführer, for which he would have earned 235 RM per month, or 2,820 RM per year. For married SS men, the respective ranks needed to earn approximately the same amount were one lower: an enlisted Sturmmann and a non-commissioned Scharführer. These numbers suggest that someone who joined the SS full-time and who rose to the higher enlisted or lower non-commissioned officer ranks most likely would have made more money on average than his non-SS affiliated counterpart working in the highest paying industries. Plus, this higher pay would have been augmented by the additional financial allowances from the SS.

For the monthly child stipends of 20–40 RM, one way to comprehend their basic value is to calculate their worth compared to a currency that existed then and now. The Reichsmark to American dollar exchange rate in 1936 was 2.48 RM to $1 and the relative worth of that dollar in

2016 is $58.10. Based on these rates, a 20 RM stipend from 1936 would equal approximately $469 in 2016 while 30 RM would equal $703 and 40 RM would equal $937.[88] Another marker by which to gauge the utility of the child stipend was its buying power. Newspapers, including *Das Schwarze Korps*, advertised household goods, thus providing a simple way to determine the Reichsmark's basic buying power. For example, an eight-piece bedroom set was advertised for 140 RM. A bookshelf cost 18 RM; to have an edition of *Mein Kampf* to place on it would cost 6–24 RM, depending on whether a person purchased a paper or leather-bound edition. A doll stroller ran between 8 and 10 RM, while a child's bicycle cost approximately 15 RM. More mundane items such as toothpaste cost 25–45 pfenning per tube (100 pfenning equaling 1 RM), while headache tablets ran between 60 pfenning and 3 RM.

These prices give a basic indication that the extra 20–40 RM per month for the child stipend would have provided an additional financial cushion. It most likely would not have convinced an SS man and his wife to have children, but it would have been of value to a couple who already wished to have children. This subsidy was also, as noted above, flexible, covering more than the traditional family of a husband, a wife, and their children. Family was not solely determined by biological relations, but by the ability and willingness of an SS man to care for children that included but were not limited to his legitimate, biological offspring.

This definitional flexibility correlates with another issue: illegitimacy. Despite the fact that most children were born in wedlock, the SS paid a substantial amount of attention to illegitimate children. This was a somewhat precarious issue. In general, German society disapproved of single mothers and their children, an attitude encouraged by both the Catholic and Protestant churches.[89] Even in the Nazi Party, there was no standard position, and many leaders opposed anything beyond the traditional norms of matrimony and family.[90] For example, in the Office for Racial Policy, Walter Groß was against illegitimate children. After his office received numerous inquiries on the issue, it released a statement indicating that while the unmarried mother and her child were a historic problem, the only sound solution was a coherent population policy. Nonetheless, despite his opposition, Groß thought that defaming unmarried mothers and their children was of no benefit, and that these women deserved protection from economic or social disadvantages that would be detrimental to the upbringing of their children.[91]

Himmler had a rather different opinion; he espoused some of the most liberal views on illegitimacy, views he encouraged SS men to accept. Himmler laid out his position in the mid-1930s. In one article, he noted that marriage and family represented "the best and most fertile solution" to Germany's low birth rate because they provided the most suitable environment to raise children and to incorporate them into the *Volk*. He further proclaimed "the family is the small Reich of which the larger Reich is made."[92] Nonetheless, Himmler thought it imperative that society "break through the small and holier-than-thou civil judgment against the unmarried mother and illegitimate children."[93] While he recognized that some illegitimate children were begotten through careless behaviour, and therefore had no value for the *Volk*, this could not be said of all of them. Many unmarried mothers were racially worthy and of good character; Himmler contended that so long as these women were valuable, and if the fathers of their children were worthy, too, then their children should be embraced as a beneficial addition to the *Volk*.[94]

Beyond accepting illegitimate children, Himmler wanted the SS to become the avant-garde when it came to changing the sexual and social mores of the German people. He did not want illegitimacy to replace marriage and legitimate children, believing that the erosion of marriage would lead to the dissolution of the family, which in turn would lead to the degeneration of the nation into Bolshevism.[95] Yet Himmler acknowledged that men and women did not abstain from sex before marriage, and he wanted the SS to break from Christian mores.[96] It was not that Himmler directly encouraged or even demanded that SS men have illegitimate children, but he did want to make sure that those men who wanted to have children outside of marriage felt free to do so. Among the men who did not wish to have extramarital offspring – the majority – he still wanted them to accept illegitimate children as equally valuable members of the SS and the *Volk*.

Himmler also did not tolerate members of the officer corps speaking poorly of unmarried mothers. Any time he heard of an officer making a snide comment, he requested to see that officer's genealogical tree. Himmler then examined the officer's ancestry to see if he had descended from a purely legitimate line. Oftentimes, Himmler claimed that he found at least one or two illegitimate ancestors, thus proving to his own satisfaction that the officer in question might very well have never been born were if not for his own less than perfect ancestry; in criticizing unmarried mothers, that officer had also berated his own ancestors.[97] Himmler pointed out that history – including the personal histories of some of his men – was replete with examples of unmarried women giving birth to children of good blood. He had no objections to this practice continuing, particularly when a father took care of his offspring.[98]

Himmler supported this rhetoric with action. Upon facing the dilemma of "brave and decent women of the most valuable blood" refusing to name the fathers of their children, he remarked that he had allowed the mother and the father to come to him and secretly acknowledge their child.[99] These acknowledgments were written down and locked up in a safe. Himmler also knew of cases where couples had made similar declarations before Hitler; they claimed that even though circumstances prevented them from recognizing their child publicly, they wanted the child to know his ancestry. Himmler made these comments before the Expert Council for Population and Racial Policy (i.e., a non-SS audience). By relating such comments to an audience of state officials and prominent scientists, he was probably suggesting that the private acknowledgment of paternity could be applied to the entire population.

An even larger project designed to assist mothers and children was the Lebensborn association. Meaning "fountain of life," the program was not created solely to aid unmarried mothers and illegitimate children, but it benefitted them as much as married mothers and legitimate children. Lebensborn homes were maternity hospitals where women – primarily those engaged or married to SS men, or those whose sexual relations with an SS man had resulted in a pregnancy – could receive care before, during, and after the birth of their children. The association also supported child-rich SS families.[100] The Lebensborn was founded in December 1935 by the RuSHA Office for Family Affairs. However, after January 1938, it was dissociated from RuSHA, subordinated to the SS Personal Staff, and reorganized under a board of directors led by Himmler.[101] The three men primarily responsible for the program were commissioned SS officers: Dr. Gregor Ebner served as the chief medical officer while first Dr. Guntram Pflaum, and later Max Sollmann, were responsible for administrative matters.

For a woman to enter a Lebensborn home, she had to be racially acceptable. Women who were engaged or married to an SS man already met such a standard, but single women had to prove their racial worth. They also had to divulge the name of the father, for he, too, had to be vetted.[102] While the father's name was revealed to Lebensborn officials and kept on file by the SS, the program supported an unmarried mother if she desired to keep these details confidential. Only she and the father received birth certificates, although the father's name might not appear on it to preserve his anonymity, particularly if he were married. No government official, private person, or party organization could obtain this information.[103] While using the privacy offered by the Lebensborn to shield themselves from scrutiny, especially for extramarital affairs, fathers had to take responsibility for their children. The Lebensborn did have several sources of income, allowing it to accept women regardless of their economic situation, but it did obligate men to provide for their children financially. Lebensborn authorities determined the amount each father had to pay based on his income and economic circumstances.[104]

Besides the father's personal obligation, Himmler declared that SS men had a "self-evident honorary duty" towards the Lebensborn program.[105] He desired that part-time officers and all men join, but he did not mandate their participation, whereas he did insist that all full-time officers join.[106] Monthly contributions were withdrawn from officers' salaries starting in October 1936. These were based on gross salaries, not including child allowances and other stipends, although Himmler could bend these rules when he saw fit.[107] Men holding the two lowest commissioned officer ranks, Untersturmführer and Obersturmführer, had to pay 1 RM per month. From the next rank, Hauptsturmführer, through the top of the officer ranks, the rates were determined by a sliding scale. The figure a man paid was not a set amount, but rather a percentage of his salary.[108] There was a general pattern to these rates. The higher a man's rank, the more he paid; the older a man was, the more he paid; if he were not married, he paid more. However, for each child a man had, he paid less. All biological children – legitimate and illegitimate – as well as other children he had taken responsibility for, were counted in his favour. Also, if an officer were divorced and supported his ex-wife, then the rate at which he was assessed was not based on his gross salary, but was adjusted to compensate for alimony payments.[109] Once an officer had joined the Lebensborn, he received a membership card and a receipt acknowledging his payments. A space in his personnel file was also marked off to indicate his membership, something that did not exist on the forms for enlisted men and non-commissioned officers.[110]

The point of these contributions was to ensure that every officer was paying for the upkeep of the family community; this became another duty, regardless of whether a man procreated or not. However, as in many cases, what Himmler wanted and what actually occurred were two different things. In the first year after he requested that officers join the program, only 4,600 of approximately 8,000 officers enrolled. That number increased slightly in early 1937, and by the beginning of 1939, the program had 13,300 members, 12,500 of whom were officers and enlisted men; at this time, the SS had more than 238,000 members.[111]

Part of the problem was that many men remained unaware of the program. Efforts were therefore made to rectify this matter. When the program was part of RuSHA, its employees working in each Oberabschnitt, along with officials employed in the Standarte support agencies, were tasked with informing the men in their units about the Lebensborn homes.[112] RuSHA even commissioned an educational primer. In addition, articles were placed in *SS-Leithefte*, a monthly magazine produced by the Education Office that served as a training guide.[113] Its articles on the Lebensborn program would have been useful for any unit training sessions or meetings with individual men.

More than a dozen articles in *Das Schwarze Korps* addressed some aspect of illegitimacy. Several indicated that single motherhood was not ideal because the best situation for the children was to have the parents together; when this was not possible, a father still had the moral obligation to care for his children. In addition, the newspaper took a notable stance on bourgeois morality, attacking the fact that women were scorned for illegitimate pregnancies when men were not.[114] One piece argued that men were just as responsible, while another indicated that men and women needed to be held to the same standards. With the related issue of adultery, the newspaper generally opposed it: "Once again, it is repeated: we still neither defend nor excuse the 'infidelity' of a man."[115] Yet when it came to the issue of reproduction, the newspaper did allow some leeway, suggesting that each man needed to decide which was the worse violation of nature: betraying his wife or not having children.[116]

These caveats aside, the newspaper was quite liberal in its support for illegitimate children. One article even pointed out that more than half of firstborn children were illegitimate because they were conceived prior to marriage – a fact the editors would have known to be relatively true in the SS if they had any knowledge of the marriage applications Himmler had approved due to pregnancy.[117] Beyond this particular statistic, the general purpose of these articles was to dispute the commonly held view that an illegitimate child was an aberration.

The newspaper argued that it could not subscribe to such a view, and that not all unwed mothers and illegitimate children should be looked down upon because every racially suitable illegitimate child deserved a place in the *Volksgemeinschaft*. It consistently contended that the state had a responsibility to find this place without devaluing marriage, and it mentioned on several occasions that the Lebensborn program had been designed for this very purpose.[118]

Two articles directly conveyed information about the program, one in January 1937 and the other from the following December.[119] The first showcased the original Lebensborn home located in Steinhöring, east of Munich. Accompanying photographs showed a home situated in an idyllic setting with clean medical facilities and comfortable accommodations. The article described the home as a place for a mother and her hereditarily worthy offspring. It indicated that these women and children were accepted regardless of the parents' marital status, thus publicly disclosing official approval of illegitimacy in the SS. The second article reported on an educational meeting for applicants of an SS unit in Berlin. Gregor Ebner spoke at this gathering, informing new recruits about the purpose of racial selection in the SS and membership in the Lebensborn. To a casual reader, these articles were just two among the dozens that appeared in each edition. But to an SS member, they served as a reminder about the program and his obligations towards it.

Again, the work of the Lebensborn was twofold: to care for racially worthy mothers and their children and to assist child-rich SS families. Regarding the second task, the Lebensborn provided money to each Oberabschnitt, which then distributed the funds to qualifying families in its section. These funds were exceedingly limited, as indicated in records from Oberabschnitt Fulda-Werra.[120] The division only had 200 RM per month, which it allocated in increments of 20 RM to ten families. When soliciting applications for this money, the division requested that its subordinate units advertise the Lebensborn program. According to the Fulda-Werra memorandum, only 4 per cent of SS members belonged to the program. The memo did not specify whether that figure referred specifically to the Oberabschnitt or to the entire SS. Regardless, it did point out that the more men who joined the Lebensborn, the more money that would be available for stipends for child-rich families.

The amount of funding available from the Lebensborn did not appear to increase in later years. At the beginning of 1939, Himmler received a report that reviewed the Lebensborn's work over the previous two years.[121] It indicated that the association paid monthly support to 110 child-rich families, a number that represented less than 6 per cent of child-rich SS families.[122] A total of 3,000 RM per month was allocated for this purpose; stipends ran between 20 and 50 RM per family, each determined by the family's size and its financial situation. In order to receive this money, a family had to submit an application, and a committee comprised of child-rich officers decided which families would obtain funding. Although meager – the 3,000 RM was intended for the entire SS – this stipend indicated that promoting the family was more than just rhetoric. The SS in general and the Lebensborn in particular were willing to back up their ideals when possible with concrete measures, in this case money. As with other SS stipends, Lebensborn funds alone were unlikely to encourage a man and his wife to have children, but this would have been a boon to a couple that already had or wanted to have a large family.

While financial assistance for child-rich families was emphasized in documents about and publicity for the Lebensborn program, far more attention was given to aiding the mothers and children residing in Lebensborn homes. Just over half of these children were illegitimate, while the remainder were the legitimate offspring of SS men, SA men, and police officers.[123] After caring for a mother during the end of her pregnancy and the birth of her child, Lebensborn officials encouraged mother and baby to leave the home. For married women, this request presented no problems, but the same could not always be said for unmarried mothers. If it were not possible for a woman to take her child, there were two possible solutions.[124] The first was to place the child in the home of an SS family temporarily. Preference would be given to childless couples, although already having offspring did not rule out the possibility of providing foster care. However, membership in the SS, or even the Nazi Party, was not a prerequisite. Lebensborn officials were most concerned about finding foster parents who would care for the child. They did not have many families from which to choose; as of mid-1937, only twenty-seven families had requested a child.[125]

In any case, the foster family would raise the child until the mother was able to resume her maternal responsibilities. Lebensborn authorities recognized that asking foster parents to care for a child only to take it away would create a hardship for them. Yet with regards to SS families, this hardship was seen as another sacrifice that a man and his wife should be willing to make. Furthermore, it was suggested that foster parents could still have a relationship with the child as honorary godparents.[126] Himmler never commented on this issue, but there is little reason to believe that he would have opposed it. He served as the godfather for scores of children, primarily the offspring of SS officers and men. He was also the godfather of any Lebensborn child born on his birthday – 7 October – whom he routinely provided with gifts, mainly money deposited into a savings account.[127]

If the mother were unable to take her child, there was a second solution: the foster parents had the option of adoption.[128] The child would not be their biological offspring, but as only racially worthy children came out of Lebensborn homes, any adopted child would have been just as valuable to the family community. *Das Schwarze Korps* promoted adoption in several articles, claiming that it was a perfectly viable option. "Children are the most precious property of our Volk," one article proclaimed. "They should all have a home and a family in our Reich."[129] In other articles the paper admitted that an adopted child might not take the place of a biological one, but this option would provide a couple otherwise denied children with the opportunity to contribute to the *Volk*.[130]

This perspective resonated with readers, leading some of them to write to *Das Schwarze Korps*. One of these letters, written by an SS-Scharführer, began by acknowledging that the goal should remain a marriage with many healthy children along with the smallest number of orphaned or illegitimate children. But reality had shown that there would always be couples who, through no fault of their own, were unable to have children; likewise, there would always be children in need of a good home. The Scharführer proclaimed that adoption would resolve both of these problems. To substantiate this claim, he relayed his own experience. The pain of wanting but not being able to have a child was great, especially for his wife. They did not initially consider adoption; no one in their families had adopted before, and their acquaintances tried to warn them against it by bringing to their attention some of the possible difficulties involved.

The Scharführer and his wife nonetheless chose to adopt, and he made it quite clear that they could not have made a better decision. "While today, on Easter Sunday, I am writing these lines, there are echoes of laughter and shouts from the nursery about the many small gifts that the 'Easter bunny' has brought, and my wife, with beaming eyes, brings the soup to our two little gorgeous blond heads of three and two years, a girl and a boy."[131] The Scharführer did not specify whether either of his children were illegitimate, although he did praise the state for emphasizing heredity, which would allow prospective adoptive parents to choose genetically healthy children. He also commended *Das Schwarze Korps* for including articles that sought to overturn the prejudice against illegitimate children.

While adoption could have been an ideal solution, very few were carried out. Biological mothers were generally unwilling to give up their children permanently, and most SS families showed little interest in adopting. Despite Himmler's efforts to have his men eschew middle-class, Christian morality, SS couples were disinclined to adopt the children of unwed mothers, whom they perceived to have loose morals.[132] Beyond this problem, the Lebensborn developed a less than wholesome reputation, and although historians have pointed out that the homes were not brothels or stud farms, this reputation has persisted.[133] Part of the reason is that most Lebensborn records are not available, and the men and women who either worked at or took advantage of a home chose not to speak about their experiences after the fact. Furthermore, those few stories that are known have created a distorted perception.

For example, some of the women who had illegitimate children were teenagers who came from the League of German Girls or the Reich Labor Service.[134] One such young woman, Hildegard Trutz, spoke of her experience to journalist Louis Hagen in the late 1940s. Even after the collapse of the Third Reich, Trutz held fast to Nazi ideology, believing in her position as a "Nordic Beauty with the 'child-bearing pelvis.' "[135] Having finished her education in the mid-1930s, she had spoken to her league leader about what she could do with her time. The leader suggested that Trutz could give a child to the Führer. It was also from this same woman that Trutz learned about the Lebensborn homes, which she thought "sounded wonderful."[136]

Trutz went to a "luxurious" home in Bavaria. There she learned about the Führer's desire to have the Reichsführer pair a small group of women of good Nordic stock with equally superior SS men in order to found a racial elite. This task was an honourable duty, one that Trutz proudly completed. She and the other young women were introduced to SS men and were given a week to choose a specific man. Once Trutz had chosen, she was given permission to receive him at night, although she noted he was having sexual relations with more than one woman. Trutz told Hagen that she and the SS man "had no shame or inhibition of any kind" because they "believed completely in the importance of what we were doing."[137] She was quite proud that it did not take long for her to get pregnant. From that point, she lived in the home until the

birth of her son, whom she kept for only two weeks. Lebensborn officials thanked Trutz for her work and told her that she could come back
in a year if she were interested. She never did. Still, her willingness to
devote almost a year of her life to conceiving and carrying a child for
no other reason than to fulfil the biological expectations of the Nazi
state and its leader is telling. As seen with the issue of adoption, many
couples did not reject traditional views of premarital sex and illegitimate children. Yet Trutz's story shows that the ideal of breeding, not
to build a family, but to contribute to the racial state, did resonate with
some women.

Trutz ended up marrying another SS man a few months prior to the
war. Interestingly, while she was proud of her premarital maternal
duty, her husband did not approve. "I was rather surprised," Trutz told
Hagen, "to find that he was not as pleased about it as he might have
been. Of course, he couldn't very well say anything against it, seeing
that I had been doing my duty to the Führer, but he didn't like it mentioned."[138] These comments must be read with care. By the time Trutz
gave this interview, she hated her husband (now a prisoner in a British
camp). She blamed him for all of her problems, and she had been trying
to divorce him since the end of the war. Her portrait of him was therefore anything but flattering. Yet given her own positive impression of
her experiences at the Lebensborn home and her husband's negative
reaction to it, Trutz's story suggests that many SS men did not abandon
conventional morality when it came to marriage and children.

While most SS men did not have children before marriage or commit
adultery, there were several notable men who did, thus adding to the
Lebensborn's sordid reputation. Among them was one of the highest-
ranking officers in the SS: Karl Wolff. In 1937, Wolff had an affair with
Ingeborg Bernstorff that resulted in a pregnancy. To avoid any gossip,
Wolff turned to fellow SS-Gruppenführer Reinhard Heydrich, head of
the Reich Security Main Office. Given his experience handling delicate
and secretive matters, Heydrich was able to arrange for Bernstorff to
travel under a false name and passport to the clinic of a well-respected
gynecologist in Budapest. After giving birth, Bernstorff returned home
while her son was placed in the Steinhöring home. Several months later
she took in her own son as a foster child.[139]

Cases like this were not common. But they happened frequently
enough that Lebensborn officials accommodated the needs of married
men, whether that meant allowing the biological mother to take the
child or arranging for the biological father and his unsuspecting wife

to adopt his child. The Lebensborn was more than willing to aid an unfaithful man in order to keep his marriage intact, thereby allowing him to produce as many children as possible.[140] This decision to place biological duty above marital vows reinforced the Lebensborn program's purpose of aiding in the creation of valuable children, regardless of the specific circumstances. Although few people used the program, it showed how Himmler implemented concrete measures to further his desire to create a "master" race. He saw no problem with bending traditional morality as long as it meant producing racially pure children that would be of good use in the future, be it as soldiers or mothers. Such flexibility fit perfectly with his conceptions of blood, race, and *Volk*.

It was these same conceptions that brought Himmler into conflict with eugenicists. They advocated strengthening the institutions of marriage and family, and they questioned the value of an unmarried mother. "The family is irreplaceable," Fritz Lenz wrote in 1932, "not only as the life and educational community, but also for the conservation of the race."[141] This perspective – which was in line with what Lenz and his co-authors Baur and Fischer had advocated more than a decade earlier – was also promoted by other eugenicists and medical professionals.[142] Otmar von Verschuer commented that "the human being is no breeding animal," and he argued for the protection of traditional marriage.[143] Physician Hermann Paull wrote a guidebook in 1934 designed to convince Germans of the value of eugenics and of the necessity of selecting a healthy marriage partner. He argued that "the sentiment must be hammered into the heads of the people: *the moral, hereditarily healthy child-rich family is the basic cell of the state.*"[144] Only the family could safeguard Germany's future welfare.

Martin Staemmler concurred with Paull's sentiment in the same book in which he praised the SS engagement and marriage command, hence doubly proving his staunch adherence to the value of marriage. However, Staemmler did indicate – much like Walter Groß – that the question of illegitimate children could never be avoided completely, and that the state should help the unmarried mother and her illegitimate child if the father was known and if both parents were hereditarily worthy.[145] Yet Hermann Siemens warned in his 1934 book that supporting illegitimate children too extensively would have an unfavourable effect. Illegitimate children, he claimed, tended to suffer from mental weaknesses more commonly than legitimate ones. He also argued that illegitimate children should not be counted when it came to birth policies designed to aid the population. Overall, he asserted, "an increase in illegitimate births is not in the interest of our race and our Volk."[146] Siemens was an important voice on this issue, not only for what he said, but where he said it: the KWI-A used his book in its medical courses for SS doctors. RuSHA also promoted Siemens's book to all SS members interested in learning more about population politics.[147]

For all of these reactions against illegitimacy, none was as problematic as the comments made by Fritz Lenz in 1937. In June of that year, the Reich Ministry of the Interior held a conference on illegitimate children. Lenz expressed his opposition to illegitimacy at this meeting, claiming that such children were undesirable because they were of lesser genetic and intellectual value.[148] In addition, in an article published in the scientific journal *Volk und Rasse*, he stated "that illegitimate births are undesirable from a racial hygienic population policy point of view."[149] Measures should be taken, Lenz argued, to reduce the number of illegitimate births.[150] Himmler was not pleased by Lenz's speech or article, which he sought (but failed) to suppress – a surprising failure given that the SS had controlled *Volk und Rasse* since 1933.[151] Himmler's displeasure also did not prevent the journal from publishing a second article on the subject later that year.[152]

The conflict with eugenicists once more illustrates how Himmler selectively chose the eugenic ideals best suited to his purposes and ignored any idea that did not buttress his model of the SS as a racial order. Still, this one conflict should not be blown out of proportion. Himmler might not have liked the approach taken by Lenz, let alone any other scientist and physician, but he did not rebuff them for their opposition.[153] He even favoured granting party membership to Lenz, among other eugenicists, in the year after Lenz's less than supportive commentary was published. In a letter to Hitler's deputy, Rudolf Heß, Himmler acknowledged Lenz's contributions, as well as those of Eugen Fischer, "to the substantiation and scientific recognition of the racial part of the National Socialist world view."[154] He proclaimed that "despite some surely existing misgivings," both men should be accepted into the party. Himmler even suggested that membership was "a certain political necessity" because it would otherwise be impossible to use these men's ideas as a "scientific underpinning for the party." Lenz, along with Alfred Ploetz, subsequently joined the party in 1938; Fischer and Otmar von Verschuer accepted membership a few years later.[155]

In all of these efforts – emphasizing the value of good blood, exhorting SS men to fulfil their duty to have children, prohibiting homosexuality and abortion, providing financial allowances, and abetting illegitimate births – Himmler had the same goal: fostering the birth of as many "superior" children as possible. However, despite all of the appeals and incentives aimed at fostering the creation of child-rich families, SS men came nowhere near to achieving the population goals their leader set for them. The ideal of at least four racially healthy children per man was nothing more than a fantasy.

Statistics compiled in 1936, 1937, and 1938 reveal just how far below this ideal the numbers were. The *Statistical Yearbook* for each of those years assessed the numbers of children per family. In 1936, there were over 50,500 marriages; included in this count were nearly 700 widowed and divorced men. Of those couples, almost 14 per cent were childless. Among couples with children, 52 per cent had 1 child, 30 per cent had 2 children, and 12 per cent had 3 children. Only 6 per cent had 4 or more children. Altogether, all marriages produced an average of 1.5 children. When the average was broken down by Oberabschnitt, only one division, Oberabschnitt Südost, had an average of 2 children per marriage; Oberabschnitt Mitte had the lowest average, at 1.2. When compared with the averages for the Reich, the report in the 1936 *Statistical Yearbook* stated that the SS had produced 32 per cent fewer children. It also stated that part of the reason for this disparity could be that the average age when an SS man married (32 years) was higher than the federal average.[156]

In 1937, the average number of children decreased, with 1.2 children per marriage.[157] The numbers in 1938 were even lower: 1.1 children. Almost 40 per cent of marriages were childless, although among those marriages about 45 per cent of couples had been wed for a year or less. In addition, fewer than 5 per cent of marriages had 4 or more children, and the SS still, as it had in 1936, lagged behind the federal birth rate. The 1938 statistics are notable for one other reason. Beyond accounting for the number of children produced by each marriage, the 1938 *Statistical Yearbook* included the number of children born to single SS men. Children born out of wedlock accounted for just over 0.75 per cent of the children.[158] Still, including them reconfirmed the lack of official stigma towards illegitimacy.

Beyond the SS as a whole, statistics were compiled on the officer corps by the SS Personnel Chancellery. These reports were far more detailed as the author(s) broke down the numbers by marital status, age, and full- or part-time service in the SS. They also listed comprehensive numbers. For 1936, just over 25 per cent of married officers had no children, 31 per cent had only 1 child, 25 per cent had 2 children, and

12 per cent had 3 children; only 7 per cent were child-rich. In 1937, the percentages remained comparable.[159] The average number of children per married SS officer was 1.52 children, a number that declined to 1.48 children in 1938.[160]

These averages, while slightly higher than those for the entire SS, were well below the four children per marriage needed to aid the growth of the *Volk* and slightly lower than the number of children per non-SS family in approximately the same time frame.[161] Himmler told his Gruppenführer that while he understood the SS had a large contingent of young officers whom he could not yet expect to marry and have children, he found such low numbers "fatal."[162] He characterized the birth deficit among the higher ranks as particularly problematic in a second speech before the police: "The higher the rank, the fewer the children. That is ingratitude against the Volk and Führer."[163] This speech was just as significant as the ones routinely given to the Gruppenführer, as many police officers belonged to the SS and were responsible for adhering to all edicts regarding their marital and familial choices.

Unlike the marriage statistics examined in the previous chapter, in which statisticians in the SS Personnel Chancellery attempted to explain the possible reasons for the high marriage ages of SS men, no such comparable explanations were given for children. More time was spent projecting how many children men could have if they married at an appropriate age (twenty-seven – the average age in the Reich and five years below the SS average) and had a child at least every three years through age forty-one.[164] Space was also dedicated to lamenting the fact that physically and racially healthy men were not procreating.[165] However, these statistical documents also acknowledged that the number of children per marriage was related to the man's age when he married. Higher marriage ages could to some extent account for the low birth numbers.[166] For this reason, one of the reports noted that a high marriage age and a low birth number would have devastating consequences for the SS after one generation. If members did not recognize their duty to have child-rich families, then the SS would have to take special care to recruit from outside its current families. Otherwise, a perpetual cycle of small families would doom the bearers of the best blood from contributing to the racial renewal of the *Volk*.[167]

Over the course of the 1930s, Himmler sought to mould the SS into an organization that could meet the present and future needs of the Reich. Part of this plan included assuring the continuation of the genetic lineage of his men. Measures were designed to encourage the creation of biologically valuable, child-rich families. These pre-war measures included the use of rhetoric emphasizing the value of Nordic blood, letters and speeches exhorting men to have children, articles promoting families and fatherhood, prohibitions against homosexuality and abortion, financial stipends, and support for illegitimacy. Altogether, these components emphasized that the formation of a family was as vital a duty for each SS man as any other responsibility to the organization. They established an ideal for which quality and quantity were seen as crucial elements of success. Reality, however, failed to reflect this ideal, especially the desire for each family to have at least four children. The outbreak of the war would only magnify this problem as the responsibility for every man to preserve his lineage by establishing a family grew more imperative.

Chapter Three

Marriage during the Second World War

Himmler did not want the war to prevent him from achieving his aim of moulding the SS into a racial elite. Of the measures meant to achieve this goal, the majority remained in place. However, with the onset of the war, the SS did revise existing measures relating to marriage and implement new initiatives. Many alterations came in the form of commands, although men were given some leeway in complying due to the war. By making these changes and allowing this leniency, Himmler sought to balance his goal of building a family community that could ensure a victory in the cradle with his desire of establishing a military branch that could contribute to the Reich's overall victory. In doing so, Himmler demonstrated his ability to modify his priorities, at least in the short term.[1] While adjusting policies as needed, he remained committed to his core objectives and aspirations, which included transforming marriage into the cornerstone of a racial elite.

The Race and Settlement Main Office remained responsible for overseeing engagements and marriages. Günther Pancke continued to supervise the office until early July 1940. Of the four RuSHA chiefs, he was the only one who needed Himmler's permission to marry as well as the only one to have four children.[2] He was replaced by Otto Hofmann, who administered RuSHA until mid-April 1943, and was followed by Richard Hildebrandt.[3] Unlike Darré, neither Pancke, Hofmann, or Hildebrandt had any formal education or publications relating to the Nordic race or blood and soil ideology. Only Hofmann had any prior experience with RuSHA, first as a Race and Settlement leader in Düsseldorf and then as the head of the RuSHA Office for Family Affairs and its Office for Racial Affairs.[4]

The Office for Family Affairs remained responsible for the engagement and marriage process during the first half of the war, but as of

1942, its responsibilities were divided between two departments: the Genealogical Office (Ahnentafelamt) and the Marriage Office (Heiratsamt), which took over the majority of the tasks related to engagements and marriages.[5] The looming threat of war in the summer of 1939 led to some relaxation of the regulations governing that process. These changes were not hastily conceived; the need to modify the marriage and engagement process had been discussed since the previous summer. At the time, SS-Sturmbannführer Helmut Poppendick, who worked in RuSHA's Office for Population Politics and Hereditary Health Care, and who also served as Arthur Gütt's adjutant in the Interior Ministry, reported that the ministry intended to relax marriage policies in case of war and suggested that the SS do the same.[6]

RuSHA began working on this task at some point during the next year, and Günther Pancke submitted a draft of an order to Himmler in late June 1939. Within less than a week, Himmler had approved Pancke's draft and requested that the RuSHA chief resubmit it to him in due time for his signature. He resubmitted the order on 26 August, explaining that he planned to announce the changes only after mobilization.[7] Himmler signed off on the command, which was announced on 1 September, the day Germany invaded Poland.[8]

Any SS member who wished to expedite the marriage process because of mobilization only had to submit the race and settlement questionnaire and the genealogical tree. The two medical forms were desired, but they were not necessary – a move that placed military mobilization ahead of racial demands for the time being. RuSHA officials made their decision within a few hours, most often approving the application as long as the questionnaire and the genealogical tree revealed no serious hereditary flaws on the part of the SS man or his fiancée. If further verification uncovered medical or racial problems, the SS man had to accept the consequences – namely, his possible dismissal from the SS.

When the command was issued, Himmler did not clarify why he had allowed these changes. However, in a March 1943 letter to SS-Obergruppenführer Udo von Woyrsch, Himmler wrote that at the beginning of the war he had wrestled with the question of whether he should promote marriages without first educating SS men about the proper life laws and racial regulations.[9] He subsequently told Woyrsch that he wanted to promote marriage among his men, and that he was willing to allow for mistakes that might result from this decision. The important thing, Himmler wrote, was that each man had at least one child before he fell. In order to facilitate the birth of these children, he was willing to risk the possibility that a minority of them would not meet SS racial standards. Even if a few of the children were not racially impeccable, Himmler argued, poor blood was better than no blood, especially when it came to boys who could later serve in the armed forces.

Five months later, in January 1940, Himmler issued a supplementary command returning the required paperwork to pre-war levels.[10] As with the September 1939 order, he did not indicate why he had changed the requirements, although it would not be unreasonable to presume that Germany's favourable military situation might have influenced his decision. With Poland divided between Germany and the Soviet Union and fighting on the western front yet to begin, the war would not have inhibited men from gathering and submitting the full paperwork. Several months later, the SS court confirmed the significance of the January command by declaring that it, along with the original December 1931 command, was a basic law (*Grundgesetz*) of the SS, and that violation of any basic law was grounds for expulsion.[11]

Outside of this court decree, Pancke issued detailed instructions on the re-expanded engagement and marriage process.[12] Among the guidelines given by Pancke and reconfirmed by additional decrees, medical examinations for both the man and his future bride were strongly encouraged. Evaluations by SS doctors (the preferred method) were still free, but these doctors' availability had decreased due to the need for their services in the armed forces. As a result, if an SS doctor were unavailable, a man had permission to visit the military doctor responsible for his unit and a woman could request an examination from a non-SS-affiliated doctor.[13] Once RuSHA received the completed medical questionnaires along with the other requisite forms, its officials evaluated the application. As with the September 1939 order, the January 1940 command proclaimed that if further investigation revealed hereditary problems, the SS man might have to leave the organization.

By this time, the regulations applied to anyone who belonged to the SS. The original 1931 command had affected only the Allgemeine-SS, then the organization's sole branch, but two others had been formed in the mid-1930s. The first was the Totenkopfverbände (or Death's Head Unit). Its members primarily worked as guards in the concentration camps. The second was the Verfügungstruppe, an infantry division that also provided a bodyguard unit for Hitler.[14] All engagement and marriage commands applied to members of these two branches, and in July 1938, the regulations were extended to Himmler's other domain, the police. In addition, after Germany annexed Austria and the Sudetenland in, respectively, March and September 1938, the rules were extended to new SS members from these territories.[15]

Further expansion took place during the war. In January 1940, Himmler widened his orders to include the Waffen-SS, the militarized branch that had been created from the four Verfügungstruppe units that had existed at the start of the war.[16] Many members of the Allgemeine-SS transferred into the Waffen-SS while others were called up for duty in the Wehrmacht. Irrespective of what branch a man served in, the engagement and marriage requirements were equally applicable. As in the pre-war period, reassignment to the armed forces did not negate an SS man's responsibility to obtain authorization from RuSHA to wed – a fact soldiers were repeatedly reminded of throughout the war.[17]

The early movement of men into the Waffen-SS and the Wehrmacht initially included only German citizens, but as the war continued the SS turned to foreign recruits. These individuals fell into three categories: *Volksdeutsche* (ethnic Germans that did not live in Germany); Germanic volunteers (foreign nationals who were acceptable because of their Nordic heritage); and other volunteers from Western and Eastern Europe. For the first half of the war, recruitment to the Waffen-SS was primarily voluntary. Unofficial conscription began in the middle of 1942; by 1943 it had spread to most countries allied with or occupied by Germany.[18]

Adding foreign volunteers and conscripts changed the composition of the SS. In 1940, the bulk of membership came from Germany, but by 1944, *Volksdeutsche* represented the largest population in the SS.[19] This shift meant that while Himmler might have wanted to maintain the organization's racial purity, the exigencies of war and the corresponding need for a large military force tempered the realization of such an ideal. And yet, regardless of when and how these men had joined, Himmler continued to insist that SS members who did not have German citizenship request permission to marry.[20] High-ranking Waffen-SS officers passed on these decrees reiterating that the engagement and marriage process applied to everyone. The continual publication of commands informed new members that their service was multifaceted and included familial obligations.

There was one other group affected by wartime expansion. In 1943, Himmler required female employees of the SS and the police to seek his approval before getting married. These women needed to submit genealogical records and the medical examination forms, but their future husbands, if they did not belong to the SS or the police, merely had to submit a genealogical tree.[21] The order did not indicate how far back the women and their future husbands had to prove their descent, but it would be reasonable to presume the standard cutoff of 1800.

Despite the increasingly inclusive nature of the engagement and marriage command, some people were exempt. In October 1940, the RuSHA Office for Family Affairs issued a letter that clarified who did not need to request permission. Anyone who had joined the Waffen-SS, including the Death's Head Units, during the war but who did not intend to remain in the SS following it were not obligated to obtain authorization. The Office for Family Affairs recommended that the Waffen-SS command record the names of these men. Over a month later, the Waffen-SS published this exception in its ordinance gazette.[22] Neither the RuSHA letter nor the ordinance was signed by Himmler, but the publication of the information in the ordinance gazette suggests that he approved it, at least for the time being. Less than two years later, RuSHA rescinded this exemption.[23] Henceforth, all Waffen-SS members had to obtain authorization to wed, even men who had volunteered for the war and had no intention of joining the Allgemeine-SS afterwards. The Waffen-SS announced this policy change in its ordinance gazette in October 1942 and again in February 1944. The February edition also stated that men in training needed to be informed about the basic laws of the SS, especially its marriage regulations.[24]

It appears that there were only two later exemptions. In May 1944, Himmler exempted those men who had joined the SS guard units (Wach-verbände) from the Wehrmacht.[25] Later that month, SS-Brigadeführer Otto Heider, chief of the Marriage Office, wrote that enlisted and non-com Waffen-SS members who were from a "foreign Volk and state affiliation" and who were not regarded as compatible with the SS could marry without approval from RuSHA.[26] They only needed authorization from their company leader or battalion commander. Officers, on the other hand, still needed Himmler's approval. Combined with the earlier exemptions, these two exceptions demonstrated that marriage policies were hardly static. Racial ideals demanded rigidity, but the reality of war necessitated periodic flexibility.

This flexibility probably affected few Waffen-SS soldiers. Most men needed permission to marry, and based on the available documentation, most seemed to obtain it, even when circumstances were less than ideal. As in the pre-war period, Himmler approved the marriages of officers and reviewed applications where rejection was highly possible.[27] One case involved a candidate named Fritz C. In the summer of 1940, he requested permission to marry, but the medical examination revealed that Fritz was infertile due to gonorrhea. The RuSHA physician who reviewed these findings recommended that Fritz's final acceptance into the SS be denied. Himmler disagreed; he was willing to allow Fritz to join and to approve his marriage if his future bride notified RuSHA that she was aware of his infertility and still wished to marry him. In addition, Himmler mandated that the couple agree to adopt at least three children if they had not conceived within one year of their marriage.[28] Upon learning of this qualified approval, Fritz submitted a short letter to RuSHA in which he declared, "it is not possible for me to accept your conditions."[29] He intended to marry his bride without prerequisites, and so he requested an honourable discharge. Himmler granted Fritz's request, dismissing him in September.[30]

While Fritz C. did not take Himmler's offer, his situation might have convinced Himmler that some latitude was necessary when it came to cases of infertility. He did not issue an order, but, according to a physician working in the Family Office, he made a private statement on the subject around the same time.[31] Himmler declared that if a couple were willing to adopt if they did not have any biological children within ten years, then he was willing to release responsibility to them. As in the 1930s, this conditional approval meant that they could marry but could not join the family community. The reason behind this shift, at least according to the physician, was that infertility could not be determined with certainty unless reproductive organs had been removed. It was equally possible that Himmler simply did not want to lose men during the war; adoption was therefore a viable alternative to dismissal.

Even then, there was some flexibility, as seen in the situation of Adolf K., another applicant. The paperwork revealed that the hereditarily healthy Adolf, a Wehrmacht soldier and Iron Cross recipient, was an ideal candidate for the SS; the issue was with Friede, the woman he wished to marry. Friede's medical examination revealed that pregnancy was unlikely because her right ovary and half of her left ovary had been removed during a surgery.[32] A follow-up medical examination in the summer of 1943 confirmed her inability to conceive, leading Himmler to agree to approve the marriage only after a confirmed pregnancy.[33] This stipulation was slightly at odds with his standard reluctance to approve a marriage application from a man who submitted paperwork only after his bride was pregnant. Moreover, there was no way to confirm whether Adolf and Friede were willing to disregard societal norms and engage in premarital sexual relations to meet this condition. Whether or not they tried to conceive, Friede was not pregnant when Adolf resubmitted his application later in the year. Despite the remaining concerns about Friede's inability to conceive, Himmler released the marriage to Adolf's responsibility after reviewing the material a second time.[34] The paper-work did not reveal if Himmler made the same demand of Adolf that he had of Fritz C. – that he and his wife adopt if they could not conceive – but it is plausible that this issue would have been raised eventually.

A third case sent to Himmler involved SS-Unterscharführer Kurt A., who submitted his request to marry Lieselotte A. in the summer of 1939. He asked for a quick decision because she was pregnant, but by the start of the war RuSHA had not yet responded to his petition. Both Kurt and Lieselotte wrote to RuSHA in September asking for an update; they learned at the end of the month that their case had to be submitted to Himmler.[35] Lieselotte wrote to RuSHA again at the end of the following month. She requested a favourable response. She did not get one; the Family Office informed Kurt that Himmler refused to grant him permission because Lieselotte did not appear to meet the physical requirements of the SS.[36]

Although unmentioned in the rejection letter, the basis of this judg-ment was not only Kurt's and Lieselotte's application, but also a follow-up report filed with RuSHA by SS-Untersturmführer Oehl, the Race and Settlement leader in Oberabschnitt Fulda-Werra. He had met with Lieselotte and her mother, and his appraisal of Lieselotte was not posi-tive. Oehl wrote that she had Asian features, including yellow-brown skin and a round face, which he surmised she had inherited from her father. He commented that she had a fair mental disposition, but had suffered some health problems during the early months of her preg-nancy.[37] Now rejected on the basis of these findings, the Family Office instructed Kurt to report back on whether he would withdraw his mar-riage application, thus indicating that he had ended his relationship with Lieselotte, or if he preferred to resign from the SS.

Displeased with this decision, Lieselotte, and not Kurt, replied in late December 1939 with a letter – though not to RuSHA, or even to Him-mler, but to Hitler himself. She began by apologizing for burdening him, but made it clear that she was heartbroken and had turned to him for help. She explained her situation – including the fact that she was eight months pregnant – and begged Hitler to intervene because she wished to marry the father of her child before she delivered so that her child would be legitimate. "I truly know that you, my Führer, now have very much work and great concern for our Volk," she wrote, "but I believe that you nevertheless understand my request and letter and I would be very much indebted to you if you would get in touch with Reichsführer-SS Himmler in this issue and check the matter again."[38]

Once again, she requested a favourable outcome, especially because she sought to fulfil her duty as a wife and mother.

The Führer's chancellery received her letter and promptly passed it along to Himmler. This led to an exchange in early 1940 between Himmler and Philipp Bouhler, the chief of Hitler's chancellery and an SS-Obergruppenführer. Himmler explained why he had refused to grant the couple permission to wed, but also asked Bouhler for his opinion. Bouhler agreed that Lieselotte did not appear to be racially suitable for the SS. However, he stated that while he was "of the opinion that only you can decide the case … I must openly confess to you that exactly in consideration of the war and the existing child, I would personally be inclined to let clemency prevail here." He then reiterated that this was only his opinion, and that he did not want to anticipate or influence Himmler's decision.[39]

Lieselotte had no knowledge of this correspondence, but the chancellery had informed her that her request had been sent to Himmler. This prompted her to write to Himmler in January, again asking for a prompt and favourable response. In consideration of the war, Himmler showed the couple leniency and released the marriage to their "own responsibility." The couple wed in late April.[40] By this time, Lieselotte had given birth to their child.

Aside from demonstrating Himmler's involvement in situations where rejection was probable, this case also shows that he reviewed cases with exceptional circumstances, such as when the fiancée was pregnant.[41] Lieselotte was hardly the only woman whose application Himmler reviewed for this reason. Wartime statistics show that 13–15 per cent of officers and 20–25 per cent of enlisted men requested permission to wed due to pregnancy.[42] However, whereas before the war Himmler lambasted his men and their superiors for submitting the paperwork because of pregnancy, he complained less frequently once the conflict began.

Nonetheless, on one occasion Himmler did write an officer to tell him that requesting permission to marry his pregnant fiancée was "cavalier and unchivalrous … [and] unworthy of an SS man."[43] These sentiments reinforce the now well-known discrepancy in Himmler's opinions on marriage and fatherhood. He accepted illegitimate children of good blood, but at the same time took offence when SS men sought to get married only after their girlfriends were pregnant. He could bend traditional morality in the name of producing children of "good blood" in the first instance, but not in the second. In Himmler's view, violating the engagement and marriage order represented a worse transgression than having an illegitimate child.

But while Himmler's response to pregnancy demonstrated a certain amount of flexibility because of his desire to have his men produce as many children of good blood as possible, there were other issues that he was less inclined to overlook. As in the pre-war period, approval was often denied if a bride were deemed unacceptable because of her nationality. For example, while a woman from Alsace or Lorraine was a suitable choice, a woman from another region of France was not.[44] In addition, a woman who had previously been married to a Jew was barred from marrying an SS man.[45] The presence of a Jewish ancestor was likewise grounds for rejection.[46] When dealing with this particular question, the position of second-grade *Mischling* – people declared by the Nuremberg Laws to be one-quarter Jewish who were to be treated as German – and the possible influence of Jewish blood led to a series of statistical analyses throughout 1943.[47]

A woman was also rejected if her family history revealed hereditary defects or diseases.[48] This was the case with Anna H., who sought to wed SS-Untersturmführer Walter J. in 1942. Her cousin had committed suicide, her aunt suffered from schizophrenia, her grandmother was insane, and her grandfather was supposedly a drunk.[49] After learning this information, Himmler wrote to Walter's superior, SS-Gruppenführer Bruno Streckenbach, asking him to speak with his subordinate and explain why he could not marry Anna. Streckenbach complied and then reported back on his conversation. He had told Walter that he could remain in the SS, but he needed to understand that it was not possible to marry a woman who could not give him many healthy children; such a union, he informed Walter, would give him no personal satisfaction. Walter, according to Streckenbach, refused to concede. He also refused to acknowledge the hereditary illnesses among the members of his potential bride's family, claiming that the doctors had assured him of the opposite. Walter furthermore told Streckenbach that due to his age and his current wartime service, he was not in a position to look for another woman to wed. Finally, he informed his superior that he did not want to break his word to Anna.[50]

Walter also wrote to Himmler. He stated that after considering his situation and reflecting on his conversation with Streckenbach, he had decided to marry Anna. Having reached this decision, and because he was soon leaving for the eastern front, he asked for a prompt answer.[51] In relaying his final decision to RuSHA, Himmler declared that he "did not expect such a lack of understanding of the principles of the SS from an SS officer," and that he did "not understand how [Walter] could simply say the he did not believe in the possibility of inherent illness in the family of his bride."[52] He was evidently baffled that Walter did not understand that the point of a marriage was to have children. Himmler therefore not only rejected his marriage application, but ordered his release from the SS in early January 1943.[53]

Nationality, Jewish ancestry, and hereditary illness all served as grounds for rejecting a woman and denying a marriage application. But in terms of what Himmler would allow, the boundary between ideal and reality was often blurry, as the cases of SS-Obersturmführer Mayr, SS-Brigadeführer Walter Schellenberg, and SS-Gruppenführer Walter Krüger illustrate. Himmler learned that Mayr's wife was one-quarter Jewish. Such information would have led to the refusal of a new application, but Mayr and his wife had married prior to this discovery and already had three children. Himmler allowed Mayr to remain in the SS provided that he and his wife had no additional children, and he was informed that his children would never be allowed into the organization.[54]

This lenient response was almost exactly the opposite of the one SS man Karl M. had received prior to the war. He had been expelled in 1934 because he had learned that his wife, who he had married in early 1930, was half-Jewish. Karl explained to his superiors that while he had been unaware of her Jewish heritage, the only reason he had married her was out of consideration for their daughter, who had been born in late 1929. His unit did not accept this justification and applied for his expulsion, which was granted.[55] Karl divorced his wife in 1934 and then requested readmission to the SS in late 1935. His status as an old party member, along with his service to both the SA and SS, stood in his favour.

However, upon reviewing Karl's paperwork, the RuSHA Racial Office expressed concern. The office questioned his motivation for divorcing his wife, suggesting that he used the knowledge of her Jewish heritage as an excuse. In a letter to the Family Office, the Racial Office also raised concerns about Karl's lack of racial instinct:

> The SS, as an association of Nordic men and families, must reject in principle having men in its ranks that have had or still have any form of kinship or sexual relations with foreign races (non-Aryans). If the person concerned has also not been aware that he has come into a close relationship with a Jewish-blooded girl, this clearly shows that his healthy racial instinct for good blood is lacking. Even if they realize their mistake, one never has with such people the security that such a failure in matters of racial instincts will not recur in any form. Since the SS should become

a family association with clearly drawn reproductive goals, it must place more value on healthy instincts in blood questions that really manifest itself in the life of the person than on deliberate avowals.[56]

Even with the positive reports on Karl's character, the Racial Office found that having an SS member with a "Jewish-blooded child that carries his name" was simply untenable.[57] Therefore, the Racial Office did not advocate allowing Karl to rejoin.[58] These objections were forwarded to the SS Main Office, which rejected Karl's readmission application in early 1936.[59] Not enough information is available in either case to determine if there might have been additional reasons for why Karl's expulsion for lack of "healthy racial instinct" was not overturned, while Mayr was neither dismissed from the SS nor required to end his marriage to remain in good standing with the organization. Still, based on the available information, Himmler's lenience toward Mayr was just one of the many exceptions he granted during the war.

As for Walter Schellenberg, neither his first nor his second marriage conformed to SS requirements. His first wife, whom he married in early 1938, was eight years older; he had needed Himmler's approval due to this age difference. He encountered a different problem when he sought to marry a second time in 1940: his future mother-in-law was Polish. Knowing that his application would likely be rejected, Schellenberg elicited help from his superior in the Reich Security Main Office, Reinhard Heydrich. Heydrich intervened on Schellenberg's behalf in September 1940, and within less than a week, he had secured Himmler's approval. A letter in Schellenberg's RuSHA file referenced the meeting between Heydrich and Himmler, but did not specify what Heydrich had said to persuade Himmler to approve Schellenberg's second marriage.[60]

Schellenberg probably did not know the content of their conversation either, as he did not provide any details in his post-war memoirs. But he did note that Heydrich's intercession had come at a high price. Six months after he was married, Schellenberg received a copy of the dossier that the Gestapo had compiled on his wife's family. The Reich security chief maintained this file until his assassination in 1942. Schellenberg commented in his memoirs that by asking for and receiving aid from Heydrich, he had given his boss the means to entrap him, which he already suspected his superior had been trying to do. Yet beyond this consequence, Schellenberg's second marriage was apparently successful and led to three children.[61]

In the case of Walter Krüger, because he had been married almost a decade prior to the engagement and marriage command, the issue was not with him, but with his children. When his daughter Elisabeth sought to marry an SS-Sturmbannführer, permission was denied. Although Krüger's lineage was impeccable, his wife Ellie's family tree revealed that she had a Jewish ancestor in 1711. Even though officers and their wives only needed to trace their lineages back to 1750, knowledge of this Jewish ancestor prevented Krüger's daughter from receiving approval. Himmler wrote to Krüger and explained the reason for the rejection. He also stated that he had not issued a rejection to the Sturmbannführer who sought to marry Krüger's daughter; rather, he was leaving the matter for Krüger to handle. He suggested that his Gruppenführer find some other way to reject the marriage, such as indicating that he could not give permission because his daughter was too young.[62]

The Krüger family's situation became more complicated when Krüger's son Gerhard sought to enter the SS. Gottlob Berger, the officer in charge of Waffen-SS recruitment, reviewed boy's application in October 1943 and provided Himmler with a positive evaluation of the sixteen-year-old. Himmler granted Gerhard permission to serve in the Leibstandarte-SS Adolf Hitler as a volunteer and stated that he would make a final decision on Gerhard's placement following the war.[63] With this decision, Himmler again demonstrated his willingness to bend his rules in order to facilitate the growth of the Waffen-SS.

But while he accepted Gerhard, Himmler refused to change his mind about Elisabeth's marriage, a topic that Ellie Krüger raised during a meeting with Berger. She could not understand why the SS rejected her daughter but accepted her son. Berger reiterated that the refusal of the marriage was based on the hereditary health of the applicants. He not only cited Ellie's Jewish ancestry, but also mentioned that the prospective fiancé had a sister suffering from tuberculosis. Berger told Ellie that due to this combination of ancestry and illness, it was unlikely that hereditarily healthy children could emerge from such a marriage. In his subsequent letter to Himmler about his conversation with Krüger's wife, Berger requested that Himmler adopt this explanation. Himmler did; he also refused to speak further about the matter with Ellie, stating that negotiating the issue with her was not possible due to her "prejudice as a mother." If the subject were to be raised again, Himmler said, all discussions should be handled by "the head of the family" – that is, SS-Gruppenführer Krüger. This was probably nothing more than a ploy to ensure that the issue would not be raised again, as it came less than two weeks after Himmler had issued another edict declaring that Krüger should not be bothered with this issue during his current deployment.[64]

Outside of these exceptions, Himmler still objected to marriages where the bride was older than the groom because few if any children could emerge from such a union. He did not stand alone on this issue; state registrars also rejected marriage applications during the war if no children could be expected due to the bride's age.[65] After Himmler denied a request, he oftentimes notified the superior officer of the man whose application he had rejected. The Reichsführer requested that this officer explain to his subordinate why his application had been refused, clarify the racial laws of the SS, and remind him of the necessity of having children.[66]

Yet here, too, there were exceptions. If the age difference were minimal, if both the bride and groom were young, and if there were no other misgivings about either applicant, then Himmler approved their application without any further objections.[67] He occasionally granted permission even when a sizeable age difference did exist.[68] While granting such leeway, Himmler tended to inform either the groom or the bride that, in principle, he opposed marriages where the woman was older, but that he had consented against his better judgment and was releasing the marriage to the responsibility of the couple.[69]

There was one other area where Himmler re-evaluated the engagement and marriage process because of the exigencies of the war. In 1935, he had issued a command dismissing any man who had married without requesting approval. Over the next three years, several hundred men had subsequently received honourable and dishonourable discharges, but shortly after the war began, Himmler decided to pardon them. He wanted every able-bodied man serving in the Waffen-SS. After communicating with the SS Personal Staff, Legal Main Office, and RuSHA, he issued an order in November 1940 that granted amnesty to men who had left the SS in 1935, 1936, and 1937. These men could seek readmission if they met three conditions: first, if they had been dismissed solely for violating the engagement and marriage command; second, if an assessment demonstrated that their character and attitude still met the standards required for admission; and third, if RuSHA gave belated approval for their marriage.[70]

Although this clemency was originally designed to benefit men who had left the SS prior to the war, its scope expanded after the conflict began. One officer who benefitted from this policy change was SS-Obersturmführer Louis E. He had married without authorization in December 1939. He tried to request authorization after the fact in early 1940, but his request was denied. Upon evaluating his wife, Senta, RuSHA officials discovered that several members of her family had been incarcerated. A police report from Bremen submitted to RuSHA also pointed out that an earlier fiancé of Senta's was serving a term in prison for swindling and that Senta had a criminal procedure brought against her due to an abortion. The case had been dropped due to a lack of evidence, but in combination with the other factors, RuSHA found Senta to be an unsuitable wife for an SS man, and Louis was released from the organization in April 1940.[71]

He appealed this decision in September 1941, claiming that he sought to divorce his wife and requesting re-entry into the SS. By this time, Louis was serving in the Wehrmacht as a lieutenant and he had earned Iron Crosses, both first and second class, for his service on the eastern front. Himmler agreed to allow him to rejoin if he divorced his wife, which Louis did by October. Once the SS Personnel Main Office received the couple's official divorce documentation, Louis was allowed to re-enter the SS in December 1944 at his previous rank.[72] Himmler requested that Louis report to him about his marital status every six months.[73] In one of these reports, Louis indicated his desire to remarry, this time with proper authorization, but he also mentioned that finding a wife proved to be difficult because he remained stationed in the East. Whether due to this posting or for other reasons, he did not remarry during the war.[74]

Louis's case represented another example of how Himmler enforced his standards on a selective basis. He sought to balance his desire for a racial elite with the need to maintain a strong military branch. The former required strict rules guiding the admission of wives into the family community, while the latter necessitated including as many men as possible into the Waffen-SS. The war forced Himmler to readjust his priorities. Although he wanted to re-evaluate the situation following the war, he was willing to show some leniency in order to achieve a more immediate goal – that of having the Waffen-SS contribute to a military victory.

Himmler indicated his desire to re-evaluate the situation in the November 1940 amnesty order. However, in late March 1944, SS-Gruppenführer Harald Turner, a jurist who served in both RuSHA and the Reich Security Main Office, sent Himmler a letter requesting that he reconsider his position regarding punishing men who violated the engagement and marriage command. He based this suggestion on his work for RuSHA, which at the time included running the office in his capacity as Richard Hildebrandt's deputy, a position he had held since December 1943.[75] In particular, Turner suggested that establishing new penal regulations was imperative if Himmler were to maintain his authority within the SS, because violations against the engagement and marriage order were more numerous than initially presumed. He did not back up this claim with specific numbers, but he insisted that new rules would prevent a further decline of discipline within the ranks. Turner wanted members of the Waffen-SS who violated the order to be punished for military disobedience, and he sent Himmler an outline for a command to this effect.[76]

It was perhaps unbeknown to Turner since it predated his time at RuSHA, but Himmler had punished violations of the engagement and marriage order in 1942 and again in 1943. Based on a November 1942 order, any man who had not obtained authorization from RuSHA and who failed to report his affiliation with the SS when registering his marriage with civil authorities was to be expelled. At least two men were ousted the following year, but judging from the response Turner received two months after sending his letter, this order must have been suspended sometime between then and March 1944.[77] The response came not from Himmler, but from the senior jurist, SS-Standartenführer Horst Bender. According to Bender, Himmler currently saw no need to punish violators. Nonetheless, the Reichsführer wished to be informed of men who married without first seeking permission; furthermore, he asked that civil registrars report to RuSHA all marriages in which the groom belonged to the SS.[78] Turner complied, and starting in August, he submitted monthly reports containing the names of SS men who had married without authorization. Approximately one hundred and fifty were listed between August 1944 and early 1945.[79] While a very small number, the list nonetheless indicates that a small minority of SS men did not obey racial and marital directives. But at the same time, the fact that Himmler was not punishing these men suggests that he might have had larger concerns, in this case a decline in morale and the loss of men as Germany came under siege at this late stage of the war.

Turner's reports hardly represented the only statistical data on these matters. RuSHA kept track of engagement and marriage petitions. As in the pre-war period, these statistics included who was single, married, divorced, or widowed. Comprehensive numbers do not exist for the entire war, but the available data from 1939–42 provides a general idea of the marital status of SS members. For example, according to one report from the end of 1939, 44 per cent of the entire SS and 78.6 per cent of officers were married. Additional reports from late 1939 and early 1940 show that the number and percentage of married officers, non-coms, and enlisted men had increased from one year earlier.[80]

RuSHA also compiled monthly reports outlining the number of men and officers applying for and receiving approval for engagements and marriages. Based on the available reports, most of which come from the second half of 1941 and early 1942, an average of approximately 2,500 requests were filed per month.[81] This average represented an increase from the pre-war period, when approximately 1,700–2,000 requests had been submitted each month. In keeping with the pre-war position that men below age twenty-five should not attempt to get married, the majority of wartime applications were submitted by officers and men who were twenty-five years and older.[82]

The wartime increase to 2,500 submissions meant that the number of marriages per month did not greatly increase even though the number of men in the SS more than tripled between 1939 and 1945. However, it is not possible to render definitive conclusions without comparable numbers from 1943 to 1945. It is nonetheless reasonable to presume that the number of applications submitted per month probably increased as the number of members increased throughout the war. It is also reasonable to conclude that an increase in numbers would not have necessarily meant an increase in the percentage of married men and officers. With just 44 per cent of SS members married as of the end of 1939, it is highly unlikely that the percentage would have drastically increased throughout the war. Within the entire SS, only one group came close to 100 per cent compliance: officers who had obtained one of the four highest ranks (Brigadeführer, Gruppenführer, Obergruppenführer, and Oberstgruppenführer). This conclusion is not based on statistics created by RuSHA, but on an analysis of SS personnel files. SS promotion records indicate that by late 1944, 479 officers held these four ranks.[83] The Berlin Document Center contains dossiers for 471 of them. Based on the information in those files, 458 officers – or 97.2 per cent – were married. More than half had wed prior to the 1931 command, but they still would have set an example for their subordinates.

That example may have been useful, but for men seeking to marry, a prompt response from RuSHA would have been more useful. As mentioned earlier, RuSHA had a backlog of applications by 1937, and to a limited extent, this problem still existed during the war. In a December

1942 letter to Otto Hofmann, Himmler expressed his displeasure over the amount of time it took for RuSHA to process an application before sending it to him for approval. He demanded that Hofmann find out why it took so long and insisted that he arrange for his subordinates to work longer hours to ensure that all applications were swiftly processed.[84]

Hofmann must have directed this inquiry straightaway to Otto Heider, the chief of the Marriage Office, as Heider provided an explanation to the RuSHA chief just two days later.[85] Heider defended his subordinates' work, and he pointed out that the Marriage Office's workload during the war vastly exceeded its pre-war levels. On average, 500–600 requests had been processed per month in the pre-war period, but in 1942 the office had processed 1,777 requests between 1 November and 10 December.[86] Heider also informed Hofmann that this increased workload was being handled by fewer personnel. He stated that the office had employed thirteen doctors before the war, but now only had two, neither of whom could commit of all of their time to processing applications. This was in part due to the requests – six to twelve per day – of troops on leave for a physical. The soldiers rightly assumed, Heider wrote, that "a medical examination in RuSHA brings about an essential acceleration in the conclusion of the engagement and marriage process" – an important consideration for anyone who received limited time off from the front. Heider claimed that most requests were nonetheless processed within two or three days, and that no outstanding files existed unless there were special circumstances. Given the above-mentioned cases handled by Himmler, special circumstances did exist and did cause some delay. However, with well over 1,000 requests handled per month, the approval process appeared to work for most applicants.

These statistics, along with the aforementioned examples, highlight an important fact about the engagement and marriage process during the war. Regardless of whether Himmler and RuSHA officials adhered to pre-existing guidelines for evaluating applications or whether Himmler allowed exceptions, many men had little difficulty finding women to marry. However, some men serving in the Wehrmacht or the Waffen-SS struggled to find a spouse during their limited leaves from the front. This dilemma prompted Hofmann to write to Himmler in early 1941.[87] He pointed out that although common events were held between the SS and female party organizations, these events were few and far between for a variety of reasons, including the difficulties created by the war.

Accordingly, Hofmann requested permission to establish a new function for the Marriage Office. He wanted it to work with female party leaders to establish questionnaires that would be completed by interested SS men and racially suitable women in order to facilitate suitable matches. Hofmann requested Himmler's comment on the issue. This amounted to a short rejection: "I do *not* hold the suggestion supplied to me as viable and request that it not be pursued."[88] Himmler did agree, however, that methods to facilitate the marriage of SS men should be pursued after the war.

Himmler's response may have motivated Hofmann to send him a suitable form for the process created by the party's Office for Racial Policy. Himmler's response, this time through his private administrative officer Rudolf Brandt, was simply to acknowledge receipt of the form and state that he would speak with Martin Bormann, a high-ranking Nazi functionary, about the subject.[89] Regardless of whether this discussion took place, it was highly unlikely, due to the lack of subsequent documentation, that anything came of Hofmann's suggestion. Yet Hofmann was not the only person who thought matchmaking might be a viable option. In the summer of 1942, Reich Health Leader Dr. Leonardo Conti submitted a proposal advocating three methods of increasing the number of children born.[90] One of those methods was matchmaking. Again, Himmler rejected the suggestion, telling Conti that the medical profession was overburdened with other responsibilities.[91]

At least one other person approached Himmler about matchmaking. In two letters from 1943, Otto Heider informed him that not all SS members were complying with the engagement and marriage regulations.[92] While he would have had first-hand knowledge of SS men's compliance, or lack thereof, due to his position as chief of the Marriage Office, Heider provided no specifics regarding the nature of this disobedience. He did, however, mention in his second letter that a possible solution would be to facilitate the meeting of SS men and racially worthy women. That Heider was raising this issue in December 1943 confirmed the lack of action on Hofmann's and Conti's earlier proposals. It likewise confirmed that Himmler's rejection of matchmaking must not have been common knowledge. There is no evidence to suggest he changed his mind and authorized Heider or any other official to pursue the matter of matchmaking.[93]

There was one additional matter associated with the engagement and marriage process during the war. On 31 December 1941, the original command had existed for a decade. Praised at its creation, many still commended it ten years later. Although it is unclear if he sent it, then RuSHA chief Hofmann wrote Himmler an enthusiastic letter on 31 December 1941 stating that his 1931 order "might represent the most beautiful gift that the SS ever received."[94] He claimed that SS men were increasingly "aware of the significance of their actions and choose their life-time companion with full consideration." These men, Hofmann claimed, were also mindful of the need to have children, and he pointed out "that there is hardly a marriage in which the first child is not born within a year." This recognition of the importance of a suitable spouse and healthy children was, Hofmann professed, the most "beautiful effect of the engagement and marriage command!" He ended his letter by commending Himmler for his forward-thinking approach over the past decade, an approach that the entire *Volk* might embrace one day.

Approval of the engagement and marriage command was not limited to in-house praise. A short article appeared in the *Völkischer Beobachter*, the Nazi Party newspaper, informing readers about the command and praising SS families for having at least one child.[95] *Das Schwarze Korps* also lauded the order.[96] The SS newspaper reminded its readers that the command had been issued because the Reichsführer had recognized that the future of the German *Volk* depended on the existence of a large number of racially and hereditarily healthy families. Over the past decade, SS men had been selected to carry out this service to the *Volk*; their descendants would be the bearers of the best blood and have the most valuable racial qualities. With this piece, the newspaper not only reminded its readers about the command, but also stated that the decree was one of the many ways in which the SS and its members were securing the nation's future.

Das Schwarze Korps was not the only SS periodical to commemorate the anniversary. In early 1942, SS-Standartenführer Bruno K. Schultz wrote an article for *Volk und Rasse*. Schultz, an anthropologist, was the editor of the journal.[97] He had also been one of the instructors at the KWI-A courses for SS medical personnel and had led the RuSHA Race Office from 1932 to 1935 and again from 1942 to 1944.[98] These positions gave him plenty of experience on which to draw for his piece. In it, Schultz called the command "the most exemplary racial measure in an organization of the NSDAP."[99] He claimed that it contained "the essential and crucial guidelines for the entire attitude of the SS to the question of race, hereditary health, [and] family."[100] Because the order enlightened SS men about their responsibility to produce future generations, the children born from these marriages, he argued, validated both the order and the marriages. He also praised the command for having set an important trend for the Reich: in the decade since its creation, the government had followed a similar path by taking steps towards regulating the marriages and racial health of the *Volk*.

Additional praise for the command came from the scientific community; this included two articles in *Archive for Race and Societal Biology*. The first was written by a doctor named Derkmann, who praised the command for its practical response to questions of race hygiene.[101] He commented that the commitment of SS men to this order demonstrated their willingness to take the first step in obliterating negative hereditary traits in Germany. Ernst Rüdin, a psychiatrist and co-editor of the journal, wrote the second article.[102] He praised Hitler's government for its willingness to take decisive steps towards implementing racial hygiene measures that put into practice what had previously been only scientific theory. Rüdin listed various laws implemented by the government, and he specifically discussed the SS engagement and marriage command. He noted that this order was the primary means through which the SS sought to conserve and increase the hereditary endowment and health of the German *Volk*.

Altogether, the engagement and marriage process continued to evolve between 1939 and 1945. This evolution took into account new complications that arose as a result of the war. It likewise reflected the changing composition of the SS with the addition of *Volksdeutsche* and foreign nationals. Even with numerous changes, the wartime regulations still sought to maintain a high standard when evaluating each couple's racial and reproductive value. In addition, while exceptions were granted, the hundreds of applications approved each week indicate that most men were able to comply with the policies. They filed the required paperwork, and, as long as no issues were discovered, they received approval to wed in a relatively prompt manner. Thus, while policies shifted due to the war, very few members violated the engagement and marriage command or resigned from the organization rather than accept the demands made of them by Himmler and/or RuSHA. The resulting wartime marriages demonstrated the commitment of old and new members alike to the racial ideals of the SS, which in turn allowed Himmler to continue to pursue his objective of establishing a racial elite. However, as in the pre-war period, marriage was only the first step in the process of creating the family community. When it came to children, here, too, the war had a decisive influence.

Chapter Four

Sustaining the Family Community during the War

As with marriage, the war greatly influenced the development of SS families. The need to populate the family community, while crucial in the pre-war years, took on greater significance during the war. This chapter will assess the continuity of many pre-war measures, including promoting fatherhood in *Das Schwarze Korps*, offering supplemental funding to married fathers, and supporting illegitimacy. It will likewise analyse the new measures used to persuade men to have children and to provide them with the opportunity to do so in the midst of the war. These measures included new rhetoric and orders, guidance from high-ranking officers, and medical research on infertility and sex ratios. With these measures, Himmler and other officials wanted to convince each man that the fate of the Third Reich not only depended on his military service, but also on his ability to generate a biological legacy. He needed to understand that his family was a vital component in the empire that Hitler sought to establish.

One of the first means designed to influence men to have children was a change in rhetoric. Wartime rhetoric continued to emphasize a point made in the pre-war period – that having racially healthy children was a duty. But orders, speeches, and booklets issued after 1939 indicated that this responsibility had become more significant. In many regards, SS rhetoric during the Second World War echoed concerns that eugenicists had raised during the First World War. During the earlier conflict, physicians and scientists had worried about the dysgenic effects of the war – namely, the consequences of millions of deaths, which deprived Germany not only of its most fit men, but also their potential offspring.[1] Whereas the Wilhelmine government had not taken any action to allay these concerns, the Nazi government's reaction was vastly different in

1939. Racial survival was seen as the core of the Nazi war effort, and the SS was at the forefront of this so-called struggle for life. Procreation was an essential element of this struggle.

The first command connecting Germany's military fight with the development of the next generation was released on 28 October 1939. Issued to the SS and police, Himmler began by proclaiming that "[e]very war is a bloodletting of the best blood."[2] By this, he did not just mean the loss of men who had perished on the battlefield, but also the absence of their unborn children. Himmler urged his men to accept "the old wisdom" that a man can die knowing he has left children behind and that a military victory in the present had little meaning if there were not enough children to sustain this legacy.

Beyond the appeal to have children, in this order Himmler also noted that unmarried women of good blood had the moral responsibility to carry the child of a soldier. This claim led to resistance, not from the SS, but from the army. Once word of Himmler's order reached the soldiers, they expressed concern about the welfare of their wives and daughters to their superiors, who in turn relayed the men's apprehension up the chain of command. The issue quickly reached the highest levels, leading the commanders of the army groups stationed on the western front to write their commander-in-chief, General Walther von Brauchitsch, to protest what was by now known as the SS procreation order.[3] General Wilhelm Ritter von Leeb was among the group commanders who protested. He censured Himmler's command "not only on moral grounds, but also because in it I see a destruction of the German family, the bearers of the state and the Wehrmacht."[4] That it provided young men with the licence to "give into their sex drives recklessly" would cause nothing but confusion, which could destroy discipline within the ranks. Leeb ended his letter by demanding that the army compel the SS to withdraw this command.

The army never issued that demand. Rather, the procreation order remained a subject of debate within the higher ranks; simultaneously, the army sought to determine the opinion of the navy and the air force. All the while, the troops continued to seethe about it among themselves and complain about it to their superior officers. While the army deliberated on how to respond to Himmler's call for women to fulfil their "sacred obligation," the SS proactively defended its position. In early January 1940, *Das Schwarze Korps* published an article discussing the merits of the October command and offering support for racially worthy illegitimate children.[5] In his book *Call of the Empire*, Nazi poet laureate and SS-Gruppenführer Hanns Johst also defended the order. The book included part of the October command along with a discussion between the narrator and a friend. The friend expressed outrage over the order while the narrator defended it, arguing that "there are no illegitimate children, there are only *German* children."[6] Johst's defence echoed Himmler's pre-war claim that legitimacy was less important than the racial value of each child and the contribution that child could make to the nation.

Himmler personally addressed the misunderstanding with the army when he released a letter to all SS men and police officers at the end of January. While stating bluntly that illegitimate children existed and would continue to exist in the future, he clarified that no decent SS soldier would attempt to establish a sexual relationship with a woman whose husband was at the front. Should one of his SS men (most of whom were also at the front) do so, Himmler pointed out that there were two people involved in a seduction – the seducer and the woman who allowed herself to be seduced. Therefore, while "one does not approach the wife of a comrade," a woman was the best guardian of her honour, and any man who rejected such a perspective insulted German women.[7]

Differences of opinion were further worked out when Himmler met with Brauchitsch a few days later. The general subsequently released a statement acknowledging that he agreed with the Reichsführer that "the vitality of the Volk rests in the assured growth of its children."[8] He asserted that "marriage is the basis of the family" and encouraged all racially valuable people to marry and have many children because they were the "highest good" and represented the best means to preserve the *Volk*. Extramarital relations and the children that resulted from them could not replace the family, Brauchitsch claimed, although he did concede that the state should protect illegitimate children from any disadvantages.

The misunderstanding between the SS and the army appeared to be resolved.[9] However, Leeb's fear that young men would "give into their sex drives recklessly" was raised by the SS court in early 1942. In a February letter to the Berlin-based justices, SS-Obersturmbannführer Günter Reinecke stated that the number of cases in which SS men and police officers had engaged in sexual relations with soldiers' wives had increased.[10] Most of the time, the culprit was a young man who had fallen in love with a married woman. Although he gave no specific data, Reinecke claimed that such cases would only increase the longer the war went on and the harder it became for the army to allot vacation time. He therefore suggested that, in accordance with Himmler's January 1940 letter, men who had intercourse with soldiers' wives should be punished for military disobedience. Reinecke did acknowledge there should be some exceptions, such as when a loving relationship had developed and a serious intent to marry existed. He also recognized that married women bore some culpability – for example, if they were looking for an opportunity to have an affair by frequenting pubs where soldiers gathered. He ended his letter by asking the jurists to present the matter to Himmler and ask him to provide clarification.

That clarification came a month and a half later in late March 1942.[11] Himmler did not want every case of adultery punished as military disobedience; rather, each case would be determined on an individual basis. In general, a judicial punishment was possible when a man clearly took advantage of a husband's absence or when a wife behaved indecently. Otherwise, the basic principle that neither an SS man nor a police officer should approach the wife of a soldier was thought to be a sufficient safeguard against extramarital affairs. While not addressed in this March response, the fact that Himmler refused to create an all-encompassing policy for adultery is hardly surprising. He had begun an extramarital relationship two years earlier, and the first of his two illegitimate children had been born in February.[12]

In addition to twice attempting to resolve concerns raised by his October 1939 procreation order, Himmler continued to press SS men to have children. He expressed these aspirations in private letters and speeches. Himmler stressed that he would be content to let his men wait to father children if he were certain they would survive the war. However, as this certainty did not exist, he wanted each man to have at least one child who could in the future not only sustain the Nordic blood and his personal family lineage, but also, if he were a boy, take his rightful place fighting for Germany.[13] To emphasize the significance of establishing a family, Himmler created new guidelines in November 1942 that made the fulfilment of an officer's familial obligations a prerequisite for promotion.[14] This meant that an officer must have married by age twenty-six and have had a suitable number of children – a number determined by the age of the couple and the length of their marriage. Pre-war requirements had stipulated four children by age forty, and there is nothing to suggest these numbers had changed.

If the officer were not married or did not have children, he had to justify his single and/or childless status. According to a February 1944 amendment to the directive, the officer had to explain why he had failed to have multiple children when his wife was under forty years old and/or the birth of their last child had been more than two years prior.[15] Despite these two orders, not having a wife or enough children did not prevent most officers from being promoted.[16] Based on statistics produced in the early 1940s, more than 50 per cent of officers who requested permission to marry were over thirty years old.[17] In addition, an examination of the personnel files of the officers who held one of the four highest ranks show that by early 1945, less than 30 per cent had four or more children. Other factors, such as exemplary job performance, the ability to continue to serve the SS and the party well, and affiliation with any Nazi organization before 1933, were just as significant when weighing whether or not to promote an officer. Combined with the fact that the SS was already losing "good blood" due to the war, these factors might have convinced Himmler to overlook low marriage and child numbers when issuing promotions, thus encouraging officers to remain in the organization instead of alienating them because of their familial choices. This did not, however, prevent Himmler from lamenting the low numbers in a June 1942 speech before the leadership corps of a Waffen-SS division: "the number of children [born to SS members] does not replace even half of those who had fallen ... A terrible loss, much more terrible than the death of the men themselves."[18] Coming from Himmler, who had never served as a soldier, such a comment probably did not go over well with the division's officers, who, along with their men, were fighting at the front.

Other prominent officials encouraged Himmler's quest to make sure that SS men produced children. First and foremost was Hitler himself, who on occasion spoke privately about the need for many children: "everyone should be persuaded that a family's life is assured only when it has upwards of four children – I should even say, four sons."[19] Himmler knew of this four sons comment, and he sought to ensure that SS men were aware of it, too.[20] Hitler also expressed the opinion that many great men in the past had come from large families, and that a two-child system would deprive Germany of future geniuses. He proclaimed that the nascent German elite would descend from the SS because "only the SS practices racial selection."[21] He wanted this practice to continue, especially because he recognized that part of the job of the SS was to set an example. Furthermore, the Führer rejoiced in the knowledge that during the war, when blood was being lost in vast quantities, SS men were fulfilling their duty by convincing young women to have children.[22] These children represented the future of the nation, and Hitler acknowledged that Germany would automatically know where to turn for its leaders.

Himmler likewise had the backing of SS-Oberstgruppenführer Kurt Daluege, chief of the uniformed police. In late 1942, Daluege submitted a draft for a command outlining how the police should serve as a model in the SS and the German *Volk* when it came to generating large families. Unlike Himmler, Daluege spoke from personal experience. He and his wife had four children, the last of whom had been born only a few months before he wrote his draft.[23] In it, he proclaimed the by then standard line that child-poor families, defined as two children per marriage, would lead to the annihilation of the *Volk*. The excuses used by police officers in the Weimar period to have small families could no longer apply. In fact, the opposite must become true. As a leading social class, the police had a duty to create families that could serve as role models; only medical reasons or advanced age should prevent a man from creating a child-rich family. However, because previous admonitions had gone unheeded, Daluege wanted superior officers to commit themselves to urging their subordinates to have children. He encouraged officers and their wives to pursue all medical avenues to ensure their ability to procreate. Himmler did not directly dismiss this order, although he only gave Daluege permission to forward it to his commanders as an educational guideline for personal conversations and instruction.[24]

Less than a year later, the SS chief medical officer, SS-Obergruppenführer Dr. Ernst Robert Grawitz, briefly addressed the necessity of children in the SS medical community. He was prompted to address the issue after Himmler expressed displeasure over the fact that few SS doctors had child-rich families. About to become a father for the fifth time, Grawitz concurred with this sentiment, adding: "It should be unnecessary to remind SS doctors about the crucial meaning of the child-richness of our generations for the life and security of our children and with it for the future of the Reich."[25] He praised the efforts of doctors' wives who had taken it upon themselves to provide the nation with new life. It was their "strength of heart" that would "secure the future of the Reich against the hatred of our enemies." These offspring would provide the *Volk* with the strength it would need to achieve its future goals after the successful conclusion of the war.

The SS newspaper also continued to emphasize the importance of children. Article after article stressed the fact that "the victory of arms must also be the victory of the commitment to the child."[26] Reproduction was defined as an integral duty. Children had the potential to even out the wartime loss of blood, and they preserved the lineage of men who had sacrificed themselves protecting Germany. This was vital, especially because many soldiers came from one- and two-child families and might have been the last surviving male.[27] Thus, men could not wait until after the war to ensure their lineage. One article implored its military readers: "We say to the soldiers, they should, if possible, not delay in giving life to a child; we advise them to marry early; we charge them and their wives not to postpone the child-luck until the peace. The German future, the security of the hard-won victories, will depend on whether our Volk will also prove to be a victor in the cradle of its children."[28] With this article, and many others like it, the newspaper sought to inculcate the idea that the future of the nation depended on more than a military victory.

The family, as the germ cell of the *Volk*, was the centre of that future.[29] Yet convincing men that they needed to ensure the continuation of their families proved easier said than done. From the correspondence submitted to and printed by *Das Schwarze Korps*, it seems that many men agreed with the concept of marrying and having children. It was the execution that proved to be problematic. One such quandary was raised in a letter submitted by an unnamed twenty-five-year-old soldier. Both a party and SA member, the man indicated that he would gladly marry his fiancée and have a child as "Germany's future is in our offspring."[30] However, he faced a dilemma: due to the war, he had never finished his education. This soldier asked the newspaper for advice on how he could take care of his wife and child after the war. The newspaper did not answer him directly, but instead reproduced a letter from a father to his son that, the editors claimed, would give everyone something to think about.

The son in question was in a similar position – twenty-six years old, serving in the field, with a twenty-one-year-old fiancée. During his last conversation with his father, he had indicated that he considered it inappropriate to marry during wartime. The father used his own experiences from the First World War to convince his child that he was wrong. He noted that a widow from the first war would have been happy had she been left with a child to raise, and that those widows who did have children had been able to live securely in the post-war era. In addition, many women had married returning soldiers, even those who had been injured (another concern raised by his son), and these couples had built prosperous lives together. The father commented that the future of Germany was probably already secured through triumph on the battlefield – a view that seemed self-evident when this letter was written in November 1939. But the future would only be completely ensured with a young and strong *Volk*, one founded through the fertility of its mothers.

This letter from father to son evidently gave readers, especially soldiers, plenty to think about because the newspaper published several more notes over the course of the war raising the same issue. Soldiers who had not finished their education or vocational training before the war were worried about providing for their families afterwards. The newspaper was not unsympathetic; through the articles it ran, it showed that it understood their dilemma.[31] Nonetheless, *Das Schwarze Korps* held to its original position: children must be born. "That one does not have any occupation," one article proclaimed, "does not alter [that a man should marry]. Life does not put itself on hold."[32] Even with the belief in an inevitable German victory early in the war, the fate of each individual was uncertain, and therefore, the newspaper argued, he must secure his family lineage.

For all of the emphasis placed on the dual victory on the battlefield and in the cradle, the newspaper did understand that reality was complicated, and that its advice – "marry, comrade, and give your Volk children" – was difficult to achieve.[33] The article "Marry – but whom?" acknowledged that finding a wife and having a family in the middle of a war was not as easy as films and novels made it seem.[34] Yet the difficulty of the task did not make it any less necessary. The newspaper tried to personalize the issue for its male readers by suggesting that they should not only fight for the survival of their country, but of their very blood as well. As one article proclaimed, "If, however, a war for the future is a war for the children, then the thoughts of a soldier also revolve around the child: around his child, that is his future blood. He fights for his child in the war; he is willing to bleed for his child; he is willing to die, if necessary, for his child."[35] It should be noted that these words were written less than half a year into the war, well before anyone associated with the newspaper started reporting routinely from the battlefront. Whoever wrote these words did so from the safety of the editorial office in Berlin.[36]

To reinforce its argument and to attach a stronger significance to the idea of a man fighting for his children, the newspaper featured the words of individual fathers. For example, in one article a young soldier named Werner N. had just seen his wife and learned of her pregnancy. After returning to the field, he told the paper that, "now I know what I have to protect because under the heart of my wife grows a child, my child, and I believe that I do my duty all the more today ... because I know this."[37] *Das Schwarze Korps* subsequently printed additional letters from fathers, showing them taking pride in their children from far away. This included reporting the immense joy felt by SS-Obersturmführer Jurgen V. when he became the father to both a son and a daughter within two years of getting married. "Through my splendid children," he wrote, "whom I could only hold in my arms a few days, I became infinitely rich."[38] In their children, these men found a reason to fight, as did other soldiers who professed that, despite the hardship of being separated from their offspring, they fought now so that their sons would not have to in the future.[39]

Beyond showing that their children were a reason to fight, these letters demonstrated how fathers remained a part of their children's lives during the war. *Das Schwarze Korps* featured correspondence between several fathers at the front and their children; the intention was to demonstrate how men could still influence their children's upbringing. In one letter a father used his front-line experiences to teach his son about the value of vigilance. As a soldier in the Waffen-SS, he related everything in terms of military preparation. He advised his growing boy to perform his duties thoroughly, and he warned his son never to hesitate, but to act decisively, especially when facing an opponent.[40]

The newspaper reprinted a letter that Alfons P. wrote to his son on his birthday. The pride he felt for his child was evident from his opening words: "With much love, I think of you on your birthday. Nine years ago, your mom gave you life and made us all quite happy with you. Because a child is the sunshine in the family. You are a healthy, faithful, and really good German boy, [who] brings us much joy."[41] Alfred conveyed his best wishes to his son, and he implored the boy to live righteously. Like the letter above, Alfred offered practical advice, such as reminding his son to "always be a good and helpful comrade." He used a gentle tone to counsel his boy, as if he understood that his letter represented what was possibly the last opportunity he had to communicate with his child.

A third letter, written by SS-Hauptsturmführer Karl S., showed how a father and his children could still commune with one another at Christmastime.[42] Karl told his children to go to the park one night and decorate a tree, and then show their festive tree to the moon and stars. If they did so, the moon and stars would be able to reach him and tell him all about them because he also saw the same skyline no matter where he was. Through this celestial communication, Karl told his children, he would know how much they loved him, and they would know the same.

For the most part, communication between a father and his children was conducted through letters, although occasionally he had the opportunity to see them when on leave. This time at home allowed the father to influence his children, as shown in the article "Father on Leave."[43] It shared the daily interactions of a father with his family while on a reprieve from military service. Neither the father nor his children could conceal their elation at seeing one another. The boys vied for their father's attention and bombarded him with questions about the front, which he patiently answered. The article related how the family found comfort in one another's presence. And yet even after the father had returned to the front, his sons did not let his memory slip away. They relived the encounter over and over and recalled what their father had said and done while at home. This article also included photographs of the father playing games with his children, tucking them into bed, and demonstrating what he did on the front. These pictures proved that even during a war, a man could serve as a father as well as a soldier.

Each of these articles and reprinted letters demonstrated that many soldier-fathers found solace through their children. However, some soldiers remained unconvinced of the need to have children. One of them, Werner W., expressed his position in a letter to the newspaper, in which he insisted that his duty as a soldier did not automatically correlate with fatherhood. He respectfully argued that, "you [the newspaper] think that we fight for our children. No, we fight for our eternal Germany. You think one struggles more easily if one has a child at home … I have no children … [but] I know what I struggle for – for Germany. However, Germany is more than our children."[44] Werner asserted that Germany had to win the war first and then concern itself with raising families in peacetime.

The newspaper refuted Werner's perspective. It asked, rhetorically, what would become of a victorious Germany that had no children to succeed the present generation? Germany was losing its best blood in the war, and if these men did not procreate now, then the nation would forfeit its most valuable racial heritage. "And therefore," the article insisted, "every soldier who would like to transmit his blood to the German future shall have the right to be a soldier and a father."[45]

The newspaper further reasoned that "the German man of the present is responsible not only for victory on the battlefield. Soldiers and Germans can no longer be separate concepts. The responsibility for the future of the Reich with all of its demands weighs on all of us."[46] Simply put, one obligation could not supersede the other.

With these articles and letters, *Das Schwarze Korps* stressed the mutually reinforcing nature of the victories on the battlefield and in the cradle. Yet as Germany was fighting a war, the newspaper could not ignore the issue of death. One way it addressed this matter was by reprinting the last wills of soldiers, some of whom were fathers. One of the most somber examples came from a war reporter named Walter S., who wrote from the perspective of a man cognizant that he might never see his unborn child (as indeed, the newspaper confirmed Walter's death in the introduction to his letter). He acknowledged that his "fate is uncertain because it lies in the darkness of the war. Whether I will see you, whether you will ride on my knees, whether I admire your first step, and whether I can ever be a playmate and comrade for you, I do not know this because death marches at the side of the soldier."[47] Walter explained that he, too, had had to stand at his father's grave at a very young age and to provide solace to his widowed mother in the days after the First World War. In his letter, he recognized that his unborn child might have to comfort his wife in the same way.

Walter described how close birth and death were for him; mortality stood as his daily companion, not unlike the baby growing in his wife's womb. He knew that if he died, his child still lived, and in this way a small part of him would remain alive. Until his death, he fought to protect his wife and child during the day and at night looked at the stars while thinking of them. This letter showed that soldierly duties did not prevent Walter from attending to his paternal responsibilities, even from afar. It reminded fellow fathers of their obligations, and it informed soldiers that their lineage did not end with their deaths.

Encouragement from *Das Schwarze Korps*, along with Himmler's commands and letters, knowledge of Hitler's opinion on the duty of fatherhood, and/or the guidelines given by a high-ranking officer, may have influenced the reproductive decisions of an SS man. However, even if he were persuaded of the need to have children, it meant very little if he and his wife did not have the opportunity to conceive because they were not in the same location. To overcome this problem, Himmler issued new policies to facilitate conjugal relations. In early August 1941, when Germany's military position was still favourable,

Himmler ordered any SS man who was the last surviving adult male in his family and who did not have at least two male descendants to be withdrawn from the front. He required these men to report to him to receive a new assignment.[48]

Less than a year later, Himmler drafted another decree designed to pull all childless SS men from the front. After consulting with and receiving Hitler's approval, Himmler released the "SS Order to the Last Sons" in mid-August 1942.[49] In three simple points it announced the removal of every last surviving son on the "Führer's orders."[50] The purpose of the extraction was to provide each man with one year to secure his family's lineage; after all, the Reich had a vested interest in ensuring that the families of its best men did not expire. Producing "children of good blood" and guaranteeing that each man was "no longer the last son" represented an obligatory duty because "it has never been the way of SS men to accept fate and not contribute anything to change." The future of the Third Reich depended as much on the reproductive contributions of these men as their prowess as soldiers. After a man had fulfilled his paternal obligation, he would return to his military post.

One month later, RuSHA released a supplementary decree reminding SS men about the last sons order.[51] The office subsequently coordinated its efforts with the Waffen-SS to determine which men were last sons.[52] This process required filing reports with Himmler, who – as with just about every matter in the SS – wanted to remain apprised of any changes.[53] In addition, Himmler, never content to leave matters solely in the hands of his subordinates, periodically intervened, as happened in the case of SS-Brigadeführer Alfred Arnold. The issue was not with Arnold, but with his son, an SS-Hauptsturmführer also named Alfred.[54] Upon learning that the younger Arnold had not married, Himmler wrote him a short letter in June 1943 saying that he needed to marry because he was his father's only son. Himmler sent a copy of this letter to the father, urging him to persuade his son to marry.[55] The younger Arnold wrote back just over two months later. He indicated his desire to comply with Himmler's wish, but also explained why he had not done so. In short, his military service kept him with his troops and away from Germany. His limited vacation did not provide him enough time to find a suitable wife who was prepared to raise their children alone in the event he did not return from the war.[56] This concern was somewhat prescient, as Alfred died in October 1944 having never married nor had a child.[57]

Alfred Arnold was hardly the only last son, or even soldier, for whom the war was an impediment to finding a wife. Furthermore, implementing the last sons order and finding sufficient time for men to father children became increasingly difficult as the tide of war turned against the Nazi regime. The closer the front lines came to Germany, the more difficult it became to transfer last sons to less dangerous assignments, such that by August 1944, only those last sons with "special cases of hardship" could be withdrawn from the front.[58] By temporarily removing men from the war, the last sons order relied on rather drastic measures in an attempt to assure the continuation of the family community. Although ostensibly designed for unmarried men, men who were married benefitted from it more than their single counterparts who had to use the same time to find a wife and have a child.[59]

The SS did implement policies solely designed to aid married men. In particular, when allotting time for vacations, married men, especially those with children, were favoured over single men.[60] Himmler also wanted married men to have an additional opportunity to meet with their wives, leading him to initiate a plan in October 1943.[61] His idea was to have these men take a leave of absence so they could rendezvous with their wives for five to six days. The point of this extra time was not to reward the men for their service; rather, it had everything to do with Himmler's goal of increasing the birth rate. As he wrote in a letter to SS-Gruppenführer Benno Martin, "we cannot otherwise expect that the desired and necessary children [will] sprout from these marriages."[62] To facilitate these trysts, the responsible Oberabschnitt had to arrange for quarters where the men could meet with their wives. These SS units also paid for the railway costs because, depending on where a husband was stationed and where his wife was living, both might have to travel to take advantage of the furlough. The Oberabschnitt could settle these expenses with Himmler's personal staff; with these expenditures covered, each couple was responsible only for the cost of meals.[63] According to the paperwork filed by several Oberabschnitt, these trips ranged in cost from 30 to 170 RM per couple, meaning that the Personnel Staff routinely reimbursed each Oberabschnitt thousands of Reichsmarks. Between November 1943 and June 1944 alone, the SS spent over 111,000 RM on this program.[64]

Because the goal of these extra vacations was to produce children, each meeting had to be planned accordingly. For instance, upon requesting a vacation for her husband, Paula Wagner was informed by

Rudolf Brandt that he had forwarded her appeal to the appropriate SS officials. While they waited for a response, Brandt recommended that she make an appointment with her gynecologist in order to determine the most favourable time for conception. With this knowledge, her husband could time his vacation when there was the highest possibility of conceiving.[65]

Husbands needed to understand the magnitude of this extra vacation, a point Himmler doubted most of them grasped. Therefore, he wanted all men to receive a copy of "Reminder and Obligation," a 1943 article by Hans Sievers, a naval doctor working at the women's clinic at the university in Greifswald.[66] Sievers proclaimed that the loss of life throughout the war had already begun to negate the rising birth rates that Germany had experienced between 1934 and 1939. According to him, every lost soldier meant a lost child, and "each unborn [child], therefore, means a military relinquishment from our political ascent."[67] The physician further noted that a high-quality marriage remained unfulfilled if it did not produce children. He defined a sterile marriage as one in which, given regular possibilities for conception, a child had not been produced after two years, and he suggested that young women in infertile marriages should consult with their doctors. Sievers, moreover, asserted that married soldiers needed scheduled vacations to meet with their wives at a time favourable for conception. Although he was not associated with the SS, Sievers reinforced the message already introduced by SS propaganda.

Taken together, the last sons order and the additional vacation demonstrate that Himmler did not want the war to impede his reproductive goals. Neither program added significantly to the growth of the population, but the vast majority of married men did have at least one child. As in the pre-war period, a man had to report the birth of his children to RuSHA, although he also had to notify the SS Personnel Main Office, which was responsible for maintaining a file on each SS man.[68] Many officers chose to inform Himmler personally about additions to their families, and oftentimes Himmler, or Brandt on his behalf, replied with a congratulatory letter.[69]

In addition, SS men continued to receive financial benefits for their children. Pay tables for the Waffen-SS indicate that a man who was married and had children received more money than one who did not, and the amount of money he received increased with each child.[70] If the father worked for the party or the state, he received supplementary allowances for legitimate children.[71] The state also provided funding to child-rich families to assist with educational expenses.[72] Funding offered by the party or the state would have been available to any eligible father, SS member or not. However, for SS men, wartime party and state subsidies would have been, as in the pre-war period, additional financial incentives beyond what they received from the SS.

There was one major difference with the allocation of funding for SS families. As the Waffen-SS grew, it came to include non-German citizens. Financial benefits for married men and fathers issued by the SS appeared to be available to all members regardless of their nationality or ethnic background.[73] The same appeared to be true for special subsidies. For example, in September 1941, Max Sollmann, the administrative head of the Lebensborn, issued a letter announcing the availability of child allowances from the program.[74] Funding was granted for all legitimate children as well as adopted children, foster children, and stepchildren in the amount of 20 RM per month for the first and second child, 30 RM for the third and fourth, and 40 RM for the fifth and every additional child. Prior to the war, the recipients of Lebensborn funds had been child-rich SS families, but that was not the intent here. Rather, this subsidy was for salaried employees of the Lebensborn. As many Lebensborn homes were located outside of Germany, it is conceivable that some recipients were not German, either by ethnicity or nationality, thus demonstrating the financial flexibility of the SS and its subsidiary programs.

The subject of funding raises one other issue. State and party funds were available solely for legitimate children, demonstrating that both bodies remained steadfast in their decision to recognize and support only legitimate offspring. The SS, on the other hand, continued to abet illegitimacy. Himmler continued to espouse it, and in this case, he actually practised what he preached. With his wife Marga, he had a daughter, Gudrun. By all accounts, Püppi, as she was called, was doted on by her parents, and she adored her father.[75] But despite their desire to have more children, especially on the part of Marga, they were unable.[76] They did adopt a son, Gerhard, who was approximately one year older than Gudrun. According to Himmler's brother, Gebhard, the boy was the son of an SS officer who had been killed prior to the war.[77] While Himmler and Marga took him in, Gebhard claimed that they never adopted Gerhard, a point confirmed by Marga when she mentioned in her diary having contact with Gerhard's biological mother. However, this was contradicted by Himmler's personnel file, which listed the boy as an adopted child.[78] Regardless of his status, he was a member of the family – both

Himmler's family and the SS family community. The son of SS men two times over, Gerhard joined the organization late in the war.[79]

As for his marriage, any affection Himmler may have felt for his wife had apparently dissipated before the war. While he remained devoted to his daughter, the same could not be said of his wife. He was not with her on their tenth wedding anniversary, and early in the war, when she was living in Berlin, he rarely came home.[80] Contemporary accounts confirm their marriage had become unhappy, although Himmler maintained the union out of respect for his wife.[81] He may have also chosen to stay with Marga because his marriage gave him the appearance of a respectable family man. This image was ironic, given how he sought to undermine the idea of bourgeois morality in the SS, but it would have been beneficial for him as a public figure, particularly as chief of police.

Himmler may also have wanted to avoid subjecting himself to the humiliation associated with a bad marriage, not to mention risk incurring Hitler's anger with a divorce. This concern would have been based on his knowledge of the incident involving Propaganda Minister Joseph Goebbels, who had a very public affair with a Czech actress. The situation grew perilous for Goebbels in the summer of 1938 when he and his wife sought to divorce. This was not to Hitler's liking because he did not want this scandal interfering with his regime or the work of his minister. He spoke personally with Goebbels and then his wife, and told them to reconcile.[82]

Himmler knew of this debacle and that many Nazi leaders, himself included, had privately vented against Goebbels.[83] With this knowledge, Himmler might not have wanted to suffer Hitler's wrath for ending his own marriage. While it is unlikely that Hitler would have removed Himmler from power, he probably would have expressed his displeasure in the same manner he had with Goebbels – by temporarily disfavouring him. An awareness of Hitler's views on divorce – or more importantly a scandal leading to divorce – might also have influenced Himmler's decisions regarding divorce within the higher ranks of the SS. For example, when Karl Wolff sought permission to divorce his wife in 1942, Himmler refused. Wolff subsequently petitioned Hitler, who, upon learning that his wife consented to it, agreed to the divorce, which in turn freed Wolff to marry the mother of his illegitimate child.[84]

Himmler did not blame Marga for their unhappy marriage or their lack of children. Yet he did not wish to be impeded from having more children. This led him to take Hedwig Potthast as his mistress in 1941. Potthast, who was twelve years Himmler's junior, had served as his personal secretary from 1936 to 1941.[85] After she left her job, she bore two children, a son named Helge in February 1942 and a daughter named Nanette Dorothea in June 1944.[86] The same month his daughter was born, Himmler appeared before an SS judge to claim paternity for both offspring, and in mid-September 1944, he acknowledged himself as their father and guardian in a legal document.[87]

As with everything else relating to his views on population policy, Himmler justified the decision to take a mistress with the biological need for more children. As he commented to Felix Kersten, his masseuse and unofficial confidant:

> The fact that a man has to spend his entire existence with one wife drives him first of all to deceive her and then makes him a hypocrite as he tries to cover it up. The result is indifference between the partners. They avoid each other's embraces and the final consequence is that they don't produce children. This is the reason why millions of children are never born, children whom the state urgently requires. On the other hand the husband never dares to have children by the woman with whom he is carrying on an affair, much [as] he would like to, because middle-class morality forbids it. Again it's the state which loses, for it gets no children from the second woman either. The law is in direct contradiction to our crying need – children and still more children. We must show courage and act decisively in this matter.[88]

Kersten's memoirs are not always the most reliable source.[89] However, in this case the remarks relayed by him are not far-fetched. To Himmler, neither marriage nor infidelity was about pleasure or happiness; everything in his belief system related to reproduction. He only approved of an affair for its ability to create more children. The promotion of children for the benefit of the state exceeded all personal desires. Himmler wanted SS men to have children with their wives *and* their mistresses. He aspired to have them forsake middle-class, bourgeois morality in order to achieve this end. To Kersten he lamented the scorn that society placed on illegitimate children, which in essence robbed a father from having an open and personal relationship with them.[90] Although Himmler made these comments a year after the birth of his illegitimate son, and therefore may have been indirectly airing his own grievances, his statement was in line with his views on illegitimacy before the war and prior to his affair. His commands continuously indicated that he believed Germany had no future without more offspring, and his stance on infidelity and illegitimacy again proved his intention to amass good blood through any means.

Himmler was not the only SS leader to have illegitimate children. SS-Obergruppenführer Oswald Pohl, chief of the Economic and Administrative Main Office, had a son by his secretary in 1942.[91] This child was in addition to the son and two daughters he had with his first wife and the daughter he had with his second wife.[92] SS-Obergruppenführer Ernst Kaltenbrunner, who succeeded Heydrich as the head of the Reich Security Main Office, had twins in March 1945 with his mistress, who had been employed in Himmler's Berlin headquarters.[93] Kaltenbrunner already had three children with his wife.[94] There is nothing to suggest that either Pohl or Kaltenbrunner had these affairs because Himmler had promoted illegitimacy, but his support worked in their favour. Himmler would have been pleased if he knew about these dalliances, just as he was delighted to learn from SS-Obergruppenführer Sepp Deitrich that many men in the Leibstandarte-SS Adolf Hitler had fathered illegitimate offspring.[95]

Himmler also found limited support among the party leadership, most notably from Rudolf Heß, the deputy to the Führer. Heß commented on the issue in a letter addressed to an unmarried mother published early in the war in the *Völkischer Beobachter*. He argued that a strong family formed the nucleus of the German state, and as such, the Nazi government had worked and would continue to work to maintain its integrity. Times of crisis, however, forced people to depart from traditional mores. Eligible young women must push aside moral scruples and guarantee that a healthy soldier did not enter the battlefield without first leaving behind his valuable blood through children. Even though the war prevented marriage between these mothers and soldiers, Heß indicated that the women could still receive widows' benefits if the men died.[96]

Despite this proclamation, Heß and Himmler stood in the minority when it came to illegitimacy. Officially, the government rejected Heß's letter. State and party propaganda touted the opposite perspective, and unmarried women who worked as civil servants or for party offices were oftentimes dismissed when they became pregnant.[97] In essence, as noted by Goebbels in a 1941 diary entry, "the legitimate child must remain at least the norm."[98] This is not to suggest that Goebbels did not support the idea of illegitimacy; other diary entries indicated that he agreed with some of Himmler's policies, and he reported that Hitler looked favourably on at least some aspects of illegitimacy.[99]

Nonetheless, most people rejected illegitimacy, putting Himmler in an awkward position. He knew that he had to approach the issue carefully, especially when it came to young women who were left vulnerable without the protection of their male relatives who were off fighting. Himmler even issued an order in April 1942 – not even two months after his illegitimate son was born – reminding his men to be mindful of their duties, one of which was to protect underage women from harm. "Never forget," he cautioned them, "how enraged you would be if your own daughter or sister were ruined. You would justifiably demand the harsh prosecution of the accused."[100] In essence, Himmler was telling his men that impregnating an unmarried woman was acceptable, so long as she was a consenting adult. But any SS man or police officer who violated this April command would be sent to the SS court and punished for disobedience. Punishments likely occurred, although how many men were affected remains unclear because Himmler prohibited the court from publishing the judgments in these cases. According to SS jurists, he did not want the public to assume that such cases occurred frequently, thereby forming an erroneous impression of the SS or the police.[101]

Beyond this matter, Himmler still found himself at odds with eugenicists, many of whom continued to denounce illegitimacy and advocate marriage as the sole place for reproduction. Among the medical professionals who espoused this position was Ernst Koch, a physician and senior medical officer in Leipzig. In a 1940 book, he claimed that one-third of the cases of idiocy and inferiority among children could be traced to unmarried mothers. Koch also argued that having such children ruined these women's future marriage prospects. He even asked his readers if they would want their daughters or their sisters in this position. Finally, Koch contended that the best place to assure the continuation of the *Volk* was through marriage.[102]

Fritz Lenz, for his part, remained steadfast in his opposition to illegitimacy. In May 1940, he wrote a letter to the editorial board of *Das Schwarze Korps* in response to an article about unmarried mothers.[103] Lenz argued that no one wanted unmarried motherhood to be preferred over matrimony, and he insisted that the state should not – as one woman had requested – entitle them to higher incomes and benefits from their employers.[104] In addition, while he found the current ratio between men and women unbalanced because of the loss of lives in the World Wars, he stated that affairs between married men and unmarried women had moral implications. Furthermore, he argued that the excess of women would not damage the *Volk* in the long term because there were enough married couples to sustain the population. As per the arguments made by him and his fellow scientists in the past, he noted that each person had a responsibility to rear four children, and that anyone who failed in this regard should be required to pay the state the equivalent cost of raising that number of children.[105]

With this letter Lenz enclosed an article he wrote entitled "Ways of further advancing population politics."[106] In it he contended that the current generation of young adults expected to produce children during the present war were part of the very generation who were lacking in numbers because of the losses sustained in the previous war. He argued against providing money to families for having children because not enough funds were available for such programs and because too many families who had taken advantage of this money did not use it to have more than one child. Lenz suggested that the taxation system should be revised after the war; among other measures, he proposed taxing people at a rate inverse to the number of children they had so that a family with four or more children would pay no taxes. He specifically addressed illegitimate children, claiming that each one should only count as half a child; both the biological father, if he were paying child support, and the full-time caregiver, either the child's mother or stepfather, would get credit for half a child.[107]

Lenz ended his letter by saying that he did not expect the SS newspaper to print it, but he requested that the editorial staff at least recognize the issues he had raised in it and in his article.[108] Over a month later, he had not heard back from *Das Schwarze Korps* or anyone else in the SS, as he reported in a letter to his KWI-A colleague Otmar von Verschuer. In his own correspondence with Lenz from the same month, Verschuer showed support for Lenz's letter and article by offering to publish them in *The Hereditary Doctor*, a medical journal he edited. Lenz expressed his appreciation, but declined the offer, citing the fact that his suggestions for overhauling the tax system were critical of current government ministers and that he was going to speak with a member of RuSHA soon.[109] That meeting must have gone favourably for Lenz, as the following spring Himmler was reported to have said that he was impressed with many of the scientist's suggestions.[110]

Besides the general issue of support for or disapproval of illegitimacy, the practice raised other concerns, including the complicated relationships between SS men and their wives and/or mistresses. One such situation involved a young man named Sepp F. In December 1939, he had gotten involved with a woman named Hella, only to find out after the fact that she was half-Jewish and pregnant by him. Distraught by the news, Sepp sought to sever all ties with Hella. She wrote to him in early February 1940, pleading for him not to abandon her.[111] He replied the following day, making his position quite clear by not only reiterating his dedication to National Socialism, but by bluntly declaring his anti-Semitism: "I consider Jewry to be the greatest enemy of the German Volk again today. We owe this war not to the English or French people, but to the Jewish manipulators that prepared for this war against Germany long beforehand."[112] Sepp repeated that because of his world view, he could not be involved with Hella any further. He could not understand why she could not comprehend these facts, and he found it inconceivable that she wanted to devote herself to him. Were she a German woman, he admitted, things would be different, but as matters stood he was devastated to learn that he was volunteering to serve in the Wehrmacht while leaving behind a Jewish child. Sepp ended his letter by claiming that Hella might think him cruel, but nothing could alter his position.

The same day he penned his letter to Hella, Sepp wrote a second letter to the editorial board of Das Schwarze Korps explaining his situation and feelings on the matter: "If this woman was at least a German woman! Then I could ... marry her or at least take over material responsibility for the child. But to marry a half-Jew ... no, I prefer the pistol. And to draw near a Jewish offspring ... the thought is simply dreadful."[113] Although he sought advice for his predicament, the newspaper did not respond, but instead forwarded his letter to Himmler's personal staff. Less than two weeks later, Sepp received a reply from Rudolf Brandt relaying the conversation he had had with Himmler about the situation. Through Brandt's letter, Himmler wanted Sepp to know that there was no "reason for you to reach for the pistol."[114] Himmler not only recognized that Sepp had made a mistake with his relationship with the Jewish woman, but also that Sepp understood the gravity of his error. Shooting himself, Brandt told Sepp, would not solve the problem. Brandt confirmed that marrying the child's mother was not possible, but still reminded Sepp that he did have a child for whom he had to take responsibility. He suggested that Sepp submit further information about himself as Himmler had consented to the possibility of him joining the Waffen-SS.

This was an interesting response. In his letter to Das Schwarze Korps, Sepp had all but directly admitted to violating the Nuremberg

Laws – namely, the Law for the Protection of German Blood and Honour, which prohibited sexual relations between Jews and non-Jews. At
the time of the violation, Sepp held Swiss citizenship (he did not gain
German citizenship until 1943).[115] However, the correspondence relating to his dilemma came from early 1940 and indicated that he lived in
Vienna. All Nazi racial laws had been applicable in Austria since shortly
after the *Anschluß* in March 1938. Besides the Nuremberg Laws, this
included the Reich Citizenship Law of November 1935, which defined
who was and was not a Jew. Sepp's unborn child only had one Jewish
grandparent, making the child a second-degree *Mischling* – technically,
not a Jew.[116] That might explain why Brandt informed Sepp that he had
to pay for the child's upkeep.

Brandt's reply greatly relieved Sepp, who declared that he accepted
his obligation to provide for the child. In addition, Sepp seized upon
the opportunity to enlist in the Waffen-SS.[117] By the end of February, the
matter had been turned over to Gottlob Berger, then an SS-Brigadeführer
responsible for recruitment for the Waffen-SS. Requests for further
information about Sepp were directed to the relevant SS authorities in
Vienna, who provided a positive character report by April. This reference allowed him to be called up for service by the middle of the month,
and he was still serving in the Waffen-SS as of September 1944.[118]

With Sepp's case, Himmler once again showed leniency. In this
particular situation, the needs of the newly founded Waffen-SS and
the branch's ability to bolster his position in the party and the state
trumped racial ideology in Himmler's eyes. Prior to the war, he would
not have given any man who had had a sexual relationship with a Jew
a chance to redeem himself. As in the the case of Karl M. (examined
in the last chapter), rejection was nearly absolute for an SS man who
unknowingly had sexual relations with a Jew. Yet during the war, circumstances necessitated some flexibility. However, not all situations
involving illegitimate children related to racial matters. In other cases,
adultery resulted in illegitimate children. In November 1943, Ruth H.,
the wife of SS-Untersturmführer Dr. Alfred H., wrote to Himmler for
help. After almost a decade of marriage and the birth of three children,
Ruth had learned that her husband was having an affair with his secretary; the relationship had already resulted in one child, and, at the
time of her letter, a second was on the way. According to Ruth, her
husband was demanding a divorce, and she sought Himmler's advice.
She asked him, "Can I, as a German wife and mother of three children,
be forced into a divorce? I am innocent in this situation and now must

fight for my rights and the rights of my children."[119] Ruth ended her letter by imploring Himmler to protect her and her children.

This situation put Himmler in a precarious position because he was in the same situation as Alfred. German law and his own regulations for the SS and police further complicated the situation. In 1938, the Nazi government had amended marriage laws by expanding the grounds for divorce. One of the new provisions allowed for a divorce if the marriage had all but dissolved because the spouses had lived apart for three years or more.[120] Ruth's letter indicated that she and her husband had not lived together for some time, first because of his assignments for the SS and then because of his choice to live with his mistress. For this reason alone, Alfred could have requested a divorce, and the court would have looked favourably on his petition because he had already begun to have children with another woman. But, while this law might have aided him, he would have simultaneously found himself in trouble with the SS court. In April 1941, SS-Gruppenführer Paul Scharfe, chief of the court, released a memorandum indicating that SS men could be disciplined for adultery. The court issued additional decrees in 1942.[121]

In response, Himmler requested that the Personnel Main Office forward a copy of Alfred's file to him. He did not reply directly to Ruth, but had an officer in his personal staff send her a letter in mid-December 1943. This letter did not indicate that Himmler was looking into the matter, but suggested that because her husband served in the Security Service, Ruth should take up the matter with the chief of that office.[122] This situation remained unresolved. Officials in Himmler's personal staff and the Security Service corresponded about the matter until at least late March 1945, debating whether or not to proceed with disciplinary actions against Alfred and determining the suitability of his mistress. Alfred's personnel file, which never listed a divorce, confirmed the lack of resolution in this matter.[123]

These two cases of illegitimacy only involved a few individuals. The vast majority of illegitimate offspring were produced through the Lebensborn program, although not all fathers belonged to the SS. During the war, the number of homes expanded; most were located in Germany and Norway. Contemporary accounts leave the impression that, contrary to later historical analysis, the homes were nothing more than a breeding ground for the master race. Himmler even contributed to this perception, at least as recorded by Felix Kersten. The Reichsführer claimed that the Lebensborn program had given a woman who would have otherwise remained childless the opportunity to have "the happy experience of being a mother" while simultaneously playing "her full part in the life of the community."[124] Himmler admitted that only the most valuable and racially pure men were allowed to conceive children with these women, and he anticipated that more women would take advantage of this possibility after the war.

One SS man who participated in this attempt to make Himmler's wish a reality was Peter Neumann. According to his post-war autobiography, he was sent to a Lebensborn home in early 1940. On his first day there, he met a young woman named Lotte. As he recalled it, both were willing to fulfil their biological duty after having known each other for only a few hours. Neumann described their brief sexual encounter as "an astonishing experience in a man's life."[125] He and Lotte succeeded in conceiving a boy whom she named after him. While at the home caring for their newborn, Lotte wrote to Peter with an update about their son. On receiving this information, Neumann reflected that, "it's funny, but I don't feel at all like a father."[126] His story, like that of Hildegard Trutz, appears to deviate from the norm. A more typical account was that of SS-Obergruppenführer Fritz Schleßmann who, after having four children with his wife, impregnated his secretary in late 1944. He turned to Himmler for assistance in placing her into a Lebensborn home – a task Himmler was more than pleased to do.[127]

Altogether, of the seven to eight thousand children born in Lebensborn homes, between 50 and 60 per cent were illegitimate.[128] Despite attempts to encourage SS families to adopt them, there was limited success. There were perhaps one hundred childless couples registered with the Lebensborn who sought to adopt, but many families were not interested in adopting in general and from the Lebensborn in particular.[129] In addition, the legal system made adoption a cumbersome process, and most unwed mothers wanted to keep their children.[130] Günther Tesch, who served as a lawyer for the Lebensborn for most of the war, later testified that fewer than a hundred children were adopted; his former colleague Inge Viermitz affirmed that the number of mothers who gave up their children was minimal.[131] Of the unmarried mothers, some wished to have a relationship with the fathers of their children. Regardless of whether this wish came to fruition, fathers were held financially responsible for their offspring. SS officers were still required to support the Lebensborn program during the war, their contributions again determined by marital status and rank.[132] Men who placed their wives, girlfriends, or mistresses in a home paid additional support. This money would have been crucial because, as Max Sollmann claimed after the war, membership fees were insufficient to support the Lebensborn's wartime tasks.[133]

Convincing men to have children – whether legitimate or otherwise – and providing them with the means to have offspring throughout the war were major concerns. But they were not the only matters in which the SS was interested. In particular, all of these issues were contingent upon one crucial factor: that a man and the woman with whom he was in a relationship were each capable of having children. For the majority of couples, the birth of their children proved this a non-issue, but for a minority, infertility was a matter with which they had to contend. Therefore, it was a matter with which the SS and its medical community had to contend as well.

Ernst Robert Grawitz worked with SS-Gruppenführer Dr. Karl Genzken, the chief of the Waffen-SS medical department, to eradicate childlessness in SS marriages. To this end, special departments for women's health and obstetrics were founded in SS military hospitals in Berlin, Prague, Dachau, and Marienbad.[134] However, a great deal of this work was not handled by SS medical personnel, but by specialists, typically university personnel specially recruited by these departments. Among the recruited physicians were Dr. Carl Clauberg and SS-Untersturmführer Dr. Hans Mackenrodt, as well as SS-Standartenführer Dr. Günther von Wolff, who produced a short commentary about female infertility at the request of Grawitz.[135] As none of these men worked at SS medical facilities, they charged fees for their services, leading Grawitz to contact Oswald Pohl and request funding. Grawitz did so on the basis that it was Himmler's desire to have SS men "sire as numerous offspring as possible."[136] This was not the first time that money had been requested to pay for infertility treatment. Over eighteen months earlier, Otto Hofmann had asked Himmler to grant RuSHA special funding to reimburse couples for expenses relating to medical treatment.[137] It is unclear whether Himmler authorized money for RuSHA, but after receiving this request from Grawitz, Pohl agreed to fund treatment in exceptional cases.[138]

Waffen-SS medical officers were notified of the funding available for infertility treatment by specialists.[139] SS medical officials communicated with both specialists and SS men in order to resolve infertility issues. In some cases, an investigation revealed a problem with the husband, in others with the wife; some investigations revealed that nothing appeared to be wrong with the reproductive organs of either spouse. When a problem was diagnosed, various treatments were suggested, among them hormone therapy and visiting additional specialists.[140] One of the more unique remedies proposed for female sterility was bathing in a natural bog bath.[141]

Aside from treatments by outside specialists, the most prominent Nazi official researching infertility was Leonardo Conti. Among the solutions he suggested was artificial insemination. His proposal was not the first time artificial insemination had been brought up in the SS; *Das Schwarze Korps* had run an article in February 1940 that discussed the statistics and causes of infertility and suggested artificial insemination as a possible solution.[142] Conti submitted an article to Himmler in June 1942 – the same article in which he suggested matchmaking as a method to increase the number of children born. With regards to artificial insemination, Conti recognized that with this proposition "the fertilization process would become somewhat mechanically soulless," but he argued that it was unnatural for a healthy woman to remain childless and be deprived her natural function as a mother.[143] He suggested that it would be possible to determine the descent of the child, especially if the sperm came from a man known to the woman, thus tacitly acknowledging that racial criteria could be upheld.

Despite his desire to have his men increase the size and quality of the *Volk* by just about any means possible, Himmler rejected Conti's proposal. To him, fertility by all possible means meant by all possible *natural* means, which excluded artificial insemination. He communicated his concerns to Conti, stating that tasking the medical profession with solving this issue would be of no benefit, particularly when it could be handled by other organizations.[144] Himmler was even leery about the overuse of artificial insemination when it came to breeding animals. In a March 1943 letter to Dr. Heinz Henseler, director of the Institute for Animal Husbandry and Breeding Biology in Munich, he commented that, "for our total breeding and passing of genetic material, I consider [artificial insemination] dangerous." He wrote that such an opinion was also "valid in the area of human reproduction."[145] Grawitz held this position, too; he rejected such methods as unnatural. Nonetheless, Conti continued developing potential methods of artificial insemination.[146] He also established the program Help for Childlessness in Marriage. It was designed to direct infertile couples to appropriate medical facilities and to help procure financial means to pay for examinations, operations, and other procedures. RuSHA was aware of this work; in a letter to all Oberabschnitt and welfare advisers, Harald Turner pointed out that SS officials needed to ensure that the men in their units were aware of this program.[147]

The concern over infertility was not limited to physicians and officials; SS men and their wives also expressed distress over their inability to conceive. They often communicated their worries through letters, a few of which were directed to Himmler, but many others were sent to the Lebensborn. Their grief was certainly personal; as one man declared, having children would be the "greatest wish" and a source of happiness for him and his wife.[148] The men and women also conveyed their sorrow at being unable to contribute to the family community. In her letter to the Lebensborn, a woman named Isle commented: "As the responsible wife of an SS officer, I would realize the pointlessness of the marriage if I would not have the certainty of bearing children."[149]

Another wife lamented that the SS would reject her marriage and would look upon her as inferior because of her lack of children. In this particular case, her fears stemmed from a talk she had attended given by Gregor Ebner. He replied to her letter, apologizing for any misunderstanding caused by his speech and clarifying his remarks:

> You can be assured that I in no way had the intention to hurt you or any other woman present at the hall. I have never said and will never say that a childless marriage is immoral. However, I did not leave any doubt that I consider an intentionally childless marriage, in which the husband or the wife abstains from having descendants for reasons of convenience, as immoral … It is quite different with childless marriages due to nature. I know only too well as a doctor with over fifteen years of practice how tragic it is for a woman if she would like to have children to go from doctor to doctor to reach this goal and finally remain unsuccessful with all efforts.[150]

Ebner ended his letter with the wish that his words would dispel the woman's anxiety. He offered to visit her and speak with her about the issue further, but there are no supplementary records indicating whether he had any additional contact with this woman.

When writing to the Lebensborn about infertility, the issue of artificial insemination came up. SS men and their wives asked whether the Lebensborn program performed such procedures or had information about medical facilities that did.[151] Guntram Pflaum considered allowing physicians at the Pommern home in Bad Polzin to carry out infertility treatment. Ebner became aware of this plan in April 1940, around the time when Max Sollmann replaced Pflaum. He was curious to know why Pflaum had promised that one of the homes would participate in infertility treatment. He expressed his concerns in correspondence with SS-Untersturmführer Dr. Düker, the leader of the Pommern home, and Dr. Hans Mackenrodt, an advisory specialist associated with the Lebensborn program.[152] Ebner opposed the plan on both legal and medical grounds. His legal rejection rested on one argument: the program's statute did not entitle it to go into that area of medical work. Among the medical reasons, he noted that women's infertility was a relatively new field in gynecology; thus, Ebner argued, work on the subject should be handled by experienced doctors and nurses working in clinics and research institutions. He commented that "some inept press articles" had led the public to expect too much from infertility treatment, whereas in reality the success rate was quite low, which could damage the prestige of the Lebensborn program.[153]

Dücker's response to Ebner's concerns is unknown, although Mackenrodt held an unfavourable opinion about the prospects of infertility treatment through the Lebensborn homes. Ebner subsequently raised his objections to Sollmann in late May, asking the new administrative head to raise the issue with Himmler.[154] Sollmann did and replied about a month later, briefly stating that "the Reichsführer-SS is of the opinion that the Lebensborn should not deal with sterility treatment. He agrees with [the opinion] that the necessary sterility treatment is transferred to a gynecological hospital."[155] Given Himmler's refusal, along with his own opposition, Ebner made it clear when corresponding with anyone interested in infertility treatment that the Lebensborn program did not "currently have any facilities in which artificial fertilization can be performed."[156] Instead, he directed the interested party to specialists contracted by the SS, most often Mackenrodt.[157]

Despite Himmler's refusal to promote artificial insemination, he did support other research projects, including an examination of the relationship between fertility and menstruation. This interest led Brandt to write Ebner and Grawitz, requesting if it would be possible to determine if there were a correlation between the age when a woman got her first period and the length of time she remained capable of bearing children.[158] Both doctors replied within approximately a week. Ebner stated that the Lebensborn program should have no difficulty compiling statistics clarifying when each mother in its homes had her first period.[159] Lebensborn physicians already gathered such information for home admissions and recorded it in each woman's medical history. Grawitz also thought that it would be possible to analyse the relationship between a woman's first period and the duration of her fertility.[160] He noted that most women began to menstruate between the ages of 13 and 16, and were capable of having children until between the ages of 45 and 47, although only about 0.2 per cent of births were to women over age 40.

Grawitz furthermore told Brandt that he had raised the issue with SS-Hauptsturmführer Dr. Günter K.F. Schultze, the director of the university gynecological hospital at Greifswald. Schultze promptly replied to Grawitz, who then sent the letter to Brandt, who in turn forwarded it to Ebner.[161] Schultze did provide a little statistical data. In addition, he pointed out that the larger concern with women who began to menstruate late was not the duration of their ability to conceive, but the fact that late menstruation might indicate a weakness in their ovaries. Although there did not seem to be a strong connection between weak ovaries and infertility, Schultze stated that attention needed to be given to this issue during SS engagement and marriage examinations. Due to his belief in the importance of the issue, he had started to investigate this relationship. Presumably, Brandt kept Himmler informed of this dialogue among the physicians.

Another subject that elicited Himmler's interest was sex ratios.[162] He paid particular attention to analyses that proposed methods for increasing the number of males born. This type of research was not uncommon within the larger scientific and sociological milieu of which the German scientific community was a part. Studies conducted prior to and during the Second World War addressed which social factors influenced the gender of children.[163] Among the research that garnered Himmler's attention was that done by Richard Korherr, a prominent demographer and statistician that he had recruited in December 1940 to be his inspector for statistics.[164] As such, he was initially responsible for overseeing the statistical work of nearly every SS department and office.[165] Korherr used the information made available to him to conduct his own studies, among which were two reports from 1942 concerning the sex ratios of legitimate children.

The first study examined the relationship between the difference in the parents' age and the gender of their children; this was based on married SS couples who had a child in 1941.[166] His report showed three significant facts: one, in 84 per cent of marriages, the father was older than the mother; two, within the SS, 109 boys were born for every 100 girls, a ratio more favourable than the Reich's 106:100 ratio; and three, the younger the mother, the larger the number of boys born. The second study delved into the gender of children and their birth order.[167] For the SS, Korherr determined that for every 100 girls born as the first child, 123 boys were born. His work also revealed that this number increased to 134 boys when it came to children conceived prior to their parents' marriage. This ratio might have given Himmler pause before he censured another SS man for asking permission to marry after his girlfriend became pregnant. In both studies, Korherr made it very clear that because he was only working with numbers for 1941, he was working with a small sample and could draw no general conclusions. These were temporary results that could only be validated or refuted with additional studies. Himmler was nonetheless pleased with the results, as a letter from Brandt to Korherr indicated that he wanted his inspector for statistics to pursue the issue.[168]

Besides Korherr's statistical reports, Himmler received information on gender ratios from other sources, including Artur Dombek, who worked for the party. Dombek wrote to Himmler in January 1944 and explained when, based on his years of observation, it was most likely for a couple to conceive a boy. He concluded that a boy was more likely for the first, second, and even third child when the man was about ten years older than the woman. More male offspring were produced during wartime, which, Dombek concluded, was due to the physical and mental fatigue experienced by the men.[169] This research intrigued Himmler, as Brandt wrote in his reply to Dombek.[170] However, Himmler would have looked highly upon any work that bolstered his already existing opinions, in this case his opposition to marriages between older women and younger men. Furthermore, learning that more boys were born in wartime would have most likely convinced him that he was correct in attempting to persuade his men to have children during the war.

Around the same time as he received Dombek's letter, Himmler had a conversation with Gottlob Berger in which the SS-Obergruppenführer informed him about a tradition from his home in the Swabian Alps. If a boy was desired, the couple had to follow a certain ritual. For one week, neither the man nor the woman consumed alcohol; during this same time frame, the wife refrained from work and got plenty of sleep. After this week, the man marched a 40 kilometre roundtrip to the city of Ulm. He could not stop during this trek, and once he had returned, he and his wife had sex, which resulted in the birth of a boy.[171]

Dombek's and Berger's theories were forwarded to Grawitz, who found both methods problematic. He proclaimed that if such formulas actually worked and were consciously used to generate offspring of one sex or the other, "it would probably mean the end of the human race."[172] Then, after providing an overview of the fertilization process where he confirmed that the father determined the sex of a child, Grawitz commented that the ratio of boys to girls was approximately 1006:1000, a number in line with the ratio reported by Korherr. As the formulas that claimed to produce boys over girls had not been tested on so large a scale, it was difficult to determine their validity. At the end of his letter, Grawitz contended that "it is impossible to generate intentionally a child of a certain sex," something that he believed would remain impossible in the future.[173] Despite Grawitz's naysaying and Korherr's caution about drawing broad conclusions from limited statistics, the information provided by Dombek and Berger intrigued Himmler to the point where he requested that the Lebensborn program investigate the question of producing boys or girls.[174] This research would have represented one more factor in Himmler's quest to create a sustainable family community.

There was one additional element to this quest. The family community's objective was to serve as the nation's racial aristocracy, but the boundaries of the Reich expanded during the first years of the war. This expansion led to the creation of grandiose plans for the reconstruction and resettlement of Eastern Europe, most notably a proposal called General Plan East. Its architects, Konrad Meyer and Walter Christaller, were experts in mapping spaces and populations. They started to lay out their designs following the conquest of Poland, and Himmler asked them to expand their work after the invasion of the Soviet Union. Their blueprint called for three large areas of German settlement in the East, which would have required the extermination of millions of people.[175] Meyer and Christaller's plan did not directly outline the role that the SS would play in this process, but the organization undoubtedly would have been at the forefront of first destroying and then reconstructing a brutally decimated Eastern Europe. In Himmler's fantasy of the future Nazi empire, SS families would have been part of this reconstruction. Fortunately, General Plan East remained an unfulfilled proposal, but it nonetheless serves as a chilling reminder that Himmler's ambitions had no bounds.

While General Plan East remained in the planning stages, the attempt to foster SS families progressed and evolved during the war. All of the measures implemented demonstrate that the survival of each man's genetic legacy remained a crucial goal for Himmler. Many of the policies he supported, including authorizing a year-long leave from the front for last sons to start a family as well as scheduling and paying for short rendezvouses between husbands and wives to promote reproduction, illustrate how he did not want the war to impede his efforts to construct the family community. The victory in the cradle was designed to work in conjunction with a military victory; both bolstered the position of the SS by strengthening the Nazi state. In an effort to solidify this connection, Himmler sought to have each man embrace the notion that fathering children represented as significant a duty to the SS and the Reich as any other. By treating fatherhood as a duty, Himmler had eroded any boundary between an SS man's private life and his service to the organization and the state. That erosion, much like his promotion of illegitimacy, shows that Himmler aspired to replace the traditional bourgeois family. The war provided him with the opportunity to promote these aspirations further, although, as will be seen in chapter 6, SS men did not completely fulfil their familial obligations.

Chapter Five

Belonging to the Family Community

The 1931 engagement and marriage command had established relatively straightforward guidelines. Successive regulations, however, resulted in a rather labyrinthine process. Throughout this evolution, each man was expected to keep up with every order regulating his marriage, and once married, he had to understand the expectations laid down for establishing a family. To facilitate staying informed, the SS provided its men with ideological education. But guidance was not limited to men. Officials incorporated wives and children into the process to ensure that family members understood that they, too, had an important place. In particular, ceremonies were created to receive wives and children into the family community. Once they belonged, the SS sought to provide care for these families. Organizational concern for their well-being was evident by the mid-1930s, although it became an increasingly larger task during the war. Examining how men were educated, along with how women and children were incorporated into the family community, is crucial to understanding the community's position in the SS. This chapter will explore the process of education and incorporation and show how cultivating a sense of belonging was an integral part of creating the family community.

A systematic attempt to educate SS men began in 1934. Initially, RuSHA was responsible for this task. It established an Education Office and assigned training leaders to serve in each unit from the Oberabschnitt down to the Sturm. Solidification of the duties of this office and these leaders continued over the next couple of years, but overall, training leaders became responsible for ideological education in the SS and the police. RuSHA remained in charge of education until August 1938, when Himmler transferred the Education Office to the SS Main Office.[1]

Even with the shift from one office to another, the same person, Joachim Caesar, remained in charge of education from 1937 until 1942.[2] Continuity in leadership meant there was relative continuity in education, the goal remaining not simply to inform men about ideology, but to show how it bound them together.

First RuSHA and then the Main Office provided training leaders with guidelines outlining the themes that each leader needed to cover in his lessons. Each training leader also worked with the officer in charge of the unit in which he served because that officer was responsible for the development of the men under him, including their educational development.[3] The training leader had to create programs that encompassed a wide range of activities. Calisthenics and exercise, for example, were important because SS men had to earn the SA and Reich sports badges, and even men who had earned them needed to remain in shape.[4] Besides fitness, there were lectures on ideology. The balance between physical activity and ideological lectures depended on the season, with more attention given to the latter in the winter. The guidelines emphasize that ideological education was not propaganda, nor was it about rote memorization. Training leaders had to explain to their men why they needed to learn particular material, which had to be presented in a lively and engaging manner. SS men needed to remain aware of daily politics by reading the Nazi press, especially *Das Schwarze Korps*, which training leaders were required to purchase regularly.[5] Each unit was also supposed to purchase at least one subscription so that the newspaper was available to its men.[6] With politics a minor subject, the purpose of ideological education was to convey the core principles of the SS, which meant highlighting the "positive" elements of SS philosophy.[7]

When a training leader organized a session, he did not improvise. Rather, he created a program based upon the material provided to him.[8] Officers working at the Oberabschnitt level periodically convened conferences to train leaders in the subordinate units of the Oberabschnitt; lower-level units did the same.[9] One of the most proactive divisions was Oberabschnitt West. Under the leadership of SS-Obergruppenführer Fritz Weitzel, it created several books designed for education. One was released in early 1938.[10] It covered a range of subjects relating to family and population policies, including spousal selection, the engagement and marriage process, the role of the family, and caring for wives and children. The book conveyed the relevant information about each subject through a series of question and answers. That layout was probably an intentional decision because it provided officers with a format that would assist them in preparing lectures and holding individual meetings with the men in their units.

While guidance from the Oberabschnitt would have been useful, most of the time the Education Office supplied training leaders with the necessary material. Among the items available were theme-based photo reels. The subjects covered by these reels included Bolshevism and Judaism along with a review of National Socialism in the context of European and German history.[11] Other reels were dedicated to family matters. It is highly likely that the images of model families in these reels came from SS men. In 1935 the RuSHA Race Office, which seemed to be in charge of producing the reels, asked training leaders to request photos of families, especially shots where the husband/father was recognizable as an SS member. The Race Office noted its intention to make these photographs available for educational purposes, although publication in *Das Schwarze Korps* was also possible.[12]

The most relevant photo reel for family matters was entitled "Spousal Selection of the SS Man," which was available by at least early 1939.[13] It contained nearly a hundred and fifty pictures along with explanatory notes for each photograph. Collectively, these images created a narrative that explained the process of spousal selection. The photo reel began by explaining how an SS man would find a suitable woman to marry. Many pictures showed ideal women, but to emphasize what an SS man should look for, images of unsuitable women were included, too. In addition, several slides showed racially acceptable women with their parents – a reminder to the men that they had to evaluate a woman's heritage because that heritage would be reflected in their children. SS men were then shown pictures of healthy and unhealthy women and children. With these images, the training leader could point out that each man had to think about what type of family he wanted to create. He could also inform the men that they had a duty to the *Volk* when making decisions about their future families. At the end, the notes called for the training leader to remind the men that their honour was called loyalty – in this particular case, loyalty to SS racial ideals.

A training leader certainly could have used a photo reel like "Spousal Selection" to send the appropriate message about SS marriage rules. He could have used it to generate a conversation with his men, clarify any misunderstandings, and address their concerns. However, the training leader had to order photo reels in advance, meaning that he would have needed to utilize other resources for many lessons.[14] The primary source he relied on most often was readings. Typically, the selections were short, as many programs were held at night, and the men, most of whom would have worked all day, would have been tired and unable to focus on lengthy readings.[15] The training leader would have had access to the books in his unit's library, especially as he was responsible for its upkeep.[16] Among the standard National Socialist works, passages from *Mein Kampf* were frequently assigned. Another commonly used source was the pamphlet *The SS as an Anti-Bolshevik Fighting Force*. Based on a speech given by Himmler at the Reich Peasants' Rally in November 1935, it was published by the party press the following year.[17] In it Himmler addressed several key ideological issues. Given its title, he spoke – unsurprisingly – of the evil of Bolshevism along with the associated nemesis in the Nazi pantheon of foes, Judaism. He reviewed the history and virtues of the *Volk* and the history of Germany up to the present. The foundation of and the principles held by the SS, including selection, loyalty, honour, and obedience, were highlighted as well.

Such information would have provided training leaders with ample material to generate discussions with their men about the core ideals of the SS. The pamphlet also reviewed the principle behind the engagement and marriage command – namely, that gathering men of good blood into one organization would be pointless unless each SS man could contribute to the foundation of a community that would show reverence for his ancestry and would guarantee the continuation of the *Volk* by marrying a woman who was of equal racial and biological value. Together, each couple would then take the next step in building that community by having children. Without those children, the Nazi Party's years of political struggle, as well as the founding of the Nazi state, would have been useless. Here Himmler used the phrase "victory of the German child."[18] This was one of the earliest examples of Himmler using this expression, although, as mentioned earlier, in letters and speeches to both SS and non-SS audiences, he linked the victory in the cradle first with the party's political victory and then with the state's military victory.

The theme of the dual victory likewise appeared in SS publications. The Education Office disseminated pamphlets during the war that were designed to elicit support for large families. Among these publications was *Victory of the Arms – Victory of the Child*, published in late 1940.[19] The title of the document summed up its purpose: to convince men through words and images that Germany's military achievement must be followed by an equivalent success in the cradle. Only an early and child-rich marriage could sustain the German *Volk* and ensure the continuation of National Socialism. In order to maintain a growing and

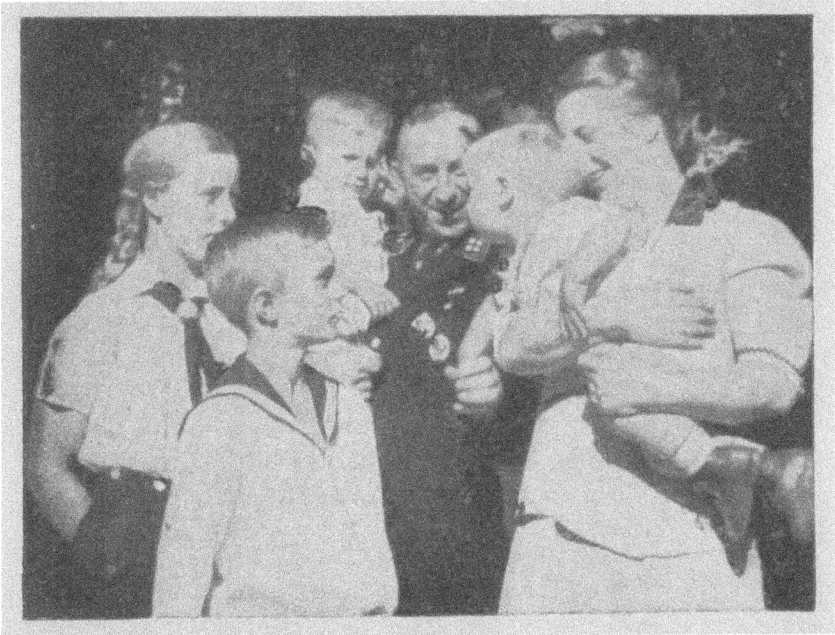

Sieg der Waffen – Sieg des Kindes, p. 27

healthy *Volk*, each man had to embrace the obligation to preserve and increase Nordic blood, which meant accepting that his family needed to have four to six children. By becoming "the happy parents of a large and healthy flock of children," SS men and their wives would prove their commitment to the *Volk* and the nation.[20]

A second pamphlet underscoring the dual-victory theme, *SS Man and the Question of Blood*, was released in 1941.[21] It emphasized the needs of the *Volk* over those of the individual. Fertility alone guaranteed the survival of the genetic material of the Nordic race, it claimed, but a decline in the willingness of the German people to have children in the first decades of the twentieth century, combined with the demographic decline caused by war, had threatened this survival. The vitality of the *Volk* therefore depended on the conservation of its best members, particularly through these people's readiness to marry early and have many children. Only when "the number of cradles [was] larger than the number of coffins" would an individual family and the entire *Volk* be saved and the military victory in the Second World War be solidified.[22]

Sieg der Waffen – Sieg des Kindes, p. 8

A third publication from 1943, *Race Politics*, stressed the idea of community – or more precisely, the *Volk* as a living community. Within that community, the pamphlet claimed, the SS embodied a community of the best bearers of Nordic blood.[23] As a selective elite within the *Volk*, the SS had the obligation to eschew the traditional two-child system and to have families with at least four children. By assuming this responsibility, each man had to acknowledge that his private decisions regarding offspring required him to place the needs of the SS and the *Volk* above his personal desires. As guardians of the Nordic race, he and his wife had to accept that passing on their blood to their offspring was their highest duty and honour.

While collectively these readings contributed to the ideological education of SS men, they merely complemented the organization's main

Sieg der Waffen – Sieg des Kindes, p. 6

source of written instruction, *SS-Leitheft*, which the Education Office began publishing in 1935.[24] The Education Office insisted that it serve as the basis of ideological education. So did Himmler. He mandated that the themes in each edition had to be timeless – that is, its content had to be equally appropriate for a current SS man as for a future member.[25]

Each edition contained articles on a wide variety of subjects. Many of them were not directly about the party or the SS. For example, articles on a broad range of historical topics were juxtaposed with ones on astronomy, anatomy, and paleontology. Other articles were more directly relevant. Unsurprisingly, some vilified the Jews. Another common topic was the history of the SS. Also included were articles on the Hitler Youth, the burden of the hereditarily ill, the role of women in the family, and the importance of farmers and agrarian policy. During the war, there were reminders about the need for good soldierly conduct as well as short histories of non-German Waffen-SS units. The publication's wide range of subjects demonstrated the breadth of information that officials in the Education Office and/or Himmler felt was necessary for each SS man to know.

There were also articles directly relevant to the theme of family and its relationship to Nazi racial ideology. An early article by Joachim Caesar not only reviewed the purpose of the marriage process, but proclaimed that SS men "must be grateful to the Reichsführer that he is concerned about your welfare and happiness" and had created the engagement and marriage command for their benefit.[26] Another prewar article thanked Himmler on behalf of all SS men for the order, "because he wants that your marriage and your children should be healthy and happy," while a wartime article reprinted the order and summarized its purpose.[27] Other articles provided advice on how to choose a wife, primarily by advising a man to examine a woman's family history carefully because her heritage would become the heritage of his children – the very same lesson conveyed in the photo reel "Spousal Selection."[28] A healthy wife would lead to a healthy marriage, leading to the creation of a racially and biologically worthy family that was the smallest yet most valuable unit in the Reich. The formation of these families and the family community represented a grave responsibility, but it was a responsibility that, as one article noted, had been vested in the SS by the Führer when he gave the organization the motto "My honour is called loyalty."[29]

While their Führer entrusted them with loyalty, their Reichsführer entrusted them to give life to Germany. To emphasize the importance of children, *SS-Leitheft* included several articles that stressed the value of offspring. One offered a two-century genealogical chronicle of a prolific family. The author pointed out that the reader should learn from the history of this family that it was possible for a family to contribute to the *Volk* in times of war as well as peace.[30] A second article highlighted great luminaries in German history who had come from large families; among the figures listed were Friedrich the Great, Wolfgang Amadeus Mozart, Johann Sebastian Bach, Richard Wagner, Otto von Bismarck, Werner Siemens, and Immanuel Kant. Every new child represented a possible future luminary, the article proclaimed, and the responsibility for ensuring the birth of these potential great men lies with the present generation.[31]

Another way in which *SS-Leitheft* demonstrated the importance of family was by using contributions about fatherhood written by SS men. In mid-1941, the journal requested submissions in which men reflected upon the theme "my mother, my wife, my dear children."[32] The editors announced that they had received many contributions, and that despite the effort it took to read all of them, it had been a worthwhile endeavour. They published several, with the intention to print more in later editions.[33] One, for example, was a poem in which a father gave his son advice on how to live as a "brave, loyal, and pure" comrade for Germany.[34] In another, an SS man described his reunion with his eight-month-old son, whom he had last seen the day the baby was born. He depicted his interaction with the baby, relishing in his son's daily development, "smother[ing] him with joy and love," and making up for missed time due to his service at the front.[35]

These testimonies to fatherhood contrasted starkly with later articles containing the last testaments of men who had died at the front. In one of these testaments, the author, Leo R., recorded that he wanted his children to respect their mother as she had given them life. He furthermore advised them that "they should always be simple, loyal, and true."[36] In a second testament, Heinz H. wrote to his parents, brother, and wife. He beseeched his brother to carry on the family name because he did not know if his wife were pregnant. However, if she were with child, then he had certain requests: if the child were a boy, he wanted his son to have his name and to be raised as a healthy and honest lad; if the child were a girl, Heinz desired that she be made aware of her maternal duties to the nation.[37]

These testaments reminded each man of his responsibilities as a husband and father. This message was reinforced in a letter written by an SS widow. The woman spoke of her late husband, their life together, and his service at the front. She wrote about their children, whom she indicated completed her life. The widow even commented that she felt sorry for German women who intentionally did not have children; they were missing out on the joy of being a mother, she said, while lamenting that she and her late husband had only been able to have three. Yet in those children, the woman recognized that her husband had never died. He lived on through them, through his son who had his eyes and his daughter who had his laugh.[38] She wanted every woman to know of her continuing love for her husband through their children, a message that would have been equally applicable to any SS man. He, too, would have been reminded from this letter that his children represented his future, a point that echoed Himmler's October 1939 order, in which he implored men to have children before they risked dying.

Beyond these individual articles, *SS-Leitheft* included a semi-regular section called "From the Practice of the Family Office." Published when

RuSHA controlled the Education Office, the articles in this section presented issues that the Family Office commonly encountered while processing engagement and marriage applications. They underscored the importance of filling in the genealogical tree completely and the consequences of finding a Jew in a family's lineage. They explained the necessity of the hereditary health questionnaire, with one article stating that each man should understand that "everything which a human being represents physically, mentally, and in character, he owes ... [to] his predecessors and passes it down to his children."[39] Other articles provided guidelines for how a man could apply for the state marriage loan. They clarified why he should only wed a physically and racially suitable woman, noting that it would be impossible for healthy children to come from a woman whose family lineage showed signs of hereditarily illness.[40]

There was one other way in which SS-Leitheft showcased the importance of family. Each edition contained pictures, and sometimes those shots featured children. In these photos, the children looked relatively innocent and sweet, not to mention physically in accord with the appropriate racial stereotypes.[41] Other pictures showed children with their fathers and/or SS men.[42] These images all presented the same basic content: a man interacting with a child in a positive manner. For example, one picture portrayed an SS soldier holding a young girl, while another showed a father teaching his son how to play the piano.[43] Such images would have been valuable in educating men to accept the creation of racially healthy children as an integral part of their community.

Altogether, the variety of themes and topics covered in SS-Leitheft provided training leaders with ample material. Prior to the war, they used the readings to foster dialogue during weekly education sessions. During the war, such personal interaction would have been difficult for men serving at the front. Still, the Education Office provided copies of SS-Leitheft to Waffen-SS units in an attempt to disseminate SS ideology. Starting in 1941, it also created foreign-language editions for non-German units. The articles in these editions mostly covered the same topics as the German edition, but there was some tweaking to demonstrate how SS ideology was applicable to all racially suitable members of the organization.[44]

The consistent publication of SS-Leitheft fostered the expectation for Himmler, the Education Office, and the training leaders, that if SS men understood the racial ideology, then they would understand the orders stemming from it, including those regulating their marriages and families. They would recognize the connection between ideology and practice and would use this knowledge as they made personal decisions. And yet reality showed that these expectations were not always met. Reports from training leaders are limited, but the available information shows that when it came to SS men participating in education sessions and comprehending ideological material, the results were mixed.[45] Several accounts listed the topics covered in meetings, but many did not, leaving much to speculate as to what subjects each training leader reviewed and how he covered them.[46] Some accounts reported attendance among individual units to be as high as 80–100 per cent, while others were lower.[47] Explanations for a lack of attendance were occasionally given; for example, sometimes men could not attend due to school or work schedules, including service in the Wehrmacht, or they were absent because they were on vacation or attending special events. Some training leaders accounted for low numbers at an individual meeting because they held multiple sessions on the same topic and did not expect repeat attendance.[48]

Training leaders routinely reflected on their men's knowledge, as well as their enthusiastic participation. Training leaders noted that their men appeared to gain a stronger understanding after group discussions, especially those following a question-and-answer format, and through personal conversations with the training leader in which they could raise specific concerns. The lectures based on photo reels were typically well received. In addition, the men took a greater interest in a subject when their unit leader showed interest in it and participated in teaching the men about it, as was sometimes the case.

Other times, training leaders observed the reverse and mentioned that involvement was lackluster. This lack of interest was most evident when the men did not know the answers to the questions posed to them. When the men appeared to lack basic knowledge, the training leader found it necessary to review past material, and he often simplified it in order to ensure that his men understood. Another problem was exhaustion; for example, training leaders stated that their men's attention strayed during evening programs. They also commented that it was difficult to improve upon poor participation when the men, even new recruits, lacked enthusiasm, a problem that was exacerbated in any unit that seemed to lack a sense of solidarity or comradeship.[49]

Another problem related more to the training leaders than the men themselves. Beyond their educational responsibilities, they had the task of assisting men with preparing their engagement and marriage paperwork.[50] By August 1935, however, the Family Office had already noted that it had to send back more than half of the genealogical trees because they were incomplete.[51] It concluded that the training leaders were not sufficiently educated about the genealogical paperwork; for this reason, officials in the Family Office wanted to provide training leaders with a course preparing them to assist the men in their units. In addition, being able to offer this help would have provided each training leader with the opportunity to interact on an individual basis with the men in his unit. Through this personal interaction, he could reinforce family-related ideology. This one-on-one time, however, was apparently not enough to remedy every problem relating to incomplete paperwork. This might have contributed to Himmler's decision in August 1937 to have RuSHA establish support agencies in each unit to assist men with the engagement and marriage forms before they submitted them to RuSHA. These new agencies did not resolve all of the difficulties raised by the engagement and marriage process.[52] But agency officials represented another set of people that SS men could turn to, first as they navigated the engagement and marriage process, and then as they established a family.

In addition to these general problems, there were concerns with *SS-Leitheft*. Some training leaders commented on the quality and usefulness of its articles, while others reported that the articles could not hold the men's attention. Another common complaint was that there was too much material to cover each month.[53] These issues were apparently never resolved. In a post-war interview, Gottlob Berger, who led the Main Office during the war, said that the Education Office continued to have difficulties with *SS-Leitheft*. Oftentimes, Berger stated, the troops rejected the ideas presented in it. He did not specify what ideas the soldiers did not accept, but simply noted that the publication "remained a permanent object of concern."[54] Thus, while *SS-Leitheft* was officially the main resource for education, the problems with it, combined with the general problems raised by training leaders in their reports, suggest that ideological education was of limited success.[55]

Joachim Caesar also briefly addressed this lack of success in a post-war affidavit. Part of it, he claimed, was due to the difficulty of creating a "uniform system" because of the "existing conditions of leadership," by which he might have meant the quarrel between Himmler and Darré and the shifting of the Education Office from RuSHA to the SS Main Office.[56] The wartime expansion of the SS created another obstacle: "The instruction could not keep up with this terrific increase of the strength of the troops, and therefore it was altogether *impossible* to think of an ideological indoctrination on a sufficient scale in addition to the military training, which in wartime in any case had priority."[57] A lack of training leaders exacerbated these problems, leading to education being pushed further and further into the background – to the point, Caesar proclaimed, that "no systematic instruction was possible."[58]

Even though a fully formed education system was never implemented, it still represented one attempt to inform men about race and to show them its connection with the establishment of their individual marriages and families as well as the family community. Yet men were only one component of that collective. Of equal significance were their wives. A woman who had married an SS man prior to the organization's existence, the creation of the 1931 command, or his acceptance into the SS, was scrutinized only so far as to ensure that their children would be worthy of joining the family community. However, for women who completed the engagement and marriage process with their future husbands, the approval of their union by RuSHA was simply the first step in their incorporation into the family community. Once permission had been granted, the next step was their wedding. Religious ceremonies were not forbidden, and many SS men had church weddings. When a man justified doing so, he typically claimed that it had been at the behest of his bride, or his or her parents.[59] If a church ceremony took place, then an SS man was, with limited exceptions, forbidden from wearing his uniform.[60]

In light of the fact that many men had, as Himmler had wanted, left their denomination and professed themselves to be believers in God (*Gottgläubig*), SS rituals were designed to replace a traditional wedding service. That the SS built its own particular marriage celebration is hardly surprising. This was in line with the Nazi government's attempt to reinvent many rituals and holidays as a way to celebrate the national community and encourage people to support the regime.[61] SS men began to express interest in holding a non-religious ceremony by mid-1935. This interest led to correspondence among RuSHA officials from the central office down through the various units as they sought to figure out the appropriate format for an SS celebration and determine whether the unit to which an SS man belonged should pay for the service.[62]

Outlines were also passed around some units laying down the basic parameters of an SS wedding.[63] Common features included the use of music, the exchange of rings, and the inclusion of the tradition of giving the bridal pair salt and bread. Another facet was having an SS officer conduct the ceremony. Himmler made it quite clear in a November 1936 speech that training leaders were forbidden from organizing ceremonies or speaking at them in any official capacity. His objection was grounded in his belief that he did not want to create a new priesthood in the SS.[64] And so the superior officer of the SS man, or the commander of the unit to which he belonged, was responsible for the speech; on occasion, this even included Himmler.[65] There was, however, a potential problem with this directive. When SS men had a positive experience attending a new wedding ceremony, it inspired them to embrace it.[66] However, as one training leader reported, men seemed disinclined to have an SS ceremony when their unit leaders appeared inept or indifferent to it. In addition, some unit leaders, knowing the amount of preparation required, felt unqualified to give a speech. The training leader therefore suggested that higher-ups needed to provide a framework for ceremonies.[67]

By the time this particular training leader had written his report, attempts to create comprehensive guidelines had already been started – though not by RuSHA, but by Oberabschnitt West. Otto Hofmann, then RuSHA leader for the Oberabschnitt, worked with another officer in the division in 1937 and 1938 to create the book *The Formation of Celebrations in the Year and Life in the SS Family*. He later stated that he had the support of the Oberabschnitt West leader Fritz Weitzel. He also claimed that part of the book's content was based on a conversation with Himmler, and that Himmler had recommended it during a speech to all Oberabschnitt leaders. Copies were available for purchase not only in Oberabschnitt West, but in all SS units.[68] Subsequently, when working for RuSHA in Berlin, Hofmann recommended that all members of RuSHA use the book as a reference, and then-chief Günther Pancke agreed to provide each support agency with a copy free of charge.[69] Later, as chief of RuSHA, Hofmann sought to assume responsibility for distributing the book throughout the entire SS. He worked out an arrangement with the new leader of Oberabschnitt West, SS-Obergruppenführer Friedrich Jeckeln, that made RuSHA responsible for distribution while providing the division with part of the profit from its sale.[70]

As its title suggests, the book's purpose was to provide guidelines for family celebrations, among them the admission of a wife into the family community through marriage. The instructions began by providing some background information on the state's attitude toward marriage, noting that the Nazi state viewed a marriage as the "germ cell of the

Volk."[71] It then transitioned to the details of the celebration. The ritual was to be simple, yet festive, and it should take place during a banquet; this meal did not have to be lavish, but could be served at the SS man's home or a nearby inn. The room in which the ceremony took place was to be modestly decorated. An SS flag would stand in the background surrounded by a flower arrangement containing fir sprigs, holly, and ivy. Chairs would be set out for the guests, including the officers who would perform the ceremony.

The service would begin with a musical prelude. *The Formation of Celebrations in the Year and Life in the SS Family* did not list specific songs, but suggested that ideologically appropriate composers should be used.[72] After the music, a speaker would commence the ceremony with a short prologue, such as a poem or a quotation from *Mein Kampf* or a speech by the Reichsführer. This prologue would be followed by an address by an officer, preferably the groom's immediate superior because he most likely knew the couple and could speak about the development of their relationship. In his address, the officer would emphasize the significance of the marriage as a means to sustain the vitality of the *Volk* and the family community. He would personally accept the wife into the family community and suggest that the phrase "My honour is called loyalty" become a guiding principle for her as she was now subordinate to the laws of the SS. Following this acceptance, the woman would receive a gift relating to her marriage or suitable for her future role as a mother. She, along with her husband, would also receive a wooden platter with salt and bread on it, along with two cups; this offering served to remind the couple of a simple standard of living. At some point during the ceremony, the man and woman would exchange vows and rings, although the instructions did not clarify when that was to take place. It did specify, however, that the ceremony should be followed with festivities and dancing.

A similar service developed for the Lebensborn, although there are limited records on it.[73] Those files that exist demonstrate that marriage ceremonies took place in Lebensborn homes, with an SS officer conducting the ceremony on behalf of the bride and groom.[74] The lack of information makes it difficult to draw many conclusions, other than the fact that the ceremonies did not seem to differ in any significant regard from the consecrations held outside Lebensborn homes; thus, the Oberabschnitt West book might have served as a guideline for these ceremonies, too. However, the lack of information may reflect the fact that few weddings took place because almost half of the children in Lebensborn homes were born to mothers who were already wed. Indeed, statistics submitted by the program to RuSHA conveyed the marital status of the mothers along with the limited numbers of weddings that took place.[75]

The new SS ceremony was not an officially recognized ritual. As with a church wedding, an SS man and his fiancée had to register their marriage with the appropriate government office. This registration could be done prior to the ceremony or during it. Based on an agreement between RuSHA and the Reich Ministry of the Interior, the civil registrar accepted approval from RuSHA as proof of the couple's racial suitability when issuing a marriage licence.[76] Once married, either the newlyweds or an officer in the unit to which the husband belonged notified RuSHA and the SS Main Office of the marriage.

While internal reporting was required, external accounts of ceremonies were forbidden. The first time an SS wedding took place in Frankfurt in the early fall of 1935, the local Nazi newspaper reported on it and included a picture of the ceremony.[77] Approximately a month later, the SS Main Office released a memo stating that "reports about marriage consecration in the SS are inappropriate. Therefore, it is forbidden to send in such reports to the newspapers or to ask the editorial staff for coverage."[78] The memo did not clarify why the SS Main Office did not want publicity. Nor did a letter by the press adviser for an SS unit in Mainz; the adviser only declared that "such publications are undesired and conceivably lead to complications."[79] He did not state what those complications might be, but the reason for the prohibition could have been as simple as not wanting SS news printed in any newspaper other than the recently founded *Das Schwarze Korps*.[80]

There are limited statistics about religion and weddings. The *Statistical Yearbook* for both 1937 and 1938 show that a minimal number of SS men (18.7 per cent and 25.8 per cent, respectively) had severed their ties to a formal religion.[81] The available wartime statistics show much higher numbers. They also list the number and percentage of SS men who chose not to have a church wedding. About 77–78 per cent of men and non-coms did not have a church wedding during the war; for officers, the rates were higher, between 95 and 99 per cent.[82] Not holding a religious ceremony did not necessarily mean that SS men and their fiancées chose the SS ceremony; many of them may have simply opted for a civil ceremony. Yet it is unlikely that Hofmann would have persisted in disseminating the Oberabschnitt West book if he did not perceive a growing interest in the non-religious ceremony. The creation of a new ritual was an important method of incorporating wives into the family community. It was a process through which SS officials could show these women that they belonged to the community.

In addition, the ceremony represented an attempt to modify a well-known ritual and to found an "invented tradition" for the SS.[83] Each union signified the beginning of a hereditarily and racially healthy family, at least according to how Himmler and RuSHA officials interpreted and applied the tenets of eugenics (though as noted already, the SS found many people in the scientific community willing to authenticate its interpretation of racial hygiene). Now married, these couples were poised to join an elite community that had the potential to serve as the vanguard of the Third Reich. To ensure they understood their place in this community, the SS established events that women were encouraged to attend.[84] The most significant was the family night (*Sippenabend*). These were routine gatherings organized and paid for by the units, supported by RuSHA, and publicized by *Das Schwarze Korps*.[85] They were used to foster unity among SS members and to promote awareness of the family community, as well as to encourage women to take an interest in the SS. It was important for wives and fiancées to attend because they needed to understand the community to which they and their men belonged and in which they were expected to participate.[86]

To facilitate this understanding and participation, most family nights were divided into two parts. While a visit to a museum was not uncommon, the first part of the evening typically consisted of a speech. Any ideologically relevant topic was suitable, but RuSHA preferred the theme of the SS as a family community.[87] Training and unit leaders could speak on this topic; so, too, could the Race and Settlement leader in an Oberabschnitt, although it was not unheard of for a unit to invite a high-ranking officer to deliver a speech.[88] For example, George Ebrecht, a high-ranking RuSHA official, gave a speech entitled "The SS as an Order and a Family Community" in late 1936 and again in early 1938 at family nights in various SS units.[89] Once the ideological part of the program had concluded, the family night shifted to a social occasion. Men and women had the opportunity to talk, listen to music, sing, and dance.[90] This informal interaction was as crucial as any formal lecture in solidifying the bonds among families.

Just as this community did not focus solely on men, neither did it focus only on couples. The purpose of marriage in the SS, like the Nazi state, was to have numerous racially suitable children. These children had a place in the family community, a place that was first recognized with a birth announcement in *Das Schwarze Korps*. The newspaper had

two sections related to family matters. The first was called "On Relations and Family" (Aus Sippe und Familie). The idea for this segment
came from Himmler, who wanted all family news published under this
heading. He requested that the men be made aware that they needed
to report their family news to RuSHA, which then forwarded the material to *Das Schwarze Korps*.[91] Presumably, the RuSHA press department
was responsible for this task, although most units had press personnel who could submit material, too.[92] "On Relations and Family" ran
periodically from 8 May 1935 through the last edition of the paper
on 29 March 1945. As a semi-regular section in which men could list
their nuptials and the birth of their children, "On Relations and Family" communicated the everyday reality of SS families. Throughout *Das
Schwarze Korps's* tenure, the style of this section and its position in the
paper varied, but the information it presented remained relatively consistent. Early editions listed engagements and marriages first and then
births in a column primarily located on page 4. The section divided the
engagements, marriages, and births by the Oberabschnitt in which the
fiancé, husband, or father served; the child's date of birth and gender
were often listed as well.

In August 1936, Himmler decided that engagements should no longer be included.[93] The section otherwise remained the same for most
of the pre-war period. The only variation was in the first five issues
of 1939. The title changed to the lengthier "We Have the Will for the
Victory of the Children and We Are Gaining this Victory," and it only
recorded births. After this alteration, the title returned to "On Relations
and Family." For the remaining months of 1939, when the newspaper
included this section, it appeared on page 5 and took up the entire page.
The most dramatic change was that the section now contained pictures
of newborns, infants, and toddlers. Starting with the 18 May edition,
one final change occurred: the articles arranged the birth announcements by the number of children per family. Although there were sometimes as many as ten children per family, the majority of families were
celebrating the birth of their first, second, or third child.

After a hiatus from mid-August 1939 to mid-May 1941, "On Relations and Family" resumed with a text-only format. Marriage notices
were placed above birth listings, which had a new layout. Sons were
listed first and then daughters, and within this gendered division, the
children were ordered by date of birth. These announcements also gave
the first name of the baby. Later editions, from 1942 to 1945, continued
this format, although when it came to reporting children, they often

declared how many children an SS man had altogether. Most of the articles were located on page 6, although they occasionally turned up on pages 7, 8, or 9. This placement situated them closer to the end of the newspaper, which typically had eight to ten pages per issue. In fact, in the final edition, "On Relations and Family" was the last article on the last page.

Appearing almost three hundred times over the course of a decade, "On Relations and Family" catalogued the birth of Germany's new elite, thus giving credence to the central role played by the family community in the Nazi state. In addition, these birth announcements promoted the merits of having a large family, especially during 1939 when the section organized the children by how many existed in a family. Because publishing the birth of one's child revealed that an SS man and his wife were fulfilling their biological duty, this type of advertisement created peer pressure. It likewise conflated the victory in the cradle with military triumph during the early years of the war. SS children represented the Germans who would safeguard in the future those gains won by their fathers.

The second section that related family matters was "Family Announcements" (Familien Anzeigen). First appearing on 19 June 1935, the section was featured in *Das Schwarze Korps* well over four hundred and fifty times. It, too, reported engagements, marriages, and births. However, "Family Announcements" differed from "On Relations and Family" in several ways. To begin with, it was a form of paid advertisement. The newspaper routinely ran a notification indicating when and where information had to be sent as well as how much it would cost to include it in the paper. And like most advertisements, "Family Announcements" was located towards the end of the paper. Depending on how many advertisements were purchased, the section took up anywhere from one-fifth of a page to two full pages.

Most advertisements were purchased by SS families. While the parents of a couple periodically placed ads, most couples announced their own engagements and marriages. In each case, a couple listed their names, the date of their engagement or marriage, and the groom's rank and unit. As for the birth of children, again ads were primarily purchased by an SS man and his wife, although on occasion just the SS man made the announcement or sometimes a unit placed a collective announcement on behalf of its men.[94] The parents typically listed the name, gender, and date of birth of their newborn. Frequently, they stated that the child was healthy, and they occasionally noted the birth order of the child. Sometimes they even phrased the announcement in a light-hearted manner – for example, by stating that their son was going to be a big brother or their three boys had a baby sister to welcome into the family.[95]

Among the officers who announced the birth of their children were three RuSHA chiefs: Darré, Pancke, and Hildebrandt.[96] Other high-ranking officers included Erich von dem Bach-Zelewski, Werner Best, August Heißmeyer, Reinhard Heydrich, Friedrich Krüger, Karl Wolff, and Udo von Woyrsch.[97] These announcements promoted the celebration of life and the expansion of the family community. They also set a good example for SS men, especially when high-ranking officers purchased announcements; the inclusion of such information sent a stronger message than the listings in "On Relations and Family" because the officers chose to share their family news as opposed to letting RuSHA supply the details.

Beyond birth announcements, the newborns, like their mothers, received a ceremonial initiation into the family community. Here, too, the SS sought to replace the traditional Christian baptism. However, the ceremony was preceded by a medical examination. Himmler required that an SS doctor evaluate the baby to determine if he were racially healthy.[98] Just because the father and mother had been vetted did not mean their child was accepted automatically. The baby needed to have a medical official proclaim his worthiness to enter the family community.

The SS called its new ceremony a name consecration. The ceremony's development followed a similar trajectory as the wedding ritual. General discussion led to the creation of basic parameters that units started to use by the mid-1930s.[99] Due to the involvement of training leaders in some cases, directives from above were issued, clarifying that the name consecration was a family celebration, not an official duty.[100] At this point the ceremony described in the Oberabschnitt West book took on a new relevance, with Hofmann ensuring that anyone who inquired with RuSHA about a ceremony could purchase a copy.[101] As laid out in the book, the name consecration was to be an intimate occasion where the parents, their closest relatives, and the father's comrades received the child into the family community. The room in which the baptism was conducted had to be decorated with flowers and fir sprigs; the service would ideally take place in the parents' home. In the first part of the ceremony, the father conferred the name of the child, which was to be carefully chosen, with preference given to German names. After the naming, an SS comrade accepted the child into the family community by giving a short speech in which he addressed five points: the great Reich into which the child had been born; the Führer and his love of children; the worship of mothers; the wife's role in increasing the size and quality of the *Volk*; and each SS member's obligation to the family community. This speech concluded the consecration, after which the same comrade gave the mother a gift, such as a piece of jewellery, to commemorate the birth.

Additional letters from Hofmann, written when he was RuSHA chief, indicate that other gifts were provided to RuSHA employees, namely a book for the mother and a contribution of 50 RM for the child.[102] As of 1942–43, all children received a ceremonial candle holder known as a *Lebensleuchter*. Himmler wanted every child born in those years to receive this gift as a visible expression of thanks to their parents for having brought a child into the world. He made RuSHA responsible for this task. As soon as the parents reported the birth, RuSHA officials arranged to have a *Lebensleuchter* inscribed with the newborn's name and date of birth before shipping it to the family.[103]

New parents may have also received a Sturm cradle, as every unit was to have one or more cradles that it could provide to parents. Several newspaper articles from 1938 discussed the existence of such cradles, including one piece about a cradle in Standarte 58 in Cologne.[104] The article stated that the communal cradle was designed to spare parents expenses associated with newborns as well as to promote the family community. This particular cradle was decorated with swastikas and runes. It came with its own family book that contained the names of the SS men who had contributed to its purchase as well as the names of the newborns who had used it. With the bequeathing of the gifts and possibly the cradle, the name consecration concluded, and a small celebratory meal was held. Every year thereafter, parents were advised not only to celebrate their child's birthday, but his or her baptism, too.[105]

There are no statistics indicating how many families chose an SS name consecration. But one of the few examples of an officer doing so was Karl Wolff. In early January 1937, he had his eldest son baptized in a newly created ceremony, one that was more eccentric than the one described above. It had been designed by SS-Brigadeführer Karl Maria Weisthor, an officer on Himmler's personal staff and a self-proclaimed expert on ancient German religion and customs.[106] Wolff gave his son the name Thorisman, after the Teutonic deity. The baby also received three middle names, one for each of his *Goden*, an ancient Germanic term for godfather: Heinrich (Himmler), Karl (SS-Sturmbannführer

Karl Diebitsch, Himmler's personal art consultant), and Reinhard (Heydrich). Throughout the service, the child, in the arms of his mother, received a blue ribbon, a cup, a spoon, and a ring. The ribbon was to symbolize "birth and marriage, life and death"; the cup to remind the child that "his purpose in life" came from God; the spoon to give him nourishment; and the ring to signify "the house of Wolff."[107]

There is one other note about this ceremony. Unlike the other name consecration ceremony, which did not mention God, Weisthor did so liberally. Moreover, at the end of baptism he proclaimed that the baby "may receive the proud name of Thorisman as your Christian name for your entire life."[108] So, in spite of Himmler's desire to have his order pull away from Christianity, even the most outlandish and pagan-like ceremony did not completely deviate from church traditions. Still, there is little reason to believe that this ceremony, unlike the one described in the Oberabschnitt West book, ever gained wide acceptance.

Name consecrations were also held in the Lebensborn homes.[109] According to Gregor Ebner, Himmler had granted home leaders permission to conduct birth celebrations. His reasoning was that the mother's family may not have been available to celebrate the birth of her child due to the secrecy of the program. That reason aside, all children born in a home could participate.[110] Married couples were encouraged to hold their own ceremonies, but if that were not possible, they were permitted to join the ceremony at the home where the wife had given birth.

The available records indicate that the Lebensborn baptisms followed the same pattern as those conducted privately. The biggest difference was that multiple children participated in a Lebensborn ceremony.[111] An SS officer associated with or in charge of the home officiated the ceremony. Taking into account the limited time span in which a room full of infants could remain quiet, he would plan a short but meaningful ceremony.[112] As part of the ceremony, he would give a speech that described its purpose and meaning. He would also emphasize the significance of the child in the National Socialist state and the mother's role in rearing her child as a proper member of that state. The officer would ask each mother if she were committed to educating her child in accordance with the Nazi world view. He would also address the SS men who had been chosen to become the godfathers of the newborn children. In some cases, the mother or the parents chose the godfather. If it were possible, he participated in the ceremony; if not, an SS man associated with the home would stand in for the godfather during the ceremony.[113] The officiating officer would ask the SS men if they were prepared to ensure that the child placed in their care was raised in a manner befitting the SS. In addition, the godfathers were asked to commit themselves to protect the mother and the child. After both the mother and the godfather answered in the affirmative, the mothers – along with the fathers, if they were present – named their children.[114]

Altogether, these naming ceremonies were designed as the initial phase in the process of welcoming newborns into the family community. They were not, however, the only family ceremonies. As seen in the Oberabschnitt West book, other services were aimed at initiating children into Nazi youth organizations, and there was advice on how each family could establish a book that would contain the life stories of its members and would inform each generation about its ancestors.[115] These additional services and rituals were not necessarily designed to replace traditional ceremonies such as birthdays, anniversaries, or even Christmas and Easter. Rather, they were created to accompany existing practices and to reorient boys and girls toward the SS world view.

It appears that the Oberabschnitt West book remained the standard reference for ceremonies until mid-1942. Around that time, Himmler must have decided that Hofmann had overstepped his bounds and that the formation of celebrations, like education, should fall under the domain of the SS Main Office.[116] By 1943 the Main Office had published *The Ceremony*, its new guidelines for celebrations.[117] One volume was dedicated to name consecrations. It covered all possible scenarios – ceremonies when the father was at the front, ceremonies for illegitimate children, ceremonies for orphans – but otherwise, it did not vary significantly from previous guidelines. No information exists on the extent to which *The Ceremony* was dispersed among SS members, but, given its advertisement in *SS-Leithefte*, it would have become the preferred resource of the SS Main and Education Offices.[118]

No matter how children became full-fledged members of the family community, their parents subsequently had the responsibility to raise them to become proper National Socialists. They were not alone in this task. The SS did not typically intervene in the daily minutiae of child rearing, although some units occasionally provided financial and material assistance.[119] But it oversaw the family community and therefore sought to ensure its vitality and longevity. The prime method of oversight was the Gruppenführer oath. During the 1936 celebration of the Munich putsch, Himmler released a basic law that dealt with maintaining racial standards. He asserted that one of the "greatest dangers for the future of the SS" was the automatic admission of sons and daughters of SS men – the former as members, the latter as wives – without further examination.[120] Future generations could not be admitted solely based on the merits of their ancestors. That their fathers had belonged was not reason enough; stricter conditions for entry had to be imposed on each generation.

Thus, Himmler required every Obergruppenführer and Gruppenführer to swear an oath that bound them to serve as "the guardians of the blood and life laws of the Schutzstaffel."[121] These members were responsible for inspecting every candidate or spouse, recognizing that such scrutiny might lead to the rejection of their colleagues' children – or even their own.[122] In addition, these officers were obligated to ensure that with each new generation who joined, at least one-quarter of the men and women came from families not already associated with the SS. To satisfy Himmler, each officer had to swear on his loyalty to the Führer and to his ancestors to uphold the Gruppenführer oath. Finally, the oath was sealed by the inclusion of a document in the officer's personnel file indicating he had taken it.[123]

Beyond the Gruppenführer oath, another way the SS cared for its own was by providing for fallen soldiers as well as their widows and orphans. For the deceased men, the primary concern was creating a funeral ceremony. Many of the parameters from the wedding and baptism ceremonies applied here, too. Church funerals were acceptable, but if a man had left the church, he needed to clarify that he did not want a Christian burial.[124] The Oberabschnitt West book provided guidelines for arranging what it called "the most serious of all our celebrations."[125] The rising death toll during the war created the need for more comprehensive directives. The growing complexity of funeral rites was most elaborately displayed in the lavish spectacle organized in June 1942 for Reinhard Heydrich, but even common funerals were regulated by the new directives.[126]

Most of these instructions were released in 1942 and 1943, with the SS Main Office primarily responsible for creating and announcing updated guidelines.[127] When possible, the unit to which the deceased man had belonged was responsible for his funeral.[128] For funerals in the Reich, the Main Office worked with the relevant Oberabschnitt to arrange the service. The family was responsible for the majority of the costs, but each Oberabschnitt could contribute a small amount of funding for music and decorations. For funerals at the front, the Waffen-SS took responsibility for conducting the ceremony and caring for the graves of deceased comrades.[129] In both cases, an officer delivered a speech, there was a musical interlude, and a wreath was laid. When possible, fellow SS men or police officers formed an honour guard and fired a salute at the end of the service.[130]

The deceased were also honoured in *Das Schwarze Korps*. The majority of death announcements placed in "Family Announcements" were for SS men, although occasionally SS men and their families purchased an ad to commemorate the loss of a parent; for example, Darré, Himmler, Heydrich, and Kaltenbrunner bought ads for this reason.[131] Most advertisements were placed by SS men to honour a fallen comrade, but occasionally a widow paid for one. Under a directive issued by Himmler, only one obituary per person was allowed. The one received by the newspaper first was accepted, and later submissions were rejected, with a note returned to the sender indicating that another announcement was in print.[132] Separated from the engagement, marriage, and birth ads by a big black border, a death announcement gave the name of the deceased, his rank, age, unit, and date of death; it oftentimes included kind words about the departed and commended him for his bravery and loyalty. An obituary could not, however, contain the words "his honour was called loyalty."[133] Himmler issued this prohibition out of concern that it might diminish the gravity of this expression.

Prior to the war, death advertisements took up no more than half of the area allocated for "Family Announcements." They frequently occupied even less space or were absent altogether. Naturally, obituaries increased as the war progressed, until death occupied more space than life. Often an entire page or more was devoted to mourning those who had died fighting for the fatherland. Shortly after the start of the war, most death announcements also contained a cross with a small swastika in the centre, the same basic design as the various medals a soldier could have earned. Thus, while other ads announced the enlargement of the family community, these ads drew attention to its potential decline. As of late July 1941, "Family Announcements" and "On Relations and Family" maintained a sort of inverse relationship to each other: the former reported only deaths and the latter only marriages and births. There were a few editions where one appeared and the other did not (normally in these cases "Family Announcements" did and "On Relations and Family" did not), but on the many occasions when both were present, they appeared on the same page, one on top of the other. By the later years of the war, these sections worked in tandem to bear witness to the fortunes of the family community.

Along with the funeral ceremony, these death announcements were a chance for the living to pay their respects to deceased comrades.[134] It was also an opportunity to ensure that the bonds between the SS and surviving dependants remained strong and that the family understood that the SS intended to continue to oversee its well-being. The notion of the SS taking responsibility for the welfare of its members' families predated the war. The Oberabschnitt West book briefly mentioned the subject. Also, on 9 November 1937, Himmler announced a basic law that addressed the issue of caring for the families of the deceased.[135] It made clear that this duty was a "sacred task" for the SS as a family community and for each SS man, especially the commanding officers of the deceased. The obligation of SS men to care for the well-being of their comrades' families took on greater significance after the war started. In mid-September, Himmler required that the Personnel Main Office compile a list of fallen SS soldiers.[136] He wanted this office to convey to him the names of married members, as this information would provide a starting point from which commanders could accept responsibility for the welfare of widows and orphans; the office complied by creating the Collecting Centre for the Losses of the SS in the War.[137] Just over a month later, Himmler commented briefly on these responsibilities in the October procreation order. Near the end of this decree, he noted that unlike previous eras, when soldiers did not want to burden their wives with wartime children, SS men should not have such reservations. If an SS man died fighting for Germany, Himmler would appoint a guardian to oversee the financial and educational needs of his family. The SS would also care for any mother who gave birth during the war. In both cases, this assistance applied to legitimate and illegitimate children.

Beyond suggesting that surviving SS men had a duty to care for families of the fallen, these orders did not outline any specific measures. They did set the tone for future decrees, however. As the war progressed and the number of casualties rose, Himmler assigned tasks to various SS offices. The Personnel Main Office oversaw the development of the children of the fallen until they reached the age of majority. Along with individual Oberabschnitt, it had to maintain records tracking the economic circumstances of surviving dependants and determine when a family needed financial help from the SS beyond what it received from the state.[138] The SS Main Office advised mothers and legal guardians about schooling and occupational training for children, particularly boys who showed interest in becoming Waffen-SS officers.[139] RuSHA managed non-economic needs, including "all questions in life."[140] On occasion, this care consisted of distributing goods such as coats, mittens, stockings, and candles, as well as allocating donations to families who had lost someone at Stalingrad or who had lost their possessions due to Allied bombing. RuSHA also intervened when another office or division could not resolve an issue.[141]

Another branch given responsibility for family welfare was the Lebensborn. According to a memorandum written by Ernst Ragaller, the leader of the Oslo home and the SS officer in the Lebensborn in charge of war orphans' welfare, Himmler had mandated that the Lebensborn needed to play a central role in the care of widows and orphans to ensure that the basic needs of surviving dependants were met. It would also guarantee that the connection between these families and the SS would be sustained and that each orphan would be raised in a manner befitting a member of the family community.[142]

Participation by the Lebensborn included providing women and children with temporary lodging.[143] From nearly the beginning of the war, the wives and fiancées of fallen SS men could stay with their children in a Lebensborn home free of charge.[144] Guntram Pflaum issued an order on this subject two months into the war.[145] He assigned each home leader the responsibility of "personally" welcoming these women "in a comradely manner." He expected that they would ensure that every woman had "an agreeable stay." Pflaum wanted each woman to understand that the comrades of her fallen man saw it as their "self-evident duty" to support her and her children. She needed to recognize through the words and actions of Lebensborn officials that she and her children still belonged to the family community. As for the officials tasked with this duty, Pflaum instructed them to take act according to a single motivating guideline: "We SS comrades – above all we officers and men of the Lebensborn – have to ask ourselves to care for and protect the wives and the brides with their children, to carry out all measures that our SS comrade would have arranged for if he had not fallen in the field for the Führer and the Volk." Pflaum ended his order by stating that their deceased comrades had "fought courageously" and "died bravely" because of their faith in the family community; they knew that their comrades would protect their wives and children, thus guaranteeing that their sacrifice had not been in vain.

There are no statistics indicating how many widows stayed in a Lebensborn home. However, that the homes would have had a limited capacity for this type of assistance suggests that few women and children would have had the opportunity to take advantage of it. Instead, most of them would have received support in other ways. Most importantly, Lebensborn officials guided women through the legal complexities of their parental rights.[146] According to the law, if a father were prevented from practising his parental authority or declared dead, then the mother was entitled to exercise all parental rights.[147] The Lebensborn did not have the authority to appropriate this legal right. It did, however, have authorization from the Reich minister of the interior to assist mothers with legal matters.[148] In addition, Himmler granted the association the right to provide women with advice regarding the status of their estate, access to pensions, and the educational and vocational options available to their children. Officials were to encourage women to utilize the Lebensborn as a resource while simultaneously assuring them that this assistance did not infringe upon their rights as mothers.[149]

There were guidelines stipulating when the Lebensborn had the authority to assume custody of a child. Himmler assigned this right in the case of legitimate children when it corresponded with the mother's wishes; otherwise, the association could initially take over guardianship only for illegitimate children. In principle, this meant the children of fallen SS and police men, although there was some latitude early in the war to allow the Lebensborn to care for a child whose father had not belonged to either organization. Guidelines issued later in the war indicated that this latitude no longer existed, but they added three categories for guardianship: if the child had lost both parents; if the mother of a legitimate child was a minor; or if the mother of a legitimate child had remarried.[150] Among these new categories, the initiative for the first did not come from Himmler, but from Hitler, who wanted the Lebensborn, not orphanages, to care for parentless children. The association took responsibility for full orphans, primarily assigning the few children who fell under its care for this reason to foster families.[151] Beyond these parameters, only in special cases – such as on Himmler's orders or following authorization from Max Sollmann – could the Lebensborn assume custody of a child.[152] In all cases, guardianship could not be taken over if there were any doubts about the child's hereditary worthiness.

As with the home stays, there are no statistics indicating how many women turned to the Lebensborn for assistance, nor how many children the organization assumed legal responsibility over. One report from late 1943 referred to documentation for approximately 40,000 children, but it did not clarify the legal relationship between the association and these children.[153] Sollmann did provide some figures during his testimony as a defendant in one of the subsequent Nuremberg Trials. He stated that the Lebensborn program became the guardian for about 17,000 full and half orphans. He also testified that Lebensborn officials assisted around 8,000 surviving dependants with advice and support.[154] The testimony of fellow defendants Günther Tesch and Inge Viermetz confirmed Sollmann's account. Both affirmed that caring for the widows and orphans of deceased SS men and providing them with advice and support fell within the tasks assigned to the Lebensborn.[155]

While the Lebensborn contributed to overseeing the welfare of widows and orphans, individual SS men were involved, too; they served as an important link between the SS and surviving family members. Three months into the war, Himmler wrote a letter to Oberabschnitt leaders stating that the "welfare for family members of our fallen SS men is one of the most beautiful duties that is incumbent on the officer corps and men on the home front."[156] He requested that each Oberabschnitt leader become involved in the welfare of surviving dependants by writing condolence letters and making personal visits.[157] In addition, they had to appoint men in their subordinate units to serve as advisers for surviving dependants. Advisers had to maintain contact with the widows, orphans, and even parents of the deceased, ensuring that a strong bond continued to exist between these families and the SS.[158] The significance of maintaining this bond was best described by SS-Obergruppenführer Josias, Hereditary Prince of Waldeck and Pyrmont, in a letter to the advisers in his division, Oberabschnitt Fulda-Werra: "You must be generally informed of every sorrow, every worry, and every joy of the family assigned to you; widows, orphans, and parents must have the greatest trust in you and must see in you a loyal friend and adviser."[159]

Seeing to the needs of surviving family members meant that advisers routinely submitted reports that detailed the concerns of and care provided to individual widows, orphans, and parents.[160] Such interaction ensured that the SS would not lose these families' racially valuable genetic lineage. It also provided a venue for the organization to see that these dependants received assistance with basic necessities. Through the limited number of dossiers still available, it is possible to establish how SS divisions, in conjunction with the Lebensborn when necessary, cared for the families of the deceased. As the cases of Kurt B., Armin E., and Hermann H. demonstrate, advisers had to handle certain common issues. Yet these cases likewise illustrate that each family's needs differed slightly.

A member of the Allgemeine-SS, Rottenführer Kurt B. had served in the Waffen-SS. He died in the early weeks of the campaign against the Soviet Union. At the time of his death, he had been married less than half a year, and his wife Erna was seven months pregnant with their first child.[161] Her appointed adviser, SS-Obersturmführer Alfred Schmidt, first contacted her in late August 1941. He expressed his sympathy for her loss, proclaiming that her "husband fell for Germany's freedom and greatness. Until [his] last breath, he had performed his duty as a brave SS man."[162] Schmidt wrote that he and his fellow Sturm comrades saw it as their duty to support her; if she needed anything, all she had to do was get in touch with him. Following this contact, Schmidt, along with other officers in his unit, began the process of assisting Erna. They had two immediate concerns, the first of which was determining her financial situation. An inquiry revealed that she lived with her parents and that both her family and Kurt's family were financially stable.[163] She nonetheless received money from the SS, and the process to determine whether she was entitled to a pension, death benefits, or insurance payments was initiated.[164]

The second concern related to her pregnancy. She was due in mid-October. The officials managing her case wanted to place her in a Lebensborn home. The association was willing to accommodate her, but Erna declined the offer. She did not believe that she had enough time until her delivery to move and she did not want to be far from home when she gave birth.[165] Erna gave birth to a daughter towards the end of the month, at which point SS officials began the process of applying for a child allowance.[166] They also kept the Lebensborn up to date about the situation. Already wed to the father of her child, Erna had the right to maintain guardianship. However, the Lebensborn requested that her adviser inform her of the association's ability to assist her with legal matters and to impress upon her that she would retain all parental rights. It took several months to get the paperwork in order, partially because Erna's advisers kept getting replaced as each was successively called up for military duty. Erna nonetheless completed and submitted the paperwork, allowing the court to authorize the legal involvement of the Lebensborn.[167] In addition, reports from 1942 and 1943 indicate that all financial matters seemed to be resolved, with Erna and her daughter receiving financial support from the state and the SS.[168]

Unlike Kurt, Armin E. was not a member of the SS, but a candidate for membership. He served in the army as a non-commissioned officer and died not even three weeks into the war. His death revealed several complications, starting with the fact that his fiancée, Meta M., was pregnant.[169] Alfred Schmidt was assigned to be her adviser, and he sought to convince her to spend the remainder of her pregnancy in a Lebensborn home. She refused because her own mother did not want her away when she gave birth. The Lebensborn accepted this explanation, but pointed out that because she would give birth to an illegitimate child, it had the authority from Himmler to assume guardianship of the child upon his birth, and that Schmidt would need to keep the association informed about the progress of the pregnancy and report the birth of the child.[170] Meta gave birth to a son named Rolf in mid-January 1940. Schmidt subsequently apprised the Lebensborn, which sent him forms for Meta to complete so that the association could assume guardianship. She completed the paperwork, allowing the local court to give the Lebensborn approval to take over guardianship.[171]

Here, too, the relevant paperwork was filed so that Meta and Rolf could receive one-time financial allowances from the SS as well as a pension for the child.[172] As Armin had served in the army, some of this funding came from the Wehrmacht. Under its regulations for brides and illegitimate children, there needed to be "believable proof" that the deceased intended to wed the bride.[173] To proceed with a proposal for support, the Wehrmacht also required proof of the bride's Aryan descent, proof of paternity or recognition by the deceased through an oath, and a certificate verifying the appointment of a guardian for the illegitimate child. Schmidt provided the Wehrmacht with the required paperwork, including an emergency will that Armin had written before he went into combat, in which he acknowledged the child Meta was carrying as his heir. He also submitted an affidavit from Meta proclaiming that she had sexual relations exclusively with Armin at the time of conception and that they were engaged prior to his death.[174] The Wehrmacht accepted this paperwork, providing Meta with child support effective from the month of Rolf's birth and agreeing to pay surviving dependant welfare to her several months later.[175]

Aside from money, there were two other issues specific to this case. The first emerged in late February 1940 when Meta sought to have her and her son's last name changed to that of her dead fiancé. This was not an issue that the SS could decide, but one that had to be approved by the local court. Paperwork was filed throughout 1940 and 1941, with the issue eventually being submitted to the Thuringian Ministry of the Interior. In late August 1941, the state ministry approved the name change.[176] The second issue related to a belated marriage. By early 1942,

Hitler had empowered the Reich Ministry of the Interior to authorize a marriage between a woman and a fallen soldier if it could be demonstrated that there had been a serious intent to wed, if there was nothing to suggest that the soldier had changed his mind prior to his death, and if the Wehrmacht gave its approval. This command was, on Hitler orders, never published, but the SS was aware of it and deemed it applicable to Waffen-SS soldiers provided that RuSHA approved the union.[177]

Local officials pointed out this authorization to Meta, leading her to write a letter to the Reich minister in early November 1942 explaining her situation and requesting his permission to authorize a belated wedding.[178] Upon learning of this request, Otto Hofmann contacted Schmidt and reminded him that Meta needed to file the relevant paperwork to receive permission from RuSHA.[179] This paperwork must have been completed and filed, although it is not all present in Armin's Race and Settlement file. In addition, the Thuringian Ministry of the Interior submitted a report to the Reich minister stating its lack of opposition to the marriage, but also noting that Armin's parents did not approve, presumably because they did not want Rolf to inherit their land. They had tried to pay Meta, but she had rejected their offer, stating that she did not want their money, but the land.[180] In response to the petition, the Reich minister authorized the marriage and dated it to the day before Armin's death. With this authorization, he declared that Rolf was a legitimate child entitled to his father's family name. So as to maintain the secrecy of Hitler's original authorization, the minister forbade the publication of his order.[181]

In the third case, SS-Rottenführer Hermann H., a member of the Allgemeine-SS, had served as a soldier in a Wehrmacht panzer division. He was wounded on the eastern front in late October 1943 and died a few days later from his injuries.[182] Initial contact with his family was made by a doctor who worked in the field hospital where Hermann had died. This letter, however, was not sent to his wife, but to his mother.[183] Hermann and his wife had divorced in May 1941, and his mother, Berta, cared for his two daughters. Due to their placement with their grandmother, the initial concern of the SS was whether she could take care of them or if other living accommodations needed to be arranged. It was determined fairly quickly that, while Berta took very good care of her granddaughters, she struggled financially.[184] She owned land and employed two foreign workers to tend to it. SS officials deemed her to be diligent in managing the property, but she was nonetheless in debt. While several one-time financial contributions from the SS were provided, and while the orphan pension had been applied for, there were questions as to whether Berta was entitled to any other pension. Correspondence on this issue revealed that the state was not willing to provide her with a pension.[185]

Another concern in this case involved Hermann's ex-wife. Since the divorce in 1941, she had not been involved in her children's life. Despite this lack of involvement, SS officials worried throughout 1944 that she might apply for a widow's pension. There was also the question of whether she might try to gain custody of her daughters and thus gain access to the property that her daughters would inherit from their grandmother. The Lebensborn initially felt that it was highly unlikely that she would seek to take the children from their grandmother. Nonetheless, its legal officials began an inquiry with the Youth Office in Erfurt to determine whether it would be possible to prevent the ex-wife from gaining custody. To do so, they wanted to have the Lebensborn assume guardianship of the children. The court must have agreed with this proposal as the Lebensborn had been granted guardianship by June 1944.[186]

The cases of Kurt B., Armin E., and Hermann H. demonstrate that the family community was not simply about race and blood. SS officials believed they had an obligation to create and sustain a strong relationship with individual families. Outside of this official involvement, individual members of the family community helped out, too. One way was by providing accommodations for families. Although some offers had been made earlier in the year, the main initiative came from the SS Main Office in late 1943, when Gottlob Berger sent out a letter concerning the plight of SS families who had been affected by "the Anglo-American bombing terror." He declared it was "the duty of the SS family community to minister to these families" that had lost their homes, arguing that "the closer we come together today, the more tight-knit our community becomes and the more our victory is guaranteed."[187] Berger requested that families who had been spared the devastation of Allied bombing examine whether they could accommodate a fellow SS family and to report their circumstances to their Oberabschnitt. At least a few SS families replied and offered accommodation to wives and children. Those who lived in rural regions even offered to take in children for the duration of the war. Based on their own family situation, they sometimes requested boys or girls or children within a certain age range, but other times, no special requests were made.[188]

Individual members of the German population also helped widows and orphans. On numerous occasions, men and women submitted letters to *Das Schwarze Korps* and included money or information about money deposited in a bank account. In these letters, the writers asked that the money, ranging in amounts from 30 to 2,000 RM, be given to an SS family; they were especially eager for these funds to go towards raising the child of a deceased SS soldier.[189] The basic tenor of each letter was the same: the writer hoped the gift would express his or her gratitude to an SS man who had fallen serving Germany. Several contributions even came from soldiers. One pointed out that he gave money for the future of the happy and healthy children for whom he and his fellow soldiers fought, while another donated money to express his gratitude after returning home on his last vacation and being able to meet his second war child.[190] With their money and sentiments, these soldiers demonstrated their dedication to Germany by publicly acknowledging that their commitment to the family community, especially widows and orphans, was one of the reasons why they fought.

All of this official and individual support remained contingent on one factor, however: the surviving dependants had to maintain an honourable and decent life – that is, honourable and decent as understood by the SS. If a widow did not, the SS reserved the right to bring her before the SS court. Guidelines regulating the steps that could be taken against surviving dependants were first created in 1941, although officials in both the SS court and RuSHA continued to discuss what actions they were legally entitled to take. Under the system they established, if the court ruled that a woman's behaviour was unbecoming of an SS widow, the judges had the right to expel her and her children from the SS community and to cease to support them financially. In addition, the court had the authority to initiate proceedings against a widow to terminate her parental rights if it believed such action was in the best interest of the children.[191] The fact that these judicial procedures existed emphasizes the seriousness with which SS leaders took their welfare responsibilities, as well as the importance they placed on maintaining an organization that met their moral standards.

From the initial engagement and marriage order until nearly the end of the war, marriage and family policies were constantly amended, yet the goal of creating and sustaining an elite family community remained consistent. So, too, did the notion of convincing SS men, along with their wives and children, that they belonged to this community. To foster unity, officials sought to connect with men and their families through various methods. Education was one. Training leaders used formal sessions and one-on-one meetings to ensure that the men in their units were properly informed about the family community and their place in it. The creation of new marriage and name consecration ceremonies likewise cultivated a sense of belonging. In both cases, an SS man's comrades celebrated the beginning of his family by welcoming his wife and/or child into their community. These same comrades bound themselves to care for the well-being of these families, especially the welfare of widows and orphans. These avenues of engagement demonstrated that the family community was not simply about official policies. It was also about making and sustaining personal relations, thus adding a layer of complexity to the racial ideals and demographic ambitions of the SS.

Chapter Six

Assessing SS Population Politics and the Family Community

Beginning with the engagement and marriage command at the end of 1931, the family community developed over the course of a decade and a half as part of the overall evolution of the SS. But this development remained incomplete. Marriage rates were well below 100 per cent. This deficit was far less problematic than reproduction rates; here, the average number of children per family was less than two. This outcome raises the question why: for an organization conceptually bound by an ideology that stressed loyalty above all else, why did SS men not fulfil their marital and reproductive duties? Which factors influenced how these men perceived the relationship between their personal lives and their allegiance to the SS? Many historians who study the SS briefly mention family and children, particularly the significance of racial selection and the engagement and marriage command. However, most of them gloss over why Himmler failed to achieve his population policies. At best, they state that the birth rate remained low because he could not convince enough men to eschew traditional "bourgeois morality."[1] This is a valid explanation, but it must be explored in greater detail. The purpose of this chapter is to explore the development of the family community in a larger context that incorporates social, economic, and educational factors that could have affected the decision or the ability of each SS man to marry and have a child-rich family. In doing so, it takes into account the balance between ideology and personal desires, the possibility of evading ideological orders, and Himmler's willingness to compromise on ideology during the war.

One way to ascertain what SS men thought about their personal lives is by looking at works by and about them. While there are a limited number of sources in which men mention their wives and children, it is possible to gain some insight from them. The most widespread example was the *Lebenslauf*, the one-page personal and professional vita; each officer was required to write one. During the war it was maintained in his personnel file; the remaining copies are now held in the Berlin Document Center files. In the *Lebenslauf*, an officer succinctly recounted his personal history, starting with when and where he was born, and continuing on to his education, employment, and service in the military, party, and SS. If he were married at the time, he indicated who he had married and when. The officer also had to mention his children. Common information included their names or gender, dates of birth or current ages, and possibly familial status if they were adults. Periodically, a picture of the couple or the family was submitted. Along with the rest of the information provided, the family details simply complimented an officer's brief life history. They were typically presented formally and dispassionately, although occasionally an officer noted that his family was hereditarily healthy.[2] Nonetheless, the inclusion of family information demonstrates that such material was as important as any other detail.

Since the collapse of the Third Reich, other resources, including biographies of leading SS officials, have revealed salient personal information. Works published soon after the war focus mainly on providing detailed accounts of their subject's life and career, whereas books written more recently place these individuals' lives and careers into the framework of the time and place in which they lived.[3] Regardless of the shifting nature of these works, most include information about their subject's families. Sometimes this is nothing more than a factual account of who a man married, when he married, and when his children were born. Other times the sources include salacious details about affairs and illegitimate children, although in the case of Karl Brandt, his biography vindicated him. According to his biographer, when he was asked about his mistress, "Brandt did not give the impression of someone who had committed adultery: 'My wife will be very surprised. Only too bad that you cannot tell me the name ... [My wife and I] actually have led a very happy life.' "[4]

A few biographies provide an inkling of a man's relationship with his offspring. The most notable in this regard were Brandt's and Ernst Kaltenbrunner's. These men were on trial – Brandt during the Doctor's Trial and Kaltenbrunner during the Nuremberg Trial. Both were found guilty and executed, but prior to sentencing each attempted to leave a record for his children. Brandt kept a notebook in which he recorded his life in prison in an attempt to show his son how he stayed strong during the trial. He wanted to prove to his son and his wife that he remained a caring father and a loving husband as well as a dedicated doctor.[5] Kaltenbrunner wrote a memoir for his children in which he proclaimed that the "truth" of what had happened would eventually come out. At that time, his children would know that they could be "proud of your Daddy as a man who sacrificed all for the greater good." He beseeched his children to look after their mother, "since I can no longer come home to you."[6] The only thing he felt guilty for was having betrayed his wife with an affair.

In these two accounts, each man attempted to show himself, in his own words, as a good and moral person. They also, if their words are taken at face value, demonstrate affection towards the children and wives they left behind. Yet these works do not reveal what either man thought of the racial standards to which he and his family had formerly adhered. Among the selected biographies, only one – Karl Wolff's – showed acceptance of SS population policies. With his first wife, Wolff had four children, and, as examined earlier, his son Thorisman was christened in the new child-naming ceremony. If Wolff had not had faith in the order to which he belonged and the rules that governed it, he would not have consented to consecrating his child with this service.

Other individuals published autobiographical accounts.[7] One was written by Peter Neumann, who accepted SS racial rhetoric, went to a Lebensborn home, and impregnated a woman he met there. Neumann's account aside, here, too, the men focused more on their service than their families. Probably the most noteworthy of these accounts was Walter Schellenberg's memoirs. Aside from the aforementioned difficulties he encountered while trying to marry his second wife and mentioning the birth of his son, he focused more on his duties for the Reich Security Main Office.

In a related manner, interviews with former officers sometimes provide a brief glimpse into their lives.[8] The conversations with SS-Gruppenführer Jürgen Stroop are among the most striking of these accounts. In 1949 Polish Home Army officer Kazimierz Moczarski spent over eight months in jail with Stroop. He subsequently wrote a book based on the conversations he had with Stroop and a third inmate, a former enlisted SS soldier. Throughout their discussions, Stroop remained unswervingly committed to SS ideology, and this is reflected in his views on marriage and family. For example, during the First World War, he had been billeted with a Polish family and had fallen for a local girl. The way in which Moczarski relayed Stroop's story shows how emotional his cellmate became as he reminisced about this girl decades later. He related how Stroop insisted that it had been in his best interest that he had never married her. "With a wife who was Polish" he stated, "I could have never joined the SS, and my children would have been mongrels."[9] He later married a woman whom he deemed to be more suitable, and they had three children. Stroop also had a child via the Lebensborn program, and although he appeared to know nothing about this child, he was proud of this dalliance.[10] Finally, he remained dedicated to SS racial ideology, not only continuing to admire Himmler as "one of the great experts concerning race," but also using his racial knowledge to classify Moczarski, and even to analyse why he himself was not a perfect Nordic specimen; apparently, his brow was too broad and his blue eyes were flecked with green.[11] In all of these matters, he remained loyal to the racial and family ideals of the SS.

A second officer who provided insight was Richard Hildebrandt. Most relevant information comes from his testimony in the post-war trial against RuSHA officials at Nuremberg.[12] Hildebrandt had been associated with the Lebensborn as a member of its board of directors. He did not have an illegitimate child, but he did assert that claims that the Lebensborn had immoral aims were wrong. The officers who paid mandatory fees to the program were generally interested in its purpose, Hildebrandt said, and based on his experience, he testified about the value of the program, stating that its objective was "to improve the fate of the unmarried mother or illegitimate child in a tactful manner."[13] He asserted that the program not only sought to do away with the prejudice associated with illegitimacy, but actually succeeded in this endeavour.

Hildebrandt, moreover, contended that the Lebensborn homes were in no way "an attack against matrimony." In defending the program, he also defended the integrity of the marriage ideals promoted in the SS: "Matrimony is and remains the foundation of every people and of every state. This very consideration and this very conception was strongly advocated and promoted in our ranks. It was an important part of the ideals which were those of the SS, because we do know that from matrimony only can originate those things that render a people in the last analysis valuable and noble."[14] Further testimony supported his contention that establishing and caring for families was one of the prime goals of the SS.[15] That Hildebrandt spoke these words when he was on trial for his work with RuSHA reveals that seeking to foster families through the bonds of matrimony was an ideal that most SS men could accept. His defence of the Lebensborn program also indicates a measure of flexibility, especially with regards to the interaction between bourgeois morality and personal decisions. An SS man did not have to take advantage of the program in order to defend its integrity.

As seen in earlier chapters, very few men challenged the idea of the family community. Only a limited number refused to comply with the engagement and marriage process and requested permission to leave the organization. The fact that so few men availed themselves of this option indicates that most of them agreed to belong to the family community, as did the women they married. Their subsequent decision to have children, even in low numbers, and the growing use of special wedding and name consecration ceremonies demonstrated their willingness to sustain this community. So did their individual and collective efforts to care for the widows and orphans of fallen comrades. The notion of an elite racial order clearly resonated with those who belonged to it.

Another way to approach the question of how much an SS man might have believed in this ideology is through his children. There is a body of literature containing interviews with and autobiographical accounts by the children of Nazis. Some of them knew their fathers, although many did not. However, in all cases, these children, now adults, sought to come to terms with who their fathers were and what they did. This task was somewhat difficult for illegitimate children born in Lebensborn homes, as they had scant records in which to look for answers to the most basic questions, including in some instances the identity of their fathers.[16] Not all of these situations were hopeless, as demonstrated by the case of Gisela Heidenreich, who not only met her father, but established a relationship with him and her half-sister.[17]

These people's reactions to their fathers' past varied. Dagmar Herzog, the daughter of SS-Hauptsturmführer Max Herzog, discovered that her father had been willing to forgo marrying her mother when the verification of his engagement and marriage application revealed that his future father-in-law was an alcoholic. Herzog then forced his fiancée's father to enter a rehabilitation program, and he told RuSHA officials that if they believed his future offspring could have a genetic disposition towards alcoholism, he would cancel his submission. Nothing came from the RuSHA check; in the end the couple married and had two children. Many years later, when she found out about his crimes, Dagmar disassociated herself and her children from her father.

Although she had trouble reconciling the image of the father who raised her with the man indicted as a criminal, she remained fearful of both the genetic and environmental influence he might have on her children were they to have a relationship with their grandfather.[18]

On the opposite end of the spectrum was Gudrun Himmler. She spoke publicly about her father once, to a journalist in 1959. At the time, she did not believe he had committed suicide and saw it as her goal to rehabilitate him.[19] "I look on it as my life's work to show him to the world in a different light," Gudrun declared. "Today my father is branded as the greatest mass murderer of all time. I want to try to revise this image. At least to get the facts straight about what he thought and why he acted as he did."[20] She proclaimed that she was going to write a book about him. She never did, nor did she publicly speak about her position again. When given the opportunity decades later by Katrin Himmler, the granddaughter of Himmler's younger brother, to contribute to her book on the Himmler brothers, Gudrun declined.[21]

While Dagmar and Gudrun had vastly different memories of their fathers, not all reactions were as stark. Such was the case for Leonardo Conti's daughter Irmgard. Like the other two women, she, too, adored her father when she was a child, and she had many fond memories of the time they spent together. She cherished these memories, writing that "my joy was complete when my father, my beloved Vati, took the time to join me in my play and examined [my doll] and bandaged a hurt leg and showed me how to do it. He had so little time to be just with me, but when he did, he gave me his undivided attention, and we were doctor and nurse making a doll patient better."[22] His suicide devastated her, and for a long time Irmgard did not want to believe that he had been complicit in anything malevolent: "Other officials maybe, but not him."[23] She eventually came to terms with her father's actions. She recognized that he was two men: the gentle and loving Vati of her childhood, whom she will always love, and the other man, the one she did not know but who, she acknowledged, was responsible for his actions.

All of these sources provide a partial view of what SS men may have thought about their organization's racial and family goals. But again, the low birth rate among SS members indicates that not all of them were committed to the official ideology, or that they may have chosen to interpret it selectively – for example, by not believing in the necessity of producing both quality and quantity. However, the decisions human beings make are dependent on a constellation of factors, notably demographic, economic, political, and social ones.[24] It is therefore necessary to look beyond ideology and to examine what other factors affecting Germany, and the larger Western world, most likely influenced SS men not to have child-rich families, or even impeded them from doing so. Such context would allow scholars to critique the supposition that bourgeois morality was the sole barrier to the realization of SS population policies.

To start with, there was a general decline in fertility among Western countries. The extent of the decline and the pace at which it occurred varied from country to country, but it was evident from the turn of the twentieth century, as publications from the time attest.[25] Just as the decline was widespread, so, too, was concern about it. Various nations began to compile statistics about their demographic situations. Among the most concerned was France; it had one of the earliest declines, dating back to the mid-nineteenth century.[26] France's low birth rate was compounded by its losses in the First World War – the country had one of the highest casualty rates.[27] Worried about the consequences of a shrinking population, the Third Republic created family welfare policies. Most notably, as of 1932 the government provided fathers with an allowance for their children. A new family code expanded these allowances in July 1939, but the onset of the war and France's subsequent defeat in June 1940 derailed some of these plans. Several Vichy leaders, Philippe Pétain included, blamed France's loss on its declining population. As a result, Vichy's National Revolution, which focused on the social renewal of the nation, placed families, especially fathers, as its centre. But this revolution had limited success.[28]

A similar situation existed in Italy. The rate of decline was not as dire, yet the government was still concerned. Benito Mussolini expressed his views on the matter during his Ascension Day speech in May 1927. From this point forward, Italy initiated a series of pronatalist policies. The regime also constantly published demographic statistics to keep the population aware of Italy's impending decline. With such publicity, the government wanted to encourage a revival, especially among the lower classes; unlike most countries, Germany included, where the focus was on reproduction in the middle and upper classes, Mussolini praised the peasantry for their familial contributions. Yet here, too, the state's campaign to increase fertility failed.[29]

The situation in Germany did not differ greatly.[30] Despite claims that Germany had followed an alternate developmental route compared to other politically and industrially modernized countries, there was no "special path" when it came to demography.[31] The Nazi government was aware of the decline in the national birth rate.[32] From an average of 41.8 births per 1,000 inhabitants in 1874, it had fallen to 35.2 in 1904 and to 14.7 in 1933.[33] While the government tried to reverse this trend, the SS also understood the gravity of the situation, and sought to combat it. For example, the SS Main Office developed guidelines for community meetings to be attended by SS men and their families.[34] Among the topics for discussion were statistics emphasizing the nation's demographic deterioration. The claim that this decline resulted from small families was attacked as wrong, although, beyond the platitude that each couple should have a child-rich family, no suggestions were given as to how the SS could solve this problem. It would have been difficult for the SS to arrest this long-standing and widespread decline within its own membership – let alone all of Germany – without a more concrete plan.

A second factor that must be considered when weighing why SS members did not have more children is sexuality – specifically, the regulation of sex.[35] Himmler spent a great deal of time and effort attempting to control the sexual lives of other people. Sex was a topic that preoccupied him before he became a member of the party. As noted by his early biographers, "no other [subject] elicited so many commonplaces from his pen."[36] This fixation even shaped his perception of women. In a diary entry from late 1921, Himmler defined his views of women as follows:

> A woman is loved by a man on three levels: as a dear child who has to be chided, perhaps even punished on account of her unreasonableness, and who is protected and taken care of just because she is tender and weak and because one loves her. Then as a wife and a loyal, understanding comrade who fights life's battles alongside [the man], and stands everywhere by his side without hemming in and fettering the man and his mind. And as a goddess whose feet he must kiss, who gives him strength through her feminine wisdom and childlike, pure sanctity [which] does not weaken during the hardest struggles and bestows upon him in ideal hours the soul's most divine gift.[37]

As exemplified by this entry, Himmler viewed women as nothing more than objects around which men dedicated their lives. In writing these sentiments, Himmler was espousing a perspective in line with his traditional, Bavarian, and Catholic upbringing. He placed women in an almost saintly role, one defined by Klaus Theweleit as the "white nurse," an emblem rather than a real figure who is strong, but at the same time needs to be protected.[38]

Yet in less than a decade, Himmler's views had shifted and, as his most recent biographer shows, they continued to shift based on changes in his personal life. His education in agriculture, his exposure to Nordic ideals from the Artamanen League, and his introduction to the blood and soil ideology added a key dimension to his views. Women were not only symbolically children, wives, and goddesses; they were also mothers who had the responsibility to bear healthy children. By the time Himmler had become Reichsführer, this fourth role shaped how he perceived women in relation to their husbands and the submissive role that they were to assume in both their individual families and the family community.

When subsequently formulating commands to regulate families, he discounted what his men may have thought or wanted, and he certainly did not take into account the opinions of their wives. Himmler expected that he could issue decrees that his men would follow and that they would persuade their wives to obey. He reconfirmed his position on the relationship that he believed husbands and wives were supposed to have in a wartime speech: "Gentlemen, there is only one possibility here. Either the man leads in the marriage, or if he cannot do this, if he is not capable of leading, then he either retires from us ... or he parts from his lifetime companion ... [who] is not internally willing to go along."[39] For Himmler, the issue was clear-cut. He never understood the complexities of his men, let alone their wives, when he sought to manage their family decisions. Even if he could have convinced every married SS man to agree to have at least four children, their wives would have needed to be persuaded, too. Instead, he objectified women as passive agents. Of course, such a view was well within the parameters of Nazi society, in which females had a select number of acceptable roles.

Himmler's disregard for women's status as active players was further confirmed during a conversation with Felix Kersten, his massage therapist. When Kersten learned of Himmler's desire to legitimize bigamy, he asked if he really thought women would accept such a proposal. Himmler clearly did, suggesting that the first wife would have special rights. To this statement Kersten replied, "I pity from the bottom of my heart the wretched husband who has to daily listen to and smooth down the quarrels of his two wives and their various children." He then pointed out another drawback: "just think, two mothers-in-law. In my opinion, it would be easier to win the Knight's Cross than to endure that for long. You must create a special award for bravery under domestic fire."[40] Kersten tried to call attention to the fact that ideology and the needs of the state would not convince women to go along with this plan. He suggested that Himmler ought to listen to the opinions of the women before implementing a law to allow bigamy. Once again, Himmler brushed off Kersten's objections, leading Kersten to report that his patient seemed amused by them. Himmler then continued by stating that education and propaganda would solve any resulting problems.[41] Here again, Kersten's reflections corroborate other sources. He reiterated that Himmler expected ideology to have a stronger hold over men and women than personal desires, a position that Himmler held on to tenaciously, and that undoubtedly influenced the failure of his population policies.

Beyond the general decline in population and the obstacles to regulating sexuality, another factor that hindered success was the relationship between class and education on one side and fertility on the other. By the early twentieth century, there was a strong correlation among these factors.[42] Simply put, among Europeans and people of European descent, the higher a person's socio-economic status and/or the greater his/her level of education, the fewer children he/she had.[43] The connection between the two is the basis of the bourgeois-morality explanation. The middle and upper classes had established a lifestyle in which education was used to foster economic comfort, a position partially maintained by abstaining from the creation of a large family. As the populations of Western countries declined in the late nineteenth and early twentieth centuries, the birth rate dropped the most severely in these groups. Eugenicists were well aware of (and displeased with) this inverse relationship between class, education, and fertility, as were sociologists, psychologists, and statisticians.[44]

This relationship is relevant to SS population policies because of the organization's demographic composition. The exclusive nature of the SS made it more appealing than other party organizations to some. Aristocrats, for example, were especially well represented in the officer ranks. An examination of the men who held one of the four highest ranks in the SS provides evidence of a relationship between social status and membership. Just under 10 per cent of the upper leadership had a noble heritage. This correlates with the conclusions drawn by Michael Kater in his social profile of the Nazi Party. He found that the elites in German society were overrepresented among the rank and file of the party, and "the higher the cadre, the greater the degree of elite representation."[45] There was no higher cadre than the SS.

During the Nuremberg Trial, the defence attorney for the SS, Horst Pelckmann, questioned Friedrich Karl von Eberstein about the relationship between the aristocracy and the SS. Eberstein confirmed the nobility's endorsement of the organization. He provided several reasons why princes, barons, and counts wanted to belong. Some wanted to show their loyalty to the new government, whereas others enjoyed the pleasures of sport and comradeship offered to members. Personally, Eberstein had "very willingly" entered the SS because service to Germany was a tradition in his family, and he thought that membership would allow him to fulfil his patriotic duty. Pelckmann subsequently asked him if he believed "that the membership of such prominent personages made an impression" on the German people. In response, Eberstein acknowledged that the admission of such people did strengthen the notion that the SS had a valuable and good purpose.[46]

Beyond the nobility, a second group swelled the ranks of the SS and its officer corps: those who had obtained some university education. According to Manfred Wolfson, more than half of the officers in his statistical survey had a graduate education, one-fourth held a doctorate, and one-fifth had obtained but not completed some form of secondary education. A second sample of officers analysed by Gunnar Boehnert reveals similar trends. After 1933, more people from high educational strata joined the SS. Thirty per cent of the men from his sample had a university education, compared with 2–3 per cent of the population. Herbert Ziegler draws similar conclusions in his book on the SS leadership corps. He suggests that so many well-educated people belonged not because the organization intrinsically valued them more, but because the nature of their work with the SS oftentimes required the skills of doctors or lawyers.[47] In his recent study of the Reich Security Main Office, Michael Wildt confirms this assessment.

In his memoir, Walter Schellenberg indicated why students like himself found the SS attractive. He claimed that because many people already considered the SS an elite group, it appealed to the best recruits. In turn, once these people joined, they enhanced the organization's prestige. "I cannot deny," Schellenberg wrote, "that at the age of twenty-three such things as social prestige and, shall we say, the glamour of a smart uniform, played quite a large part in my choice."[48] Another former officer, Helmut Poppendick, reported a similar first impression: "I joined the SS ... because a number of my friends whom I knew to be idealists were members."[49] As with Eberstein and Schellenberg, Poppendick saw value in the SS. He viewed it as an organization to which he, as a physician, could make a positive contribution. Werner Best, one of the many lawyers who joined, expressed comparable sentiments; the elite status of the SS, especially compared to the SA, was appealing.[50]

By joining the SS, aristocrats and university-educated men lent credibility to the organization. They were admitted as a result of their ability to prove their Nordic heritage, although many of them fit the elite standards – based on class, education, and social productivity – set by eugenicists for decades. Not all SS members were from prominent backgrounds or were well educated, but the organization did, as shown in its statistical surveys, contain a smaller percentage of people from uneducated or rural backgrounds compared to the general population.[51] Neither these surveys nor other SS statistics categorized birth rates according to level of education, which means that definitive conclusions between education and birth rate cannot be made. Nonetheless, the general point holds that the very types of people who already produced the lowest number of children joined the SS in droves and had an impact on the overall child statistics. When the relationship between social class/education and fertility was combined with the widespread decline in fertility in the West, it created a difficult predicament for the SS to overcome. Commands, rhetorical persuasion, ideological education, and monetary incentives – all of which existed in vast quantities – were not enough to prevail against the social and educational factors that had been influencing familial decisions long before the SS existed.

With social class and education came a related factor: age. People in this higher-class, well-educated group tended to marry later in life than their fellow countrymen with less education and in lower socio-economic classes.[52] Postponing marriage meant that a couple had a shorter time span to have a family; it also increased the possibility of complications due to infertility. Although a man's reproductive capacity does diminish over his lifetime, this decline is more rapid for women. It begins in the early thirties and accelerates over the next decade.[53] Both of these age-related complications would have affected the SS. Men had a median marriage age of thirty-two, and over 10 per cent of women were thirty years or older when they got married.[54]

Although they would have differed according to individual circumstances, each of these reasons could have contributed to limiting reproduction. However, there are two other factors to evaluate: the Great Depression and the Second World War. Germany was not alone in suffering the dire effects of these two events, but they would have influenced whether SS men and their wives chose to or had the opportunity to have children. During the Depression, one of the largest crises in Germany was unemployment. This economic woe in turn affected social conditions. People waited to get married and those who were already wed delayed having children.[55] These postponements made an already dire population situation worse. When the Nazi government came to power, one of the first problems it had to tackle was the economic predicament. Through a series of measures, the regime appeared to create a system that stabilized the country's economy.[56]

This apparent recovery affected familial choices. Once the financial crisis ended, people who had postponed getting married now did so. With a rise in marriages, there followed an increase in births.[57] However, waiting to get married increased the average age of marriage, thereby limiting the time period in which a couple could have children. Nonetheless, the birth rate rose. From a low of 14.7 births per 1,000 inhabitants in 1933, there were 19 births per 1,000 inhabitants in 1936. This number continued to climb, peaking at just over 20 births in the first years of the war.[58] This increase made Germany stand out from nearby countries where birth rates either remained the same or decreased, leading contemporary sociologists to suggest that Nazi policies geared towards increasing the birth rate were successful.[59]

SS members who were already adults during the Depression would have been influenced by these problems. Even men who were teenagers and who joined the SS later would have had a clear memory of this time and its impact on their family lives. The economic turmoil of the period would have most likely affected how they viewed their ability to have a financially secure life. Thus, the experience of the Depression, combined with the class and educational backgrounds of these men, was a formidable confluence of factors that the SS failed to overcome. If educated SS men were already well ensconced in the middle-class bourgeois values of the day, and if they had memories of unemployment and material deprivation, then there is little reason to think that they would have used the supplemental income provided by the SS to increase the size of their families. It is far more likely that such funds would have been seen as a means to establish a small but financially secure family. There is also the related issue of peer influence, a factor that, as already seen, explains why the nobility and the highly educated found the SS appealing. A man and woman might have chosen to limit the number of children they had based on working and socializing with couples from similar educational and social backgrounds who had small families.[60]

Furthermore, Germany's economic recovery was short-lived. No one had the opportunity to become accustomed to the country's newfound stability before the Second World War started. New obstacles arose, many of which – unsurprisingly – had a direct impact on procreation. The First World War had already demonstrated the debilitating effects of modern warfare.[61] During the Second World War, the belligerent powers knew that no country had been able to recover demographically from the losses of the first great conflict of the twentieth century.[62] The Nazi regime sought to avoid repeating the mistakes of the imperial government, and in some regards it succeeded. One major success was food rationing. To prevent malnutrition, and also to mitigate possible discontent among the population, the government began to reserve grain before the war. A few days before Germany invaded Poland, the Reich Ministry for Food and Agriculture began a rationing system. It was relatively effective in providing the population with enough calories and nutrients.[63] The availability of food staved off a potential source of disgruntlement, but it also affected fertility as a healthy diet is crucial to a successful pregnancy.[64]

But while nutrition was not an issue, other factors impeded reproduction. One of those factors was stress – namely, men on the front fighting and women at home concerned about those men. Related to this wartime stress were the continually worsening conditions on the home front. Since late 1940, German cities had been subject to Allied bombing. The targets were primarily industrial, but as post-war American studies reveal, strategic bombing was inaccurate, and civilians suffered as a result.[65] The fear and reality of bombardment caused stress for the women living through it, as well as for the men on the front who knew that they could not prevent it. The bombings also deprived people of their homes, making day-to-day survival more important than seeking to expand one's family. Such a predicament was a problem for every German, as secret reports compiled by the SS Security Service revealed.[66] There is simply no reason to believe that SS families would have been able, or would have chosen, to surmount such difficulties to have children.

Outside of these issues, which affected the entire country, there were problems specific to the SS. Himmler was among the people who recognized the impact of war, and as discussed previously, he encouraged reproduction to prevent a repeat of the demographic loss seen in the First World War. For example, the SS provided married men with extra vacation time to meet with their wives in the hope of each couple conceiving a child during the rendezvous. But the very fact that special efforts had to be made to promote reproduction indicates the difficulties inherent in conceiving during the war.

Beyond the issue of physical separation, there were two particular factors that impeded Himmler's goals. The first was the age of recruits. Waffen-SS recruits got younger every year. Initially, the call-up age for volunteers and conscripts for both the Wehrmacht and the Waffen-SS was 19. By 1943, this had dropped to 17. The average age of a Waffen-SS division throughout the war was 18. Even the vaunted Leibstandarte Adolf Hitler division was not that old. The average age among enlisted soldiers was 19.35 years, and for non-commissioned officers it was 25.76 years, leading to a unit average of 22.5 years.[67]

Following the loss at Stalingrad in early 1943, new Waffen-SS divisions were formed, including the Hitler Jugend. The name was not a random choice. Himmler worked in conjunction with the head of the Hitler Youth to form a unit recruited from that organization. After receiving Hitler's approval in early February, the new division was formed, allowing the boys to hold joint membership in the Hitler Youth and the Waffen-SS. About ten thousand boys joined, the majority of them enthusiastic volunteers. After training from summer 1943 through winter 1944, the boys, who were only seventeen or eighteen, were sent to the front under the leadership of commissioned and non-commissioned officers from the Leibstandarte. Their presence on the front was known not only in the German ranks, but also to the enemy, who dubbed this group the "Baby Division."[68]

Recruiting among the youth inhibited Himmler's population goals for several reasons. First, a boy in his late teens was unlikely to be married. By going off to war, he would have reduced his chances of getting married by being away from the home front and losing the opportunity to meet and marry someone. He also risked being killed while fighting. Second, prior to the war, Himmler had not expected a young SS man without sufficient means of caring for a family to have gotten married. He wavered when it came to the specific age, but the age was always in the early to mid-twenties, an age supported by wartime statistics showing when SS men married.[69] Nonetheless, young men recruited to fight prior to completing their education and/or securing employment would hardly have had the financial means to support a family – a dilemma that, as examined earlier, soldiers had raised in letters to *Das Schwarze Korps*. Third, while Himmler encouraged each man to have a child before going off to fight, SS policies favoured men who were already married and had children, which made it more difficult for an unmarried soldier to change his marital status.

Overall, with the average age of SS members declining throughout the war, Himmler could have had no reasonable expectation that the number of marriages among SS men, let alone the number of children born to them, would rise significantly. By recruiting young men, which was seen as a military necessity to stave off defeat, Himmler was essentially repeating a mistake from the First World War. He allowed a younger generation to risk dying before they had the opportunity to get married and father children. While the military victory was supposed to work in tandem with the victory in the cradle, in reality, trying to achieve the former greatly impaired the success of the latter.

The other factor that impeded the population goals of the SS was Himmler himself. Whereas he sought to control his men's personal behaviour, he also allowed leniency and granted exceptions to the rules. For example, as examined earlier, while several hundred men were discharged for disregarding the engagement and marriage command, many of them were later readmitted. Himmler likewise showed leniency when it came to promoting officers. Wartime regulations stipulated that an officer's marital and familial status were relevant criteria for advancement, but lacking a wife or not having enough children did not prohibit most officers from being promoted.

Himmler's willingness to grant his men latitude to make decisions affecting their personal lives was not limited to marriage and children; religion was another area in which enforcement of the rules was inconsistent. Himself a lapsed Catholic, Himmler was quite hostile, at least in private, to Christianity.[70] He wanted his men, their wives, and their children to break with their churches, but his orders regarding religious belief never demanded they do so. Church affiliation and participation in church-related activities did not affect a man's standing in the SS.[71] As Himmler told a priest who inquired about the issue, "Each SS man is at liberty to be in a church or not. This is his personal issue that he is responsible to before God and his conscience."[72] The only exception was for men who served in a leadership capacity in their church. As of October 1934, they had to choose between their religion and the SS, although if they chose their church, they received an honourable discharge.[73]

When a man left his church, Himmler preferred that he not state he was renouncing formal religion because of his membership in the SS. He felt that such a reason would tarnish the organization's reputation; he preferred instead that a man specify that his choice had been prompted by an "end of personal conviction."[74] While granting his men a choice in this area, Himmler refused to tolerate atheism.[75] Belief in God was an absolute necessity, most likely because the Nazis had spent years haranguing the Communists for being godless. This need for a belief in God, along with the hostility towards Communism, might have influenced Himmler's decision during the war to tolerate religion in at least two foreign Waffen-SS divisions: Catholicism in the Ukrainian Galicia division and Islam in the Bosnian Handschar division.[76] This overall tolerance for religious belief was reflected in the available numbers. By the late 1930s, only 18–25 per cent of SS men had declared themselves to be *Gottgläubig*, or believers in God. Approximately the same percentage of men remained Catholic, while more than half proclaimed themselves Protestant.[77] As with other statistics, the group that best complied with Himmler's wishes was the highest-ranking officers, just over 70 per cent of whom proclaimed themselves to be *Gottgläubig*.

This position on religion, much like the rules regulating the family community, showed that no aspect of a man's personal life was off limits to Himmler's intervention. Likewise, the religious exceptions detailed above demonstrate that leeway in complying with official policy was not uncommon. The fact that an SS man could evade ideological orders does not suggest that Himmler was not serious when it came to regulating personal affairs and decisions, but there were circumstances where evasion was possible. Even when it came to commands relating to one's official position, the ability to elude obeying existed. This is most evident in the case of the Einsatzgruppen, the mobile killing units composed of SS and police personnel responsible for executing Jews in Eastern Europe. Bourgeois morality unfortunately did not inhibit most men in these battalions from committing murder – yet, as Christopher Browning shows, a minority were able to decline participating in the executions without punishment.[78]

These men's choice not to obey belies the impression given by many high-ranking SS officers after the war that disobeying an order was not possible. For example, Otto Ohlendorf testified during the Nuremberg Trial that disobedience would have resulted in a court martial. Franz Stangl, the former commandant of Treblinka, raised this point in a postwar interview, as did Erich von dem Bach-Zelewski and Richard Hildebrandt during the RuSHA Trial.[79] These men might very well have believed that disobedience was impossible, although their claims must be regarded with suspicion. On trial or in prison for their service during the Third Reich, their assertions may have been nothing more than a tactic to deflect responsibility. This is a far more plausible explanation, given that some historians have suggested that evasion was possible, and even Albert Speer, Hitler's court architect and wartime head of the Armaments Ministry, contended that an individual could mitigate the orders he had received.[80]

The possibility of evasion has relevance to commands aimed at regulating SS families. If a man were willing to risk death to avoid fulfilling a duty-related order, then he would have had no objection to being expelled from the SS for disregarding an order that impinged on his personal life. Furthermore, enforcing complete compliance would have required an effective apparatus that could dictate clear guidelines for how each order had to be obeyed and the specific process through which punishment would be administered. The SS did have a court, but without a system in place to enforce its policies consistently, some SS men avoided following orders without fear of reprisal. Even if an efficient system did exist, Himmler would have had to allow it to function without constantly intervening, which, given his predilection for getting involved in almost everything, would have been nearly impossible.

In the end, Himmler's population ideals, along with the desires and goals of many Nazi leaders, never came to fruition. While he did construct an inflated bureaucracy capable of many things – most of which were deadly in nature – his objective to create a family community that could serve as an everlasting elite came to naught. The pervasiveness of bourgeois morality is a valid explanation, but that alone cannot explain SS men's inability or choice not to cooperate. A range of social, economic, and educational factors created obstacles that could have influenced the development of family policies. Some factors were unique to the SS – the overrepresentation of the nobility and the well educated, the declining age of its members throughout the war, and Himmler's incessant micromanagement. Other factors, such as the Depression and the Second World War, were more generalized. Collectively, these factors provide a larger context in which to explore the contours and the significance of the SS family community.

Examining both the ideal and the reality of this community provides historians with a stronger understanding of the evolving ambitions of the SS. The core element in the creation of the family community was convincing each man that he had the responsibility to ensure a victory in the cradle. His contribution as a father was as significant as his efforts towards advancing first the political victory of the Nazi Party and then the military victory of the Nazi state. The SS used a variety of measures to encourage each man to establish not just a racially healthy family, but a child-rich one as well.

An entire system was created, primarily through the work of the Race and Settlement Main Office, to foster and assist families. It all began with the 1931 engagement and marriage command, which established a process whereby RuSHA could ensure that each man and his future wife were racially suitable to found a child-rich family. Once each couple had been vetted, a barrage of rhetoric encouraged them to begin a family. Both the state and the SS backed up this encouragement with financial assistance, and RuSHA provided material support in addition to promoting ceremonies to celebrate couples' unions as well as the birth of their children. The availability of these resources meant that any SS man who wanted to take advantage of them could do so. Based on the low numbers of children born, the majority did not avail themselves of these incentives and did not have large families. For various reasons, they were either unable to or chose not to do so, and even granting them a modicum of leeway during the war did not alter this outcome. Nevertheless, the very existence of this system, the quantity of resources dedicated to it, and the efforts expended on implementing it demonstrates the importance of the family community to the SS. Its construction was designed to work in conjunction with the Nazi Party's crusade to reshape the nation into a racial state.

However, the measures employed by the SS to found this community were not of its own making. Himmler and other SS leaders, notably RuSHA chiefs Richard Walther Darré and Otto Hofmann, embraced and implemented the ideals of the then internationally respected science of eugenics. Eugenicists had wanted for decades to find a humane means of improving the quantity and quality of the population. Based on their individual class, racial, religious, and national biases, they wanted to limit certain people's ability to reproduce while encouraging other people to have more children. In seeking to control these people's reproductive rights, eugenicists suggested a wide range of measures, many of which Himmler adopted. He selectively used the ideas that best suited his plans while ignoring any suggestion that did not fit his racial view of the world. In this way Himmler and the SS, particularly RuSHA, attempted to turn rhetoric into reality by applying eugenic ideals.

The employment of eugenics to construct the family community did not come without consequences. To manage this vast enterprise and to supervise every phase of family life, RuSHA became a large bureaucracy that rendered all personal decisions subject to organizational oversight. The engagement and marriage procedure represents the best example of this management. When the SS only had fifteen thousand members, it was simple enough for Himmler to require a thorough review of each application and to evaluate most if not all of them personally. As the SS grew and additional regulations were created, this process became more cumbersome. RuSHA consequently had to expand to meet the needs presented by this steep increase in applicants.

This expansion demonstrates the complicated nature of oversee-ing the personal lives of other people – something that eugenicists had not anticipated, or had at least not acknowledged in their works. One can only imagine what type of massive and complex bureaucracy would have been needed to implement the measures used in the SS on a nationwide scale. This difficulty was compounded by the fact that there were many reasons that inhibited an SS man and his wife from having a child-rich family. Eugenicists could not have accounted for all of these reasons when they proposed how to improve the population. Therefore, the inability of the SS to use eugenics to create a supposedly superior master race was not just a failure for the organization and for Himmler's plans, but for the science of eugenics as well.

The attempt to increase the population through positive eugenic mea-sures failed. Unfortunately, negative measures, primarily exemplified by sterilization, euthanasia, and genocide, were far more effective. Due to this destructive use, along with the connection to racism and anti-Semitism, eugenics was discredited following the Second World War. Many of its constituent fields, however, did not suffer repercussions. For example, scientists and social scientists remain interested in the declin-ing birth rate in Europe. They seek to understand the causes along with the short- and long-term effects of a low birth rate. One such research endeavour was the European Fertility Project, based at Princeton Uni-versity. Its purpose was to create a quantitative record of the birth decline as well as to assess the social changes resulting from it. More recently, the World Health Organization has taken an interest in this subject as part of its larger focus on sexual and reproductive health. So, too, has Eurostat, the statistical office of the European Union. In 2013 it released a report analysing the relationship between fertility trends and the economic recession.[81] Outside of the scientific community, the media frequently comments on European countries' demographic status and the influence of the changing birth rate on the political situation.[82]

In addition to demographic research, the idea of using science to create healthier offspring flourishes in the field of genetics. Genetic engineering, gene therapy, genetic counselling, and in vitro fertilization are
just a few ways in which this science could be used to influence the biological heritage of future generations.[83] Among the most recent research,
that with the greatest potential application is the Human Genome Project. One of its explicit purposes is the application of genetic knowledge
to improve the health and well-being of human beings.[84] Fortunately,
the scientists conducting this research recognize the potential non-
scientific ramifications of their work, and this recognition will hope-
fully shape their future endeavours.

While the ideal of using science to improve mankind still exists,
eugenics has been discredited and is now primarily viewed through
the prism of Nazism. As used in Nazi Germany, it has a multifaceted
legacy. Its appropriation in the formation of SS family ideology is a vital
part of this legacy. Heinrich Himmler applied eugenic principles to a
select group as no individual, organization, or state had ever done. He
sought to establish an elite aristocracy whose members were chosen
based on a common bond of race and blood. His commitment to building this eugenic-based community remained steadfast, although he
amended policies as needed to adapt to the changing circumstances.

Yet the SS family community did not develop as a one-way conduit,
with orders issued from above and obeyed from below – that was certainly Himmler's intention, but reality did not reflect this ideal. Himmler set the process in motion and stayed intimately involved in its
development, but other SS leaders contributed to the evolution of the
family community, too, as did SS men and their wives. Their participation was vital, but it also revealed the limitations of this community –
namely, its lack of children. The inability or the choice not to create
prolific families of "good blood" left the SS without a biological legacy
to sustain the racial empire that the Nazi regime sought to construct.
Without a solid family foundation, there could be no Thousand Year
Reich ruled by an SS aristocracy. The racial elite so imagined is therefore
nothing more than a part of the horrid legacy of destruction wrought
by the SS in one of the darkest chapters in European history.

Appendices

Appendix A: The Engagement and Marriage Command

Munich, 31 December 1931

1. The SS is an association of German, particularly Nordic, men who are chosen according to selective criteria.
2. In accordance with the National Socialist world view and with the realization that the future of our *Volk* is based on the selection and preservation of the racial and hereditary health of good blood, I introduce, effective as of 1 January 1932, the "marriage authorization" for all unmarried members of the SS.
3. The goal to aim for is the hereditarily healthy family of German Nordic type.
4. The marriage authorization is given or refused solely on racial and hereditary health criteria.
5. Every SS man who intends to marry has to obtain the marriage authorization of the Reichsführer-SS.
6. SS members who marry despite having been denied the marriage authorization will be dismissed from the SS; they will be given the option of resigning.
7. The appropriate processing of marriage requests is the task of the "Race Office" of the SS.
8. The Race Office of the SS is in charge of the "Family Book of the SS," in which the families of SS members are written down after the granting of the marriage authorization or approval of the request for registration.

9. The Reichsführer-SS, the leader of the Race Office, and the advisers of this office are bound to secrecy by their word of honour.
10. The SS is aware that with this order it has taken a step of great importance. Mockery, scorn, and misunderstanding do not affect us; the future belongs to us!

The Reichsführer-SS
[signed] H. Himmler

Appendix B: Development of the SS

Date	Notable event	Number of members
9 November 1925	Founding of the SS	8
31 December 1925		100
6 January 1929	Himmler appointed RFSS	280
31 December 1929		1,000
31 December 1930		2,727
31 December 1931		14,964
13 April 1932		25,000
14 June 1932		41,000
31 December 1932		52,048
30 January 1933	Hitler appointed chancellor	52,174
30 June 1933		113,094
31 December 1933		209,014
30 June 1934	As of the Röhm purge	221,025
31 December 1934		196,075
31 December 1935		199,915
31 December 1936		200,129
31 December 1937		208,364
31 December 1938		238,159
31 December 1939		258,456
1 July 1940		254,529
31 December 1940		331,731
30 June 1941		222,252
31 December 1941		397,668
31 December 1942		465,798
31 December 1943		706,797
30 June 1944		794,941

Appendix C: Rank Comparisons

SS	German Army	American Army
Reichsführer-SS	Generalfeldmarschall	General of the Army

Commissioned Officer grades:

SS-Oberstgruppenführer	Generaloberst	General
SS-Obergruppenführer	General	Lieutenant General
SS-Gruppenführer	Generalleutnant	Major General
SS-Brigadeführer	Generalmajor	Brigadier General
SS-Oberführer	(no equivalent)	(no equivalent)
SS-Standartenführer	Oberst	Colonel
SS-Obersturmbannführer	Oberstleutnant	Lieutenant Colonel
SS-Sturmbannführer	Major	Major
SS-Hauptsturmführer	Hauptmann	Captain
SS-Obersturmführer	Oberleutnant	First Lieutenant
SS-Untersturmführer	Leutnant	Second Lieutenant

Non-Commissioned Officer grades:

SS-Sturmscharführer	Stabsfeldwebel	Sergeant Major
SS-Standarten-Oberjunker	Oberfähnrich	(no equivalent)
SS-Stabscharführer	Hauptfeldwebel	(no equivalent)
SS-Hauptscharführer	Oberfeldwebel	Master & First Sergeant
SS-Oberscharführer	Feldwebel	Technical Sergeant
SS-Standartenjunker	Fähnrich	(no equivalent)
SS-Scharführer	Unterfeldwebel	Staff Sergeant
SS-Unterscharführer	Unteroffizier	Sergeant

Enlisted grades:

SS-Rottenführer	Stabgefreiter & Obergefreiter	Corporal (NCO grade)
SS-Sturmmann	Gefreiter	(no equivalent)
SS-Oberschütze (SS-Mann)	Oberschütze	Private First Class
SS-Schütze (SS-Mann)	Schütze	Private
SS-Anwärter	Rekrut	(no equivalent)

Appendix D: Organization of the Allgemeine-SS

Oberabschnitt
By 1944, there were eighteen in Germany and four in the occupied territories.

Abschnitt
There were approximately two to four in each Oberabschnitt.

Standarte
There were approximately two to four in each Abschnitt.

Sturmbann
There were approximately three to five in each Standarte.

Sturm
There approximately four to five in each Sturmbann.

Zug and Schar
These were two units below the Sturm.

Notes

Introduction

1 "Schlüssel zum Leben," *Das Schwarze Korps*, 3 June 1943.
2 *Trial of the major war criminals before the International Military Tribunal, 14 November 1945–1 October 1946* (Nuremberg: n.p., 1947–49), 4: 176 (hereafter cited as *IMT*).
3 Ibid., 161.
4 Herbert Ziegler, *Nazi Germany's new aristocracy: The SS leadership, 1925–1939* (Princeton, NJ: Princeton University Press, 1989).
5 Bruce Campbell, *The SA generals and the rise of Nazism* (Lexington: University Press of Kentucky, 1998), 30–3; Edgar Erwin Knoebel, "Racial illusion and military necessity: A study of SS political and manpower objectives in occupied Belgium" (PhD diss., University of Colorado, 1965), 1–6; Robert Lewis Koehl, *The SS: A history 1919–1945* (Stroud, UK: Tempus, 1989), 32–4; Gunter d'Alquen, *Die SS: Geschichte, Aufgabe, und Organisation der Schutzstaffel der NSDAP* (Berlin: Junker und Dünnhaupt, 1939), 6–7; and *IMT*, vol. 29: document 1992(a)-PS and document 2284-PS.
6 "Richtlinien der 'Schutzstaffeln' der Nationalsozialistischen Deutschen Arbeiter-Partei," BA NS19/1934, pp. 4, 12, and 13; Richard Bessel, *Political violence and the rise of Nazism: The storm troopers in eastern Germany, 1925–1934* (New Haven, CT: Yale University Press, 1984), 45.
7 "Verfügung," BA NS19/1934, p. 34.
8 Felix Kersten, *The Kersten memoirs, 1940–1945*, trans. Constantine Fitzgibbon and James Oliver (New York: Macmillan, 1957), 297; Peter Padfield, *Himmler* (New York: MJF Books, 1990), 297 and 377.
9 Koehl, *The SS*, 237.

10 Anthony Marx, *Faith in nation: Exclusionary origins of nationalism* (Oxford: Oxford University Press, 2003); Oliver Zimmer, *Nationalism in Europe, 1890–1940* (New York: Palgrave Macmillan, 2003).

11 Benedict Anderson, *Imagined communities: Reflections on the origin and spread of nationalism* (London: Verso, 1983), 6–7. Eric Hobsbawm also suggests that a nation is a cultural construct in *Nations and nationalism since 1870: Programme, myth, reality* (Cambridge: Cambridge University Press, 1990), 9–11.

12 Michael Burleigh and Wolfgang Wippermann, *The racial state: Germany, 1933–1945* (Cambridge: Cambridge University Press, 1991).

13 John Connelly, "The uses of the Volksgemeinschaft: Letters to the NSDAP Kreisleitung Eisenach, 1939–1940," *The Journal of Modern History* 68, no. 4 (December 1996): 299–330; David Welch, "Nazi propaganda and the Volksgemeinschaft: Creating a people's community," *Journal of Contemporary History* 39, no. 2 (April 2004): 213–38; Martina Steber and Bernhard Gotto, eds., *Visions of community in Nazi Germany: Social engineering and private lives* (Oxford: Oxford University Press, 2014).

14 Oskar Hertwig and Ernst Bumm did not advocate it. Paul Weindling, "The medical profession, social hygiene, and the birth rate in Germany, 1914–1918," in *The upheaval of war: Family, work, and welfare in Europe, 1914–1918*, eds. Richard Wall and Jay Winter (Cambridge: Cambridge University Press, 1988), 429; Weindling, *Health, race, and German politics between national unification and Nazism, 1870–1945* (Cambridge: Cambridge University Press, 1989), 292 and 366.

15 Robert Proctor, *Racial hygiene: Medicine under the Nazis* (Cambridge, MA: Harvard University Press, 1988), 22; Sheila Faith Weiss, *Race hygiene and national efficiency: The eugenics of Wilhelm Schallmayer* (Berkeley: University of California Press, 1987), 18; Weiss, "The race hygiene movement in Germany, 1904–1945," in *The wellborn science: Eugenics in Germany, France, Brazil, and Russia*, ed. Mark Adams (Oxford: Oxford University Press, 1990), 9–14; Weiss, "Wilhelm Schallmayer and the logic of German eugenics," *Isis* 77, no. 1 (March 1986): 33; Peter Weingart, "Eugenics: Medical or social science?" *Science in Context* 8, no. 1 (1995): 202.

16 Weiss, "The race hygiene movement," 22–3; Peter Weingart, "German eugenics between science and politics," *Osiris*, second series (1989), 5: 261–62.

17 Karl Binding and Alfred Hoche, *Die Freigabe der Vernichtung lebensunwerten Lebens. Ihr Mass und ihre Form* (Leipzig: F. Meiner, 1920). See also Henry Friedlander, *The origins of Nazi genocide: From euthanasia to the Final Solution* (Chapel Hill: University of North Carolina Press, 1995), 14–16.

18 Erwin Baur, Eugen Fischer, and Fritz Lenz, *Menschlichen Erblichkeitslehre und Rassenhygiene. Band I* and *Band II* (Munich: J.F. Lehmanns Verlag, 1921).

19 "KWI-A Jahresbericht 1927/1928," MPG Abt. 1, Rep. 3, Nr. 4, p. 1; Paul Weindling, "Weimar eugenics: The Kaiser Wilhelm Institute for Anthropology, Human Heredity, and Eugenics in social context," *Annals of Science* 42, no. 3 (May 1985): 303–18.

20 Weingart, "German eugenics," 266–7; "KWI-A Jahresbericht 1927/1928," 27; "KWI-A Jahresbericht 1930," MPG Abt. 1, Rep. 3, Nr. 6, p. 41; "KWI-A Jahresbericht 1934," MPG Abt. 1, Rep. 3, Nr. 10, p. 141; Adolf von Harnack, *Handbuch der Kasier-Wilhelm-Gesellschaft zur Förderung des Wissenschaften* (Berlin: Verlag von Reimar Hobbing, 1928), 199–200; "Niederschriften 71 über die Sitzung des Senates der Kaiser-Wilhelm-Gesellschaft zur Förderung der Wissenschaften," MPG Niederschriften von Sitzungen des Senats der Kaiser-Wilhelm-Gesellschaft, 1933–1943, pp. 5–6.

21 Sheila Faith Weiss, "Human genetics and politics as mutually beneficial resources: The case of the Kaiser Wilhelm Institute for Anthropology, Human Heredity, and Eugenics during the Third Reich," *Journal of the History of Biology* 39, no. 1 (2006): 52; Thomas Berez and Sheila Faith Weiss, "The Nazi symbiosis: Politics and human genetics at the Kaiser Wilhelm Institute," *Endeavor* 28, no. 5 (December 2004): 174.

22 Weiss, "Human genetics," 70; Proctor, *Racial hygiene*, 45; Sheila Faith Weiss, *The Nazi symbiosis: Human genetics and politics in the Third Reich* (Chicago: University of Chicago Press, 2010).

23 Michael Wildt, *An uncompromising generation: The Nazi leadership of the Reich Security Main Office*, trans. Tom Lampert (Madison: University of Wisconsin Press, 2009), 110. See also Christopher Browning, "The Holocaust: Basis and Objective of the *Volksgemeinschaft*?" in *Visions of Community in Nazi Germany*, 217–25.

24 Ian Kershaw, *Hitler: Hubris, 1889–1936* (New York: W.W. Norton & Company, 2000), xxi.

25 See Wildt, *An uncompromising generation*.

26 Jutta Mühlenberg, *Das SS-Helferinnenkorps: Ausbildung, Einsatz, und Entnazifizierung der weiblichen Angehörigen der Waffen-SS, 1942–1949* (Hamburg: Hamburger Edition, 2011).

27 Kershaw, *Hitler: Hubris*, xxi, and Christopher Browning, *Ordinary men: Reserve Police Battalion 101 and the Final Solution in Poland* (New York: Harper Perennial, 1998), xix–xx.

28 Robert Gerwarth, *Hitler's hangman: The life of Heydrich* (New Haven, CT: Yale University Press, 2011), x.

29 Anke Schmeling, *Josias Erbprinz zu Waldeck und Pyrmont: Der politische Weg eines hohen SS-Führers* (Kassel: Verlag Gesamthochschul-Bibliothek, 1993), and Gudrun Schwarz, *Eine Frau an seiner Seite: Ehefrauen in der "SS-Sippengemeinschaft"* (Hamburg: Hamburger Edition, 1997). Using documents in the US National Archives, Robert Shalka wrote a history of Fulda-Werra: "The General-SS in central Germany 1937–1939: A social and institutional study of SS Main Sector Fulda-Werra (PhD diss., University of Wisconsin, 1972).

30 For a brief overview of SS officer [SSO] and RuSHA [RS] files now in the BDC, see Jens Banach, *Heydrichs Elite: Das Führerkorps der Sichheitspolizei und des SD 1936–1945* (Paderborn: Ferdinand Schöningh, 1998), 27–8.

31 William Combs, *The voice of the SS: A history of the SS journal "Das Schwarze Korps"* (New York: Peter Lang, 1986), and Mario Zeck, *Das Schwarze Korps: Geschichte und Gestalt des Organs der Reichsführung SS* (Tübingen: Maz Niemeyer Verlag, 2002).

32 Weiss, "Wilhelm Schallmayer"; Weiss, *Race hygiene and national efficiency*; Daniel Gasman, *The scientific origins of National Socialism: Social Darwinism in Ernst Haeckel and the German Monist League* (New York: American Elsevier, 1971); Jochen-Christoph Kaiser, Kurt Nowak, and Michael Schwartz, eds., *Eugenik, Sterilisation, "Euthanasie": Politische Biologie in Deutschland 1895–1945; Eine Dokumentation* (Berlin: Buchverlag Union, 1992); Peter Weingart, Jürgen Kroll, and Kurt Bayertz, *Rasse, Blut, und Gene: Geschichte der Eugenik und Rassenhygiene in Deutschland* (Frankfurt: Suhrkamp, 1988).

33 Proctor, *Racial hygiene* and Proctor, "Nazi medicine and the politics of knowledge," in *The "racial" economy of science: Toward a democratic future*, ed. Sandra G. Harding (Bloomington: Indiana University Press, 1993).

34 For more on biological determinism, see Stephan Jay Gould, *The mismeasure of man* (New York: W.W. Norton and Company, 1996).

35 Julian Huxley and Alfred Haddon, *We Europeans: A survey of "racial" problems* (New York: Harper and Brother Publishers, 1936), 13. Clifford Kirkpatrick raised the same point two years later: *Nazi Germany: Its women and family life* (Indianapolis, IN: The Bobbs-Merrill Company, 1938), 41–2. Amram Scheinfeld made a similar point the year after that: *You and heredity* (New York: Frederick A. Stokes Company, 1939), 354.

36 Hans Buchheim, "The SS – instrument of domination," and "Command and compliance," both in *Anatomy of the SS state*, ed. Helmut Krausnick et al. and trans. Richard Barry et al., 127–302 and 303–96 (New York: Walker and Company, 1965); Buchheim, "The position of the SS in the Third Reich," in *Republic to Reich: The making of the Nazi revolution*, ed. Hajo

Holborn and trans. Ralph Manheim (New York: Pantheon, 1972); and
Gerald Reitlinger, *The SS, alibi of a nation* (New York: Viking Press, 1957).

37 Robert Lewis Koehl, *RKFDV: German population and resettlement policy,*
1933–1945: A history of the Reich Commission for the Strengthening of
Germandom (Cambridge, MA: Harvard University Press, 1957); Koehl,
"Toward an SS typology: Social engineers," *American Journal of Economics*
and Sociology 18, no. 2 (January 1959): 113–26; Koehl, "The character of the
Nazi SS," *The Journal of Modern History* 34, no. 3 (September 1962): 275–83;
Koehl, *The black corps: The structure and power struggles of the Nazi SS*
(Madison: University of Wisconsin Press, 1983).

38 James Weingartner, "The Race and Settlement Main Office: Toward an
order of blood and soil," *The Historian* 34, no. 1 (1971): 62–77.

39 Isabel Heinemann, " 'Another type of perpetrator': The SS racial experts
and forced population movements in the occupied regions," *Holocaust and*
Genocide Studies 15, no. 3 (Winter 2001): 387–411, and Heinemann, *Rasse,*
Siedlung, deutsches Blut: Das Rasse-und Siedlungshauptamt der SS und die
rassenpolitische Neuordnung Europas (Göttingen: Wallstein Verlag,
2003).

40 Herbert Ziegler, "Fight against the empty cradle: Nazi pronatal policies
and the SS-Führerkorps," *Historical Social Research* no. 38 (April 1986):
25–40; Ziegler, *Nazi Germany's new aristocracy*; Manfred Wolfson,
"Constraint and choice in the SS leadership," *The Western Political Quarterly*
18, no. 3 (September 1965): 551–68; and Wolfson, "The SS leadership" (PhD
diss., University of California Berkeley, 1965).

41 Geoffrey Giles, "Straight talk for Nazi youth: The attempt to transmit
heterosexual norms," in *Education and cultural transmission: Historical*
studies of continuity and change in families, schooling, and youth cultures, ed.
Johan Sturm (Ghent, BE: CSHP, 1996); Giles, "The institutionalization of
homosexual panic in the Third Reich," in *Social outsiders in Nazi Germany,*
eds. Robert Gellately and Nathan Stoltzfus (Princeton, NJ: Princeton
University Press, 2001); Giles, "The denial of homosexuality: Same-sex
incidents in Himmler's SS and police," *Journal of the History of Sexuality* 11,
no. 1–2 (January/April 2002): 256–90.

42 George Mosse, *Nationalism and sexuality: Respectability and abnormal*
sexuality in modern Europe (New York: Howard Fertig, 1985).

43 Stefan Maiwald and Gerd Mischler, *Sexualität unter dem Hakenkreuz:*
Manipulation und Vernichtung der Intimsphäre im NS-Staat (Hamburg:
Europa Verlag, 1999).

44 Michel Foucault, *The history of sexuality: An introduction* (New York: Vintage
Books, 1990), 1: 11, 34, 39, 108–9, and 147.

45 Dagmar Herzog, "Hubris and hypocrisy, incitement and disavowal:
   Sexuality and German fascism," *Journal of the History of Sexuality* 11, no.
   1–2 (January/April 2002): 3–21; Herzog, ed., *Sexuality and German fascism*
   (New York: Berghahn Books, 2005); Herzog, *Sex after fascism: Memory and
   morality in twentieth-century Germany* (Princeton, NJ: Princeton University
   Press, 2005); and Herzog, *Sexuality in Europe: A twentieth-century history*
   (Cambridge: Cambridge University Press, 2011), 66–7.
46 Robert Waite, "Teenage sexuality in Nazi Germany," *Journal of the History of
   Sexuality* 8, no. 3 (January 1998): 434–76. The remaining articles come from
   Journal of the History of Sexuality 11, no. 1–2 (January/April 2002): Elizabeth
   Heineman, "Sexuality and Nazism: The doubly unspeakable?" 22–66;
   Julia Roos, "Backlash against prostitutes' rights: Origins and dynamics of
   Nazi prostitution policies," 67–94; Birthe Kundrus, "Forbidden company:
   Romantic relationships between Germans and foreigners, 1939 to 1945,"
   201–22; and Annette Timm, "Sex with a purpose: Prostitution, venereal
   disease, and militarized masculinity in the Third Reich," 223–55.
47 Alfred Meusel, "National Socialism and the family," *Sociological Review* 28,
   no. 2 (April 1936): 166–86; Meusel, "National Socialism and the family, part
   II," *Sociological Review* 28, no. 4 (October 1936): 389–411; Frank Hankins,
   "German policies for increasing births," *The American Journal of Sociology*
   42, no. 5 (March 1937): 630–52; P.K. Whelpton, "Why the large rise in the
   German birth rate?" *The American Journal of Sociology* 41, no. 3 (November
   1935): 299–313; Kirkpatrick, *Nazi Germany*; Clifford Kirkpatrick, "Recent
   changes in the status of women and the family in Germany," *American
   Sociological Review* 2, no. 5 (October 1937): 650–8; and Conrad Taeuber and
   Irene Taeuber, "German fertility trends, 1933–39," *The American Journal of
   Sociology* 46, no. 2 (September 1940): 150–67.
48 Jill Stephenson, *Women in Nazi society* (New York: Barnes and Noble Books,
   1975); Tim Mason, "Women in Germany, 1925–1940: Family welfare and
   work, part I," *History Workshop* 1 (Spring 1976): 74–113; Mason, "Women in
   Germany, 1925–1940: Family welfare and work, part II," *History Workshop* 2
   (Summer 1976): 5–32; Gisela Bock, "Antinatalism, maternity, and paternity
   in National Socialist racism," in *Maternity and gender policies: Women and
   the rise of the European welfare states, 1880s–1950s*, eds. Gisela Bock and Pat
   Thane (London: Routledge, 1991); Claudia Koonz, *Mothers in the fatherland:
   Women, the family and Nazi politics* (New York: St. Martin's Press, 1987);
   Gabriele Czarnowski, " 'The value of marriage for the *Volksgemeinschaft*':
   Policies towards women and marriage under National Socialism," in
   Fascist Italy and Nazi Germany: Comparisons and contrasts, ed. Richard Bessel
   and trans. Pamela Selwyn (Cambridge: Cambridge University Press, 1996);

Lisa Pine, *Nazi family policy 1933–1945* (Oxford: Berg, 1997); Michelle
Mouton, *From nurturing the nation to purifying the Volk: Weimar and Nazi
family policy, 1918–1945* (Washington, DC: German Historical Institute,
2007); and Annette Timm, *The politics of fertility in twentieth-century Berlin*
(Cambridge: Cambridge University Press, 2010).

49 Bertram Schaffner, *Father land: A study of authoritarianism in the German family*
(New York: Columbia University Press, 1948); David Rodnick, *Postwar
Germans: An anthropologist's account* (New Haven, CT: Yale University Press,
1948). See also Helmut Schelsky, "The family in Germany," *Marriage and
Family Living* 16, no. 4 (1954): 331–5.

50 See Göran Therborn, *Between sex and power: Family in the world, 1900–2000*
(London: Routledge, 2004); R.W. Connell, "The state, gender, and sexual
politics," *Theory and Society* 19, no. 5 (October 1990): 507–44; Robert
Moeller, *War stories: The search for a usable past in the Federal Republic of
Germany* (Berkeley: University of California, 2001); Roy Jerome, ed.,
Conceptions of postwar German masculinity (Albany: State University of
New York Press, 2001); and the following articles from *Signs* 24, no. 1
(Autumn 1998): Robert Moeller, " 'The last soldiers of the Great War'
and tales from family reunion in the Federal Republic of Germany,"
129–45; Heide Fehrenbach, "Rehabilitating fatherland: Race and German
remasculinization," 107–27; and Susan Jeffords, "The 'remasculinzation' of
Germany in the 1950s," 163–9.

51 Katharina Pohl, "Fatherhood in East and West Germany: Results of the
German family and fertility survey," in *Fertility and the male life-cycle in the
era of fertility decline*, eds. Caroline Bledsoe, Susana Lerner, and Jane Guyer
(Oxford: Oxford University Press, 2000).

52 Katharina Tumpek-Kjellmark, "From Hitler's widows to Adenauer's
brides: Towards a construction of gender and memory in postwar
Germany, 1938–1963" (PhD diss., Cornell University, 1994).

53 Van Rahden, "Demokratie und väterliche Autorität. Das Karlsruher
'Stichenscheid'-Urteil in der politischen Kultur der frühen
Bundesrepublik," *Zeithistorische Forschungen* 2, no. 2 (2005); van Rahden,
" 'Germ cells': The private realm as a political project in the Bonn Republic:
On some similarities between the fifties and the late sixties," paper
presented at "Gender and the Long Postwar: Reconsiderations of the
United States and the Two Germanies, 1945–1989," German Historical
Institute, Washington, DC, May 30–31, 2008 (thanks to the author for
providing me with a copy); and van Rahden, "Paternity, rechristianization,
and the quest for democracy in postwar West Germany," *Forschungsberichte*
(aus dem Duitsland Instituut Amsterdam) 4 (2008): 53–71.

1 The Engagement and Marriage Command

1 Padfield, *Himmler*, 103.
2 Weiss, *Race hygiene and national efficiency*, 54–6 and Baur-Fischer-Lenz, *Menschliche Erblichkeitslehre und Rassenhygiene*, 2: 133.
3 Richard Weikart, *From Darwin to Hitler: Evolutionary ethics, eugenics, and racism in Germany* (New York: Palgrave Macmillan, 2004), 93 and 139.
4 "SS-Befehl – A – Nr. 65," BA NS19/1934, p. 147.
5 Fritz Lenz, "Die Stellung des Nationalsozialismus zur Rassenhygiene," *Archiv für Rassen-und Gesellschaftsbiologie* 25 (1931): 300–8.
6 Fritz Lenz, "Notizen: Ein Versuch rassenhygienischer Lenkung der Ehewahl," *Archiv für Rassen- und Gesellschaftsbiologie* 26 (1932): 461.
7 For more on the selective use of terror, see Nathan Stoltzfus, "Tactical terror: Exceptions to Nazi reliance on terror for repressing dissidents and its social causes," in *Terror: From tyrannicide to terrorism*, eds. Brett Bowden and Michael Davis (Brisbane, AU: University of Queensland Press, 2009).
8 "SS-Befehl – A – Nr. 67," 31 December 1931, BA NS19/1934.
9 Johnpeter Horst Grill, "The Nazi Party's rural propaganda before 1928," *Central European History* 15, no. 2 (June 1982): 166, 172–3, and 178–9; Geoffrey Field, "Nordic racism," *Journal of the History of Ideas* 38, no. 3 (July–September 1977): 529–30; Clifford Lovin, "Blut und Boden: The ideological basis of the Nazi agricultural program," *Journal of the History of Ideas* 28, no. 2 (April–June 1967): 280; Weingartner, "The Race and Settlement Main Office," 62–3; and Peter Longerich, *Heinrich Himmler*, trans. Jeremy Noakes and Lesley Sharpe (Oxford: Oxford University Press, 2012), 128.
10 Richard Walther Darré, *Neuadel aus Blut und Boden* (Munich: J.F. Lehmanns Verlag, 1934), 13, 40, 59, 177, 187, 188, and 190; Lovin, "Blut und Boden," 282–4; Barbara Miller Lane, "Nazi ideology: Some unfinished business," *Central European History* 7, no. 1 (March 1974): 27–8; Anna Bramwell, *Blood and soil: Richard Walther Darré and Hitler's "Green Party"* (Bourne End, UK: The Kensal Press, 1985), 24, 26, 42, 55, 72, and 75; and Gesine Gerhard, "Breeding pigs and people for the Third Reich: Richard Walther Darré's agrarian ideology," in *How green were the Nazis? Nature, environment, and nation in the Third Reich*, eds. Franz-Josef Brüggemeier, Mark Cioc, and Thomas Zeller (Athens: Ohio University Press, 2005), 130–3.
11 Glorification of the people and the land was not unique to Germany. The idealization of the peasant cultivator, when combined with other factors, has been a key element in instigating genocide. See Ben Kiernan, "Twentieth-century genocides: Underlying ideological themes from

Armenia to East Timor," in *The spector of genocide: Mass murder in historical perspective*, eds. Robert Gellately and Ben Kiernan (New York: Cambridge University Press, 2003), 33, 39, 41, and 51.

12 Affidavit of Darré, in *Trials of war criminals before the Nuernberg Military Tribunals under Control Council Law No. 10*, Case 8: US v. Greifelt (Washington, DC: US Government Printing Office, 1946–49), document book 1, sheets 13–23 (hereafter *US v. Greifelt*).

13 The other two were the SS Office and Security Office. This reorganization came after Franz von Papen lifted the ban on the SS and the SA that Heinrich Brüning had implemented in April. Thomas Grant, *Stormtroopers and crisis in the Nazi movement: Activism, ideology, and dissolution* (London: Routledge, 2004), 75 and 97.

14 "Aufgaben und Gliederung des Rasse- und Siedlungsamtes-SS," 21 September 1934, BA NS2/99, p. 1.

15 Longerich, *Heinrich Himmler*, 182 and 257; Weingartner, "The Race and Settlement Main Office," 62–3; Koehl, *The black corps*, 109 and 117–18; d'Alquen, *Die SS*, 23; Supreme Headquarters Allied Expeditionary Force, *Basic handbook: The Allgemeine SS (The General SS)* (Wiltshire, UK: Antony Rowe, 1993), M1 (hereafter SHAEF, *Basic handbook*); and Heinemann, *Rasse*, 684–5.

16 "SS-Befehl – A – Nr. 5," BA NS2/179, pp. 75–6. While this order did not directly reference any existing laws, the German Civil Code did have several paragraphs that defined the policies a couple had to follow in order to wed. Mouton briefly reviews these laws in *From nurturing*, 36–7.

17 Grant, *Stormtroopers*, 54, 56, 66, and 74–6; Stoltzfus, 'Tactical terror," 215–17; and Otis Mitchell, "Terror as a neo-Marxian revolutionary mechanism in the Nazi SA (1932)," *Wichita State University Bulletin* 63, no. 2 (May 1965): 3 and 10.

18 "Befehl zum Einholen der Verlobungs- und Heiratsgenehmigung," 11 March 1936, BA NS19/3902, p. 69. A follow-up decree was issued on 15 August: "Verlobung und Heirat von lebensberuflich angestellten SS-Angehörigen, sowie Angehörigen der SS-VT, SS-TV, und SS-Führerschulen," StA-M 327/2a/80.

19 "SS Befehl," May 1937, BA NS19/435, p. 3.

20 "SS Befehl," 27 April 1937, BA NS19/435, p. 2.

21 "Vorlage von Bescheinigungen über die Teilnahme an einem Mütterschulungslehrgang bei Verlobungsgesuchen," 14 August 1936, StA-M 327/2a/80 and "Mütterschulungskurse für SS-Bräute," 9 March 1938, StA-M 327/2b/120. See also Pine, *Nazi family policy*, 45.

22 "Einholung der nachträglichen Heiratsgenehmigung," BA NS2/2, p. 105.

23 "Einholung der Heiratsgenehmigung für bereits Verlobte bzw Verheiratete SS-Bewerber," 3 August 1935, StA-M 327/2a/144; Sippenamt chief to Standarte 33, 11 December 1936, StA-D N1/48, p. 694; Himmler to RuSHA, 21 April 1937, BA NS2/280; and Wolff to RuSHA, 27 May 1937, BA NS2/280.

24 "Nachweis der arischen Abstammung und Erbgesundheit," 13 December 1934, BA NS2/172, p. 14, and "Befehl zum Einholen der Verlobungs- und Heiratsgenehmigung," 11 March 1936, BA NS19/3902, p. 69.

25 Ibid., 70–1. These age/rank requirements changed over the years. Himmler to RuSHA, 10 April 1935, NA T580/333/Ordner 122; the Führer of Leibstandarte-SS to RuSHA, 13 August 1936, NA T175/148/ frame 2675356; "Heiratsgenehmigung für die aus den SS-Junkerschulen hervorgegangenen SS-Führer," 30 August 1937, StA-M 327/2b/64; Himmler to RuSHA, 7 December 1937, NA T580/330/Ordner 52, Teil 2; Heiratsamt chief to Margarete K., 3 February 1943, NA T580/326/ Ordner 18; and "Heiratsgenehmigung für die aus den SS-Junkerschulen hervorgegangenen SS-Führer," 30 January 1940, BA NS34/52.

26 "Fragebogen!" Berlin Document Center Race and Settlement file, A417, pp. 2942–3 (hereafter BDC RS).

27 "Befehl zum Heiratsgesuch," BA NS19/3079, p. 2; Himmler to Pancke, 25 March 1939, BA NS19/3079, p. 4; and "Befehl," BA NS19/3079, p. 6.

28 The RuSHA questionnaire does not indicate that this judgment must be included, but it is mentioned in a form that outlines what must be included in an application. See BDC RS A5489, p. 2915.

29 "Ehestandsdarlehen," 8 December 1936, StA-M 327/2a/80; "Ehetauglichkeitszeugnisse," 19 August 1938, StA-M 327/2b/54; "Ehestandsdarlehen," 19 November 1938, StA-M 327/2b/120.

30 Untitled document, BA NS2/8, p. 49; "Nachweis der arischen Abstammung und Erbgesundheit," BA NS2/172, p. 14; and "Abstammungsprüfung," BDC RS G106, p. 2208.

31 Peter Fritzsche, *Life and death in the Third Reich* (Cambridge, MA: Belknap Press, 2008), 76–9; Eric Ehrenreich, *The Nazi ancestral proof: Genealogy, racial science, and the Final Solution* (Bloomington: Indiana University Press, 2007); and Christopher Hutton, *Race and the Third Reich: Linguistics, racial anthropology, and genetics in the dialectic of Volk* (Cambridge: Polity, 2005), 80, 90, 93–4, and 106–7.

32 David Sorkin, *The transformation of German Jewry, 1870–1840* (New York: Oxford University Press, 1987), 28–9, 33–6, and 173; Ewald Grothe, "Model or myth? The Constitution of Westphalia of 1807 and early German constitutionalism," *German Studies Review* 28, no. 1 (February 2005): 6,

11, and 13; and Erhard Lange, *Ahnentafel-Fibel. Im Auftrage des Rasse-und Siedlungshauptamtes-SS* (Miesbach: W. F. Mayer, 1937), BA NSD 41/59, 7–8.

33 Heinrich Himmler, *Once in 2000 years* (New York: American Committee for Anti-Nazi Literature, 1938), 8; SHAEF, *Basic handbook*, 32; "Rede vor Hitler-Jugend am 25.5.1936," BA NS19/4003, pp. 111–12; and Ziegler, *Nazi Germany's new aristocracy*, 53–4.

34 Himmler to RuSHA, 21 December 1936, BA NS2/172, p. 3.

35 Lange, *Ahnentafel-Fibel*. See also: "Die arische Großmutter," *Das Schwarze Korps*, 3 December 1936.

36 "Ahnentafelfibel," 24 October 1936, StA-M 327/2a/31; Abschnitt XXX to Oberabschnitt (hereafter OA) Rhein, 5 November 1936, StA-M 327/2a/31; "Ausschnitt aus dem SS-Befehls-Blatt, Nr. 22: SS-Ahnentafelfibel," 25 March 1937, StA-M 327/2b/116; "Ausschnitt aus dem SS-Befehls-Blatt, Nr 20: Sippenbücher," 25 June 1937, StA-M 327/2b/116; and "Familienbuch," 31 May 1937, StA-M 327/2b/115.

37 As seen in the case of Richard H., if a person lived in a town without an SS doctor, RuSHA preferred to arrange for transportation to another town that had one. StA-D N1/2, pp. 364, 368, and 373.

38 "Allgemeine, SS-ärztliche Untersuchung für Verlobungs- und Heirats-Genehmigung," 18 May 1937, BA NS2/179, p. 2.

39 "Heiratsgesuch," 13 September 1934, BDC RS E387, p. 480; "Vordrucke zum Verlobungs Heirats Gesuche," 29 October 1935, BA NS2/166, pp. 3–4; "Abzug aus den Ergänzungsbestimmungen zum Verlobungsbefehl, soweit sie für die Erläuterung seiner Durchführung wichtig sind, [part] B, P.P.," BA R187/669, p. 227.

40 Robert Proctor, "Nazi doctors, racial medicine, and human experimentation," in *The Nazi doctors and the Nuremberg Code: Human rights in human experimentation*, eds. George Annas and Michael Grodin (Oxford: Oxford University Press, 1995), 19.

41 Mouton, *From nurturing*, 56–8.

42 "Allgemeine, SS-ärztliche Untersuchung für Verlobungs- und Heirats-Genehmigung," pp. 2–3. The need to remain tactful may have emanated from the uneasiness that some women felt toward the invasive examinations also required of non-SS couples applying for a state marriage loan. See Mouton, *From nurturing*, 137.

43 An *Erbgesundheitsbogen* can be found in BDC RS A417, pp. 2294–2300. There were three variations of the *Ärztlicher Untersuchungsbogen*. The one discussed here can be found in NA T611/11/Ordner 446 (Teil 2). The other two versions are variations from 1934 and 1935; copies can be found in BDC RS B0335, pp. 178–82, and BDC RS B282, pp. 1680–2.

44 Instructions for returning the forms were provided in "Allgemeine, SS-ärztliche Untersuchung für Verlobungs- und Heirats-Genehmigung" cited in note 38, and relevant information, including the doctor's credentials, was noted in a list of material that each applicant had to submit. See BDC RS A5489, p. 2915.

45 "Die Aufgaben des SS-Arztes in der Schutzstaffel von SS-Brigadeführer Dr. Grawitz, Reichsarzt-SS," IfZ MA284/frames 2520621 and 2520625.

46 Leonardo Conti, "Grundzüge nationalsozialistischer Bevölkerungspolitik," *Ärztlicher Lehrhefte der SS*, BA BDC 31.30. BDC here refers to the Berlin Bundesarchiv library; the copy of the article does not list a publication date, but online catalogues list the year as either 1935 or 1939.

47 "Ärzte unter sich," *Das Schwarze Korps*, 26 September 1935; Thomas Maibaum, "Die Führerschule der deutschen Ärzteschaft Alt-Rehse" (PhD diss., University of Hamburg, 2007).

48 SHAEF, "Germany Basic Handbook, Part II," NA RG331/54, p. 145; "SS Lazarett Berlin," *Das Schwarze Korps*, 10 March 1938; Proctor, *Racial hygiene*, 86; Weindling, *Health, race, and German politics*, 534; Michael Kater, *Doctors under Hitler* (Chapel Hill: University of North Carolina Press, 1989), 72; "Soldat und Arzt," *Das Schwarze Korps*, 11 May 1944; and Richard Schulze-Kossens, *Die Junkerschulen: Militärischer Führernachwuches der Waffen-SS* (Osnabrück: Munin Verlag), 43–4.

49 Hans-Walter Schmuhl, *Crossing boundaries: The Kaiser Wilhelm Institute for Anthropology, Human Heredity, and Eugenics, 1927–1945* (London: Springer, 2008), 137–9.

50 Proctor, *Racial hygiene*, 348; Schmuhl, *Crossing boundaries*, 205; Benno Müller-Hill, *Murderous science: Elimination by scientific selection of Jews, Gypsies, and others, Germany 1933–1945*, trans. George Fraser (Oxford: Oxford University Press, 1988), 37; Berez and Weiss, "The Nazi symbiosis," 175; and Weiss, "Human genetics," 70.

51 SS-Amt chief to OA Rhein, 14 November 1934 and "Schulungskurse für SS-Aerzte," 27 August 1935, StA-M 327/2a/145.

52 "Tätigkeitsbericht von Professor Dr. Fischer vom 1.4.1934-31.3.1936," MPG Abt. 1, Rep. 1A, Nr. 2404, p. 52b.

53 "Schulung der SS-Ärzte. Richtlinien für Kursteilnehmer," 15 August 1935, BA NS31/184, pp. 32–4; "Schulung der SS-Ärzte. Richtlinien für Kursteilnehmer," 25 May 1936, BA NS19/3794, p. 8; and "Schulungskurse für SS-Ärzte. Lehrplan," [May 1936], BA NS19/3794, p. 4.

54 Berez and Weiss, "The Nazi symbiosis," 174 and Weiss, "Human genetics," 60–1.

55 Verschuer to Fischer, 15 April 1937, MPG Abt. 3, Rep. 86A, Nr. 291, p. 13.

56 Schmuhl, *Crossing boundaries*, 164–5 and 205 and Benoît Massin, "Rasse und Vererbung als Beruf: Die Hauptforschungsrichtungen am Kaiser-Wilhelm-Institut für Anthropologie, menschliche Erblehre, und Eugenik im Nationalsozialismus," in *Rassenforschung an Kaiser Wilhelm Instituten vor und nach 1933*, ed. Hans-Walter Schmuhl (Göttigen: Wallstein, 2003), 209–10, 217, 220, and 223.

57 "SS-Befehls-Blatt," BA NSD 41/2.

58 "Die innere Sicherung des Reichs," 21 November 1935; "Wie ich meine Ahnen suchen," 3 October 1935; "Seine Braut war zwei Zentimeter zu klein," 26 December 1935; "Eine Mahnung an Saboteure," 13 February 1936; and "Die arische Großmutter," 3 December 1936.

59 "Warum Heiratsgenehmigung?" 3 April 1935 and "Das sogenannte Privatleben," 16 March 1939.

60 "Dienstanweisung für Rassenreferenten," NA T580/333/Ordner 122; untitled document, BA NS2/8, p. 49; "Befehl zum Einholen der Verlobungs- und Heiratsbefehl," BA NS19/3902, p. 70; Robert John Shalka, "The General-SS in central Germany 1937–1939: A social and institutional study of SS Main Sector Fulda-Werra," (Ph.D. diss., University of Wisconsin, 1972), 129 and 207–8; Weingartner, "The Race and Settlement Main Office," 65–6; and *US v. Greifelt*, 3469. Heinemann's book *Rasse, Siedlung, deutsches Blut* extensively covers the responsibilities of RuSHA's racial advisers.

61 Schmidt to Waldeck-Pyrmont, 1 September 1937, StA-M 327/2b/112; "Vorläufige Dienstvorschrift für SS-Pflegestellen," 13 August 1937, NA T580/332/Ordner 95; "Änderung der vorl. Dienstvorschrift," 6 September 1938, BA NS 2/21, pp. 67–70; "Besetzung der SS-Pflegestellen," 30 March 1939, BA NS2/21, p. 90; and d'Alquen, *Die SS*, 23.

62 "Vorläufige Dienstvorschrift für SS-Pflegestellen," 30 March 1938, BA NS2/1053 and "Mitarbeit bei der SS-Pflegestelle 13," 19 November 1938, StA-L PL506/Bü 50.

63 Examples of reports from 1938 and 1939 are in StA-M 327/2b/55, 327/2b/112, and 327/2b/120; selected reports for 1944 are in BA NS47/54.

64 "Anregung zum Vortrag beim Reichsführer-SS," [May 1939], BA NS2/183, pp. 98–100; Pancke to Daluege, 27 June 1939, BA NS2/66; and Heider to Richert, 26 August 1943, NA NS2/82, p. 143.

65 "Verlobungs- und Heiratsgenehmigung," NA T175/135/frame 2663483.

66 *US v. Greifelt*, 3173. Hildebrandt also confirmed Himmler's involvement, 4004.

67 "Reichsführer Himmler am 15 Juni 1937 (Ausführungen gelegentlich der Beratungen des Sachverständigenbeirats für Bevölkerungs- und Rassenpolitik)," BA NS2/41, p. 61.

202 Notes to pages 33–5

68 Examples of Himmler approving applications can be found in the following BDC RS files: A417, p. 2926; B88, p. 476; C5116, p. 2770; G73, p. 1648; and G588, p. 1592.
69 Examples of approval letters can be found in BDC RS A41, p. 272; B335, p. 166; and C5116, p. 2768.
70 "Heiratsgenehmigung des SS-Rottf. H. K.," NA T354/407/frame 4123035; untitled document, BA NS2/8, p. 49; Sippenamt chief to SS-Unterscharführer Xaver Sch., 6 September 1938, StA-D N1/6364; BDC RS files of Sch. (RS F305, p. 2792) and Richard Gl. (B5195, p. 2800).
71 "Verlobungs- und Heiratsgesuch des SS-Unterscharführer Georg Sch.," NA T580/330/Ordner 52, Teil 2; "Verlobungs- und Heiratsgesuch des SS-Oberscharführers Hans W.," NA T580/330/Ordner 52, Teil 2; "Verlobungs- und Heiratsgesuch des SS-Untersturmführers Rupprecht Q.," NA T580/329/Ordner 47a; "Verlobungs- und Heiratsgesuch des SS-Sturmmannes Martin W.," NA T580/329/Ordner 47a; "Verlobungs- und Heiratsgesuch des SS-Mannes Friedrich M.," NA T580/329/ Ordner 47a; Helmut Heiber, ed., *Reichsführer! Briefe an und von Himmler* (Stuttgart: Deutsche Verlags-Anstalt, 1968), letter 27; and "Verlobungs- und Heiratsgesuch des SS-Sturmmannes Wilhelm W.," NA T580/330/Ordner 53, Teil 2.
72 Himmler to Lammers, 21 March 1939, BA NS2/55, pp. 139–141.
73 Himmler granted RuSHA limited autonomy to approve marriages where there were misgivings. Himmler to RuSHA, 16 June 1936, BA NS2/232, p. 133, and Himmler to RuSHA, 13 November 1937, BA NS2/40, p. 67.
74 "Erbgesundheit von SS-Angehörigen," BA NS2/179, p. 27; Himmler to Darré, 27 February 1935, BA NS2/179, p. 32; and "Entlassung aus der SS," 5 August 1935, BA NS2/168, pp. 252–3.
75 Darré to Himmler, 10 December 1935, BDC RS F5201, p. 1248; Standarte 33 Führer to Sturmbann Res-33, 27 January 1936, StA-D, N1/26; "Verlobungs und Heiratsgesuch bearbeitet im Sippenamt SS," 28 November 1935, BDC RS F5201, p. 1164; and Sippenamt chief to Hans Sch., 8 January 1936, BDC RS F5201, p. 1244.
76 Sch. to Schultze, BDC RS F5201, p. 1234.
77 Standarte 33 Führer to Abschnitt XI, 27 January 1936, StA-D, N1/26.
78 Hildebrandt to OA Rhein, 28 January 1936, BDC RS F5201, p. 1230.
79 Sippenamt chief to OA Rhein, 1 September 1936, BDC RS F5201, p. 1216.
80 Sippenamt chief to Hans Sch., 26 January 1937, BDC RS F5201, p. 1198, and Caesar to Himmler, 16 January 1937, BDC RS F5201, pp. 1206–8.
81 Longerich, *Heinrich Himmler*, 354. According to Otto Hofmann, the Sippenbuch had still not been created by early 1939. "Anregung zum Vortrag beim Reichsführer-SS," BA NS2/183, pp. 98–100.

82   Roger Manvell and Heinrich Fraenkel, *Heinrich Himmler* (New York: Putnam, 1965), 17; Padfield, *Himmler*, 93.
83   Himmler to RuSHA, 4 October 1935, NA T580/333/Ordner 122.
84   "Befehl zum rechtzeitigen Einholen der Verlobungs- und Heiratsgenehmigung," 19 March 1936, BA NS19/577, p. 10.
85   "Verlobungs und Heiratsgenehmigung für SS-Zugehörige," 7 November 1935, BA NS7/2, p. 31.
86   Complete paperwork showing successful examples include the cases of Heinz B. and Adalbert D. (StA-M 327/2b/193) as well as Erich B. (StA-M 327/2b/261).
87   Himmler to Darré, 18 May 1937, BA NS2/41, pp. 142–3.
88   20,285 according to communication between Brandt and Ebrecht in BA NS2/53, pp. 36–40.
89   "Rede des Reichsführer-SS anlässlich der Gruppenführer-Besprechung in Tölz am 18.II.1937," BA NS19/4004, p. 96 and "Heiratsgenehmigungen und Freigaben," BA NS19/577, p. 40.
90   Himmler to SS-Hauptamt, 21 March 1935, NA T175/30/frame 2537793.
91   "Genehmigung zur Verlobung und Heirat," 6 June 1935, BA NS19/577, p. 5. Heißmeyer issued further instructions, 3 July 1935, StA-M 327/2a/78.
92   Lack of knowledge due to poor education was discussed in a subsequent document ("Genehmigung zur Verlobung und Heirat," 3 July 1935, BA NS7/1194), as were the specifics regarding punishments ("Genehmigung zur Verlobung und Heirat," [1935], StA-D N1/2938, pp. 13–14).
93   Heißmeyer to RuSHA, SS-Hauptamt, and the OA, 19 July 1935, BA NS7/2, p. 26.
94   Six cases with incomplete paperwork can be found in StA-M 327/2b/207.
95   These reports are found in StA-M 327/2b/36.
96   *Statistisches Jahrbuch, 1937*, NSD 41–37, pp. 16 and 55–6.
97   *Statistisches Jahrbuch, 1938*, NSD 41–37, pp. 16, 18, and 67–9.
98   Sturm 4/33 Führer to Sturmbann I/33, 7 September 1935, StA-D N1/25, p. 373 and Standarte 33 Führer to Sturmbann I/33, 18 September 1935, StA-D N1/25, p. 371.
99   Standarte 33 Führer to Abschnitt XI, 27 September 1935, StA-D N1/25, p. 369 and Standarte 33 Führer to G, 14 December 1935, StA-D N1/25, p. 368.
100 Standarte 33 Führer to Abschnitt XI, 24 September 1936, StA-D N1/25, p. 364; Sturmbann I/33 Führer to Standarte 33, 16 October 1936, StA-D N1/25, p. 362; and Standarte 33 Führer to Abschnitt XI, 16 October 1936, StA-D N1/25, p. 361.

101 The approval of his marriage is in BDC RS B5183.
102 "Heirat des SS-Standartenführers Wilhelm H. ohne Genehmigung des RuS-Hauptamtes," BDC RS C5064, p. 2086.
103 Wilhelm H., BDC SSO 123A, p. 452. The rest of the information comes from his RuSHA file, C5064: "Heiratsgesuch," p. 2064; OA Nordost Führer to RuSHA chief, 30 April 1936, p. 2096; "Verehelichung ohne Genehmigung des RuS-Hauptamtes des SS-Sturmbannführers Wilhelm H," p. 2102; and "Heiratsgesuch des SS-Sturmbannführers Wilhelm H," p. 2130.
104 "Verstösse gegen den Verlobungs- bezw. Heiratsbefehl," 23 June 1937, BA NS2/63, p. 131.
105 "Verstöße gegen den Verlobungs- bezw. Heiratsbefehl," 16 November 1937, NA T580/332/Ordner 95. The June 1937 order remained in effect well into 1938: "SS-Oberabschnittsbefehlsblatt Nr 13 Jahrgang 2 vom 15.8.1938," StA-M 327/2b/58.
106 "Nachtrag für die bevölkerungspolitische Schrift an die SS-Führer," BA NS19/3964, pp. 18–19 and "Nachtrag für die bevölkerungspolitische Schrift an die SS-Führer," BA NS19/3965, pp. 7 and 9.
107 "Nachtrag für die bevölkerungspolitische Schrift an die SS-Führer," BA NS19/3964, p. 19; *Statistisches Jahrbuch, 1936*, NSD 41–37, p. 25; *Statistisches Jahrbuch, 1937*, p. 61; *Statistisches Jahrbuch, 1938*, p. 93; "Zahl der Verheirateten und Gesamtkinderzahl in der SS am 1.1.1939 und 31.12.1939," BA NS19/752, p. 29; and "Rede vor der Auslandsorganisation am 2.9.1938," in Heinrich Himmler, *Geheimreden 1933 bis 1945 und andere Ansprachen*, ed. Bradley Smith and Agnes Peterson (Frankfurt am Main: Propyläen Verlag, 1974), 82.
108 "Bevölkerungspolitik im SS-Führerkorps," 1 December 1938, BA NS34/30, p. 8.
109 "Nachtrag für die bevölkerungspolitische Schrift an die SS-Führer," BA NS19/3965, pp. 2 and 9; "Bevölkerungspolitik im SS-Führerkorps," 1 December 1938, BA NS34/30, p. 7; "Zahl der Verheirateten und Gesamtkinderzahl in der SS am 1.1.1939 und 31.12.1939," BA NS19/752, p. 29; and "Nachtrag für die bevölkerungspolitische Schrift an die SS-Führer," BA NS19/3964, pp. 14, 16, and 18.
110 This issue was also raised in a *Preußische Zeitung* article: "Heiratsalter und Beruf," 4 September 1937.
111 *Statistisches Jahrbuch, 1937*, pp. 68–74; *Statistisches Jahrbuch, 1938*, pp. 109–13.
112 "Nachtrag für die bevölkerungspolitische Schrift an die SS-Führer," BA NS19/3964, pp. 16–18; "Nachtrag für die bevölkerungspolitische Schrift an die SS-Führer," BA NS19/3965, pp. 14, 15, and 17.

113 Longerich, *Heinrich Himmler*, 375.
114 "Vorlage von Ehescheidungsurteilen," 14 March 1938, StA-D N1/40, p. 48.
115 Quoted in Longerich, *Heinrich Himmler*, 416.
116 Affidavit of Ebrecht, *US v. Greifelt*, document book 1, sheets 27–30.
117 "SS-Befehl," 10 September 1938, BA NS19/3901, p. 65.

2 Establishing SS Families

1 Adolf Hitler, *Mein Kampf*, trans. Ralph Manheim (Boston: Houghton Mifflin Company, 1999), 252.
2 Burgdörfer, *Volk ohne Jugend: Geburtenschwund und Überalterung des deutschen Volkskörpers: Ein Problem der Volkswirtschaft, der Sozialpolitik, der nationalen Zukunft* (Berlin: Kurt Vowinkel Verlag, 1934), 65–8; Alfred Kühn, Martin Staemmler, and Friedrich Burgdörfer, *Erbkunde, Rassenpflege, Bevölkerungspolitik: Schicksals Fragen des deutschen Volkes* (Leipzig: Quelle and Meyer, 1935), 224.
3 Ibid., 230.
4 Konrad Dürre, *Erbbiologisher und rassenhygienischer Wegweiser fur Jedermann* (Berlin: Alfred Metzner Verlag, 1933), 92; Hermann Werner Siemens, *Vererbungslehre: Rassenhygiene und Bevölkerungspolitik für Gebildete aller Berufe* (Munich: J.F. Lehmanns Verlag, 1934), 136; and Martin Staemmler, *Rassenpflege im völkischen Staat* (Munich: J.F. Lehmanns Verlag, 1934), 64.
5 Staemmler, *Rassenpflege*, 67.
6 Burgdörfer, *Volk ohne Jugend*, 87 and 491; Staemmler, *Rassenpflege*, 64; Siemens, *Vererbungslehre*, 157; Fritz Lenz, "Rassenhygiene (Eugenik)," vol. 3 of *Handbuch der Vererbungswissenschaft*, eds. Erwin Baur and Max Hartmann (Berlin: Verlag von Gebrüder Borntraeger, 1932), 20; Kühn, Staemmler, and Burgdörfer, *Erbkunde*, 265 and 293; Dürre, 87; Walter Schultze, *Die Rassenfrage und Erbgesundheitslehre und ihre Folgerungen für den nationalsozialistischen Staat* (Berlin: Beamtenpress, 1935), 24; Otmar von Verschuer, *Erbpathologie: Ein Lehrbuch für Ärzte und Medizinstudierende* (Dresden: T. Steinkopff, 1934), 2; Otmar von Verschuer, "Rassenhygiene als Wissenschaft und Staatsaufgabe," *Der Erbarzt* 3, no. 2 (15 February 1936): 17; and "Wege zur Erbgesundheit des deutschen Volkes. Vortrag, gealten von Prof. Dr. O. Frhr. v. Verschuer am 16.2.1934 in der Kaiser Wilhelm-Gesellschaft zur förderung der Wissenschaften," MPG Abt. 1, Rep. 1A, Nr. 779, p. 123.
7 Jan-Pieter Barbian, "Literary policy in the Third Reich," in *National Socialist cultural policy*, ed. Glenn Cuomo (New York: Palgrave Macmillan, 1995), 179; Jay Baird, *Hitler's war poets: Literature and politics*

in the Third Reich (Cambridge: Cambridge University Press, 2007), 238; Burkhard Stenzel, "Buch und Schwert: Die 'woche des deutschen buches' in Weimar (1934–1942). Anmerkungen zur NS-Literaturpolitik," in *Hier, hier ist Deutschland: Von nationalen Kulturkonzepten zur nationalsozialistischen Kulturpolitik*, eds. Ursula Härtl, Burkhard Stenzel, and Justus Ulbricht (Göttingen: Wallstein Verlag, 1997), 83–122; and Lynne Tatlock, "Our correspondent in Weimar: Gabriele Reuter and 'The New York Times,' 1923–1939," *German Studies Review* 22, no. 3 (October 1999): 376 and 382 n42.

8 "Werbung der SS in der Woche des deutschen Buches," 19 November 1936; "Werbung der SS in der Woche des Deutschen Buches," 20 November 1936; and "Aufstellung! 35 SS-Standarte," no date, StA-M 327/2a/31.

9 "Woche des deutschen Buches 1935," BA NS19/3902, p. 48, and "SS-Befehl," 26 October 1937, BA NS19/3901, pp. 43–4. See also: "Bücher werben für Deutschland," *Das Schwarze Korps*, 21 November 1935.

10 Staemmler, *Rassenpflege*, 132.

11 Proctor, *Racial hygiene*, 87; "Rassenpolitiches Amt," BA NS6/217, p. 56; and "Bedeutung und Aufgaben des Rassenpolitiches Amt," BA NS6/217, pp. 57–9; Bormann to the Reichsleiter and Gauleiter, 20 October 1933, BA NS6/215, p. 34; "Vereinheitlichung der Schulungs- und Propagandaarbeit auf dem Gebiet der Bevölkerungspolitik und Rassenpflege," BA NS6/215, p. 55; "Reichsbund der Kinderreichen," BA NS6/221, pp. 44–5; and "Behandlung von Fragen bevölkerungspolitischer Natur," BA NS6/227, p. 21.

12 "Schulungs und Propaganda auf dem Gebiete der Bevölkerungspolitik und Rassenpflege," BA NS19/3902, p. 20. Himmler referenced the Propaganda Office for Population Policy and Racial Welfare, the predecessor of the Office for Racial Policy.

13 *US v. Greifelt*, 435.

14 Weindling, *Health, race, and German politics*, 520–2; Burleigh and Wippermann, *The racial state*, 57–59; and Michael Kater, "Dr. Leonardo Conti and his nemesis: The failure of centralized medicine in the Third Reich," *Central European History* 18, no. 3–4 (September-December 1985): 299–302. Leonardo Conti and Karl Brandt later entered this fracas for control, as Conti succeeded Wagner and Brandt used his position as Reich commissioner for health and sanitation to undermine Conti.

15 "Gesetz zur Verminderung der Arbeitslosigkeit vom 1 Juni 1933," *Reichsgesetzblatt* [RGB], Part I, no. 60, 2 June 1933, in particular section 5, pp. 326–329, and "Durchführungsverordnung über die Gewährung von Ehestandsdarlehen vom 20 Juni 1933," RGB, Part I, no. 67, 22 June 1933, pp. 377–88.

16 Pine, *Nazi family policy*, 17–18; Mouton, *From nurturing*, 56; Stephenson, *Women*, 47; and Ziegler, "Fight against the empty cradle," 27–8.

17 Pine, *Nazi family policy*, 17.

18 "Eine Verfügung des Reichsfinanzministers bezüglich der kinderreichen Familien," BA NS2/155, p. 30.

19 Stephenson, *Women*, 47.

20 "Kind = Kind," 18 March 1937. The newspaper also criticized tax laws that were detrimental to divorced fathers. "Gleiches Recht für alle Väter!" 12 January 1939.

21 Himmler, *Once in 2000 Years*, 6.

22 "Rede vor unbekanntem Publikum im Jahre 1938," in Himmler, *Geheimreden*, 85.

23 "Gruppenführerbesprechung," November 1938, NA T175/90/frame 261259.

24 Himmler had read both volumes: Richard Breitman, "*Mein Kampf* and the Himmler family. Two generations react to Hitler's ideas," *Holocaust and Genocide Studies* 13, no. 1 (1999): 90–8.

25 Hitler, *Mein Kampf*, 404.

26 Ibid., 405.

27 Himmler to all SS-Führer, 4 June 1935, BA NS19/3902, p. 38.

28 Himmler to all SS-Führer, 13 September 1936, BA NS19/3902, p. 84.

29 "Rede des Reichsführer-SS auf der Tagung der Auslandsorganisation in Stuttgart am 2.9.1938," IfZ MA312/frame 2612585 and Himmler, *Die Schutzstaffel*, 25.

30 Ibid. Himmler expressed a similar sentiment in another Gruppenführer speech: "Rede des Reichsführer-SS anlässlich der Gruppenführer-Besprechung in Tölz am 18.2.1937," BA NS19/4004, p. 163.

31 "Rede des Reichsführers-SS bei der Gruppenführerbesprechung in München im Führerheim des SS-Standarte 'Deutschland' am 8 November 1937," IfZ MA312/frame 2612447.

32 Himmler to all SS-Führer, 13 September 1936, BA NS19/3902, p. 84.

33 "Bevölkerungspolitik im SS-Führerkorps, Stand: 1.12.1938, Bearbeitet von der SS-Personalkanzlei," BA NS34/30, p. 9.

34 For more on the Stennes revolt, see Bessel, *Political violence*, 62–5.

35 "Bevölkerungspolitik im SS-Führerkorps," 3.

36 Ibid., 11.

37 Ibid., 10.

38 "Werbung für Sturmzigaretten," 15 December 1932, StA-D N1/38; other documents in this folio indicate that the SS had good relations with cigarette companies in the early 1930s.

39 "Befehl an die gesamte SS und Polizei," 12 April 1938, NA T611/26/
Ordner 165; "Übermässiger Alkoholgenuss," 21 December 1937, NA
T611/26/Ordner 165; Heiber, *Reichsführer!*, letters 17, 154, and 311b; "Rede
vor SS-Führern des Oberabschnitts Süd-Ost in Breslau am 19.1.1935" in
Himmler, *Geheimreden*, 88–9; "Rede vor der SS-Standarte 99 in Znaim
(Sudetenland) am 11.12.1938," in Himmler, *Geheimreden*, 89–90; and Robert
Proctor, *The Nazi War on Cancer* (Princeton: Princeton University Press,
1999), 138.
40 "Reichsführer Himmler am 15 Juni 1937 (Ausführungungen gelegentlich
der Beratungen des Sachverständigenbeirats für Bevölkerungs- und
Rassenpolitik)," BA NS2/41, p. 65.
41 Ibid., 58.
42 "Rede des Reichsführer-SS anlässlich der Gruppenführer-Besprechung in
Tölz am 18.2.1937," BA NS19/4004, p. 134.
43 Ibid., 126–8; "Reichsführer Himmler am 15 Juni 1937 (Ausführungungen
gelegentlich der Beratungen des Sachverständigenbeirats für
Bevölkerungs- und Rassenpolitik)," BA NS2/41, pp. 58–9.
44 Florence Tamagne, *A history of homosexuality in Europe: Berlin, London,
Paris, 1919–1939*, vols. 1 and 2 (New York: Algora Publishing, 2004); Jeffrey
Weeks, *Making sexual history* (Malden, UK: Polity Press, 2000); and John
D'emilio, *Sexual politics, sexual communities: The making of a homosexual
minority in the United States, 1940–1970* (Chicago: University of Chicago
Press, 1983).
45 Ullmann to Grawitz, 10 June 1938, NA T175/84/frame 2609744 and Jansen
to Ullmann, 8 December 1936, NA T175/84/frame 2609746. Himmler later
requested that children in Lebensborn homes be broken of left-handed
or ambidextrous tendencies. "Allgemeine Anordnung Nr. 109," 21 March
1939, 4.1.0/82448553/ITS Digital Archive/Bad Arolsen.
46 Nicholas Edsall, *Toward Stonewall: Homosexuality and society in the modern
Western world* (Charlottesville: University of Virginia Press, 2003), 212;
Tamagne, *A history of homosexuality*, 366.
47 "Rede vor den Gruppenführern am 18.2.1937," in Himmler, *Geheimreden*,
97–8; Gerhard Rempel, *Hitler's children: The Hitler Youth and the SS* (Chapel
Hill: University of North Carolina Press, 1999), 51.
48 Hans-Georg Stümke, "From the 'people's consciousness of right and
wrong' to 'the healthy instincts of the nation': The persecution of
homosexuals in Nazi Germany," in *Confronting the Nazi past: New debates
on modern German history*, ed. Michael Burleigh (New York: Palgrave
Macmillan, 1996), 154 and 158; Eric Johnson, *Nazi terror: The Gestapo, Jews,
and ordinary Germans* (New York: Basic Books, 2000), 287; and Christian

Goeschel, *Suicide in Nazi Germany* (Oxford: Oxford University Press, 2009), 88.

49 "Rede vor den Gruppenführern am 18.2.1937," in Himmler, *Geheimreden*, 97.

50 This persecution intensified during the war; see: "Erlaß des Führers zur Reinhaltung von SS und Polizei," NA T175/66/frames 2582266–2582267; "Erlass des Führers zur Reinhaltung der SS und Polizei vom 15 November 1941," in Jeremy Noakes, ed., *Nazism 1919–1945, Vol. 4, The German home front in World War II, a documentary reader* (Exeter, UK: University of Exeter Press, 1998), 390 and 393; and Giles, "The denial of homosexuality," 257, 263, 265–6, and 269–70.

51 "Im Mittelpunkt: das Kind," 21 October 1937.

52 "Ein Wort zur Ehescheidung," 12 November 1936; "Die Ehe – ein Geschäft," 10 December 1936; "Ein Rechtswahrer zur Ehescheidungsreform," 24 December 1936; "Ahnenehrung einst und heute," 18 February 1937; and "Das Kind heiligt die Ehe," 21 October 1937.

53 "Wann sollen wir heiraten?" 10 September 1936; "Ein Problem, das noch nicht geklärt ist," 31 December 1936; "Eine unerläßliche Voraussetzung," 21 January 1937; "Weitere Vorschläge erwünsche," 18 February 1937; "Unsere Leser schalgen vor," 4 March 1937; and "Jung gefreit," 8 June 1939.

54 "Ein Problem," 31 December 1936; "Deutschlands wichtige Frage," 16 March 1939; and "Der Wille zum Kind," 20 January 1944.

55 "Die Tanten sollten lieber helfen," 13 July 1939. Another case is in "Frage und Antwort," 30 July 1942.

56 "Kinderreichtum um jeden Preis?" 11 May 1939 and "Für Deutschlands Zukunft entscheidend," 1 June 1939.

57 "Die innere Sicherung des Reichs," 21 November 1935. Emphasis in original.

58 "SS siedelt elfköpfige Familie auf eigener Scholle an," 12 December 1935; "Die Weltanschauung voran," 12 December 1935; "Deutschlands Führer und Deutschlands Zukunft," 7 May 1937; and "Kinderliebes Rostock," 18 August 1938.

59 " 'O diese Kinder …!" 25 May 1939 and "Für Kinderreiche verboten!" 3 August 1939.

60 "Ein Volk hat größere Güter nicht," 23 June 1938. The other poems: "Ewigkeit," 20 March 1935; "Unser Junge," 20 March 1935; "An meinen Sohn," 29 May 1935; "Des Ahnen Ruf," 7 August 1935; "Ewiges Blut," 28 August 1935; "Der Väter Blut," 31 October 1935; "Kind und Sonne," 21 January 1937; "Sieg Heil … Ihrem Kindchen," 19 May 1938; "Für meine

Kinder," 7 July 1938; "Bange Frange," 30 March 1939; and "Sein Kind," 14 March 1940.

61 Combs, *The voice of the SS*, 31 and 44; "Befragung von Herrn Günter d'Alquen am 13/14 Januar 1968 im Mönchen-Gladbach," IfZ ZS/2, p. 36.

62 See "Wie man die deutsche Mutter nicht ehren sollte," 22 May 1935; "Aussicht auf Mutterschaft," 22 May 1935; "Die Mutter," 19 June 1935; "Frauen sind keine Manner!" 12 March 1935; "Junge Mutter," 28 May 1936; "Noch einmal das Generationsproblem," 11 June 1936; "Frau soll Frau sein," 3 December 1936; "Mutter," 7 October 1937; "Heilig ist uns," 30 December 1937; "Die ganze Aufgabe der Frau," 22 June 1939; and "Das Wunder nach einmal erleben," 22 February 1940.

63 "Gesundheit, Liebe, Kinder," 1 October 1942.

64 "Der patriotische Papi," 16 July 1936.

65 "Ist das ünmännlich?" 10 August 1939, p. 14.

66 Ibid., 13.

67 "Die besten Freunde," 17 August 1939.

68 Ibid., 8.

69 Ibid., 9.

70 Examples of SA pay differentials can be found in documents in StA-D N1/38.

71 "Berechnung der Grundgehälter der Besoldungsordnung der SS unter Berücksichtigung der Gehaltskürzungen und der Zehrzulage (in Berlin einschliesslich Sonderzuschlag)," BA NS31/262, pp. 10–13, and "Bestimmungen über die Gewährung der Besoldung in der allgemeinen-SS," BA NS3/1565, pp. 13–14. There was also a pay differential based on the location; the numbers here were for men and officers in Berlin, who had the highest pay.

72 "Tagesbefehl Nr. 2/36," BA NS2/10, p. 3.

73 "Reichsparteitag 1937," 11 August 1937, StA-M 327/2b/505; "Oberabschnittsverwaltungsbefehl Nr. 1 zum Reichsparteitag 1938," 5 August 1938, StA-M 327/2b/58; and "Tage- u. Verpflegesgelder während des Reichsparteitages 1939," [August 1939], StA-M 327/2b/505.

74 "Gewährung von Kinderbeihilfen an kinderreiche Familien," BA NSD 41/2, p. 19, and "Kinderbeihilfen an kinderreichen Familien," BA NS2/2, p. 85. According to the salary charts provided by Otto Nathan, only 3.3 per cent of the working population in 1938 earned 600 RM or more per month, meaning the majority of the population would have been eligible. See Otto Nathan, "Consumption in Germany during the period of rearmament," *The Quarterly Journal of Economics* 56, no. 3 (May 1942): 361.

75 "Bestimmungen über die Gewährung der Besoldung in der allgemeinen-SS, Teil I: Haushalt und Besoldung," BA NS3/1565, p. 11;

"Durchführungsbestimmung zur Haushaltplannung 1935," 14 November
1935, BA NS3/465, pp. 51–3; "Haushaltplannung der Schutzstaffel der
NSDAP für das Rechnungstab 1936," BA NS3/466, p. 7; "Kinderzuschläge," 2
September 1936, StA-M 327/2a/180; and "Haushaltplannung der Schutzstaffel
der NSDAP für des Rechnungsjahr 1938," BA NS3/468, p. 7.

76 "Durchführungsbestimmung zur Haushaltplannung 1935"; "Zahlung von
    Kinderzuschlag," 25 February 1937, StA-M 327/2b/505; and "Tagesbefehl
    Nr. 2/36," BA NS2/10, p. 3.

77 "Geldbedarfsanmeldung d. SS-Oberabschnitts Rhein f. d. Monat Oktober
    1935," 17 September 1935, StA-M 327/2a/13; "Geldbedarfsanmeldung d.
    SS-Oberabschnitts Rhein f. d. Monat März 1936," 18 February 1936, StA-M
    327/2a/12.

78 "Weihnachtszuwendung 1936," 16 December 1936, StA-L PL506/
    Bü72; "Weihnachtsbeihilfe 1937," 21 December 1937, StA-M 327/2b/13;
    "Weihnachtsbeihilfe 1937 [letter from Pohl]," 7 December 1937, StA-M
    327/2b/13; "Weihnachtsbeihilfe 1937," 3 December 1937, StA-M
    327/2b/13; "Weihnachtsbeihilfe 1937," 2 December 1937, StA-M
    327/2b/13; "Auszahlung von Weihnachtsgratifikation," 14 December 1937,
    StA-M 327/2b/13; "Weihnachtsbeihilfe 1937 [letter from Tschentscher],"
    7 December 1937, StA-M 327/2b/13; and "Veränderungsmeldung zur
    Geldbedarfsanmeldung Januar 1938," 6 December 1937, StA-M 327/2b/13.

79 "Besondere Zuwendung anläßlich des Julfestes 1938," BA NS2/65, p. 47.

80 "Weihnachtsbeihilfe 1939," 18 December 1939, StA-M 327/2b/26;
    "Jelleuchterverteilung 1940," 18 October 1940, StA-M 327/2b/56; and
    Gabriele Huber, *Die Porzellan-Manufaktur Allach-München GmbH: Eine
    "Wirtschaftsunternehmung" der SS zum Schutz der "deutschen Seele"*
    (Marburg: Jonas Verlag, 1992), 133–7.

81 The average number of copies sold is printed in each edition on page 2.
    Two articles also mention circulation: "Ein Jahr 'Das Schwarze Korps,' " 5
    March 1936, and "Über 500,000 Auflage in 3 Jahren," 24 March 1938. For
    more information, see: "Befragung von Herrn Günter d'Alquen am 13/14
    Januar 1968 im Mönchen-Gladbach," IfZ ZS/2, p. 34; Combs, *The voice of
    the SS*, 20; Norbert Frei and Johannes Schmitz, *Journalismus im Dritten Reich*
    (Munich: Beck, 1989), 102; Fritz Schmidt, *Presse in Fesseln: Eine Schilderung
    des NS-Pressetrusts* (Berlin: Verlag Archiv und Kartei, 1947), 218.

82 "An alle SS-Männer!" *Das Schwarze Korps*, 18 February 1937.

83 "Werbprämien der Reichspropaganda-Aktion 'Das Schwarze Korps'
    1937," BA NS3/565, p. 59; "Werbprämien der Reichspropaganda-Aktion
    für das 'Schwarze Korps' 1937," BA NS33/75, p. 86; "Werbprämien der
    Reichspropaganda-Aktion für das 'Schwarze Korps' 1937," BA NS33/75,

p. 87; "Verteilung von Patenschenken aus der Werbeprämie 'Schwarze Korps,' " NA T611/18/Ordner 487 (Teil 2); and "Geburtenhilfe 'Schwarze Korps,' " 23 October 1944, BA NS2/22, p. 158. For letters about men receiving money, see StA-M 327/2b/62 and BA-MA RS14/12.

84 Gerhard Bry, *Wages in Germany, 1871–1945* (Princeton, NJ: Princeton University Press, 1960), 58. Bry did examine net wages, but gross wages are used here because it appears that SS salaries were listed by gross amounts. A fifty-two-week work year is used here because neither he nor René Livchen in his study indicate if the average worker was given time off. Thus, fifty-two weeks is used to give the highest possible earnings for comparison. See Livchen, "Wage trends in Germany from 1929 to 1942," *International Labour Review* 48 (December 1943): 714–32, and "Net wages and real wages in Germany," *International Labour Review* 50 (July 1944): 65–72.

85 Bry, *Wages in Germany*, 251. Adam Tooze stated that in 1936, 62 per cent of German taxpayers earned annual incomes of less than 1,500 RM, 21 per cent earned between 1,500 and 2,400 RM, and 17 per cent earned more than 2,400 RM. See Tooze, *The wages of destruction: The making and breaking of the Nazi economy* (New York: Penguin Books, 2007), 141–2.

86 As cited above in note 75, these SS pay rates are from "Bestimmungen über die Gewährung der Besoldung in der allgemeinen-SS."

87 "Der Weg des SS-Mannes," IfZ MA356/frames 2685441–2685446.

88 Harold Marcuse, "What is old German money worth?" *Historical dollar-to-marks currency conversion page*, http://www.history.ucsb.edu/faculty/marcuse/projects/currency.htm (accessed 26 August 2014), and Samuel Williamson, "Seven ways to compute the relative value of a US dollar amount, 1774 to present," *Measuring Worth* https://www.measuringworth.com/uscompare/ (accessed 6 September 2016). My thanks to Williamson for informing me that the correct option for comparison is "production worker compensation." Email to author, 26 August 2014.

89 Catrine Clay, *Master race: The Lebensborn experiment in Nazi Germany* (London: Hodder & Stoughton, 1995), 56–7.

90 Pine, *Nazi family policy*, 38–9, 53, and 180.

91 "Die Stellung des unehelichen Kindes: Eine Erklärung des Rassenpolitischen Amtes," BA NS22/520, originally published in *Münchener Neueste Nachrichten*, 5 May 1939. Georg Lilienthal, *Der "Lebensborn e.V.": Ein Instrument nationalsozialistischer Rassenpolitik* (Stuttgart: Gustav Fischer, 1985), 25.

92 "Die Schutzstaffel und das deutschen Frauengeschlecht," BA NS2/51a, p. 11.

93 Ibid., 13.

94 Ibid., 13–14.

95   "Stellungnahmen zu dem Problem 'uneheliche Kinder,' " 28 April 1936, BA NS19/4090.
96   Longerich, *Heinrich Himmler*, 370.
97   "Bemerkungen des Reichsführer-SS zum Vortrag 'Zwei Jahre Lebensborn Arbeit,' " BA NS48/31, pp. 35–6.
98   "Ausführungen gelegentlich der Beratungen des Sachverständigenbeirats für Bevölkerungs- und Rassenpolitik," BA NS2/41, pp. 61–2 and 71.
99   Ibid., 69.
100   "An alle SS-Führer," NS19/3902, p. 84, and "Abschrift. Neuer Entwurf. Satzung des Vereins 'Lebensborn' e.V.," BA NS3/878, p. 38.
101   Koehl, *The SS*, 132; Lilienthal, *Der Lebensborn*, 44; Longerich, *Heinrich Himmler*, 372; Clay, *Master race*, 61 and 65; and *US v. Greifelt*, 41.
102   An example of a Lebensborn questionnaire can be found in BA NS19/3031, pp. 2–3.
103   Clay, *Master race*, 7; Lilienthal, *Der Lebensborn*, 79; Marc Hillel and Clarissa Henry, *Of pure blood*, trans. Eric Mossbacher (New York: McGraw Hill, 1976), 51; and Dorothee Schmitz-Köster, *Deutsche Mutter, bist du bereit: Alltag im Lebensborn* (Berlin: Aufbau-Verlag, 1997), 183.
104   "Aufgaben und Ziele des Lebensborn," BA NSD41/103, p. 17, and Larry Thompson, "*Lebensborn* and the eugenics policy of the *Reichsführer-SS*," *Central European History* 4, no. 1 (March 1971): 62.
105   "Entwurf. An sämtliche SS-Führer im RuS-Wesen beim SS-Oberabschnitt," BA NS2/65, p. 162.
106   "An alle SS-Führer," BA NS19/3902, pp. 84–5, and "Zwei Jahre Lebensborn-Arbeit," BA NS48/31, p. 17.
107   "Beiträge zum Verein Lebensborn e.V.," 23 September 1936, StA-L PL506/Bü80, and "Befehl," 2 March 1939, BA NS34/21.
108   "An alle SS-Führer," BA NS19/3902, pp. 84–5, and "Beitragstabelle zum 'Lebensborn e.V.,' " BA NS19/3358, pp. 3–7.
109   "Ergänzung zu der Beitragstabelle des Lebensborn e.V.," August 1939, 4.1.0/82449963/ITS Digital Archive/Bad Arolsen.
110   A copy of Walter Schellenberg's membership card and receipts are in NA T175/572/frame 9449646. There were different cards for enlisted men: StA-L PL506/Bü 95 and StA-D N1/6364.
111   "Nachtrag für die bevölkerungspolitische Schrift an die SS-Führer," BA NS19/3964, p. 20; "Aufstellung," 9 April 1937, BA NS34/93, pp. 51–63; "Zwei Jahre Lebensborn-Arbeit," BA NS48/31, p. 17.
112   "SS-Pflegestellen," NA T580/332/Ordner 95 and "Änderung der vorl. Dienstvorschrift," BA NS2/21, p. 70.

113 "Entwurf. An sämtliche SS-Führer im RuS-Wesen beim SS-Oberabschnitt," BA NS2/65, p. 162, and "Lebensborn Fibel," BA NS2/23, p. 31.
114 "Kinder – ausserhalb der Gemeinschaft," 9 April 1936; "Das uneheliche Kind," 9 April 1936; "An die Herrn Männer," 29 February 1940; "Altpapier – weg damit!" 14 August 1941; "Die Sprachen der Zahlen," 4 September 1941; and "Offene Aussprache," 25 June 1942.
115 "Im Mittelpunkt: das Kind," 21 October 1937.
116 The following articles discuss adultery: "Keine konstruierten Ehebrüche mehr," 21 October 1937; "Sinn und Unsinn der Ehe," 28 October 1937; "Die sittliche Bewertung," 28 October 1937; and "Der Sippenanwalt," 1 April 1943.
117 "Kinder – ausserhalb der Gemeinschaft," 9 April 1936. A second article proclaims Austria had a regional average where one out of four children was illegitimate. "An ihren Früchten," 9 July 1936.
118 "Kind = Kind," 18 March 1937; "Darauf können wird stolz sein," 16 November 1939; "Ich fand wieder zu mir selbsts zurück," 9 May 1940; and "Gute Gelegenheit," 4 July 1940.
119 "Mütterheim Steinhöring," 7 January 1937, and "Bewerber Vereidigung," 2 December 1937.
120 "Unterstützung kinderreicher SS-Familien," NA T354/485/frames 4232986–4232987. Related letters can be found in BA-MA RS14/13.
121 "Zwei Jahre Lebensborn-Arbeit," BA NS48/31, p. 18. A later report provided additional statistics: "Bericht der Finanzverwaltung des Lebensborn e.V. für die Zeit vom 1.1. bis 30.6.1939," 4.1.0/82449977–78/ITS Digital Archive/Bad Arolsen. Support continued during the war: "Unterstützung kinderreicher SS-Familien durch Lebensborn," 17 November 1943, LA-D RW0134/16, p. 75.
122 Lilienthal, *Der Lebensborn*, 40.
123 Ibid., 58, 66–7, and 244; Lilienthal, "Ärtze und Rassenpolitik: Der 'Lebensborn e.V.,'" in *Ärtze im Nationalsozialismus*, ed. Fridhof Kudlien (Cologne: Kiepenheuer and Witsch, 1985), 156; and Schmitz-Köster, *Deutsche Mutter*, 35.
124 Ebrecht to Himmler, 26 January 1938, BA NS2/65, pages 188–90.
125 *US v. Greifelt*, 1379, and "Ausstellung der bis jetzt an den Verein Lebensborn e.V. erbeten Vermittlungen von Erziehungskindern," 28 May 1937, BA NS2/65, p. 106. For more on foster care in general, see Mouton, *From nurturing*, 254–68.
126 Ibid., 190.

127 Lists of Himmler's godchildren can be found in BA NS19/482, NS19/629, and NS19/3672.
128 Ebrecht to Himmler, 26 January 1938, BA NS2/65, p. 190.
129 "Kinder auf Widerruf?" 21 July 1938.
130 "Adoption," 22 December 1938; "Aufgabe der Krankenkassen," 27 April 1939; "Geschäfte mit Adoptivkindern," 27 July 1939; and "Adoption und Patenschaft," 22 February 1940.
131 "Das uneheliche Kind," 30 April 1936.
132 Schmitz-Köster, *Deutscher Mutter*, 36; Schmitz-Köster, "A topic for life: Children of German Lebensborn homes," in *Children of World War II: The hidden enemy legacy*, ed. Kjersti Ericsson and Eva Simonsen (Oxford: Berg, 2005), 216; and Kåre Olsen, "Under the care of Lebensborn: Norwegian war children and their mothers," in *Children of World War II*, 17.
133 Koehl, *The SS*, 210; Robin Lumsden, *Himmler's black order: A history of the SS, 1923–1945* (Stroud, UK: Sutton Publishing, 1997), 73; Thompson, "*Lebensborn* and eugenics," 71, and Schmitz-Köster, "A topic for life," 214.
134 Hillel, *Of pure blood*, 81.
135 Louis Hagen, *Follow my leader* (London: A. Wingate, 1951), 254.
136 Ibid., 263.
137 Ibid., 265.
138 Ibid., 268.
139 Jochen von Lang, *Top Nazi: Karl Wolff, the man between Hitler and Himmler* (New York: Enigma, 2005), 130–1 and 203.
140 Lilienthall, *Der Lebensborn*, 151; Hillel, *Of pure blood*, 53.
141 Lenz, "Rassenhygiene," 31.
142 Baur-Fischer-Lenz, *Menschliche Erblichkeitslehre und Rassenhygiene*, 2: 133.
143 Quoted in Georg Lilienthal, "Rassenhygiene im Dritten Reich," *Medizinhistorisches Journal* 14 (1979): 127.
144 Emphasis in original. Hermann Paull, *Deutsche Rassenhygiene, II Teil: Erbgesundheitspflege (Eugenik), Rassenpflege* (Görlitz: Verlag für Sippenforschung und Wappenkunde, 1934), 31.
145 Staemmler, *Rassenpflege*, 70.
146 Siemens, *Grundzüge der Vererbungslehre*, 152.
147 "Verzeichnis wertvoller Bücher für den SS-Mann," December 1935, BA NS2/129, pp. 163–8.
148 Müller-Hill, *Murderous science*, 76; Weindling, *Health, race and German politics*, 535; and Friedlander, *The origins of Nazi genocide*, 19.
149 Lenz, "Zur Frage der unehelichen Kinder," *Volk und Rasse* 12, no. 3 (1937): 93.

150   Ibid., 92.
151   Himmler to Buch, 21 April 1937, BA NS2/51a, pp. 118–19; Himmler to
      Schultz, 30 May 1933, BDC SSO 111B, p. 181; Field, "Nordic racism," 531;
      and Weindling, *Health, race, and German politics*, 500.
152   Wilhelm Lange, "Der erbbiolgische Wert der uneheliche Mutter mit
      drei und mehr unehelichen Kindern," *Volk und Rasse* 12, no. 10 (1937):
      376–9. In contrast to this and Lenz's articles, the journal only printed a
      short description about the Lebensborn: "Der Lebensborn e.V.," 14, no. 1
      (January 1939): 20.
153   A claim of unconditional rejection, particularly of Lenz, by Himmler
      and RuSHA was posited by Peter Emil Becker, *Zur Geschichte der
      Rassenhygiene: Wege ins Dritte Reich* (Stuttgart: Georg Thieme, 1988), 199.
      Sheila Faith Weiss addressed this claim in "Race and Class in Fritz Lenz's
      Eugenics," *Medizinhistorisches Journal* 27 (1992): 19.
154   Himmler to Stab des Stellvertreters des Führers, 17 August 1938, BDC
      DS/G0117, p. 170.
155   Schmuhl, *Crossing boundaries*, 153; Weindling, *Health, race, and German
      politics*, 511–12; and Hans-Peter Kröner, *Von der Rassenhygiene zu
      Humangenetik: Das Kaiser-Wilhelm-Institut für Anthropologie, menschliche
      Erblehre, und Eugenik nach dem Kriege* (Stuttgart: G. Fischer, 1998), 28 and
      33. There are discrepancies among the dates given by these authors, but
      the point about it being politically incorrect to use these scientists' ideas
      without granting them party membership is still valid.
156   "Familienstand und Kinderzahl," *Statistisches Jahrbuch, 1936*, 25. The
      Reich average given here was thirty years, although other reports (see
      note 165) claimed twenty-seven.
157   "Familienstand und Kinderzahl," *Statistisches Jahrbuch, 1937*, 62.
158   "Familienstand und Kinderzahl der SS-Angehörigen am 31.12.1938,"
      Statistisches Jahrbuch, 1938, 94 and 96, and "Kinderzahl der
      SS-Angehörigen nach der Dauer der Ehe," *Statistisches Jahrbuch, 1938*, 98.
159   "Nachtrag für die bevölkerungspolitische Schrift an die SS-Führer," BA
      NS19/3965, p. 2.
160   Ibid., 8, and "Bevölkerungspolitik im SS-Führerkorps," BA NS34/30, p. 16.
161   "Ehedauer und Kinderzahl 1933 und 1939," *Wirtschaft und Statistik:
      Herausgegeben vom Statistischen Reichsamt* 22, no. 5 (May 1942): 171 in NA
      RG165/box 2599; and *Statistik des Deutschen Reiches, Band 452, 1: Volks-,
      Berufs- und Betriebszählung vom 16. Juni 1933. Volkszählung. Die Familien
      und Haushaltungen nach den Ergebnissen der Volks- und Berufszählung 1933.
      Heft 1: Die Ehen im Deutschen Reich nach der Zahl der geborenen Kinder*

(Berlin: Verlag für Sozialpolitik, Wirtschaft und Statistik, 1937), 9 in BA R3102/RD75/1–452.

162 "Rede des Reichsführer-SS anlässlich der Gruppenführer-Besprechung in Tölz am 18.II.1937," BA NS19/4004, p. 96.

163 "Zur Statistik der Kinderzahlen bei der Polizei," in Himmler, *Geheimreden*, 85.

164 "Nachtrag für die bevölkerungspolitische Schrift an die SS-Führer," BA NS19/3965, pp. 11–13, and "Nachtrag für die bevölkerungspolitische Schrift an die SS-Führer," BA NS19/3964, pp. 25–9.

165 "Bevölkerungspolitik im SS-Führerkorps," BA NS34/30, p. 12.

166 *Statistisches Jahrbuch, 1936*, 25.

167 "Nachtrag für die bevölkerungspolitische Schrift an die SS-Führer," BA NS19/3964, p. 29.

3 Marriage during the Second World War

1 Family affairs was hardly the only realm under Himmler's control that frequently shifted. Longerich, *Heinrich Himmler*, 264.

2 BDC SSO files: Darré SSO 136, p. 1280; Pancke SSO 364A, p. 3; Hofmann SSO 111A, p. 765; and Hildebrandt SSO 097A, p. 810.

3 *US v. Greifelt*, 40, 683, 3179, 3262, 3838, 3978, 3995–6, and 4002, and Heinemann, *Rasse*, 684–5.

4 *US v. Greifelt*, 655–7, 706, 1301, 3171–6, 3995–7, and 4002.

5 Untitled RFSS order, 31 December 1941, BA NS19/3903, p. 105.

6 "Aktenvermerk," 29 June 1939, BA NS2/55, p. 30.

7 Pancke to Himmler, 30 June 1939, BA NS2/55, p. 28; Persönlicher Stab RFSS to Pancke, 5 July 1939, BA NS2/55, p. 27; and Pancke to Himmler, 26 August 1939, BA NS2/55, p. 26.

8 "Befehl," 1 September 1939, BA NS19/577, p. 23.

9 Himmler to Woyrsch, 22 March 1943, BA NS2/240, p. 1. This letter was in response to earlier letters that raised problems with the medical examination: BA NS2/21, pp. 56–60.

10 "Verlobungs- und Heiratsgenehmigung," 26 January 1940, BA NS2/21, p. 127.

11 "4. Sammelerlaß," 1 April 1940, BA NS7/3, pp. 13–16. Other punishments for violating a basic law were in "Heerwesen: SS-Diziplinar – Staf- und Beschwerordnung," [1943], BA-MA RS13/18.

12 "Verlobungs und Heiratsgesuch" and supplementary documents, StA-L, PL506/Bü86.

13 Wolff to Radtke, 1 April 1941, BA NS19/3479, p. 47; Heiratsamt II, 15 June 1942, BA NS2/70, p. 104; and Heiratsamt chief to Schwalm, 4 September 1944, BA NS2/84, p. 12.
14 George Stein, *The Waffen SS: Hitler's elite guard at war, 1939–1945* (Ithaca, NY: Cornell University Press, 1966), xxx–iv.
15 "Verordnung zur Durchführung und Ergänzung des Gesetzes zur Vereinheitlichung des Rechts der Eheschließung und der Ehescheidung im Lande Österreich und im übrigen Reichsgebiet (Ehegesetz)," *Reichsgesetzblatt*, Teil I, Nr 116, 27 July 1938, pp. 923–34, available at the Österreichische Nationalbibliothek http://alex.onb.ac.at/cgi-content/alex?aid=dra&datum=1938&size=60&page=1101 (accessed 27 May 2014); "Behandlung der Heiratsgesuche aus Österreich," 30 March 1938, BA NS2/174, p. 58; and "Behandlung der Heiratsgesuche von sudetendeutschen SS-Angehörigen," 15 December 1938, StA-M 327/2b/54.
16 "Verlobungs- und Heiratsgenehmigung," 26 January 1940, BA NS2/21, p. 127.
17 "Heiratsordnung der Wehrmacht für die Dauer des Krieges," 28 May 1943, LA-D RW0134/21, p. 285; "Heiratsordnung der Wehrmacht für die Dauer des Krieges," 6 September 1943, LA-D RW0134/13, p. 21; and "Verlobungs und Heiratsgenehmigung," 27 January 1944, LA-D RW0134/22, p. 86.
18 On foreign recruitment and units, see Mark Philip Gingerich, "Toward a brotherhood of arms: Waffen-SS recruitment of Germanic volunteers, 1940–1945" (Ph.D. diss., University of Wisconsin–Madison, 1991); George Lepre, *Himmler's Bosnian division: The Waffen SS Handschar Division, 1943–1945* (Atglen, PA: Schiffer Military History, 1997); Sol Littmann, *Pure soldiers or sinister legion: The Ukrainian 14th Waffen SS Division* (Montreal: Black Rose Books, 2003); Kenneth Estes, *A European anabasis – Western European volunteers in the German Army and SS, 1940–1945* (New York: Columbia University Press, 2008); Martin Gutmann, "Fighting for the Nazi new order: Himmler's Swiss, Swedish and Danish volunteers and the Germanic project of the SS" (PhD diss., Syracuse University, 2011); and Gutmann, "Debunking the myth of the volunteers: Transnational volunteering in the Nazi Waffen-SS officer corps during the Second World War," *Contemporary European History* 22, no. 4 (November 2013): 585–607.
19 Stein, *The Waffen SS*, xxxi, 20, 32–5, 44–6, 94–5, 137–43, 168, 172–3, 180, and 185; Peter Scharff Smith, Niels Bo Poulsen, and Claus Bundgård Christensen, "The Danish volunteers in the Waffen SS and German warfare at the eastern front," *Contemporary European History* 8, no. 1 (March 1999): 73 and 76; Valdis Lumans, "The ethnic German minority of Slovakia and the Third Reich, 1938–1945," *Central European History* 15, no. 3 (September 1982): 275 and 287–8; Lumans, *Himmler's auxiliaries: The Volksdeutsche*

Mittelstelle and the German national minorities of Europe, 1933–1945 (Durham: University of North Carolina Press, 1993), 212; and Alfred Vagts, "The foreigner as soldier in the Second World War, II," *The Journal of Politics* 9, no. 3 (August 1947): 406–7.

20 "Verlobungs- und Heiratsgesuche von Volksdeutsche, die der SS-angehören," 8 March 1940, NA T611/11/Ordnung 446 (Teil 2); "Verlobungs und Heiratsgenehmigung anderer, als Reichsdeutscher SS-Angehöriger," 11 February 1941, StA-M, 327/2b/115; Aust to RuSHA chief, 16 June 1942, BA NS2/81; untitled regulations for Dutch SS, 23 June 1942, StA-M 327/2b/216; "Heiratsgenehmigung für alle Angehörigen der SS," 1 October 1942, BA NSD41/40, p. I/1h; "Heiratsgenehmigung für Angehörige der Waffen-SS," 14 December 1942, NA T175/152/frames 2681626–2581627; and Himmler to Heider, 28 December 1944, BA NS2/175, p. 2.

21 "Abschrift," 10 September 1943, BA NS2/231, p. 32.

22 "Heiratsgenehmigung," 4 November 1940, NA T580/326/Ordner 18 and *IMT*, vol. 42, document SS-42.

23 Hofmann to Jüttner, 28 August 1942, BA NS2/71, p. 11.

24 "Heiratsgenehmigung," *Verordnungsblatt der Waffen SS*, 1 October 1942, paragraph 359, and "Heiratsgenehmigung," *Verordnungsblatt der Waffen SS*, 1 February 1944, paragraph 57, both in NA T611/6/Ordner 431.

25 Himmler to RuSHA chief, 11 May 1944, BA NS2/231, p. 11.

26 "Heirat von ital. Hilfswilligen," 25 May 1944, BA-MA RS14/120.

27 As of July 1944, Himmler allowed RuSHA to handle some problematic cases based on precedents he had set earlier in the war. Himmler to RuSHA chief, 3 July 1944, BA NS2/231, p. 10.

28 "Sippenakte," BDC RS A5455, p. 2278, and Brandt to RuSHA, 11 August 1940, BA NS19/3480, p. 49.

29 Fritz C. to RuSHA, 26 August 1940, BDC RS A5355, p. 2290.

30 Hofmann to Himmler, 4 September 1940, BDC RS A5355, p. 2286; Sippenamt chief to Fritz C., 16 September 1940, BDC RS A5355, p. 2282; and Sippenamt chief to SS-Hauptamt chief, 16 September 1940, BDC RS A5355, p. 2280.

31 Schmitt to Hofmann, 3 September 1940, BA NS2/175, p. 67.

32 "Sippenakte für K., Adolf," BDC RS C5374, p. 956.

33 Letter to Martin, 18 June 1943, StA-L, PL506/Bü54; "Aktenvermerk," 6 July 1943, StA-L, PL506/Bü54; and "Ärztliche Zeugnis," 6 July 1943, BDC RS C5274, p. 1018.

34 Pflegestelle 13 Führer to RuSHA, 20 October 1943, StA-L PL506/Bü54 and Heider to Adolf K., 3 November 1943, BDC RS C5374, p. 968.

35 These letters come from Kurt A.'s BDC RuSHA file (A0012): Kurt A.
    to RuSHA, 19 July 1939, p. 2436; Kurt A. to RuSHA, 2 September 1939,
    p. 2428; Lieselotte A. to RuSHA, 19 September 1939, p. 2420; Kurt A.
    to RuSHA, 25 September 1939, p. 2416; and Sippenamt to Kurt A., 28
    September 1939, p. 2400.
36 Lieselotte A. to RuSHA, 29 October 1939, p. 2398, and Sippenamt to Kurt
    A., 14 November 1939, p. 2390, both in BDC RS A0012.
37 Oehl to RuSHA chief, 10 October 1939, StA-M 327/2b/120.
38 Lieselotte A. to Hitler, 23 December 1939, BDC RS A0012, pp. 2376–7.
39 Himmler to Bouhler, 23 January 1940, BA NS19/3480, p. 7, and Bouhler to
    Himmler, BA NS19/3480, pp. 5–6.
40 Lieselotte A. to Himmler, 19 January 1940, BDC RS A0012, p. 2370; Wolff
    to Bouhler, 13 March 1940, BA NS19/3480, p. 4; Brandt to Kreisleitung
    Weimar, 16 March 1940, BA NS19/3480, p. 2; Kurt A. to RuSHA, 29 April
    1940, BDC RS A0012, p. 2346, and "Sippenakte," BDC RS A0012, p. 2334.
41 Himmler to RuSHA chief, 3 July 1944, BA NS2/231, p. 10; "Verlobungs-
    und Heiratsgesuch des SS-Untersturmführers Heinrich W.," 8 January
    1940, BA NS19/3481, p. 265; "Entscheidung über das Heiratsgesuch des
    SS-Hauptsturmführers Dr. Otto V.," 12 September 1942, NA T175/116/
    frame 2640638; Himmler to RuSHA, 27 August 1944, BA NS19/3978, p. 91;
    "Verlobungs- und Heiratsgesuch des SS-Oberführers Willi K.," 3 October
    1940, BDC D60, p. 2638; Sippenamt chief to Himmler, 10 December 1940,
    BDC RS A041, p. 284; and Pancke to Himmler, 13 March 1940, BDC RS
    B440, p. 916.
42 "Statistischer Monatsbericht des Sippenamtes," July–November 1941 in BA
    NS19/3479, pp. 6, 17, 23, 31, and 38.
43 Heiber, Reichsführer!, letter 207.
44 Kaaserer to Herold, 15 January 1942, BA NS2/288, and letter from Heider,
    5 February 1943, BA NS2/231, p. 63; Himmler to Rauter, 17 May 1943, BA
    NS19/3483, p.139; and Himmler to RuSHA chief, 3 July 1944, BA NS2/231,
    p. 10.
45 As seen in the case of Emil Sch. and Valerie R., BA NS19/2988, pp. 3–6, and
    BDC SSO 119B, pp. 606–8, 611–12, 666–7, and 716.
46 Withmann to Berger, 5 August 1943, BA NS19/3483, pp. 388–9; Brandt to
    Berger, 19 August 1943, BA NS19/3483, p. 386; and Heiber, Reichsführer!,
    letters 27, 50, 62a, 288a, and 288b.
47 Correspondence by Hofmann, Hildebrandt, and Himmler along with
    assessments by Bruno Schultz, Richard Korherr, and Karl Astel on this
    issue are in BA NS19/1047.

48 Koelhe, 27 July 1942, BA NS2/237, p. 12; Himmler to Eicke, 30 November 1942, BA NS19/3483, p. 346; and Himmler to RuSHA chief, 5 October 1944, BA NS19/3978, p. 134.
49 "Sippenakte," BDC RS C5162, p. 1262.
50 Brandt to Streckenbach, 28 November 1942, BA NS19/3482, p. 119, and Streckenbach to Brandt, 10 December 1942, BDC RS C5162, p. 1280.
51 Walter J. to Himmler, 14 December 1942, BDC RS C5162, p. 1282.
52 Meine to RuSHA, 4 January 1942, BDC RS C5162, p. 1276.
53 Heiratsamt chief to SS-Hauptamt, 2 January 1943, BDC RS C5162, p. 1270.
54 Heiber, *Reichsführer!*, letter 50.
55 "Vernehmung des SS-Mannes Karl M.," 9 April 1934, StA-D N1/48, p. 583, and "Ausschluss ds SS-Mannes Karl M.," 12 May 1934, StA-D N1/48, p. 582.
56 Rassenamt to Sippenamt, 22 October 1935, BDC RS E0036, p. 2876.
57 Ibid.
58 Rassenamt to Sippenamt, 22 February 1936, BDC RS E0036, pp. 2836–8. Another related Rassenamt letter is on pp. 2852–4.
59 RuSHA Stabsführer to SS-Hauptamt chief, 22 February 1936, BDC RS E0036, p. 2834; SS-Ergänzungsamt chief to RuSHA, 3 March 1936, BDC RS E0036, p. 2830; and Ergänzungsamt chief to [Karl] M., 5 March 1936, BDC RS E0036, p. 2832.
60 RuSHA file of Schellenberg, BDC RS F270.
61 Walter Schellenberg, *Hitler's secret service*, trans. Louis Hagen (New York: Pyramid Books, 1971), 37–8, and personnel file of Schellenberg, BDC SSO 074B, p. 201.
62 Heiber, *Reichsführer!*, letters 264a and 264b, and personnel file of Krüger, BDC SSO 220A, p. 427.
63 Himmler to Berger, October 1943, BA NS19/3857, p. 13.
64 Ibid; Berger to Himmler, 22 October 1943, BA NS19/3857, pp. 7–8; and Heiber, *Reichsführer!*, letter 264b.
65 Heinz Boberach, ed., *Meldungen aus dem Reich, 1938–1945: Die geheimen Lageberichte des Sicherheitsdeinstes der SS* (Herrsching: Pawlak Verlag, 1984), 4: 1080, 6: 1892–3.
66 "Aktennotiz zu dem Heiratsgesuch des SS-Hauptscharführers Hermann H.," 24 September 1942, BA NS19/3482, p. 102; Himmler to RuSHA, 23 February 1943, BA NS19/3483, p. 248; Himmler to Berger, 9 October 1942, BA NS19/3483, p. 303; Himmler to Eicke, 30 November 1942, BA NS19/3483, p. 346; Himmler to Kaltenbrunner, June 1943, BA NS19/3978, p. 160; Brandt to Pohl, 22 January 1944, BA NS19/3978, p. 176; Brandt to

Streckenbach, 28 November 1942, BA NS19/3482, p. 119; and Brandt to RuSHA, 2 November 1942, NA T175/116/frame 2640581.

67 For example, the marriages of Henno K. (BDC RS C529) and Michael R. (BDC RS F058).

68 For example, the marriages of Erwin M. (4.1.0/82448380/ITS Digital Archive/Bad Arolsen) and Erich H. (BA NS19/3978 and BDC RS C0034).

69 Himmler to Roth, 14 May 1942, BA NS19/3482, pp. 242–3, and Himmler to Tichatschke, 22 January 1943, BA NS 19/3483, p. 348.

70 "Verstöße gegen den Verlobungs- und Heiratsbefehl," 27 October 1939, BA NS19/752, p. 24; "Amnestie wegen Vergehen gegen den Verlobungs- und Heiratsbefehl," 16 August 1940, NA T580/333/Ordner 122; and "Wiederaufnahme in die SS bei Vergehen gegen den Verlobungs- und Heiratsbefehl," 1 November 1940, BA NS7/216, pp. 2–3.

71 "Sippenakte," BDC RS B257, p. 2426, and "Wiederaufnahme in die Schutzstaffel des ehemaligen SS-Obersturmführers Louis E.," 6 January 1942, RS B257, p. 2432.

72 "Wideraufnahme."

73 Personalhauptamt to RFSS Persönlichen Stab, 3 February 1944, BA NS19/1028, p. 2; Personalhauptamt chief to RFSS Persönlichen Stab, 31 October 1944, BA NS19/1028, p. 4; and Brandt to Personalhauptamt, 13 November 1944, BA NS19/1028, p. 6.

74 "Wideraufnahme in die SS," 21 May 1944, BA NS19/1028, p. 5, and personnel file of Louis E., BDC SSO 192.

75 US v. Greifelt, 4011, 4041, and 5080–1, and "Befehl," 16 December 1943, BA NS2/22, p. 92.

76 Turner to Himmler, 28 May 1944, BA NS2/239, p. 68; and "Entwurf!" no date, BA NS2/239, pp. 2 and 69.

77 Woyrsch to Abschnitt II, XVIII, and XXXVII, 17 February 1943, NA T580/326/Ordner 18 and Ahlgrimm to OA Südwest, 7 September 1943, BDC RS D0196, p. 1778.

78 Bender to Turner, 17 July 1944, BA NS7/216, p. 6.

79 "Heiraten ohne Genehmigung des RuS-Hauptamtes-SS," BA NS7/216, pp. 9, 11, 13, 17, and 21. Additional lists of people who married without authorization: BA NS19/3978, pp. 183 and 185, and a 9 January 1945 letter on p. 182 to Schwalm in RuSHA stated that Himmler was still refraining from punishing men during the war, but wanted records kept for afterwards.

80 "Zahl der Verheitateten und Gesamtkinderzahl in der SS am 1.1.1939 und 31.12.1939," December 1939, BA NS19/752, p. 29; "Heiratsgenehmigungen und Freigaben," December 1939, BA NS2/55, pp. 133–6; and "Heiratsgenehmigungen und Freigaben," February 1940, BA NS19/577, p. 40.

81 The range of requests was quite large. For commissioned officers, it ranged from 57 requests (September 1941) to 358 requests (January 1942); for non-coms and enlisted men, it ranged from 1,009 requests (January 1940) to 4,326 requests (January 1942). "Heiratsgenehmigungen und Freigaben," BA NS19/577, p. 40; "Statistischer Monatsbericht des Sippenamtes im RuS-Hauptamt von Monat November 1941," BA NS19/3479, pp. 2–7; "Statistischer Monatsbericht des Sippenamtes im RuS-Hauptamt von Monat September 1941," BA NS19/3479, pp. 13–18; "Statistischer Monatsbericht des Sippenamtes im RuS-Hauptamt von Monat Oktober 1941," BA NS19/3479, pp. 19–25; and "Statistischer Monatsbericht über das Sippenamtes im Rasse- und Siedlungshauptamt-SS von Monat Januar 1942," BA NS19/3482, pp. 324–31. Additional reports from 1941 and 1942 do not differentiate among officers, non-coms, and enlisted men, so they were not included in the average. "Statistischer Monatsbericht des Sippenamtes im RuS-Hauptamt von Monat August 1941," BA NS19/3479, pp. 27–32; "Statistischer Monatsbericht des Sippenamtes im RuS-Hauptamt von Monat Juli 1941," BA NS19/3479, pp. 35–9; and "Verlobungs- u. Heiratsgesuche 1942," BA NS48/6.

82 Although it was preferred that men not marry before age twenty-five, they could do so as of twenty-one, the legal age for emancipation. See Himmler to RuSHA, 4 October 1935, NA T580/333/Ordner 122; Brandt to *Das Schwarze Korps*, 28 February 1940, BA NS19/3480, p. 216; Wolff to Radke, February 1940, BA NS19/3480, p. 220; Margarete K. to *Das Schwarze Korps*, 27 January 1943, NA T580/326/Ordner 18; and Heiratsamt chief to Margarete K., 3 February 1943, NA T580/326/Ordner 18.

83 *Dienstalterliste der Schutzstaffel der NSDAP (SS-Oberst-Gruppenführer – SS Standartenführer) Stand vom 9 November 1944* (Berlin: Herausgegeben vom SS-Personalhauptamt, 1944), BA NSD41/65 – 1944.

84 Himmler to Hofmann, 21 December 1942, BA NS19/3483, p. 257.

85 Heider to Hofmann, 23 December 1942, BA NS19/3483, p. 255.

86 This completion rate was higher than the rates in the six to twelve months prior, which ranged from 565 applications (October 1941) to 1,214 (June 1942). "Arbeitsbericht des Sippenamt für das 2 Halbjahr 1941," 27 January 1942, BA NS2/58, pp. 158–65, and "Vorläufige Entscheidungen von VH-Gesuchen," 13 August 1942, BA NS19/3483, pp. 310–11.

87 Hofmann to Himmler, 28 January 1941, BA NS2/56, pp. 2–3.

88 Emphasis in original; Himmler to Hofmann, 6 March 1941, BA NS2/56, p. 1.

89 Hofmann to Himmler, 18 March 1941, BA NS2/56, p. 9, and Brandt to Hofmann, 29 March 1941, BA NS2/56, p. 8.

90 Conti, "Erhöhung der Kinderzahl durch Eheanbahnung, Eheberatung, und Wahlkinder," NA T175/69/frame 2585953.

91 Himmler to Conti, 13 July 1942, NA T175/69/frame 2585949.

92 Heider to Himmler, 3 June 1943, NA T175/29/frame 2536756 and Heider to Himmler, 20 December 1943, NA T175/29/frame 2536745. Around the same time, the Reich League of German Women set up letter centres to facilitate matches, although not necessarily with SS men: Jill Stephenson, "'Reichsbund der Kinderreichen': The League of Large Families in the population policy of Nazi Germany," *European Studies Review* 9, no. 3 (July 1979): 364–6.

93 Melitta Wiedemann, editor of the journal *Die Aktion*, also submitted a proposal. Brandt requested an opinion from the Legal Main Office, whose officials rejected her proposal as untenable. See NS7/176, pp. 1–13.

94 Hofmann to Himmler, 31 December 1941, BA NS2/46, p. 199. Pancke had praised the command three years earlier during a Gruppenführer conference: "Sippenpflege und Siedlung des Rasse und Siedlungshauptamtes-SS," January 1939, BA NS19/1660, pp. 108–116.

95 "Zehn Jahre Heiratsbefehel der SS," 3 January 1942.

96 "10 Jahre 'Heiratsbefehl," 8 January 1942.

97 Weindling, *Health, race and German politics*, 500.

98 Koehl, *The black corps*, 82–3, and Heinemann, *Rasse*, 684–5.

99 Schultz, "10 Jahres Verlobungs- und Heiratsbefehl in der Schutzstaffel," *Volk und Rasse* no. 1 (January 1942). In a 10 August 1942 letter, Hofmann informed Himmler about this article and sent him a copy: BA NS19/752, p. 49.

100 Schultz, "10 Jahres."

101 Unterarzt Derkmann, "Ehetauglichkeit als rassenhygienische Maßnahme," *Archiv für Rassen- und Gesellschaftbiologie* 34 (1940): 401–432.

102 Rüdin, "Zehn Jahre nationalsozialistischer Staat," *Archiv für Rassen- und Gesellschaftsbiologie* 36 (1943): 321–2.

4 Sustaining the Family Community during the War

1 Weingart, "German eugenics," 261–2.

2 "SS Befehl für die gesamte SS und Polizei," 28 October 1939, BA NS19/3901, p. 80.

3 Longerich, *Heinrich Himmler*, 462. See also Klaus Jürgen Müller, *Das Heer und Hitler: Armee und nationalsozialistisches Regime, 1933–1940* (Stuttgart: Deutsche Verlags-Anstalt, 1969), 459–70.

4   Leeb to Brauchitsch, 20 January 1939, BA-MA N104/3, p. 15.
5   "Der Sieg der Frauen," *Das Schwarze Korps*, 4 January 1940.
6   Emphasis in original. Hanns Johst, *Ruf des Reiches – Echo des Volkes!*
    Eine Ostfahrt (Munich: Franz Eher Verlag, 1940), full conversation 51–7,
    quote 56. For more on Johst, see Rolf Düsterberg, "Mein Reichsführer,
    lieber Heini Himmler!" *Zeit Online*, 11 March 2004, http://www.zeit.
    de/2004/12/A-Johst (accessed 21 May 2014).
7   "An alle Männer der SS und Polizei," 30 January 1940, BA NS19/3901, p. 91.
8   "Abschrift Nr. 327/40," 6 February 1940, BA NS18/712, p. 1.
9   This meeting did not resolve all of the tension between the army and the
    SS. Müller, *Das Heer und Hitler*, 466–9.
10 "Bestraffung wegen milit. Ungehorsam wegen Geschlechtsverkehrs mit
    Soldatenehefrauen," 9 February 1942, BA NS7/221, pp. 1–2.
11 "Bestraffung wegen milit. Ungehorsam infolge Geschlechtsverkehrs mit
    Soldatenehefrauen," 23 March 1942, BA NS7/221, p. 3.
12 Longerich, *Heinrich Himmler*, 375 and 466.
13 Himmler to Jüttner, 29 May 1942, BA NS19/3441, p. 1; "Rede des
    Reichsführer-SS am 19.6.1942 vor dem Führerkorps der Division," IfZ MA312/
    frame 2612908; and Himmler to Woyrsch, 22 March 1943, BA NS2/240, p. 2.
14 "Richtlinien zur Einreichung von Beförderungsvorschlägen für Führer
    der Allgemeine-SS und der Waffen-SS für die Dauer des Krieges," 15
    November 1942, BA NS34/21. Himmler wrote to the Personnel Main
    Office on October 20, noting that several promotions had been rejected
    because the officers were not married; NA T175/54/frame 2568954–
    2568956. Other examples of Himmler making similar demands are in
    Heiber, *Reichsführer!*, letter 277 and Padfield, *Himmler*, 294.
15 "Einreichung von Beförderungsvorschlägen," 15 February 1944, BA
    NS34/21. This issue was also partially addressed in a letter from Brandt to
    Frank from December 1944 in Heiber, *Reichsführer!*, letter 366.
16 For a few exceptions see Zielger, "Fight against the empty cradle," 30;
    Bianca Vieregge, *Die Gerichtsbarkeit einer "Elite": Nationalsozialistische
    Rechtsprechung am Beispiel der SS- und Polizei-Gerichtsbarkeit* (Baden: Nomos
    Verlagsgesellschaft, 2002), 68; and lists of officers submitted for promotion
    in 1943 in StA-M 327/2b/521.
17 See chapter 3, note 81.
18 Quoted in Longerich, *Heinrich Himmler*, 377.
19 Hugh Trevor-Roper, *Hitler's table talk 1941–1944: His private conversations*
    (New York: Enigma, 2008), 58–9.
20 Heiber, *Reichsführer!*, letter 217, and "Rede des Reichsführers-SS am
    23.11.1942 – SS-Junkerschule Tolz," BA NS19/4009, p. 194.

21 Trevor-Roper, *Hitler's table talk*, 83.

22 Ibid., 327.

23 Personnel file of Daluege, BDC SSO 134, p. 1213.

24 Himmler to Daluege, 5 October 1942, NA T175/18/frame 2522065, and "Familiennachwuches des Führerkorps der Ordnungspolizei," NA T175/18/frames 2522066–2522069.

25 Letter from Grawitz, 7 April 1943, BDC SSO 030, p. 147; information on his children is in SSO 029, p. 1434.

26 "Neues Leben für vergossenes Blut," 15 May 1941.

27 "Das Wunder nach einmal erleben," 22 February 1940; "Die Aufgaben der Zukunft," 18 December 1941; and "Unser lieber einziger Sohn," 15 July 1943.

28 "Lebensfeinde," 30 April 1942.

29 "Ernste Frage und Antwort," 21 December 1939, and "Ausschneiden," 5 March 1942.

30 "Ernste Frage und Antwort."

31 "Front und Heimat," 23 November 1939; "Das allein ist der Maßstab," 28 December 1939; "Der Dank des Vaterlandes," 11 January 1940; "Er kann jetzt heiraten," 25 January 1940; "Ein Mann der Praxis," 8 February 1940; and "Ins Eheglück stürzen," 9 March 1944.

32 "Eine persönliche Frage?" 22 July 1943.

33 "Wohler worbene Rechte," 28 May 1942.

34 "Heiraten – aber wen?" 31 December 1942.

35 "Und wird was nachher," 25 January 1940.

36 For more on the Waffen-SS Standarte Kurt Eggers, see Combs, *The voice of the SS*, 159; William Combs, "Fatal attraction: Dueling and the SS," *History Today* 47, no. 6 (June 1997): 16; and Werner Augustinovic and Martin Moll, "Günter d'Alquen: Propagandist des SS-staates," in *Die SS: Elite unter dem Totenkopf: 30 Lebensläufe*, ed. Ronald M. Smelser and Enrico Syring (Paderborn: Ferdinand Schönningh, 2000), 108.

37 "Und wird was nachher." This letter was included in a compilation of letters edited by d'Alquen. The letters were divided thematically, and one theme was "War and Family," in which several soldiers spoke of their pride as fathers. It is not clear whether SS men wrote all of the letters, although Himmler did endorse the publication. See d'Alquen, *Das ist der Sieg! Briefe des Glaubens in Aufbruch und Krieg* (Berlin: Franz Eher Verlag, 1941), 59, 61–3, and 72. Another SS publication that reprinted letters from soldiers on the front as well as the family to the soldiers was *Aufbruch: Briefe germanischer Kriegsfreiwilliger* (Berlin: Der Reichsführer-SS, SS-Hauptamt, 1942).

38 "Ein glücklicher Vater," 1 October 1942.
39 "Für meine drei Jungen," 25 January 1940 and "Übertriebene Lebenssicherung," 7 September 1944.
40 "Frontsoldat schreibt seinem Sohn," 27 February 1941.
41 "Der Soldat an seinen Sohn," 15 May 1941.
42 "Brücke der Gedanken," 18 December 1941.
43 "Vater auf Urlaub," 4 January 1940.
44 "Soldat und Vater," 28 March 1940.
45 Ibid.
46 Ibid.
47 "Dein Vater kennt ihn," 5 August 1943.
48 "Zurückziehung aus der fechtenden Truppe," 4 August 1941, BA NS7/381, p. 1.
49 Knoebel, "Racial illusion," 75.
50 "SS-Befehl an die letzten Söhne," 15 August 1942, BA NS2/23, p. 45.
51 "Tagesbefehl 24/42. Besondere Anweisungen," BA NS2/11, p. 61.
52 Later documents show continuing cooperation: "Rasse- und Siedlungshauptamt-SS Sonderbefehl Nr. 15/44," 29.3.1944, BA NS2/17, p. 52.
53 "Letzte Söhne," 9 April [1943], NA T354/519/frame 4275238 and "Karteimäßige Erfassung der 'Letzten und einzigen Söhne,' " 29 March 1944, BA NS2/17, p. 52.
54 Telegram from the Personalhauptamt to the Persönlichen Stab RFSS, 10 June 1943, personnel file of Brigadeführer Arnold, BDC SSO018, p. 20632.
55 The 21 June 1943 letters from Himmler to father and son are in BA NS19/2970, pp. 3 and 5.
56 Hauptsturmführer Arnold to Himmler, 30 August 1943, BA NS19/2970, p. 1.
57 Groß to Brigadeführer Arnold, 14 October 1944, BDC SSO018, pp. 20627–8, and "Familien Anzeigen," *Das Schware Korps*, 30 November 1944.
58 "Schutzbestimmungen über 'einzige und letzte Söhne', Väter von 5 und mehr lebenden Kinder sowie Familien mit 5 und mehr Wehrdienst stehende Söhnen," BA R187/680, pp. 166–7; "Zurückziehung 'einziger und letzter Söhne' aus der kämpfenden Truppe in besonderen Härtefällen," 8 August 1944, BA R187/680, pp. 168–9; and "Tagesbefehl Nr. 350/44 Besondere Anweisungen," BA NS2/16, p. 59.
59 Heiber, *Reichsführer!*, letter 240.
60 "Weihnachtsurlaub," 7 November 1940, BA NS33/230, p. 55; "Urlauberplatzkarten – Jahresurlaub," 25 November 1942, BA-MA RS3–8/33; "Urlaub zu Weihnachten 1942 und Neujahr 1943," 5 November

1942, BA-MA RS3–8/33; "Urlaub zu Weihnachten 1942 und Neujahr 1943," 5 December 1942, BA NS3/1080, pp. 149–50; and "Erholungsurlaub für Waffen-SS/Allgemeine-SS Angehörige, einschl. Ziviliangestellte," 5 March 1943, BA NS2/22, p. 80.

61 "Planmäßiger Urlaub," 2 October 1943, NA T175/71/frame 2588327, and Lilienthal, *Der Lebensborn*, 137.

62 Heiber, *Reichsführer!*, letter 247a. Himmler wanted Felix Steiner to coordinate with Martin on this issue: Himmler to Steiner, 9 July 1943, BA NS19/3594, p. 224.

63 "Planmäßiger Urlaub," 5 August 1944, NA T175/71/frame 2588347.

64 "Planmäßiger Urlaub," 19 September 1944, NA T175/71/frame 2588320, and "Zusammenstellung der vom November 1943 bis Juni 1944 gezahlten Beträge für planmässigen Urlaub," 30 June 1944, NA T175/71/frame 2588414.

65 Heiber, *Reichsführer!*, letter 233.

66 Himmler to Steiner, 9 July 1943, and Himmler to Jüttner, 9 September 1943, NA T175/71/frame 2588518.

67 "Mahnung und Verpflichtung," NA T175/71/frame 2588536.

68 Hoffman to all full-time and honorary members of RuSHA, 12 August 1941, BA NS2/21, p. 146; Brandt to Hoffman, 15 December 1942, BA NS2/147, p. 1; and Himmler to all main office chiefs, higher SS and police leaders, and OA leaders, 20 March 1943, BA NS19/3904, p. 65.

69 See correspondence between Himmler and Hayler, BA NS19/3034, pp. 5–6.

70 Salary tables for the Verfügungstruppe and the Waffen-SS can be found in NA T611/7/Ordner 432 (Teil 2) and "Besoldung der Waffen-SS," 1 January 1945, BA NS3/502.

71 "Reichsschatzminister der NSDAP. Gewährt Geburtenbeihilfen," BA NS2/115, p. 34, and Frank to Allgemeine-SS, 6 February 1941, BA R187/670, p. 7.

72 "Fürsorge für Kinderreich – Ausbildungsbeihilfe," 6 July 1944, LA-D RW0134/14, pp. 40–1.

73 "Familienunterhalt," 16 November 1940, BA NS33/458; "Sonderbetreuung von kinderreichen Familien eingezogener SS-Angehöriger," 26 February 1941, BA-MA RS14/21; "Versorgungsbestimmungen," 18 April 1942, BA NS19/1954; "Erlass die Zahlung von Familienunterhalt der Waffen-SS im Ausland bei eheählichen Verhältnissen," [November 1942], BA-MA RS5/1056; "Fürsorge für die Angehörigen der SS-Freiwilligen aus Rümanien," 21 October 1943, BA NS2/299; and "Merkblatt über die Fürsorgebenachrichtigung," 4 March 1945, BA NS2/278.

74 In-house letter from Sollmann, 25 September 1941, 4.1.0/82452869–70/ITS Digital Archive/Bad Arolsen.
75 Entries from Marga Himmler's diary, 13 March 1938 and 15 March 1939, USHMM 1999.A.0092, and Stephan Lebert and Norbert Lebert, *My father's keeper: Children of Nazi leaders – an intimate history of damage and denial*, trans. Julian Evans (Boston: Little, Brown, and Company, 2000), 155.
76 This desire is most clearly manifested in an entry from 26 January 1938: "Püppi is still doing badly in diction. We often call her 'schwinekin' [little pig] and then one day she answered, 'Schwinekin Mommy.' Too bad we don't have six like this, so loveable."
77 Manvell and Fraenkel, *Heinrich Himmler*, 40 and 258 n1.
78 Marga Himmler diary, 2 April 1938 and 8 April 1938, and personnel file of Himmler, BDC SSO 099A, p. 003.
79 Marga Himmler diary, 21 February 1945.
80 Marga Himmler diary, 3 July 1938, 28 November 1940, and 7 December 1940.
81 Schellenberg, *Hitler's secret service*, 313 and Kersten, *Memoirs*, 304.
82 Helmut Heiber, *Goebbels*, trans. John K. Dickinson (New York: Da Capo Press, 1972), 242–4.
83 Viktor Reimann, *Goebbels: The man who created Hitler*, trans. Stephen Wendt (New York: Doubleday, 1976), 228–31.
84 Lang, *Top Nazi*, 205–7.
85 Padfield, *Himmler*, 233–4.
86 "Interview of Hedwig Potthast," 22 May 1945, NA RG238/M1270/27/ frame 192, and Katrin Himmler, *The Himmler brothers: A German family history* (London: Macmillan, 2007), 247 and 253.
87 Manvell and Fraenkel, *Heinrich Himmler*, 263–4 n14, and Padfield, *Himmler*, 539.
88 Kersten, *Memoirs*, 177.
89 Longerich, *Heinrich Himmler*, x and 381, and Gerwarth, *Hitler's hangman*, xv.
90 Kersten, *Memoirs*, 177–8.
91 Schwarz, *Eine Frau*, 93 and Katrin Himmler, *The Himmler brothers*, 249.
92 Personnel file of Pohl, BDC SSO 387A, p. 825. For additional information about Pohl's family life, see Dorothee Schmitz-Köster, *Kind L 364: Eine Lebensborn-Familiegeschichte* (Berlin: Rowohlt Verlag, 2007).
93 Schwarz, *Eine Frau*, 93; Peter Black, *Ernst Kaltenbrunner, ideological soldier of the Third Reich* (Princeton, NJ: Princeton University Press, 1984), 117; and Central Intelligence Agency, "The last days of Ernst Kaltenbrunner," *Center for the Study of Intelligence* 4, no. 2, https://www.cia.gov/library/center-for-the-study-of-intelligence/kent-csi/vol4no2/html/v04i2a07p_0001.htm (accessed 18 September 2014).

94   Kaltenbrunner's personnel file (SSO150A, p. 004) only lists two children, but the CIA article noted three.

95   Himmler to Dietrich, 23 July 1943, IfZ MA287/frame 2529087.

96   "Rudolf Heß an einen unverheiratete Mutter," *Völkischer Beobachter*, 24–26 December 1939.

97   Dorothee Schmitz-Köster, "A Topic for Life," 216.

98   Joseph Goebbels, *The Goebbels Diaries, 1939–1941*, trans. and ed. Fred Taylor (London: Hamish Hamilton, 1982), 321.

99   Joseph Goebbels, *Die Tagbücher von Joseph Goebbels*, ed. Elke Fröhlich (Munich: K.G. Saur, 1998–2005); 19 November 1939 (Teil I/Bd. 7, p. 201), 13 March 1940 (Teil I/Bd. 7, p. 346), and 29 October 1943 (Teil II/Bd. 10, p. 199).

100   Himmler to all SS and police men, 6 April 1942, BA NS2/187, p. 41.

101   "Erlass der Reichsführer-SS zum Schutz der weiblichen Jugend vom 6.4.1942," 2 July 1942, BA NS7/181, p. 25, and "Zwölfter Sammelerlass, [number] 45: 'Berichtpflicht bei Ungehorsam gegen den Befehl des Reichsführers-SS über den Schutz der weiblichen Jugend,' " 1 August 1942, BA NS7/5, p. 108.

102   Ernst Walther Koch, *Sichert die heutige Ehe noch den Bestand unseres Volkes?* (Leipzig: Offizin Haag-Drugulin, 1940), 11, 19, and 21.

103   "Eine Frau hat das Wort," *Das Schwarze Korps*, 11 April 1940.

104   Lenz to *Das Schwarze Korps* editorial board, 10 May 1940, MPG Abt. 3, Rep. 86B, Nrs. 1–13, Nr. 10, pp. 8–10.

105   Ibid., 12–13.

106   Lenz, "Wege weiteren Vormarsches der Bevölkerungspolitk," MPG Abt. 3, Rep. 86B, Nrs. 1–13, Nr. 10, pp. 15–16.

107   Ibid., 16, 18, and 21.

108   Lenz to *Das Schwarze Korps* editorial board, 14.

109   Verschuer to Lenz, 12 June 1940, MPG Abt. 3, Rep 86B, Nrs. 1–13, Nr. 10, p. 22, and Lenz to Verschuer, 17 June 1940, MPG Abt. 3, Rep. 86B, Nrs. 1–13, Nr. 10, pp. 24–5.

110   Kröner, *Von der Rassenhygiene*, 36.

111   Hella to Sepp F., [2 February 1940], BA NS19/3480, pp. 79–80.

112   Sepp F. to Hella, 3 February 1940, BA NS19/3480, p. 78.

113   Sepp F. to *Das Schwarze Korps* editorial board, 3 February 1940, NA T175/115/frame 2639677.

114   Brandt to Sepp F., 14 February 1940, BA NS19/3480, p. 85.

115   SD Leitabschnittes Vienna Führer to OA Donau Führer, 3 April 1940, BA NS19/3480, p. 76, and Standarte Kurt Eggers to Hauptamt Volksdeutsche Mittelstelle, 20 September 1944, BDC EWZ-W H0015.

116 Office of United States Chief of Counsel for Prosecution of Axis
     Criminality, *Nazi conspiracy and aggression* (Washington, DC: US
     Government Printing Office, 1946), 4: document 2124-PS; Raul Hilberg,
     The destruction of the European Jews (New Haven, CT: Yale University
     Press, 2003), 2: 434–43.
117 Sepp F. to the Persönlichen Stab RFSS, 18 February 1940, NA T175/115/
     frames 2639681–2639682.
118 Brandt to Sepp F. and Berger, 22 February 1940, NA T175/115/frame
     2639674; Brandt to OA Donau, 23 February 1940, NA T175/115/
     frame 2639673; SD Leitabschnitt Vienna Führer to OA Donau Führer,
     3 April 1940, BA NS19/3480, pp. 76–7; Berger to Himmler, 11 April
     1940, BA NS19/3480, p. 74; and Standarte Kurt Eggers to Hauptamt
     Volksdeutsche Mittelstelle, 20 September 1944, BDC EWZ-W-H0015.
119 Ruth H. to Himmler, 18 November 1943, BA NS19/3031, p. 4.
120 Pine, *Nazi family policy*, 18, and Czarnowski, *The value of marriage*, 104–10.
121 "Disziplinarmassnahmen wegen Ehebruchs," 16 April 1941, NA
     T175/135/frame 2663203; "Zehnter Sammelerlass," 15 January 1942,
     BA NS7/4; and "Zwölfter Sammelerlass [number] 24 Beurteilung von
     Ehebruch," 1 August 1942, BA NS7/6, pp. 98–9.
122 Meine to Alfred H., 14 December 1943, BA NS19/3031, p. 6.
123 Personnel file of Alfred H., BDC SSO 078A, p. 525. The correspondence
     can be found on pp. 578, 613–19, 622, 624, 626, 630–1, and BA NS19/3031,
     pp. 7–13.
124 Kersten, *Memoirs*, 181.
125 Neumann, *The black march: The personal story of an SS man*, trans.
     Constantine Fitzgibbon (New York: Bantam Books, 1960), 85.
126 Ibid., 162.
127 Heiber, *Reichsführer!*, letters 380a and 380b, and Schleßmann's personnel
     file, BDC SSO 081B, p. 014.
128 Lilienthal, *Der Lebensborn*, 112 and 244, and Lilienthal, "Ärtze und
     Rassenpolitik," 156.
129 Ebner to Langleist, 4 August 1941, 4.1.0/82458324/ITS Digital Archive/
     Bad Arolsen.
130 For cases of adoption of Lebensborn children: "Die Annahme an Kindes
     Statt," *Münchener Neueste Nachrichten*, 16 August 1941 and selected
     correspondence with the Lebensborn in NA T175/40/frames 2550775–
     2550792, T175/76/frames 2594383–2594391, T175/77/frames 2595490–
     2595499, and T175/210/frames 2750074–2750104. For information on
     adoption, see Lilienthal, *Der Lebensborn*, 73; Schmitz-Köster, *Deutsche
     Mutter*, 36, and Michelle Mouton, "Rescuing children and policing

families: Adoption policy in Weimar and Nazi Germany," *Central European History* 38, no. 4 (2005): 545–71.

131 *US v. Greifelt*, 4448 and 4495.
132 "Dienstanordnung Nr. 100," 18 February 1942, IfZ Fa202/frame 85.
133 *US v. Greifelt*, 4298–9.
134 Genzken to Grawitz, 30 October 1944, BA NS2/148, p. 38.
135 Grawitz to Himmler, 23 May 1942, BA NS19/711, p. 2; Himmler to Grawitz, 8 June 1942, BA NS19/711, p. 3; and "Geheimlehre der Frauenschaft," BA NS19/1632, pp. 1–29.
136 Grawitz to Pohl, 8 November 1944, BA NS2/148, p. 37.
137 Hofmann to Himmler, 11 February 1943, BS NS2/148, p. 52.
138 Pohl to Grawitz, 16 November 1944, NA RG238/190/13/4/06/entry 211/box 2/folder SS-987-C-6-Dupl-No-3352.
139 Klug to Waffen-SS medical services, 1 December 1944, BA NS2/148, p. 34.
140 Reil to Weber, 20 March 1945, BA NS2/148, p. 8; Wolff to Reil, 26 February 1945, BA NS2/148, p. 10; Reil to Wolff, 15 February 1945, BA NS2/148, p. 11; Krumfuß to the leaders of the RuSHA medial service offices, 2 December 1944, BA NS2/148, p. 12; Reil to Weber, 4 September 1944, BA NS2/148, p. 13; Heiratsamt chief to Weber, 6 July 1944, BA NS2/148, p. 15; Wolff to Pflegestelle 6, 21 June 1944, BA NS2/148, p. 16; Reil to the troop doctor of the RuSHA field office in Bohemia-Moravia, 12 February 1945, BA NS2/148, p. 17; troop doctor of the RuSHA field office in Bohemia-Moravia to Poppendick, 16 January 1945, BA NS2/148, p. 18; troop doctor of the RuSHA field office in Bohemia-Moravia to Reil, 17 January 1945, BA NS2/148, p. 19; Grümmer to Himmler, 18 January 1945, BA NS2/148, pp. 24 and 28; Reil to Wolff, 16 March 1945, BA NS2/148, p. 24; Reil to Grümmer, 2 February 1945, BA NS2/148, p. 25; Grümmer to Reil, 1 March 1945, BA NS2/148, p. 26; letter from Dibowski, no date, BDC RS B0088, p. 536; Heiratsamt chief to Kiefer, 6 November 1943, NA T611/26/Ordner 165; and Heiber, *Reichsführer!*, letter 210.
141 Brandt to Sollmann, 17 May 1944, NA T175/20/frame 2524516; Brandt to the medical inspection of the Waffen-SS and SS chief medical officer, 26 October 1944, NA T175/20/frame 2524517; Brant to the medical inspection of the Waffen-SS, 17 May 1944, NA T175/20/frame 2524519; letter to Sollmann, 6 March 1944, NA T175/20/frames 2524521–2524522. This was one of the few cases where the Lebensborn coordinated treatments.
142 "Wie kann hier geholfen werden?" 1 February 1940.
143 "Erhöhung der Kinderzahl durch Eheanbahnung, Eheberatung, und Wahlkinder," NA T175/69/frame 2585953.

144 Himmler to Conti, 13 July 1942, NA T175/69/frame 2585949.

145 Heiber, *Reichsführer!*, letter 226.

146 " 'Bevölkerungslehre und Bevölkerungspolitik im Dritten Reich,' Tagung in Berlin-Dahlem vom 30.11–1.12.2001," *Demographie: Mitteilungen der Deutschen Gesellschaft für Demographie e.V.* 1, no. 2 (July 2002): 11; Lilienthal, *Ärzte*, 162; and Ulf Schmidt, *Medical films, ethics, and euthanasia in Nazi Germany: The history of medical research and teaching films of the Reich Office for Educational Films-Reich Institute for Films in Science and Education, 1933–1945* (Hasum: Matthiesen, 2002), 204.

147 Turner to all OA main offices and welfare advisers, 21 June 1944, BA-MA RS14/16.

148 Erich B. to Lebensborn, 1 November 1943, 4.1.0/82457753/ITS Digital Archive/Bad Arolsen.

149 Isle Sch. to Lebensborn, 10 October 1942, 4.1.0/82457716/ITS Digital Archive/Bad Arolsen.

150 Ebner to Frau D., 3 May 1939, 4.1.0/82451069–70/ITS Digital Archive/Bad Arolsen.

151 Vierthaler to Lebensborn, 5 December 1943, 4.1.0/82451088/ITS Digital Archive/Bad Arolsen and Anneliesse M. to Edelmann, 13 June 1944, 4.1.0/82457771/ITS Digital Archive/Bad Arolsen.

152 Ebner to Düker, 27 May 1940, 4.1.0/82451081/ITS Digital Archive/Bad Arolsen. For Mackenrodt's association with the Lebensborn, see "Beratenden Fachärzte im Lebensborn e.V.," 1 April 1940, 4.1.0/82452486/ITS Digital Archive/Bad Arolsen.

153 Ebner to Mackenrodt, 15 April 1940, 4.1.0/82451073/ITS Digital Archive/Bad Arolsen.

154 Ebner to Sollmann, 15 April 1940, 4.1.0/82451072/ITS Digital Archive/Bad Arolsen; Ebner to Sollmann, 27 May 1940, 4.1.0/82451080/ITS Digital Archive/Bad Arolsen and Ebner to Sollmann, 29 May 1940, 4.1.0/82451082/ITS Digital Archive/Bad Arolsen.

155 Sollmann to Ebner, 28 June 1940, 4.1.0/82451083/ITS Digital Archive/Bad Arolsen.

156 Ebner to Vierthaler, 14 December 1942, 4.1.0/82451090/ITS Digital Archive/Bad Arolsen. See also Ebner to Stadler, 8 April 1944, 4.1.0/82451095/ITS Digital Archive/Bad Arolsen, and Ebner to Anneliesse M. 22 June 1944, 4.1.0/82457773/ITS Digital Archive/Bad Arolsen.

157 See Ebner to Vierthaler, 14 December 1942, 4.1.0/82451090/ITS Digital Archive/Bad Arolsen.

158 Brandt to Ebner and Grawitz, 4 August 1942, BA NS19/3684, p. 1.

159 Ebner to Brandt, 12 August 1942, BA NS19/3684, p. 4.

160   Grawitz to Brandt, 7 August 1942, BA NS 19/3684, pp. 2–3.
161   Grawitz to Brandt, 7 September 1942, BA NS19/3684, p. 5; Schultze to Grawitz, 11 August 1942, BA NS19/3684, pp. 6–7; and Brandt to Ebner, 13 September 1942, BA NS19/3684, p. 8.
162   Walter Koch also conducted research into sex ratios, some of which was done in the Lebensborn program in the 1940s. See William James, "The categories of evidence relating to the hypothesis that mammalian sex ratios at birth are causally related to the hormone concentrations of both parents around the time of conception," *Journal of Biosocial Science* 43 (2011): 167–84.
163   See Sanford Winston, "The influence of social factors upon the sex-ratio at birth," *The American Journal of Sociology* 37, no. 1 (July 1931): 1–21; Winston, "Birth control and sex ratio at birth," *The American Journal of Sociology* 38, no. 2 (September 1932): 225–31; Heinrich Rosenhaupt, "The male birth surplus," *The Scientific Monthly* 48, no. 2 (February 1939): 163–9; and Constantine Panunzio, "Are more males born in wartime?" *The Milbank Memorial Fund Quarterly* 21, no. 3 (July 1943): 281–91. These types of studies continued after the war. See C.A. McMahan, "An empirical test of three hypothesis concerning the human sex ratio at birth in the United States," *The Milbank Memorial Fund Quarterly* 29, no. 3 (July 1951): 273–93; Brian MacMahon and Thomas Pugh, "Sex ratio of white births in the United States during the Second World War," *American Journal of Human Genetics* 6, no. 2 (June 1954): 284–92; and K. Gilbert and Heidi Danker, "Investigations on the changes of sex-ratio in Germany from 1826 up to 1978," *Acta Anthropogenetica* 5, no. 2 (1981): 89–110.
164   Personnel file of Korherr, BDC SSO 201A, p. 389, and letter from Himmler, 9 December 1940, NA T580/331/Ordnung 78. Gerald Reitlinger and William Seltzer each provide an overview of Korherr's work for the SS. See Reitlinger, *The SS*, 221–2 and Seltzer, "Population statistics, the Holocaust, and the Nuremberg Trials," *Population and Development Review* 24, no. 3 (September 1998): 530–1.
165   "Gespräch mit Dr. Korherr am 9 April 1956," IfZ ZS1657, p. 1. Himmler's order from 9 December 1940 establishing the position of inspector for statistics confirmed Korherr's post-war assessment of his role. See BDC SSO 201A, p. 852.
166   Korherr to Himmler, 21 May 1942, BDC SSO 201A, pp. 698–710.
167   Korherr to Himmler, 18 September 1942, BA NS19/472, pp. 2–6.
168   Brandt to Korherr, 18 December 1942, IfZ MA287/frame 2529146.
169   Dombek to Himmler, 30 January 1944, BA NS19/444, p. 3.
170   Brandt to Dombek, 14 February 1944, BA NS19/444, p. 6.

171 Brandt to Sollmann, 12 February 1944, BA NS19/444, p. 5; Heiber, *Reichsführer!*, letter 297, which lists the date of the letter as 14 February.
172 Grawitz to Brandt, 19 February 1944, BA NS19/444, p. 8.
173 Ibid., 9.
174 Heiber, *Reichsführer!*, letter 297.
175 Mark Mazower, *Hitler's empire: How the Nazis ruled Europe* (New York: The Penguin Press, 2008), 206–11; Götz Aly and Susanne Heim, *Architects of annihilation: Auschwitz and the logic of destruction*, trans. A.G. Blunden (Princeton, NJ: Princeton University Press, 2002), 253–68; and Michael Burleigh, "Nazi Europe: What if Nazi Germany had defeated the Soviet Union?" in *Virtual history: Alternatives and counterfactuals*, ed. Niall Ferguson (New York: Basic Books, 1999), 326 and 333–40.

5 Belonging to the Family Community

1 Himmler to Schulungsamt, 1 August 1938, StA-M 327/2b/54. For possible reasons why this transfer occurred, see Longerich, *Heinrich Himmler*, 312 and 830 n80; Heinemann, *Rasse*, 65–7, 76, 91, and 98–101; and Jan Erik Schulte, *Zwangsarbeit und Vernichtung: Das Wirtschaftsimperium der SS. Oswald Pohl und das SS-Wirtschafts-Verwaltungshauptamt, 1933–1945* (Paderborn: Ferdinand Schöningh, 2001), 64–5.
2 Heinemann, *Rasse*, 685, and Bastian Hein, *Elite für Volk und Führer? Die Allgemeine-SS und ihre Mitglieder 1925–1945* (Munich: Oldenbourg Verlag, 2012), 237.
3 "Dienststellung der Schulungsleiter," 29 October 1938, StA-M 327/2b/54.
4 For more on sports badges, see David Littlejohn and C.M. Dodkins, *Orders, decorations, medals, and badges of the Third Reich (including the Free City of Danzig)* (Mountain View, CA: R. James Bender Publishing, 1973), and Berno Bahro, "Der Sport und seine Rolle in der nationalsozialistischen Elitetruppe SS," *Historical Social Research / Historische Sozialforschung* 32, no. 1 (2007): 78–91.
5 "Mitarbeiter des Rasse-und Siedlungsamtes," 23 June 1933, StA-D, N1/55, pp. 139–42; "Dienstanweisung für die Schulungsleiter," 16 [October] 1934, BA NS2/277; "Bezug der SS-Zeitung 'Das Schwarze Korps,' " 27 [March] 1935, BA NS2/73; "Richtlinien zur Weltanschauliche Grundschulung der SS," 17 February 1936, BA NS2/277; "Anlage für die Weltanschauliche Schulung," 27 August 1937, StA-L PL506/Bü 10; and "Richtlinien für die Sommerausbildung 1936 der Allgemeinen-SS," 13 Mai 1936, StA-D N1/15, pp. 4–6. Additional guidelines can be found in BA NS2/1, NS2/17, NS2/20, and NS2/74 and StA-L PL506/Bü 16.

6　"SS-Zeitung 'Das schwarze Korps,' " 27 May 1935, BA NS31/354, p. 47, and "Aushängekästen für das 'Schwarze Korps,' " 25 January 1937, BA NSD41/2, p. 8.

7　"Richtlinien für die Ausbildung der Allgemeinen-SS im Winterhalbjahr 1937/38," 27 August 1937, StA-M 327/2b/53. For more on ideology, see André Mineau, *SS thinking and the Holocaust* (Amsterdam: Rodopi, 2012).

8　The SS had officer academies that created their own education plans: BA-MA RS13/1, RS13/11, RS13/31, and RS13/62.

9　Henschel to Schramm, 3 April 1937, StA-L PL506/Bü 77; "Dienstplan für den Schulungslehrgang für Standartenführer und Standartenschulungsleiter vom 12-13 Ernting 1935," [August] 1935, StA-M 327/2a/126; "Schulungskursus für Führer von Einheiten und Schulungsmännern," 28 January 1936, StA-M 327/2a/312; "Schulungskursus für Führer von Einheiten und Schulungsmännern vom 7-10.2.1936 in der Bauernschule in Landau," 5 February 1936, StA-M 327/2a/312; and "Dienstplan des SS-Schulungskurs in Landau vom 7-9.2.1936," StA-M 327/2a/312.

10　"Prüfungsfragen für SS-Führer," LA-D RW0134/42.

11　Descriptions of these reels can be found in BA NS31/165–169.

12　"Rassenkundliches Schulungsmaterial," 5 [September 1935], BA NS2/169, pp. 271–2, and "Bildsmaterial von SS-Familien," [1935], BA NS2/168, pp. 239–40.

13　"Gattenwahl des SS-Mannes," BA NS31/168, pp. 13–55. A second photo set produced by OA West is on pp. 56–69.

14　"Richtlinien zur Weltanschauliche Grundschulung der SS," 17 February 1936, BA NS2/277. By the war, material not produced or approved by the Main Office was not permitted: "Weltanschauliche Schulung in der SS," 9 October 1943, BA NS31/155.

15　"Richtlinien für die Sommerausbildung 1936 der Allgemeinen-SS," 13 Mai 1936, StA-D N1/15.

16　"Dienstanweisung für die Schulungsleiter," 16 [October] 1934, BA NS2/277.

17　Heinrich Himmler, *Die Schutzstaffel als antibolschewistische Kampforganisation* (Munich: Zentralverlag der NSDAP, 1936), and Longerich, *Heinrich Himmler*, 261.

18　Himmler, *Die Schutzstaffel*, 25. The earliest use was probably in a letter to SS officers in December 1934. See "Gründung des Vereins Lebensborn e.V.," 13 September 1936, *IMT* vol. 31, document 2825-PS, p. 177.

19　*Sieg der Waffen – Sieg des Kindes*, BA NSD41/130, p. 31.

20 Ibid. The SS continued to promote this work through its publishing house, Nordland Verlag. "Werbung für das Bildwerk 'Sieg der Waffen – Sieg des Kindes,' " BA NS2/67, p. 95.

21 *SS-Mann und Blutsfrage: Die biologischen Grundlagen und ihre sinngemäße Anwendung für die Erhaltung und Mehrung des nordischen Blutes,* BA NSD41/128.

22 Ibid., 6.

23 *Rassenpolitik,* BA NSD41/122.

24 "Schulungsbrief," 21 [January] 1935, BA-MA N756/433a; "Rede des Reichsführer-SS auf der Ordensburg Sonthofen am 5 Mai 1944," NA T175/92/frame2613495; Heinemann, *Rasse,* 91; and Shalka, *The General-SS,* 296.

25 "Weltanschauliche Schulung," 28 June 1937, StA-M 327/2b/52; "Schulungsstoff," 3 June 1938, BA NS2/277, p. 8; Himmler decree, 1 June 1942, BA NS31/415, p. 1; and "Gedanken zur Gestaltung der SS-Leitheft in Ausführung des Erlasses des Reichsführers-SS vom 1 June 1942," BA NS31/415, pp. 2–6.

26 Caesar, "SS Kamerad an meiner Seiten," 3, no. 4 (August 1937): 39.

27 "SS Mann, du musst wissen," 2, no. 11 (February 1937): 38; Mayerhofer, "Der Sippenorden," 9, no. 2 (February 1943): 13–17.

28 "Aus der Praxis des Sippenamtes: Unklug gefreit, gar selten gedeiht!" 3, no. 4 (August 1937): 31–3; Caesar, "SS Kamerad an meiner Seiten," 38–9.

29 Mayerhofer, "Der Sippenorden," 17.

30 G.d., "Wir geben das Erbe weiter," 8, no. 3 (1942): 17–18. *Das Schwarze Korps* printed the same article on 9 July 1942.

31 "Der Wurf des Schicksals," 7, no. 5a (1941): 9–13. Citing great men from large families was a tactic used prior to the founding of the SS. See Burgdörfer, *Volk ohne Jugend,* 67–8, and Alfred Ploetz, "Rassenhygiene als Grundlage der Friedenspolitik," *Ahnen und Enkel: Beiträge zur Sippenforschung, Heimatkunde, und Erblehre* 3 (March 1936): 29.

32 "Meine Mutter, meine Frau und meine lieben Kinder: Beiträge aus eine Rundfrage der SS-Leithefte," 7, no. 6a (1941): 8–11.

33 This was probably where the poem "Mein Kind" came from in vol. 8, no. 3 (1942) between pages 16 and 17.

34 "An meinen Sohn," 7, no. 6a (1941): 8.

35 "Wiedersehen mit meinem Jungen," 7, no. 6a (1941): 11.

36 "Der letzte Wille eines SS-Mannes," 10, no. 6 (1944): 9.

37 "Das Testament eines SS-Mannes," 8, no. 6 (1942): 12. *Das Schwarze Korps* printed it, too: "Der Vermächtnis der Front," 8 August 1942.

38 "Mein Mann ist nicht tot. Er lebt in meinen Kinder weiter," 9, no. 1–2 (February 1943): 24.

39 "Vier Beispiel aus der Praxis des Sippenamtes," 2, no. 4 (April 1936): 51.

40 "Aus der Praxis des Sippenamtes: Wie erhalte ich as SS-Angehöriger meine Ehestandsarlehen?" 3, no. 1 (May 1937): 41–42; "Aus der Praxis des Sippenamtes: Aus böser Wurzel kommt üble Frucht," 3, no. 2 (June 1937): 60; and "Aus der Praxis des Sippenamtes: Unklug gefreit, gar selten gedeiht!" 3, no. 4 (August 1937): 31–3.

41 For examples, see volumes 7 (1941), 8 (1942), 9 (1943), and 10 (1944).

42 For examples, see volumes 7 (1941) and 9, no. 12 (December 1943).

43 The first image can be found in a series of pictures prior to page 13 of vol. 6, no. 12b (1940), and the second can be found before page 1 of vol. 7, no. 6a (1941).

44 See BA NS31/410 and NS31/411 for limited information on the French and Norwegian editions.

45 The largest set of training reports was in StA-L PL506/Bü 4 and PL506/Bü 10. Caesar also provided an overview during a January 1939 Gruppenführer meeting: "Erfahrung in der Schulung," BA NS19/1669, pp. 154–66. Limited wartime reports can be found in BA-MA RS3–15/20, RS3–17/38, and RS3–17/45.

46 "Schulung des SS-Sturmes 1/5, Koblenz," 30 April 1936, StA-M 327/2a/126; "Schulungs- und Sippentag des Schulungskörpers der 33 SS-Standarte in Darmstadt am 29 u 30.VIII.1936," StA-M 327/2a/126; "Tätigkeitsbericht 3 Vierteljahr 1936," 15 October 1936, StA-M 327/2a/126; "Vierteljahresbericht des Sturmbannschulungsleiter II/35," 15 January 1937, LA-D RS0134/46, p. 25; and "Bericht über die Schulungsabende im SS Sturm 2/Pi3 I Vierteljahr 1938," StA-M 327/2b/113. Other reports can be found in StA-L PL506/Bü 10.

47 "Schulungskontrolle in Hann Münden," 10 January 1938, StA-M 327/2b/214, and "Bericht Hann Münden," [December 1937], StA-M 327/2b/214.

48 "Tätigkeitsbericht des 4 Vierteljahres 1936," 9 January 1936, StA-M 327/2b/129; "Vierteljahresbericht für das 4 Vierteljahr 1936," 7 January 1937, StA-M 327/2a/129; "Tätigkeitsbericht für das 3 Vierteljahr 37," 8 October 1937, StA-M 327/2b/129; and "Schulungskontrolle in Hann Münden," 16 December 1937, StA-M 327/2b/214.

49 "Tätigkeitsbericht des 4 Vierteljahres 1936," 9 January 1937, StA-M 327/2a/129; "Arbeitsbericht 2 Vierteljahr 1936," 4 July 1936, BA NS2/131, p. 40; "Schulungsbericht," 3 October 1936, BA NS2/131, pp. 6–8; "Tätigkeitsbericht 3 Vierteljahr 1936," 15 October 1936, StA-M

327/2a/126; "Schulungskontrolle in Hann Münden," 16 December 1937, StA-M 327/2b/214; "Bericht Hann Münden," [December 1937], StA-M 327/2b/214; "Vierteljahresbericht," 30 August 1938, StA-L PL506/Bü 4; and "Standortschulung," 10 March 1939, BA-MA RS14/15.

50 "Arbeitsbericht 2 Vierteljahr 1936," 4 July 1936, BA NS2/131, p. 40; "Tätigkeitsbericht – Schulungsdienst," [1936], BA NS2/131, p. 80; "Vierteljahresbericht des Sta-SL für das 3 Vierteljahr 1937," 4 October 1937, StA-L PL506/Bü4; "Tätigkeitsbericht auf 5.10," 26 October 1937, StA-L PL506/Bü4; and "Vierteljahresbericht für das 4 Vierteljahr 1936," 7 January 1937, StA-M 327/2a/129.

51 "Schulung der SS Einheits-Schulungsleiter durch das Sippenamt," 19 August 1935, BA NS2/168, p. 206.

52 Heinemann, *Rasse*, 110–11.

53 "Arbeitsbericht 2 Vierteljahr 1936," 4 August 1936, BA NS2/131, p. 40; "Schulungsbericht," 3 October 1936, BA NS2/131, p. 7; "Auszug aus Halbjahresbericht Sommer 1937," 8 February 1938, BA NS2/64; Zeck to RuSHA, 2 February 1938, BA NS2/64, p. 152; and Ebrecht to Himmler, 8 February 1938, BA NS2/64, p. 149.

54 Quoted in Bernd Wegner, *The Waffen SS: Organization, ideology and function*, trans. Ronald Webster (Oxford: Basil Blackwell, 1990), 199.

55 The limits of education is briefly addressed in Sönke Neitzel and Harald Welzer, *Soldaten: On fighting, killing, and dying: The secret World War II transcripts of German POWs*, trans. Jefferson Chase (New York: Alfred A. Knopf, 2012), 312–13.

56 Affidavit of Caesar, document book 1 Hofmann, document no. 6, *US v. Greifelt*, sheets 32–41.

57 Ibid. Emphasis in original.

58 Ibid.

59 "Vierteljahres-Tätigkeitsbericht," 5 October 1937, StA-L PL506/Bü 4.

60 Kaul to Hofmann, 16 September 1941, BA NS2/79, p. 147; Hofmann to Kaul, 19 September 1941, BA NS2/79, pp. 143–4; Rainer to Himmler, [August 1942], BA NS19/3483, page 279; Brandt to Rainer, 20 August 1942, BA NS19/3483, p. 278; and Friedrich Zipfel, *Kirchenkampf in Deutschland 1933–1945: Religionsverfolgung und Selbstbehauptung der Kirchen in der nationalsozialistischen Zeit* (Berlin: Walter de Gruyter and Company, 1965), 108.

61 William John Wilson, "Festivals and the Third Reich," (PhD diss., McMaster University, 1994); Wolfgang Krater, "Feiern und Feste der Nationalsozialisten: Aneignung und Umgestaltung christlicher Kalender, Ritten, und Symbolie (PhD diss., Ludwigs Maximillians-Universität,

1998); and Joe Perry, "Nazifying Christmas: Political culture and popular celebration in the Third Reich," *Central European History* 38, no. 4 (2005): 572–605.

62 OA West Rassereferent to RuSA, 28 [June] 1935, LA-D RW-134/46; "Persönliche Rücksprache mit SS-Untersturmf Richert," 2 April 1937, StA-M 327/2b/114; Darré to Persönlichen Stab RFSS, 17 June 1937, BA NS19/1148, pp. 2–5; "Kosten für die Feiern anlässlich der Aufnahme der Frau in die SS-Sippengemeinschaft bei Verehelichung von SS-Angehörigen," 15 December 1937, StA-M 327/2b/53; "Kosten für die Feiern anlässlich der Aufnahme der Frau in die SS-Sippengemeinschaft bei Verehelichung von SS-Angehörigen," 24 January 1938, StA-M 327/2b/17; and "SS-Oberabschnittsbefehlsblatt Nr 3 Jahrgang 2 vom 15.2.1938. Ziff 11: Kosten für die Feiern anlässlich der Aufnahme der Frau in die SS-Sippengemeinschaft bei Verehelichung von SS-Angehörigen IV," StA-M 327/2b/260.

63 "Geburtsfeiern, Eheschließungen, und Begräbnisse der SS," 18 February 1937, StA-M 327/2b/115; "Eheweihe," StA-M 327/2b/120; "Grundgedanken zur Gestaltung von Ehe und Geburtsfeiern," StA-M 327/2b/114; "Feier der Eheschließung von Angehörigen der Partei und ihrer Gliederungen," BA NS19/1148, pp. 4–5; and "Plan für die Durchführung einer Hochzeitsfeier," BA NS19/1148, p. 6.

64 "Rede des Reichsführers-SS anlässlich der Gruppenführer Besprechung am 8 November 1936 in Dachau," BA NS19/4003, pp. 208–9. Caesar reiterated this view in a directive from 23 April 1940, BA NS31/353, p. 15; it was probably based on a draft by Himmler from 16 April, BA NS2/231, p. 116.

65 "Worte des Reichsführers-SS Himmler bei der Eheweihe des SS-Sturmbannführers D. am 2.IV.1936," BA NS2/291, and "Rede des Reichsführers-SS anlässlich der Hochzeit des SS-Obersturmführer Luitpold Sch. mit Rosamarie W. des 4.III.1937," BA NS19/4004, pp. 189–91.

66 "SS-Namensweihe des Sohnes des SS-Angehörigen Frehoff," 8 June 1936, StA-M 327/2a/131.

67 Rohrbacher to RuSHA leader in OA Südwest, 4 January 1938, StA-L PL506/Bü4.

68 Hofmann to Müller, 12 March 1941, BA NS2/79, p. 236, and Hofmann to Gutenberger, 8 October 1941, BA NS2/79, p. 221.

69 "Stabsbefehl Nr. 9/39," BA NS2/6, p. 12, and Pancke to all Pflegestellen, 20 March 1939, BA NS2/21, p. 85.

70 Jeckeln to Hofmann, 20 January 1941, BA NS2/123, p. 13; Hofmann to Müller, 19 March 1941, BA NS2/79, p. 152; and Hofmann to Jeckeln, 19 March 1941, BA NS2/79, p. 154.

71 SS-Oberabschnitt West, *Die Gestaltung der Feste im Jahres- und Lebenslauf in der SS Familie* (Wuppertal: Völkisher Verlag, [1937–8]), 71.

72 Use of appropriate music was also mentioned in "Plan für die Durchführung einer Hochzeitsfeier," BA NS19/1148, p. 6.

73 Heim Wernigerode to Zentrale Abteilung Heimaufnahme, 16 January 1940, 4.1.0/82464595–96/ITS Digital Archive/Bad Arolsen; Heim Hohehorst to Lebensborn e.V. in Munich, 26 April 1940, 4.1.0/82451126/ITS Digital Archive/Bad Arolsen; "Eheschließungen und Namensgebungen," 6 May 1940, 4.1.0/82453227/ITS Digital Archive/Bad Arolsen; Karl S. to Ebner, [May] 1940, 4.1.0/82453228/ITS Digital Archive/Bad Arolsen; Heim Hohehorst to Ebner, 9 May 1940, 4.1.0/82453229/ITS Digital Archive/ Bad Arolsen; Heim Kurmark to Ebner, 10 May 1940, 4.1.0/82453234–35/ ITS Digital Archive/Bad Arolsen; and Heim Wernigerode to Ebner, 18 May 1940, 4.1.0/82453336/ITS Digital Archive/Bad Arolsen.

74 For examples of speeches, see BA NS48/29.

75 These statistics can be found in BA NS3/431, as well as the following ITS collections: 82449165–77; 82449221–76; 82449284–87; 82449289–347; 82449354–87; and 82464595–96.

76 "Ausschnitt aus dem SS-Befehls-Blatt. Ziff. 31: Betr. Nachweis der Abstammung bei Eheschließung von SS-Angehörigen," 25 March 1938, StA-M 327/2b/120.

77 Ludwig Dotzert, "Erste Eheweihe in Frankfurt a.M.," *Frankfurter Volksblatt* (23 September 1935).

78 "Pressveröffenlichungen über Eheweihen in der SS," 25 October 1935, StA-D N1/7, p. 21.

79 "Eheweihen der SS," 10 June 1936, StA-D N1/35, p. 138.

80 The newspaper had already reported on the festivities the night before the marriage of SS-Gruppenführer Hans Prützmann: "Reichsführer-SS Himmler in Ostpreußen," 5 May 1935.

81 "Konfession der SS-Angehörigen," *Statistisches Jahrbuch 1937*, 79, and "Konfession der SS-Angehörigen," *Statistisches Jahrbuch 1938*, 105.

82 "Statistischer Monatsbericht über das Sippenamt," 6 October 1941, BA NS19/3479, p. 16; "Statistischer Monatsbericht über das Sippenamt," 10 November 1941, BA NS19/3479, p. 22; "Statistischer Monatsbericht über das Sippenamt," 17 December 1941, BA NS19/3479, p. 4; and "Statistischer Monatsbericht über das Sippenamt," 17 February 1942, BA NS19/3482, p. 328.

83 This ceremony fulfilled Hobsbawn's definition of the three types of tradition invented since the Industrial Revolution: See "Introduction: Inventing traditions," in *The invention of tradition*, eds. Eric Hobsbawm and Terence Ranger (Cambridge: Cambridge University Press, 2005), 9.

84 "Sippentag und Schulungslager sämtlicher Sturmschulungsmänner und Schulungsleiter mit Frauen und Bräuten der 33 SS-Standarte in Darmstadt," 18 August 1936, StA-M 327/2b/122; "Sprechabend der SS-Pflegestelle 83," 15 April 1939, StA-M 327/2b/112; "Tätigkeitsberichte," 10 January 1937, StA-L PL506/Bü 4.

85 SS-Befehlsblatt 4 Jahrgang, Nummer 11, 25 November 1936, Nr. 14: Betr: "Kosten für Sippenabend," BA-MA N756/13. *Das Schwarze Korps* reported on a dozen gatherings: "Sippenabend der Sanitäter," 25 March 1937; "Sippenabend der Sanitäter," 1 July 1937; "Erster Sippenabend in Linz," 7 July 1938; "Sommerfest mit unserem FM," 18 August 1938; "Sippenabend," 16 March 1939; "Sanitätsabteilung," 13 April 1939; "Sippenabend," 27 April 1939; "Sippenabend," 4 May 1939; "Sippenabend," 18 May 1939; "Sippenabend," 25 May 1939; "Sippenabend," 8 June 1939; "Sippenabend," 24 August 1939.

86 "Sippenabende des SS-Abschnitts XIV," 13 May 1936, BA NS2/24, pp. 143–4; "Ausbildungsrichtlinien für die Weltanschauliche Schulung," 27 August 1937, StA-M 327/2b/53; and "Feiergestaltung," 21 September 1942, BA NS/2/82, p. 179.

87 "Tätigkeitsbericht 3 Vierteljahr 1936," 15 October 1936, StA-M 327/2a/126; "Sippenabend," *Das Schwarze Korps*, 27 April 1939; and Harm to all OA racial advisers, 3 December 1936, StA-L PL506/Bü 2.

88 "Standortschulung," 10 March 1939, BA-MA, RS14/15, and "Sippenabend des Sturmes, 11 March 1939, BA-MA RS14/15.

89 Kunzmann to Heinz-Schmitz," 11 December 1936, StA-L PL506/Bü 2; Kunzmann to OA Südwest racial adviser, 18 December 1936, StA-L PL506/Bü 2; Kleffel to Ebrecht, 24 January 1938, BA NS2/77, p. 120; RuSHA to Abschnitt XXXIV, 27 January 1938, BA NS2/77, p. 119; and Schulungsamt to Abschnit XXXIV, 1 February 1938, BA NS2/77, p. 118.

90 Brodersen to Schwalm, 3 February 1938, StA-M 327/2b/113, and "Sippenabend des Sturmbann III/2 SS-Standarte am 9 April 1938," StA-M 327/2b/45.

91 "Familiennachrichten für 'Das Schwarze Korps,' " 30 March 1935, BA NS31/354, p. 46, and "Familien-Nachrichten für 'Das Schwarze Korps,' " 15 June 1937, BA NS2/155, p. 4.

92 The Office for Archive and Press Management in RuSHA was established in October 1935, with the press department added in February 1936. "Stabsbefehl Nr 36/35," 12 October 1935, BA NS2/4, p. 141, and "Stabsbefehl Nr 7/36," 3 February 1936, BA NS2/4, p. 138. On the press personnel in the units, see Wittje to OA press advisers, Abschnitte, and Standarten, 11 February 1935, BA NS31/354, p. 37.

93 Rolf d'Alquen to Himmler and RuSHA, 1 August 1936, NA T580/329/
   Ordnung 50.

94 For an example of the latter, see 20 March 1941, p. 12.

95 For example, 26 September 1935, p. 13; 24 October 1935, p. 12; 19
   December 1935, p. 16; 26 December 1935, p. 12; and 5 March 1936, p. 19.

96 Darré (8 September 1938); Pancke (19 November 1936 and 24 August
   1939); and Hildebrandt (16 July 1936).

97 Bach-Zelewski (27 August 1936); Best (3 August 1939); Heißmeyer (19
   March 1936, 7 October 1937, and 12 December 1940); Heydrich (20 April
   1939); Krüger (19 March 1936); Woyrsch (16 July 1936); and Wolff (23
   January 1936 and 30 March 1938).

98 "Vormerkung! Befehl des Reichsführer-SS," 19 January 1937, BA
   NS19/3902, p. 154.

99 "SS-Namensweihe des Sohnes des SS-Angehörigen Frehoff," 8 June 1936,
   StA-M 327/2a/131; Bitsch to OA Rhein race adviser, 15 October 1936,
   StA-M 327/2a/126; "Tätigkeitsbericht über das letzte Vierteljahr 1937,"
   27 December 1937, StA-M 327/2b/113.

100 Wolff to RuSHA chief, [1937], BA NS2/51, p. 176, and "Namensweihen,"
    17 June 1937, StA-Marburg 327/2b/52.

101 Two letters to RuSHA, 8 March 1941, BA NS2/68, pp. 34–5; "Eheweihen
    und Namenskundgebunden," 11 March 1931, BA NS2/68, p. 33; Braun to
    RuSHA, 9 April 1941, BA NS2/45, p. 23; and RuSHA to Braun, 17 April
    1941, BA NS2/25, p. 22.

102 Hofmann to all members of RuSHA, 12 August 1941, BA NS2/21, p. 146;
    letters to individual men from the same time are in BA NS2/36.

103 Letter from Himmler, no date, BA NS2/147, p. 5; letter from RuSHA
    chief, no date, BA NS2/147, pp. 6–7; "Entwurf für eine Veröffentlichung
    im Schwarzen Korps," BA NS2/167, pp. 8–9; and Brandt to Korherr, 3
    April 1942, BA NS48/6.

104 "Eine Wanderwiege der SS," *Münchener Neueste Nachrichten*, 4 February
    1938. *Das Schwarze Korps* ran two articles: "Ein Schöner Brauch," 19 May
    1938, and "Späteren Generationen zum Gedächtnis," 16 June 1938.

105 SS-Oberabschnitt West, *Die Gestaltung*, 66–8.

106 Hans-Jürgen Lange, *Weisthor: Karl Maria Wiligut: Himmlers Rasputin und
    seine Erben* (Engerda: Arun, 1998), 47, 53, and 62; Michael Moynihan,
    ed., *The secret king: Karl Maria Wiligut, Himmler's lord of the runes*, trans.
    Stephen Flowers (Waterbury, VT: Dominion Press, 2001), 21; and Lang,
    Top Nazi, 37.

107 Lang, *Top Nazi*, 38–9; Lange, *Weisthor*, 192–3; and Moynihan, *The secret
    king*, 122–4.

108   Lang, *Top Nazi*, 39.
109   There are limited statistics for Lebensborn ceremonies; see note 75 for the
      relevant ITS collections.
110   Ebner to Westermann, 14 October 1941, 4.1.0/82453300/ITS Digital
      Archive/Bad Arolsen, and Sollmann to Ebner and all home leaders, 9
      July 1940, 4.1.0/82453269 ITS Digital Archive/Bad Arolsen.
111   Ebner to Ebrecht, 12 May 1938, BA NS2/65, p. 149; letter from Heim
      Steinhöring, 26 October 1938, 4.1.0/82453187/ITS Digital Archive/
      Bad Arolsen; letter from Heim Polzin, 7 June 1939, 4.1.0/82453203/
      ITS Digital Archive/Bad Arolsen; letter from Heim Hohehorst, 21 June
      1939, 4.1.0/82453208/ITS Digital Archive/Bad Arolsen; letter from Heim
      Wienerwald, 11 August 1939, 4.1.0/82453209/ITS Digital Archive/Bad
      Arolsen; letter from Heim Hohehorst, 15 August 1939, 4.1.0/82453212/
      ITS Digital Archive/Bad Arolsen; letter from Heim Steinhöring, 24
      August 1939, 4.1.0/82453213/ITS Digital Archive/Bad Arolsen; and
      Heim Harz to Ebner, 11 February 1941, 4.1.0/82453283/ITS Digital
      Archive/Bad Arolsen.
112   Volker Koop, *"Dem Führer ein Kind schenken": Die SS-Organisation
      Lebensborn e.V.* (Cologne: Böhlau Verlag, 2007), 126.
113   Ebner to Hannseugen M., 5 September 1938, 4.1.0/82453172/ITS Digital
      Archive/Bad Arolsen.
114   "Programm einer Namensgebung," 11 October 1938, 4.1.0/82453161–64/
      ITS Digital Archive/Bad Arolsen; "Namensgebungen," 22 March
      1939, 4.1.0/82453197–98/ITS Digital Archive/Bad Arolsen; "Über
      Namenswahl," 4.1.0/82453132–38/ITS Digital Archive/Bad Arolsen;
      and "Ansprache zur Namensweihe am 6 Dezember 1940 in Heim
      Steinhöring," 4.1.0/92453278–82/ITS Digital Archive/Bad Arolsen.
115   SS-Oberabschnitt West, *Die Gestaltung*, 42 and 68–70.
116   Berger to Hofmann, 16 July 1942, BA NS2/70, pp. 96–7 and Berger to
      Hofmann, 15 July 1942, BA NS2/70, p. 98.
117   Der Reichsführer-SS and der Chef des SS-Hauptamtes, *Die Feier: Schrift
      für Lebensführung und Feiergestaltung in der SS* (Berlin: SS-Hauptamt,
      1943), BA NSD41/110.
118   Der Schriftleiter der *SS-Leithefte*, "An meine Kameraden!" 8, no. 3 (1942):
      38.
119   Information on assistance provided by Standarte 33 can be found at StA-
      D: N1/5, N1/14, N1/18, N1/26, N1/41, N1/44, N1/45, and N1/48.
120   "Grundgesetz über die Vereidigung der SS-Obergruppen- und
      Gruppenführer als Hüter des Blutes- und Lebensgesetzes der
      Schutzstaffel," BA NS19/3902, p. 125. Interestingly, *Das Schwarze Korps*

had promoted this responsibility nearly a year earlier. See "Die innere Sicherung des Reichs," 21 November 1935.

121 "Grundgesetz über die Vereidigung," 126.

122 Himmler mentioned this requirement in two speeches: "Rede des Reichsführers-SS anlässlich der Gruppenführer Besprechung in Tölz am 18.II.1937," BA NS19/4004, p. 97, and "Eine Rede des Reichsführers-SS Himmler anläßlich der Gruppenführerbesprechung am 8 November 1937 im Führerheim der SS-Standarte 'Deutschland' in München," BA NS19/4004, pp. 349–51.

123 Ernst Robert Grawitz's file has a copy of the oath: BDC SSO 030, p. 123.

124 "Kirchliche Beisetzungen," 22 September 1936, LA-D RW0134/36, p. 53. For wartime church burials, see Hartl to the SS-Hauptamt, 14 December 1940, BA NS33/76, p. 18, and Berger to the SS-Führungshauptamt, 17 March 1941, BA NS33/76, p. 28.

125 SS-Oberabschnitt West, *Die Gestaltung*, 74.

126 Gerwarth, *Hitler's hangman*, 1–13 and 279–80. Information on funeral planning can be found in BA NS19/3454, NS19/4009, and Heydrich's BDC file SSO 095A.

127 Reference to the Main Office guidelines can be found in "SS-Ehrenbegräbnis," 31 October 1942, BA NS33/365, and "Unterstützung des SS-Totenfeieren durch die Hoheitsträger," 17 January 1944, LA-D RW0134/21, p. 168.

128 Hofmann to all higher SS and police leaders, in-house offices, and Hauptfürsorge und versorgungsamt, 2 February 1942, BA NS2/22, pp. 3–4.

129 "Feierliche, SS-mäßige Gestaltung der Beerdigung von gefallen und verstorbenen SS-Angehörigen," 10 October 1942, BA NS33/77, p. 5; "Gräberfürsorge," 10 September 1942, BA-MA RS14/39; "Unkostendeckung für SS-Begräbnisse," 18 September 1943, LA-D RW0134/13, p. 11.

130 "Feierliche SS-mäßige Gestaltung der Beerdigung von gefallen und gestorbenen SS-Angehörigen," 31 August 1942, LA-D RW0134/22, and "Feierliche SS-mäßige Gestaltung der Beerdigung von gefallen und gestorbenen SS-Angehörigen," 16 October 1942, 4.1.0/92448383/ITS Digital Archive/Bad Arolsen.

131 Darré's mother (30 July 1936); Himmler's father (5 November 1936); Heydrich's father (1 September 1938); and Kaltenbrunner's father (15 September 1938).

132 "Einsetzung von Todesanzeigen in das 'Schwarze Korps,' " 30 May 1940, BA NS33/77, p. 21.

133   "Todesanzeigen und Nachrufe für verstorbenen SS-Angehörige,"
       15 January 1937, BA NS33/77, p. 84, and "Todesanzeigen für
       SS-Angehörige," 12 September 1940, BA NS33/228, p. 8.
134   "Beerdigung des SS-Unterscharführer Walter M.," 27 October 1943,
       BA-MA RS14/41; Stiehl to Brüggen and Hintzen, 4 November 1943,
       LA-D RW0134/12, p. 37, and "Totengedenktag," 2 November 1943, LA-D
       RW0134/12, p. 39; and "Aktenvermerk zur Beinahme für die Handakte
       Nr. 27," [April 1944], BA-MA RS14/25.
135   "Grundgesetz," BA NS19/3902, p. 180.
136   Untitled RFSS order, 16 September 1939, BA NS34/21.
137   This centre worked with the Information Center for the War Losses
       for the Waffen-SS, which was founded in early 1940 and based in the
       SS Main Welfare and Supply Office. Both were transferred to RuSHA
       in early 1942. Untitled RFSS order, 2 January 1942, BA-MA RS5/1048;
       "Die Auskunfstelle für Kriegesverluste der Waffen-SS. Eine Beitrag zum
       Melde und Auskunftswesen der Waffen-SS von Wolfgang Vopersal,"
       BA-MA N756/308b; and Rüdiger Overmans, *Deutsche militärische
       Verluste im Zweiten Weltkrieg* (Munich: R. Oldenbourg, 1999), 43–9.
138   Waldeck to Hennicke, 19 October 1940, StA-M 327/2b/29, and
       "Betreuung Hinterbliebener gefallener SS-Angehöriger zum Julfest
       1942," 12 February 1943, LA-D RW0134/22, p. 189.
139   "Chefsbefehl Nr. 19," 30 June 1943, BA NS3/1080, p. 167.
140   "Ausführungsbestimmungen zum Befehl des Reichsführers-SS," 19 June
       1940, BA NS19/3901, p. 111.
141   "Ausbildungs- und Berufsförderung für Kinder gefallener SS-Männer,"
       19 June 1943, NA T175/152/frame 2681592; "Richtlinien zur
       Durchführung der Ausbildungs- und Berufsförderung für Kinder
       gefallener SS-Männer," 30 July 1943, NA T175/190/frames 2727660–
       2727661; Hildebrantdt to all OA and Abschnitt XXXIX, 17 November
       1943, BA-MA RS14/55; Hildebrandt to all Main Offices, OA, and
       Abschnitt XXXIX, 4 December 1943, BA-MA RS14/16; and Heiber,
       Reichsführer!, letter 145.
142   "Aktenvermerk," 23 July 1942, 4.1.0/82451378/ITS Digital Archive/Bad
       Arolsen. Himmler addressed the need for Lebensborn involvement in a
       letter to Pflaum, 9 September 1939, NA T175/76/frame 2594391.
143   OA Fulda-Werra also attempted to procure homes for widows and
       orphans: "Freiplätze für Hinterbliebene gefallener SS-Kameraden," 29
       May 1941, StA-M 327/2b/57, and Waldeck to SS-Führungshauptamt,
       Verwaltungsamt-SS, 30 June 1941, StA-M 327/2b/30.

144 "Freiplätze für Frauen, deren Kindesväter gefallen sind," 4.1.0/82448808/ITS Digital Archive/Bad Arolsen.

145 "Sonderanordnung!" 7 November 1939, 4.1.0/82448597–98/ITS Digital Archive/Bad Arolsen.

146 Undated Rundschreiben, 4.1.0/82452982/ITS Digital Archive/Bad Arolsen, and letter from Sollmann, 10 July 1944, BA NS34/8.

147 "Aktenvermerk," 23 July 1942, and in-house letter to Ebner, 30 October 1939, 4.1.0/82457919/ITS Digital Archive/Bad Arolsen.

148 Reichsstatthalter in Hessen, Landesregierung, Abteilung III to the Landräte, and Oberbürgermeister (Jugendämter), 31 December 1940, StA-D, R1B/6408.

149 "Aktenvermerk," 23 July 1942, and Lebensborn Amt für Vormundschaften to Ebner, 30 October 1939, 4.1.0/82457919/ITS Digital Archive/Bad Arolsen.

150 "Bestellung des Lebensborn e.V. als Beistand für die ehelichen Kinder und Übernahme der Vormundschaft für die unehelichen Kinder gefallener SS-Kameraden," 27 October 1939, 4.1.0/82448314/ITS Digital Archive/Bad Arolsen, and "Merkblatt Nr. 3," April 1944, StA-D R1B/3966.

151 Sollmann to Wolff, 19 February 1943, IfZ MA304/frames 2590241–2590242; Wolff to Sollmann, 31 January 1943, IfZ MA304/frame 2590243; Himmler to all Hauptamtchef, 13 January 1943, IfZ MA304/frame 2590244; "Erziehung elternloser Kinder," 5 January 1943, IfZ MA304/frame 2590245; Himmler to Lammers, 5 January 1943, IfZ MA304/frame 2590254; Lammers to the Reich Ministry of the Interior, 5 January 1943, BA NS19/3606, p. 21; Brandt to Sollmann, 13 March 1943, BA NS19/3606, p. 3; and Ragaller to Brandt, 19 March 1943, BA NS19/3606, p. 1.

152 "Rundschreiben Nr. 32," 4 February 1943, 4.1.0/82453024/ITS Digital Archive/Bad Arolsen.

153 Ziesmer to Ebner, 19 November 1943, 4.1.0/82448814–15/ITS Digital Archive/Bad Arolsen.

154 *US v. Greifelt*, 4303.

155 Ibid., 4447 and 4495.

156 Himmler to OA leaders, 7 December 1939, StA-M 327/2b/55.

157 Examples of letters can be found in BA-MA RS14/34, RS14/39, and RS14/41.

158 "Betreuung von Hinterbliebenen gefallener SS-Angehöriger," 3 January 1942, StA-M 327/2b/508, and "SS-Fürsorge- und

Versorgungsbefehlsblatt des SS-Oberabschnitts Fulda-Werra," 1, no. 3–5, April-June 1942, StA-M 327/2b/88.

159 Copies of this letter are in StA-M 327/2b/492.

160 "Verluste der SS in Kriege – Erstellung von Verlustmeldungen," 11 March 1941, StA-M 327/2b/57.

161 "Verlustmeldung," 16 August 1941. All documents for this case come from StA-M 327/2b/87.

162 Schmidt to Erna B., 25 August 1941.

163 Schmidt to OA Fulda-Werra, 26 July 1941.

164 Hennicke to SS-Fürsorgeführer Fulda-Werra, 26 August 1941; Henning to SS-Sturm 57, 14 October 1941; and Führungsstab 1/57 SS-Standarte to Schulz, 3 December 1941.

165 Lebensborn Hauptabteilung A to SS-Sturmbann I/57, 18 August 1941; Schmidt to Schulz, 23 September 1941; Schulz to Schmidt, 28 September 1941; and Schmidt to Lebensborn, 6 October 1941.

166 Schulz to Schmidt, 4 November 1941, and Erbe to Abschnitt XXVII, 30 December 1941.

167 Ragaller to K. Schmidt, 14 January 1942; Erbe to Schulz, 26 January 1942; Erbe to Ozimek, 10 February 1942; letter to Schmidt, 31 May 1943; and Schmidt to Reitz, 4 June 1943.

168 "Betreuungsbericht für das I Vierteljahr 1942"; "Ergänzungsbericht zur Verlustmeldung vom [no date]"; "Betreuungsbericht für das Vierteljahr 1943"; "Bericht," June 1943; and "Pflegebericht," [June 1943].

169 Untitled report by Schmidt, 4 October 1939. Unless otherwise specified, all documents for this case come from StA-M 327/2b/87.

170 Schmidt to Lebensborn, 5 December 1939, and Lebensborn to Schmidt, 12 December 1939.

171 Lebensborn to Schmidt, 6 February 1940; Lebensborn to Schmidt, 19 February 1940; and Landrat des Kreises Hildburghausen, Jugendamt to Sturm 1/57, 30 April 1940.

172 Schmidt to Milz, 15 April 1940; Schmidt to Lebensborn, 17 May 1940; Schmidt to Lebensborn, 25 July 1940; Lebensborn to Schmidt, 3 August 1940; and Schmidt to Standarte 1/57, 14 August 1940.

173 Wehrmachtfürsorge und Versorgungsamt Erfurt to Lebensborn, 11 May 1940.

174 Schmidt to Lebensborn, 28 May 1940, and "Eidesstattliche Erklärung," 28 May 1940.

175 Gutjahr to Rolf M., 25 June 1940; Wolf to Meta M., 14 October 1940; Meta M. to Wehrmachtfürsorge und Versorgungsamt Erfurt, 16 October 1940;

Schmidt to Lebensborn, 28 October 1940; and Schmidt to Abschnitt XXVII, 20 November 1940.

176 Declaration from Meta M.; Schmidt to Hildburghausen and Milz Standesbeamten, Lebensborn, and Standarte 1/57, 27 February 1940; Lebensborn to Schmidt, 7 August 1940; Schmidt to Lebensborn, 13 August 1940; and Schmidt to Abschnitt XXVII, 11 September 1941.

177 "Hinterbliebenenversorgung für Bräute von gefallenen oder im Felde verstorbenen Angehörigen der Waffen-SS," 13 March 1942, BA-MA RS14/143.

178 Gnüg to Schmidt, 2 November 1942, and Meta M. to the Reich minister of the interior, 7 November 1942.

179 Hofmann to Schmidt, 20 January 1943.

180 State secretary and leader of the Thuringian Ministry of the Interior to the Reich minister of the interior, 30 April 1943, BDC RS B0218.

181 Reich minister of the interior to the state secretary and leader of the Thuringian Ministry of the Interior and RuSHA, 14 July 1943, BDC RS B0218. A quarterly report filed by Schmidt on 13 January 1944 listed the date of marriage as 31 July 1942.

182 "Personalangaben," 18 January 1944. All documents for this case come from StA-M 327/2b/88.

183 Abraham to Berta H., 3 November 1943.

184 Lebensborn to Schmidt, 21 January 1944, and Kirchner to Schmidt, 6 March 1944.

185 "Betreuungsbericht für das I Vierteljahr 1944"; Schmidt to Abschnitt XXVII, 10 May 1944; Schmidt to Abschnitt XXVI, 14 June 1944; Abschnitt XXVII to SS-Sturm 1/57, 13 July 1944; and Schmidt to Sturm 1/57, 4 September 1944.

186 Lebensborn to Schmidt, 21 January 1944; Lebensborn to Sturm I/57, 28 March 1944; Lebensborn to Schmidt, 2 May 1944; and note by Schmidt, 8 June 1944, on back of letter from Reise to Sturm 1/57 Führer, 15 May 1944.

187 "Unterbringung bombengeschädigter Familien von SS-Führern und SS-Männern," 21 October 1943, LA-D RW0134/16.

188 "Aufnahme eines Kindes aus einer bombengeschädigen Familie," 31 July 1943, LA-D RW0134/22, p. 126; "Verwundeten-Hinterbliebenen-Betreuung," 29 April 1943, LA-D RW0134/22, p. 170; "Unterbringung bombenschädigter Familien von SS-Führern und SS-Männern," 23 November 1943, BA-MA RS14/55; Gerhard B. to SS-Standortführung Dachau, 29 November 1943, BA-MA RS14/55; "Freiplätze für 2 Jungen

im Alter von 10-14 Jahren," 9 February 1944, LA-D RW0134/22, p. 73; "Aufnahme eines 11-12 jahrigen Mädchens aus bombengeschädigten Gebiet," 18 February 1944, LA-D RW0134/15, p. 69; and "Aufnahme eines Kindes eines bombengeschädigten SS-Führers," 27 July 1944, LA-D RW0134/14, p. 31.

189 "Dank ist nicht nötig," 18 January 1940; "Wir danken," 25 January 1940; "Wir danken," 15 February 1940; "Jeder hilft mit," 11 April 1940; "Drei neue Dankrezepte," 8 August 1940; "Drei Männer – drei Jungen," 31 October 1940; and "Eine bessondere Patenschaft," 1 April 1943.

190 "Weit vom Schuß," 6 November 1941; "Leben, dem Leben geopfert," 11 December 1941; "Echo aus der Heimat," 2 July 1942; "Die Materialisten," 6 April 1944; "Vom Widersinn," 6 April 1944; and "Lieber kleine Renate!" 22 June 1944.

191 All documents come from BA NS7/229: "Entziehung der fürsorgerischen Betreunng für die Hinterbliebenen von verstorbenen SS-Angehörigen," 17 April 1941, pp. 10–11; Hofmann to Himmler, 4 April 1942, pp. 12–13; Brandt to Scharfe, 23 March 1942, p. 14; "Erläuterungen," date unknown, pp. 17–20; Hildebrandt to Himmler, 17 June 1943, pp. 6–9; Reinecke to Bender, 2 July 1943, pp. 1–4; "Schiedverfahren zur Entziehung der Fürsorge und Förderung von Hinterbliebenen gefallener oder verstorbenener SS-Angehöriger," 8 March 1944, pp. 21–2; and Wolfson, "Constraint and choice," 557.

6 Assessing SS Population Politics and the Family Community

1 Thompson, "*Lebensborn* and eugenics," 76–7. In a more general use, Kershaw discusses the relevance of bourgeois political culture to the Führer. See *The "Hitler myth": Image and reality in the Third Reich* (Oxford: Oxford University Press, 2001), 4, 10, 254–7, and 262. Carolyn Kay examines bourgeois family ideals in turn-of-the-century Germany: "How should we raise our son Benjamin? Advice literature for mothers in early twentieth-century Germany," in *Raising citizens in the "century of the child": The United States and German Central Europe in comparative perspective*, ed. Dirk Schumann (New York: Berghahn Books, 2010).

2 See Oskar H., BDC SSO 102A, pp. 14–15; August Sch., BDC SSO 124B, p. 872; and Otto T., BDC SSO 190B, pp. 128–9.

3 On trends in biographies and in relation to their use in the study of Nazis, see Volker Berghahn and Simone Lässig, eds., *Biography between structure and agency: Central European lives in international historiography* (New York: Berghahn Books, 2008); Kenneth Silverman, "Biography

and pseudobiography," *Common-place* 3, no. 2 (January 2003); Jill Lepore,
"Historians who love too much: Reflections on microhistory and biography,"
The Journal of American History 88, no. 1 (June 2001): 129–44; and Ulrich Schlie,
"Today's view of the Third Reich and the Second World War in German
historiographical discourse," *The Historical Journal* 43, no. 2 (June 2000): 543–64.

4 Ulf Schmidt, *Karl Brandt: The Nazi doctor, medicine, and power in the Third
   Reich* (London: Hambeldon Continuum, 2007), 92.
5 Ibid., 354 and 357.
6 Quoted in Black, *Ernst Kaltenbrunner*, 272 and 276.
7 On the use of the autobiography, see Jeremy Popkin, "Historians on the
   autobiographical frontier," *The American Historical Review* 104, no. 3 (June
   1999): 725–48.
8 See Reinhard Doerries, *Hitler's last chief of foreign intelligence: Allied
   interrogations of Walter Schellenberg* (London: F. Cass, 2003), and Gitta
   Sereny, *Into that darkness: An examination of conscience* (New York: Vintage
   Books, 1983).
9 Moczarski, *Conversations with an executioner*, ed. Mariana Fitzpatrick
   (Engelwood Cliffs, NJ: Prentice Hall, 1981), 22.
10 Ibid., 31, 55, 60, 73–4.
11 Ibid., 74.
12 On the reliability of SS witnesses, see Ruth Bettina Birn, "Criminals
   as manipulative witnesses: A case study of SS General von dem Bach-
   Zelewski," *Journal of International Criminal Justice* 9 (2011): 441–74.
13 *US v. Greifelt*, 4016.
14 Ibid., 4017.
15 Ibid., 4063.
16 Tilmann Moser, *Dabei war ich doch sein liebstes Kind: Eine Psychotherapie
   mit der Tochter eines SS-Mannes* (Munich: Kössel, 1997), and Gitta Sereny,
   "Children of the Reich," in *Living in Nazi Germany*, ed. Elaine Halleck (San
   Diego, CA: Greenhaven Press, 2004).
17 Heidenreich, *Das endlose Jahr: Die langsame Entdeckung der eigenen
   Biographie – ein Lebensbornschicksal* (Bern: Scherz Verlag, 2002).
18 Dagmar's story is retold in Gerald Posner, *Hitler's children: Sons and
   daughters of the leaders of the Third Reich talk about their fathers and themselves*
   (New York: Random House, 1991), 203–6 and 211–12.
19 Gudrun's interview is in Lebert and Lebert, *My father's keeper*, 154 and 193.
20 Ibid., 106.
21 Katrin Himmler, *The Himmler brothers*.
22 Irmgard Powell, *Don't let them see you cry: Overcoming a Nazi childhood*
   (Wilmington, OH: Orange Frazer Press, 2008), 22.

23 Ibid., 172.
24 That procreation is dependent on a variety of factors was well established by the 1930s; see Frank Notestein and Clyde Kiser, "Factors affecting variations in human fertility," *Social Forces* 14, no. 1 (October 1935): 34; Rudolf Heberle, "Social factors in birth control," *American Sociological Review* 6, no. 6 (December 1941): 794; and P.K. Whelpton and Clyde Kiser, "Trends, determinants, and control in human fertility," *Annals of the American Academy of Political and Social Science* 237 (January 1945): 118 and 121.
25 See William Beveridge, "The fall of fertility among European races," *Economica* no. 13 (March 1925): 10–27; Madison Grant, *The passing of the great race or the racial basis of European history* (New York: Charles Scribner's Sons, 1921); R.R. Kuczynski, "The decrease of fertility," *Economica* 2, no. 6 (May 1935): 128–41; Leo J. Martin, "Population policies under National Socialism," *The American Catholic Sociological Review* 6, no. 2 (June 1945): 67–82; George Frederick McCleary, "Pre-war European population policies," *The Milbank Memorial Fund Quarterly* 19, no. 2 (April 1941): 105–20; Henry Shryock, "Trends in age-specific fertility rates," *The Milbank Memorial Fund Quarterly* 17, no. 3 (July 1939): 294–307; Alexander Stevenson, "Some aspects of fertility and population growth in Vienna," *American Sociological Review* 7, no. 4 (August 1942): 479–88; Taeuber and Taeuber, "German fertility trends," 150–67; and Sanford Winston, "The relation of certain social factors to fertility," *The American Journal of Sociology* 35, no. 5 (March 1930): 753–64.
26 Maria Sophia Quine, *Population politics in twentieth-century Europe: Fascist dictatorships and liberal democracies* (London: Routledge, 1996), 18 and 53.
27 John Keegan, *The First World War* (New York: Alfred A. Knopf, 1999), 422–3.
28 Quine, *Population politics*, 79–80, and Kristen Stromberg Childers, *Fathers, families, and the state in France, 1914–1945* (Ithaca, NY: Cornell University Press, 2003), 36–8, 82–3, 93–4, and 109. See also *French Historical Studies* 19, no. 3 (Spring 1996) for its forum "Population and the State in the Third Republic."
29 Aaron Gillette, *Racial theories in Fascist Italy* (London: Routledge, 2002), 41–2; Carl Ipsen, "The organization of demographic totalitarianism: Early population policy in Fascist Italy," *Social Science History* 17, no. 1 (Spring 1993): 72–99; Ispen, *Dictating demography: The problem of population in Fascist Italy* (Cambridge: Cambridge University Press, 1996), 215; and Perry Wilson, *Women in twentieth-century Italy* (New York: Palgrave Macmillan, 2010), 65.
30 See John Knodel, *The decline of fertility in Germany, 1871–1939* (Princeton, NJ: Princeton University Press, 1974).

31 On the *Sonderweg* thesis, see Hans-Ulrich Wehler, *The German Empire 1871–1918*, trans. Kim Traynor (New York: Berg Publishers, 1985); David Blackbourn and Geoff Ely, *The peculiarities of German history: Bourgeois society and politics in nineteenth-century Germany* (Oxford: Oxford University Press, 1984); V.R. Berghahn, *Imperial Germany 1871–1918: Economy, society, culture, and politics* (New York: Berghahn Books, 2005); Reinhard Rurup, ed., *The problem of revolution in Germany, 1789–1989* (Oxford: Berg, 2000); and George Steinmetz, "German exceptionalism and the origins of Nazism: The career of a concept," in *Stalinism and Nazism: Dictatorships in comparison*, eds. Ian Kershaw and Moshe Lewin (Cambridge: Cambridge University Press, 1997).

32 "Die Familien und Haushaltungen nach den Ergebnissen der Volks- und Berufszählung 1933," *Statistik des Deutschen Reiches* 452, no. 1, BA R3012/RD75/1–452, p. 9; "Die Familien und Haushaltungen nach den Ergebnissen der Volks- und Berufszählung 1933," *Statistik des Deutschen Reiches* 452, no. 3, BA R3012/RD75/1–452, p. 8; and *Germany speaks, by 21 leading members of party and state* (London: T. Butterworth Limited, 1938), 38.

33 Baur-Fischer-Lenz, *Menschliche Erblichkeitslehre und Rassenhygiene*, 2: 85, and Otmar von Verschuer, *Leitfaden der Rassenhygiene* (Leipzig: Georg Thieme Verlag, 1943), 112.

34 "Richtlinien für die politischen Gemeinschaftsstunden der SS 1942-43," BA NS2/70, pp. 36–46.

35 As Robert Gellately notes, "A racist regime inevitably devotes an enormous amount of its resources to regulating sex." See "Social outsiders and the consolidation of Hitler's dictatorship, 1933–1939," in *Nazism, war, and genocide: Essays in honour of Jeremy Noakes*, ed. Neil Gregor (Exeter, UK: University of Exeter Press, 2005), 70.

36 Werner Angress and Bradley Smith, "Diaries of Heinrich Himmler's early years," *Journal of Modern History* 31, no. 3 (September 1959): 218.

37 Quoted in Ibid., 219.

38 Klaus Theweleit, *Male fantasies*, trans. Steven Conway (Minneapolis: University of Minnesota Press, 1987), 1: 95, 99, 108, 125–6, and 134.

39 "Eine Rede des Reichsführers-SS," *Die Lage: Zentralinformationsdienst der Reichspropagandaleitung der NSDAP und des Reichsministerium für Volksaufklärung und Propaganda*, BA NSD12/35, p. 8.

40 Kersten, *Memoirs*, 178.

41 Ibid., 179–80.

42 There is also the related issue of social mobility: Jerzy Berent, "Fertility and social mobility," *Population Studies* 5, no. 3 (March 1952): 244–60; Charles Westoff, "The changing focus of differential fertility research:

The social mobility hypothesis," *The Milbank Memorial Fund Quarterly* 31, no. 1 (January 1953): 24–38; E. Digby Baltzell, "Social mobility and fertility within an elite group," *The Milbank Memorial Fund Quarterly* 31, no. 4 (October 1953): 411–20; Keith Hope, "Social mobility and fertility," *American Sociological Review* 36, no. 6 (December 1971): 1019–32; and John Kasarda and John O.G. Billy, "Social mobility and fertility," *Annual Review of Sociology* 11 (1985): 305–28.

43 Wolfgang Knorr, "Der Kinderreichtum um Handarbeiterstand," *Volk und Rasse*, no. 5 (May 1937): 193, and Erhard Hense, "Nicht Korn allein, Menschen sollen wachsen," *N.S. Landpost*, no. 4 (27 January 1939).

44 "The fertility of the professional classes," *The British Medical Journal* 2, no. 3122 (30 October 1920): 672–3; William Ogburn and Clark Tibbitts, "Birth rates and social classes," *Social Forces* 8, no. 1 (September 1929): 1–10; Edgar Sydenstricker and Frank Notestein, "Differential fertility according to social class: A study of 69,620 native white married women under 45 years of age based upon the United States census returns of 1910," *Journal of the American Statistical Association* 25, no. 169 (March 1930): 9–32; Frank Hankins, "Is the differential fertility of the social classes selective?" *Social Forces* 12, no. 1 (October 1933): 33–9; Edgar Sydenstricker and G. St. J. Perrott, "Sickness, unemployment, and differential fertility," *The Milbank Memorial Fund Quarterly* 12, no. 2 (April 1934): 126–33; Raymond Pearl, "Biological factors in fertility," *Annals of the American Academy of Political and Social Science* 188 (November 1936): 14–25; Frank Notestein, "Class differences in fertility," *Annals of the American Academy of Political and Social Science* 188 (November 1936): 26–36; John Flanagan, "A study of psychological factors related to fertility," *Proceedings of the American Philosophical Society* 80, no. 4 (15 February 1939): 513–23; Clyde V. Kiser, "Birth rates and socio-economic attributes in 1935," *The Milbank Memorial Fund Quarterly* 17, no. 2 (April 1939): 128–51; and John Kanter and Robert Potter Jr., "Social and psychological factors affecting fertility. XXIV. The relationship of family size in two successive generations," *The Milbank Memorial Fund Quarterly* 32, no. 3 (July 1954): 294–311.

45 Michael Kater, *The Nazi Party: A social profile of members and leaders, 1919–1945* (Cambridge, MA: Harvard University Press, 1983), 236.

46 *IMT*, vol. 20, 283–5.

47 Wolfson, "The SS leadership," 152; Boehnert, "An analysis of the age and education of the SS Führerkorps 1925–1939," *Historical Social Research* 12 (October 1979), 4 and 12–13; and Ziegler, *Nazi Germany's new aristocracy*, 115.

48 Schellenberg, *Hitler's secret service*, 21.

49 *Trials of war criminals before the Nuernberg Military Tribunals under Control Council Law No. 10*, vol. 2, case 1: US v. Brandt (Washington, DC: US Government Printing Office, 1946–49), 155.

50 Ulrich Herbert, *Best: Biographische Studien über Radikalismus, Weltanschauung, und Vernunft, 1903–1989* (Bonn: J.H.W. Dietz, 2001), 119.

51 *Statistisches Jahrbuch, 1937,* 68–74, and *Statistisches Jahrbuch, 1938,* 109–13. SS demographics also vastly differed from the SA; see Conan Fischer, "The occupational background of the SA's rank-and-file membership during the Depression years, 1929 to mid-1934," in *The shaping of the Nazi state,* ed. Peter Stachura (London: Croom Helm, 1978), 138–9 and 151–2, and "The SA of the NSDAP: Social background and ideology of the rank and file in the early 1930s," *Journal of Contemporary History* 17, no. 4 (October 1982): 654 and 657; Bessel, *Political violence,* 34, 41, and 44; and Campbell, *The SA generals,* 8–9 and 39.

52 "Heiratsalter und Beruf," *Preußische Zeitung,* 4 September 1937.

53 Medical literature confirms the relationship between age and the ability to procreate. For contemporary literature, see Colin Clark, "Age at marriage and marital fertility," *Population Studies* 2, no. 4 (March 1949): 417; Paul Mundy, "Fertility Variations with Education," *The American Catholic Sociological Review* 7, no. 2 (June 1946): 110–11; Pearl, "Biological factors," 22; Shryock, "Trends in age-specific fertility rates," 296, 300, and 302; and Stevenson, "Some aspects of fertility," 483–4. For more recent literature, see Jonathan Berek, ed., *Berek and Novak's gynecology* (Philadelphia: Lippincott and Williams, 2007), 1203 and 1206; Elise de la Rochebrochard and Patrick Thonneau, "Paternal age ≥ 40 years: An important risk factor for infertility," *American Journal of Obstetrics and Gynecology* 189, no. 4 (October 2003): 901–4; Cecilia Schmidt-Sarosi, "Infertility in the older woman," *Clinical Obstetrics and Gynecology* 41, no. 4 (December 1998): 940–50; and Hamish Wallace and Tom Kelsey, "Human ovarian reserve from conception to the menopause," *PLOS One* 5, no. 1 (January 2010): 1–9.

54 See chapter 3 n81 for Statistischer Monatsbericht citations.

55 Dudley Kirk, "The relation of employment levels to births in Germany," *The Milbank Memorial Fund Quarterly* 20, no. 2 (April 1942): 128 and 135. The relationship between fluctuations in the business cycle and marriage and children was already recognized; for example, see William Ogburn and Dorothy Thomas, "The influence of the business cycle on certain social conditions," *Journal of the American Statistical Association* 18, no. 139 (September 1922): 324–40.

56 Thomas Balogh, "The national economy of Germany," *The Economic Journal* 49, no. 191 (September 1938): 472–3, 479, 482, and 496, and Gordon Craig, *Germany, 1866–1945* (Oxford: Oxford University Press, 1980), 604 and 607.

57 Kirk, "The relation of employment levels to births," 128, 135, and 138, and Ogburn and Thomas, "Influence of the business cycle," 324, 334, and 338–9.

58 Friedrich Burgdörfer, "Familienstatistik und Fruchtsbarkeitsmessung. Neue Aufgaben und neue Wege der deutschen Bevölkerungsstatistik," *Review of the International Statistical Institute* 5, no. 3 (October 1937): 218, and Verschuer, *Leitfaden*, 112.

59 Taeuber and Taueber, "German fertility trends," 150, 156, and 160–1.

60 This correlation was suggested in a 1955 Indianapolis study: Robert Potter and John Kanter, "Social and psychological factors affecting fertility. XXVIII. The influence of siblings and friends on fertility," *The Milbank Memorial Fund Quarterly* 33, no. 3 (July 1955): 246–67.

61 The influence of nineteenth-century wars on marriage and population were known during the First World War; see William Rossiter, "Influence of the war upon the population," *The North American Review* 203, no. 726 (May 1916): 700–10, and A.B. Wolfe, "Economic conditions and the birth-rate after the war," *The Journal of Political Economy* 25, no. 6 (June 1917): 521–41.

62 "1940 population estimates for European countries," *Population Index* 8, no. 2 (April 1942): 81; "Effects of war on population," *The British Medical Journal* 1, no. 2890 (20 May 1916): 729; "German vital trends in war," *Population Index* 8, no. 4 (October 1942): 255; Wilson Grabill, "Effect of the war on the birth rate and postwar fertility prospects," *The American Journal of Sociology* 50, no. 2 (September 1944): 107; Earl Hamilton et al., "The economic effects of war," *The American Economic Review* 31, no. 1, part 2 (March 1942): 299; Bernard Mallet, "Vital statistics as affected by the war," *Journal of the Royal Statistical Society* 81, no. 1 (January 1918): 8 and 10–12; and "The demography of war: Germany," *Population Index* 14, no. 14 (October 1948): 291.

63 There were food shortages, but as Götz Aly points out, most problems were shunted on to people in occupied countries and Soviet POWs. See Aly, *Hitler's beneficiaries: Plunder, racial war, and the Nazi welfare system*, trans. Jefferson Chase (New York: Metropolitan Books, 2007), 169–70. See also David M. Kennedy, ed., *The Library of Congress World War II companion* (New York: Simon and Schuster, 2007), 878–9; John Lukacs, *The last European war, September 1939–December 1941* (New Haven, CT: Yale University Press, 2001), 192–3; and Frederick Strauss, "The food problem in the German war economy," *The Quarterly Journal of Economics* 55, no. 3 (May 1941): 364–412.

64 Vern Katz et al., *Comprehensive Gynecology*, 5th ed. (Philadelphia: Mosby Elsevier, 2007), chapter 9; Ernestine J. Becker, "Nutrition in pregnancy,"

The American Journal of Nursing. 41, no. 11 (November 1941): 1246–7; and Regine K. Stix, "Research in causes of variations in fertility: Medical aspects," *American Sociological Review* 2, no. 3 (October 1937): 669.

65 *The United States Strategic Bombing Survey: A collection of the 31 most important reports printed in 10 volumes*, vols. 5 and 6 (New York: Garland Publishing, 1976). See also, Conrad Crane, *Bombs, cities, and civilians: American airpower strategy in World War II* (Lawrence: University of Kansas Press, 1993), 64.

66 Boberach, *Meldungen aus dem Reich*, 10: 3766–70, and 15: 6022–33.

67 Stein, *The Waffen SS*, 207; Alan Dearn, *The Hitler Youth, 1933–1945* (Westminster, MD: Osprey Publishing, 2006), 11; Gordon Williamson, *The Waffen SS: 11 to 23 divisions* (Oxford: Osprey Publishing, 2004), 9; and Kurt Meyer, *Grenadiers: The story of Waffen SS General Kurt "Panzer" Meyer* (Mechanicsburg, PA: Stackpole Books, 2005), 34.

68 Dearn, *The Hitler Youth*, 12; Williamson, *The Waffen SS*, 8–9; Meyer, *Grenadiers*, 211–12 and 248; Michael Kater, *Hitler Youth* (Cambridge, MA: Harvard University Press, 2004), 209–10; John Keegan, *Waffen SS: The asphalt soldiers* (New York: Ballantine Books, 1970), 91; and Hubert Meyer, *The 12th SS: The history of the Hitler Youth Panzer Division* (Mechanicsburg, PA: Stackpole Books, 2005), 1: 2–4.

69 "Rede des Reichsführer-SS anlässlich der Gruppenführer-Besprechung in Tölz am 18.II.1937," BA NS19/4004, p. 96, and "Heiratsgenehmigung für Angehörige der Waffen-SS," NA T175/60/frame 2576365.

70 Longerich, *Heinrich Himmler*, 218 and 265–7, and Richard Steigmann-Gall, *The holy Reich: Nazi conceptions of Christianity, 1919–1945* (Cambridge: Cambridge University Press, 2003), 129 and 219. Himmler's own animosity notwithstanding, he did not tolerate an SS man mocking or scorning the religion of another member. "SS-Befehl," 20 September 1935, BA NS19/3901, p. 8, and "Religiöse Veranstaltungen," BA NS19/3902, p. 28.

71 "Rede des Reichsführer-SS anlässlich der Gruppenführer-Besprechung in Tölz am 18.II.1937," pp. 93–4.

72 Himmler to Friedrich, 11 March 1937, BA NS2/280.

73 "Geistliche als SS-Angehörige," 15 October 1934, BA NSD 41/2, p. 3.

74 "SS-Befehl," 7 April 1936, BA NS19/3901, p. 23. Examples of declarations are in LA-D RW0134/46 and StA-L PL506/Bü 95, p. 10.

75 "Rede des Reichsführer-SS auf der Ragung der Auslandsorganisation in Stuttgart am 2.9.1938," IfZ MA312/frame 2612587; "Eine Rede des Reichsführers-SS," BA NSD12/35, p. 4; and Himmler, *Geheimreden*, 88.

76 Heike Wolf-Dietrich, *The Ukrainian Division "Galicia," 1943–45: A memoir*, trans. Andriy Wynnyckyj (Toronto: The Schevchenko Scientific Society, 1988), xix–xxii, 18–19, and 69, and Lepre, *Himmler's Bosnian division*, 22, 35, 64, 71, and 75–7.

77 See chapter 5, notes 81 and 82.

78 Browning, *Ordinary men*, 57, 71–5, 86, 102–3, 113, and 127–30.

79 *IMT*, 4: 354; Sereny, *Into that darkness*, 52, 55, and 134; and *US v. Greifelt*, 451 and 4053.

80 Hans Buchheim, "Command and compliance," 371; Karl Patel, "The reign of the black order. The final phase of National Socialism: The SS counter-state," in *The Third Reich*, ed. Maurice Beaumont (New York: Praeger, 1954), 665; and Albert Speer, *Infiltration*, trans. Joachim Neugroschel (New York: Macmillan Publishing Company, 1981), 9.

81 "European Fertility Project: Introduction and overview," *The Office of Population Research at Princeton University*, http://opr.princeton.edu/Archive/pefp/ (accessed 21 October 2017). The 2006 volume of *Entre Nous* issued by WHO addresses these issues: http://www.euro.who.int/__data/assets/pdf_file/0010/73954/EN63.pdf?ua=1 (accessed 21 October 2017). Eurostat released a report in 2013; see Giampaolo Lanzieri, "Towards a 'baby recession' in Europe? Differential fertility trends during the economic crisis," 13 (2013), http://ec.europa.eu/eurostat/documents/3433488/5585916/KS-SF-13-013-EN.PDF/a812b080-7ede-41a4-97ef-589ee767c581 (accessed 21 October 2017).

82 See "The EU's baby blues," *BBC News*, 27 March 2006, http://news.bbc.co.uk/2/hi/europe/4768644.stm (accessed 26 October 2014); Robert Samuelson, "Behind the birth dearth," *Washington Post*, 24 May 2006, http://www.washingtonpost.com/wp-dyn/content/article/2006/05/23/AR2006052301529.html (accessed 26 October 2014); David Gordon Smith, "Demographic worries: German birthrate rising – but for how long?" *Der Spiegel*, 18 February 2009, http://www.spiegel.de/international/germany/demographic-worries-german-birthrate-rising-but-for-how-long-a-608172.html (accessed 26 October 2014); "Demography in the Balkans: A birth dearth," *The Economist*, 12 November 2009, http://www.economist.com/node/14870080 (accessed 26 October 2014); Alan Greenblatt, "Asian, European nations fret over birthrate swoon," *NPR*, 2 November 2011, http://www.npr.org/2011/11/02/141901809/asian-european-nations-fret-over-birthrate-swoon (accessed 26 October 2014); Lee Kuan Yew, "Warning bell for developed countries: Declining birth rates," *Forbes*, 16 October 2012, http://www.forbes.com/sites/currentevents/2012/10/16/warning-bell-for-developed-countries-declining-birth-rates/ (accessed 26 October 2014); Suzanne Daley and Nicholas Kulish, "Germany fights population drop," *New York Times*, 13 August 2013, http://www.nytimes.com/2013/08/14/world/europe/germany-fights-population-drop.html?hp&_r=0 (accessed 26 October

2014); and Gaia Pianigiani, "Italy's 'Fertility Day' call to make babies arouses anger, not ardor," *New York Times*, 13 September 2016, http://www.nytimes.com/2016/09/14/world/europe/italy-births-fertility-europe.html?_r=0 (accessed 26 October 2014).

83 Frank Dikotter, "Race culture: Recent perspectives on the history of eugenics," *The American Historical Review* 103, no. 2 (April 1998): 476; Weingart, "German eugenics," 282; and Christina Cogdell, *Eugenic design: Streamlining America in the 1930s* (Philadelphia: University of Pennsylvania Press, 2004), 220.

84 More on the Human Genome Project can be found at http://www.genome.gov/10001772. See also Kenneth Garver and Bettylee Garver, "The Human Genome Project and eugenic concerns," *American Journal of Human Genetics* 54 (1994): 148–58.

Bibliography

Archives

Bundesarchiv, Berlin-Lichterfelde (BA)
Bundesarchiv, Freiburg (BA-MA)
Institut für Zeitgeschichte, Munich (IfZ)
International Tracing Service, Bad Arolsen (4.1.0/ITS)
Landesarchiv Nordrhein-Westfalen, Abteilung Rheinland, Standort
    Düsseldorf (LA-D)
Max Planck Gesellschaft Archiv, Berlin (MPG)
Staatsarchiv Darmstadt (StA-D)
Staatsarchiv Ludwigsburg (StA-L)
Staatsarchiv Marburg (StA-M)
United States Holocaust Memorial Museum, Washington, DC (USHMM)
United States National Archives, College Park, Maryland (NA)

Journals and Newspapers

Das Schwarze Korps. Berlin and Munich: Franz Eher Verlag, 1935–45.
Der SA Mann. Munich: Franz Eher Verlag, 1932–34.
SS Leithefte. Berlin: Schutzstaffeln der NSDAP, 1935–44.
Volk und Rasse. Munich: J.F. Lehmanns Verlag, 1933–44.
Völkischer Beobachter. Munich: Franz Eher Verlag, 1932–34.

Articles and Books

Ackermann, Josef. *Heinrich Himmler als Ideologe*. Göttingen: Musterschmidt,
    1970.

Adams, Mark, ed. *The wellborn science: Eugenics in Germany, France, Brazil, and Russia.* New York: Oxford University Press, 1990.

Ailsby, Christopher. *SS: Hell on the eastern front: The Waffen-SS war in eastern Russia, 1941–1945.* London: Brown Packaging Books, 1998.

Aislby, Christopher. *SS, roll of infamy.* Osceola, WI: Motorbooks International, 1997.

Alexander, Leo. "Medical science under dictatorship." *New England Journal of Medicine* 241 (1949): 39–47.

Alexander, Leo. "Sociopsychologic structure of the SS: Psychiatric report of the Nuremberg Trials for War Crimes." *Archives of Neurology* 59 (1948): 622–34.

Allen, Michael Thad. "The banality of evil reconsidered: SS mid-level managers of extermination through work." *Central European History* 30, no. 2 (1997): 253–94.

Aly, Götz. *Hitler's beneficiaries: Plunder, racial war, and the Nazi welfare state.* Translated by Jefferson Chase. New York: Metropolitan Books, 2007.

Aly, Götz, Peter Chroust, and Christian Pross. *Cleansing the fatherland: Nazi medicine and racial hygiene.* Translated by Belinda Cooper. Baltimore: Johns Hopkins University Press, 1994.

Aly, Götz, and Susanne Heim. *Architects of annihilation: Auschwitz and the logic of destruction.* Translated by A.G. Blunden. Princeton, NJ: Princeton University Press, 2002.

Aly, Götz, and Karl Heinz Roth. *The Nazi census: Identification and control in the Third Reich.* Translated by Edwin Black and Assenka Oksiloff. Philadelphia: Temple University Press, 2004.

Anderson, Benedict. *Imagined communities: Reflections on the origin and spread of nationalism.* London: Verso, 1983.

Angress, Werner, and Bradley Smith. "Diaries of Heinrich Himmler's early years." *Journal of Modern History* 31, no. 3 (September 1959): 206–24.

Arnold, Bettina. "Arierdämmerung: Race and archeology in Nazi Germany." *World Archaeology* 38, no. 1 (March 2006): 8–31.

Aufbruch: Briefe germanischer Kriegsfreiwilliger. Berlin: Der Reichsführer-SS, SS-Hauptamt, 1942.

Augustinovic, Werner, and Martin Moll. "Günter d'Alquen: Propagandist des SS-staates." In *Die SS: Elite unter dem Totenkopf: 30 Lebensläufe*, edited by Ronald M. Smelser and Enrico Syring, 100–18. Paderborn: Ferdinand Schönningh, 2000.

Bachrach, Susan, ed. *Deadly medicine: Creating the master race.* Washington, DC: United States Holocaust Memorial Museum; Chapel Hill: University of North Carolina Press, 2004.

Bahro, Berno. "Der Sport und seine Rolle in der nationalsozialistischen Elitetruppe SS." *Historical Social Research / Historische Sozialforschung* 32, no. 1 (2007): 78–91.

Baird, Jay. *Hitler's war poets: Literature and politics in the Third Reich.* Cambridge: Cambridge University Press, 2007.

Balogh, Thomas. "The national economy of Germany." *The Economic Journal* 49, no. 191 (September 1938): 461–97.

Baltzell, E. Digby. "Social mobility and fertility within an elite group." *The Milbank Memorial Fund Quarterly* 31, no. 4 (October 1953): 411–20.

Banach, Jens. *Heydrichs Elite: Das Führerkorps der Sicherheitspolizei und des SD 1936–1945.* Paderborn: Ferdinand Schöningh, 1998.

Barbian, Jan-Pieter. "Literary policy in the Third Reich." In *National Socialist cultural policy*, edited by Glenn Cuomo, 155–96. New York: Palgrave Macmillan, 1995.

Bar-On, Dan. *Legacy of silence: Encounters with children of the Third Reich.* Cambridge, MA: Harvard University Press, 1989.

Baumann, Angelika, and Andreas Heusler, eds. *Kinder für den "Führer": Der Lebensborn in München.* Munich: Franz Schiermeier Verlag, 2013.

Baur, Erwin, Eugen Fischer, and Fritz Lenz. *Menschliche Erblichkeitslehre und Rassenhygiene.* 2 volumes. Munich: J.F. Lehmanns Verlag, 1921.

Becker, Anne, and Detlef Mühlberger. "Analysing the sociography of the membership of the *Schutzstaffel* [SS] in *SS-Oberabschnitt Rhein* using Access II." *History and Computing* 11, no. 3 (1999): 213–24.

Becker, J. Ernestine. "Nutrition in pregnancy." *The American Journal of Nursing* 41, no. 11 (November 1941): 1245–51.

Becker, Peter Emil. *Zur Geschichte der Rassenhygiene: Wege ins Dritte Reich.* Stuttgart: Georg Thieme, 1988.

Beddies, Thomas. " 'Du hast die Pflicht gesund zu sein.' Der Gesundheitsdienst der Hitler-Jugend, 1933–1945." Professional dissertation (*Habilitationsschrift*). Berlin: Charité Centrum für Human- und Gesundheitswissenschaften, Institut für Geschichte der Medizin, 2009.

Berek, Jonathan, ed. *Berek and Novak's gynecology.* Philadelphia: Lippincott and Williams, 2007.

Berent, Jerzy. "Fertility and social mobility." *Population Studies* 5, no. 3 (March 1952): 244–60.

Berez, Thomas, and Sheila Faith Weiss. "The Nazi symbiosis: Politics and human genetics at the Kaiser Wilhelm Institute." *Endeavor* 28, no. 4 (December 2004): 172–7.

Berg, Manfred, and Geoffrey Cooks, eds. *Medicine and modernity: Public health and medical care in nineteenth- and twentieth-century Germany.* Washington, DC: German Historical Institute, 1997.

Berghahn, Volker. *Imperial Germany 1871–1918: Economy, society, culture, and politics.* New York: Berghahn Books, 2005.

Berghahn, Volker, and Simone Lässig, eds. *Biography between structure and agency: Central European lives in international historiography.* New York: Berghahn Books, 2008.

Berry, Roberta. "Eugenics after the Holocaust: The limit of reproduction rights." In *Humanity at the limit: The impact of the Holocaust experience on Jews and Christians,* edited by Michael Alan Singer, 224–40. Bloomington: Indiana University Press, 2000.

Bessel, Richard. *Political violence and the rise of Nazism: The storm troopers in eastern Germany, 1925–1934.* New Haven, CT: Yale University Press, 1984.

Best, Walter. *Mit der Leibstandarte im Westen: Berichte eines SS-Kriegsberichters.* Munich: Franz Eher, 1944.

Beveridge, William. "The fall of fertility among European races." *Economica* no. 13 (March 1925): 10–27.

"Bevölkerungslehre und Bevölkerungspolitik im 'Dritten Reich.' Tagung in Berlin-Dahlem vom 30.11.-1.12.2001." *Demographie: Mitteilungen der Deutschen Gesellschaft für Demographie e.V.* 1, no. 2 (July 2002): 6–14.

Biddle, Tami Davis. "Allied air power: Objectives and capabilities." In *The bombing of Auschwitz: Should the Allies have attempted it?,* edited by Michael Neufeld and Michael Berenbaum, 35–51. New York: St. Martin's Press, 2000.

Binding, Karl, and Alfred Hoche. *Die Freigabe der Vernichtung lebensunwerten Lebens. Ihr Mass und ihre Form.* Leipzig: F. Meiner, 1920.

Birn, Ruth Bettina. "Criminals as manipulative witnesses: A case study of SS General von dem Bach-Zelewski." *Journal of International Criminal Justice* 9 (2011): 441–74.

Black, Peter. *Ernst Kaltenbrunner, ideological soldier of the Third Reich.* Princeton, NJ: Princeton University Press, 1984.

Blackbourn, David, and Geoff Ely. *The peculiarities of German history: Bourgeois society and politics in nineteenth-century Germany.* Oxford: Oxford University Press, 1984.

Blandford, Edmund. *Hitler's second army: The Waffen SS.* Osceola, WI: Motorbooks International, 1994.

Bleuel, Hans Peter. *Sex and society in Nazi Germany.* Philadelphia: Lippincott, 1973.

Boberach, Heinz, ed. *Meldungen aus dem Reich, 1938–1945: Die geheimen Lageberichte des Sicherheitsdienstes der SS.* 17 volumes. Herrsching: Pawlak Verlag, 1984.

Bock, Gisela. "Antinatalism, maternity, and paternity in National Socialist racism." In *Maternity and gender policies: Women and the rise of the European welfare states, 1880s–1950s,* edited by Gisela Bock and Pat Thane, 233–55. London: Routledge, 1991.

Bock, Gisela. "Racism and sexism in Nazi Germany: Motherhood, compulsory sterilization, and the state." *Signs* 8, no. 3 (Spring 1983): 400–21.

Boehnert, Gunnar. "An analysis of the age and education of the SS Führerkorps 1925–1939." *Historical Social Research* 12 (October 1979): 4–17.

Boehnert, Gunnar. "The jurists in the SS-Führerkorps, 1925–1939." In *The "Führer state": Myth and reality: Studies on the structure and politics of the Third Reich,* edited by Gerhard Hirschfeld and Lothar Kettenacker, 361–74. Stuttgart: Klett-Cotta, 1981.

Börger, Wilhelm. *Nationalsozialismus und Volk.* Cologne: Der Treuhänder d. Arbeit f. d. Wirtschaftsgebiet Rheinland, 1935.

Börger, Wilhelm. *Vom deutschen Wesen.* Würzburg: Konrad Triltsch Verlag, 1942.

Borneman, John, ed. *Death of the father: An anthropology of the end in political authority.* New York: Berghahn Books, 2004.

Bouwmeester, Han. "Beginning of the end: The leadership of SS Obersturmbannführer Jochen Peiper." MA thesis, US Army Command and General Staff College, 2004.

Bowen, Robert. *Universal ice: Science and ideology in the Nazi state.* London: Belhaven Press, 1993.

Bramwell, Anna. *Blood and soil: Richard Walther Darré and Hitler's "Green Party."* Bourne End, UK: The Kensal Press, 1985.

Brandes, O. Jean. "The effect of war on the German family." *Social Forces* 29, no. 2 (1950): 164–73.

"Brauchen wir mehr uneheliche Kinder?" *Neues Volk: Blätter des Rassenpolitischen Amtes der NSDAP* (April 1937): 21.

Breitmann, Richard. *The architect of genocide: Himmler and the final solution.* New York: Alfred A. Knopf, 1991.

Breitmann, Richard. "*Mein Kampf* and the Himmler family. Two generations react to Hitler's ideas." *Holocaust and Genocide Studies* 13, no. 1 (1999): 90–8.

Brentjes, Burchard, ed. *Wissenschaft unter dem NS-Regime.* Schöneiche bei Berlin: Lang, 1992.

Bridenthal, Renate, Atina Grossman, and Marion Kaplan, eds. *When biology became destiny: Women in Weimar and Nazi Germany.* New York: Monthly Review Press, 1984.

Brohmer, Paul. *Biologieunterricht und völkische Erziehung.* Frankfurt am Main: Verlag Moritz Diesterweg, 1933.

Browder, George. "Problems and potentials of the Berlin Document Center." *Central European History* 5, no. 4 (1972): 362–80.

Browning, Christopher. *Ordinary men: Reserve Police Battalion 101 and the Final Solution in Poland*. New York: Harper Perennial, 1998.

Bry, Gerhard. *Wages in Germany, 1871–1945*. Princeton, NJ: Princeton University Press, 1960.

Bryant, Thomas. *Himmlers Kinder: Zur Geschichte der SS-Organisation "Lebensborn" e.V., 1935–1945*. Wiesbaden: Marix Verlag, 2011.

Buch, Walter. *Niedergang und Aufstieg der deutschen Familie*. Munich: Franz Eher, 1932.

Buchheim, Hans. "Command and compliance." In *Anatomy of the SS state*, edited by Helmut Krausnick, Hans Buchheim, Martin Broszat, and Hans-Adolf Jacobsen and translated by Richard Barry, Marian Jackson, and Dorothy Lang, 303–96. New York: Walker and Company, 1965.

Buchheim, Hans. "The position of the SS in the Third Reich." In *Republic to Reich: The making of the Nazi revolution*, edited by Hajo Holborn and translated by Ralph Manheim, 251–97. New York: Pantheon, 1972.

Buchheim, Hans. "The SS – instrument of domination." In *Anatomy of the SS state*, edited by Helmut Krausnick, Hans Buchheim, Martin Broszat, and Hans-Adolf Jacobsen and translated by Richard Barry, Marian Jackson, and Dorothy Lang, 127–302. New York: Walker and Company, 1965.

Büchler, Yehoshua. " 'Unworthy behavior': The case of SS officer Max Täubner." *Holocaust and Genocide Studies* 17, no. 3 (Winter 2003): 409–29.

Bundesverband der Soldaten der ehemaligen Waffen-SS e.V. *Wenn alle Brüder schweigen: Großer Bildband über die Waffen-SS*. Osnabrück: Munin Verlag GmbH, 1975.

Burgdörfer, Friedrich. *Bevölkerungsentwicklung im Dritten Reich: Tatsachen und Kritik*. Heidelberg: K. Vowinckel, 1935.

Burgdörfer, Friedrich. "Familienstatistik und Fruchtsbarkeitsmessung. Neue Aufgaben und neue Wege der deutschen Bevölkerungsstatistik." *Review of the International Statistical Institute* 5, no. 3 (October 1937): 212–26.

Burgdörfer, Friedrich. "Statistik: Lehren der deutschen Familienstatistik 1939." *Archiv für Bevölkerungswissenschaft und Bevölkerungspolitik* 12 (1942): 315–19.

Burgdörfer, Friedrich. *Sterben die weissen Völker: Die Zukunft der weissen und farbigen Völker im Lichte der biologischen Statistik*. Munich: G.D.W. Callaway, 1934.

Burgdörfer, Friedrich. *Volk ohne Jugend: Geburtenschwund und Überalterung des deutschen Volkskörpers: Ein Problem der Volkswirtschaft, der Sozialpolitik, der nationalen Zukunft*. Berlin: Kurt Vowinkel Verlag, 1934.

Burgdörfer, Friedrich. *Volksdeutsche Zukunft: Eine biologisch-statistische Betrachtung der gesamtdeutschen Bevölkerungsfrage*. Berlin: Junker und Dünnhaupt, 1938.

Burleigh, Michael. "Nazi Europe: What if Nazi Germany had defeated the Soviet Union." In *Virtual history: Alternatives and counterfactuals*, edited by Niall Ferguson, 321–47. New York: Basic Books, 1999.

Burleigh, Michael, and Wolfgang Wippermann. *The racial state: Germany, 1933–1945*. Cambridge: Cambridge University Press, 1991.

Buss, Philip, and Andrew Mollo. *Hitler's Germanic Legions: An illustrated history of the Western European Legions with the SS, 1941–1943*. London: Macdonald and Jane's Publishers Limited, 1978.

Butler, Rupert. *The black angels: A history of the Waffen-SS*. New York: St. Martin's Press, 1979.

Calic, Edouard. *Reinhard Heydrich: The chilling story of the man who masterminded the Nazi death camps*. New York: Morrow, 1985.

Campbell, Bruce. *The SA generals and the rise of Nazism*. Lexington: University Press of Kentucky, 1998.

Central Intelligence Agency. "The last days of Ernst Kaltenbrunner." *Center for the Study of Intelligence* 4, no. 2, https://www.cia.gov/library/center-for-the-study-of-intelligence/kent-csi/vol4no2/html/v04i2a07p_0001.htm.

Childers, Kristen Stromberg. *Fathers, families and the state in France 1914–1945*. Ithaca, NY: Cornell University Press, 2003.

Clark, Colin. "Age at marriage and marital fertility." *Population Studies* 2, no. 4 (March 1949): 413–26.

Clauss, Ludwig Ferdinand. *Der nordic Seele*. Munich: J.F. Lehmanns Verlag, 1932.

Clauss, Ludwig Ferdinand. *Rasse und Charakter*. Frankfurt am Main: M. Diesterweg, 1938.

Clauss, Ludwig Ferdinand. *Rasse und Seele: Ein Einführung in den Sinn der leiblichen Gestalt*. Munich: J.F. Lehmanns Verlag, 1941.

Clay, Catrine. *Master race: The Lebensborn experiment in Nazi Germany*. London: Hodder and Stoughton, 1995.

Cogdell, Christina. *Eugenic design: Streamlining America in the 1930s*. Philadelphia: University of Pennsylvania Press, 2004.

Cogdell, Christina. "Products or bodies? Streamline design and eugenics as applied biology." *Design Issues* 19, no. 1 (Winter 2003): 36–53.

Combs, William. "Fatal attraction: Dueling and the SS." *History Today* 47, no. 6 (June 1997): 11–16.

Combs, William. *The voice of the SS: A history of the SS journal "Das Schwarze Korps."* New York: Peter Lang, 1986.

Connell, R.W. "The state, gender, and sexual politics." *Theory and Society* 19, no. 5 (October 1990): 507–44.

Connelly, John. "The uses of the Volksgemeinschaft: Letters to the NSDAP Kreisleitung Eisenach, 1939–1940." *The Journal of Modern History* 68, no. 4 (December 1996): 299–330.

Conti, Leonardo. "Anordnungen des Reichsgesundheitsführers: Anordnung 10/42; Arbeitsgemeinschaft 'Hilfe bei Kinderlosigkeit in der Ehe.' " *Deutsches Ärzteblatt* 72, no. 22 (1942): 262.

Conti, Leonardo. *Gesundheitspflicht und Geschlechtskrankheiten*. Berlin: Reichsgesundheitsverlag, 1942.

Conti, Leonardo. "Volksgesundheit, Volksschicksal." *Praktische Gesundheitspflege in Schule und Haus: Zeitschrift für die Methodik der Gesundheitsziehung* 8, no. 4 (January/February 1940): 65–70.

Cook, Stephen, and Stuart Russell. *Heinrich Himmler's Camelot: Pictorial/ documentary; The Wewelsburg Ideological Center of the SS, 1934–1945*. Andrews, NC: Kressmann-Backmeyer, 1999.

Cornwell, John. *Hitler's scientists: Science, war and the devil's pact*. New York: Viking, 2003.

Craig, Gordon. *Germany, 1866–1945*. Oxford: Oxford University Press, 1980.

Crane, Conrad. *Bombs, cities, and civilians: American airpower strategy in World War II*. Lawrence: University of Kansas Press, 1993.

Czarnowski, Gabriele. " 'The value of marriage for the *Volksgemeinschaft*': Policies towards women and marriage under National Socialism." In *Fascist Italy and Nazi Germany: Comparisons and contrasts*, edited by Richard Bessel and translated by Pamela Selwyn, 94–112. Cambridge: Cambridge University Press, 1996.

Daley, Suzanne, and Nicholas Kulish. "Germany fights population drop." *New York Times*, 13 August 2013. http://www.nytimes.com/2013/08/14/ world/europe/germany-fights-population-drop.html?hp&_r=0.

d'Alquen, Gunter. *Das ist der Sieg! Briefe des Glaubens in Aufbruch und Krieg*. Berlin: Franz Eher Verlag, 1941.

d'Alquen, Gunter. *Die SS: Geschichte, Aufgabe, und Organisation der Schutzstaffeln der NSDAP*. Berlin: Junker und Dünnhaupt, 1939.

Darré, Richard Walther. *Das Bauerntum als Lebensquell der nordischen Rasse*. Munich: J.F. Lehmanns Verlag, 1937.

Darré, Richard Walther. *Neuadel aus Blut und Boden*. Munich: J.F. Lehmanns Verlag, 1930.

Darré, Richard Walther. *Zucht als Gebot*. Berlin: Verlag Blut und Boden, 1944.

Darwin, Leonard. "On the statistical enquires needed after the war in connection with eugenics." *Journal of the Royal Statistical Society* 79, no. 2 (March 1916): 159–88.

Davenport, Charles Benedict. *State laws limiting marriage selection examined in the light of eugenics*. New York: Cold Spring Harbor, 1913.

David, Henry, Jochen Fleischhacker, and Charlotte Hohn. "Abortion and eugenics in Nazi Germany." *Population and Development Review* 14, no. 1 (March 1988): 81–112.

Davidson, Martin. *The perfect Nazi: Uncovering my grandfather's secret past.* New York: G.P. Putnam's Sons, 2011.

Dearn, Alan. *The Hitler Youth, 1933–1945.* Westminster, MD: Osprey Publishing, 2006.

Dederichs, Mario. *Heydrich: The face of evil.* Translated by Geoffrey Brooks. London: Greenhill, 2006.

Degrelle, Leon. *Die verlorene Legion.* Stuttgart: Veritas Verlag, 1952.

Deichmann, Ute. *Biologists under Hitler.* Translated by Thomas Dunlap. Cambridge, MA: Harvard University Press, 1996.

Deichmann, Ute, and Benno Müller-Hill. "Biological research at universities and Kaiser Wilhelm Institutes in Nazi Germany." In *Science, technology, and National Socialism,* edited by Monika Renneberg and Mark Walker, 160–83. Cambridge: Cambridge University Press, 1994.

de la Rochebrochard, Elise, and Patrick Thonneau. "Paternal age ≥ 40 years: An important risk factor for infertility." *American Journal of Obstetrics and Gynecology* 189, no. 4 (October 2003): 901–4.

D'emilio, John. *Sexual politics, sexual communities: The making of a homosexual minority in the United States, 1940–1970.* Chicago: University of Chicago Press, 1983.

"Demography in the Balkans: A birth dearth." *Economist,* 12 November 2009. http://www.economist.com/node/14870080.

Der Reichführer-SS. *Rassenpolitik*: Berlin: SS-Hauptamt, 1940.

Der Reichsführer-SS and der Chef des SS-Hauptamtes. *Die Feier: Schrift für Lebensführung und Feiergestaltung in der SS.* Berlin: SS-Hauptamt, 1943.

Deschner, Günther. *Heydrich: The pursuit of total power.* London: Orbis, 1981.

Deschner, Günther. *Reinhard Heydrich: A biography.* New York: Stein and Day, 1981.

Dicks, Henry V. *Licensed mass murder: A socio-psychological study of some SS killers.* New York: Basic Books, 1972.

Diehl, Paula. *Macht – Mythos – Utopie: Die Körperbild der SS-Männer.* Berlin: Akademie Verlag, 2005.

Dikotter, Frank. "Race culture: Recent perspectives on the history of eugenics." *The American Historical Review* 103, no. 2 (April 1998): 467–78.

Doerries, Reinhard. *Hitler's last chief of foreign intelligence: Allied interrogations of Walter Schellenberg.* London: F. Cass, 2003.

Dolbin, Ernest, and Claire Pohly. "The social composition of the Nazi leadership." *The American Journal of Sociology* 51, no. 1 (July 1945): 42–9.

Dürre, Konrad. *Erbbiologisher und rassenhygienischer Wegweiser fur Jedermann.* Berlin: Alfred Metzner Verlag, 1933.

Düsterberg, Rolf. "Mein Reichsführer, lieber Heini Himmler!" *Zeit Online,* 11 March 2004. http://www.zeit.de/2004/12/A-Johst.

Earl, Hilary. *The Nuremberg SS-Einsatzgruppen trial, 1945–1958: Atrocity, law, and history.* Cambridge: Cambridge University Press, 2009.

Edsall, Nicholas. *Toward Stonewall: Homosexuality and society in the modern Western world.* Charlottesville: University of Virginia Press, 2003.

"Effects of war on population." *The British Medical Journal* 1, no. 2890 (20 May 1916): 728–9.

Ehrenreich, Eric. *The Nazi ancestral proof: Genealogy, racial science, and the Final Solution.* Bloomington: University of Indiana Press, 2007.

Epstein, F.T. "War-time activities of the SS-Ahnenerbe." In *On the track of tyranny, essays presented by the Weiner Library to Leonard G. Montefiore, O.B.E., on the occasion of his seventieth birthday,* edited by Max Beloff, 77–95. London: Valentine, Mitchel, 1960.

Estes, Kenneth. *A European anabasis – Western European volunteers in the German Army and SS, 1940–1945.* New York: Columbia University Press, 2008.

Ettelson, Todd. "The Nazi 'New Man': Embodying masculinity and regulating sexuality in the SA and SS, 1930–1939." PhD diss., University of Michigan, 2002.

"European Fertility Project: Introduction and overview." *The Office of Population Research at Princeton University.* http://opr.princeton.edu/ Archive/pefp/.

Evans, Richard. *The Third Reich in power, 1933–1939.* New York: Penguin Press, 2005.

Eydt, Alfred. "Der Sinn der Heiratsgenehmigung bei der SS." *Nationalsozialistische Monatshefte* 4, no. 38 (1933): 24–30.

Fangerau, Heiner. "Der 'Baur-Fischer-Lenz' in der Buchkritik 1921–1940: Eine quantifizierende Untersuchung zur zeitgenössischen Rezeption rassenhygienischer Theorien." *Medizinhistorisches Journal* 38, no. 1 (2003): 57–83.

Fangerau, Heiner, and Irmgard Müller. "Das Standardwerk der Rassenhygiene von Erwin Baur, Eugen Fischer und Fritz Lenz im Urteil der Psychiatrie und Neurologie 1921–1940." *Nervenarzt* 73, no. 11 (November 2002): 1039–46.

Fehrenbach, Heide. "Rehabilitating fatherland: Race and German remasculinization." *Signs* 24, no. 1 (Autumn 1998): 107–27.

Ferdinand, Ursula. "Geburtenrückgangstheorien und 'Geburtenrücksgangs-Gespenster' 1900–1930." In *Herausforderung Bevölkerung: Zu Entwicklung des modernen Denkens über die Bevölkerung vor, im, und nach dem Dritten Reich,* edited by Josef Ehmer, Ursula Ferdinand, and Jürgen Reulecke, 77–98. Wiesbaden: Verlag für Sozialwissenschaften, 2007.

Field, Geoffrey. "Nordic racism." *Journal of the History of Ideas* 38, no. 3 (July–September 1977): 523–40.

Fischer, Conan. "The occupational background of the SA's rank-and-file membership during the Depression years, 1929 to mid-1934." In *The shaping of the Nazi state*, edited by Peter Stachura, 131–59. London: Croom Helm, 1978.

Fischer, Conan. "The SA of the NSDAP: Social background and ideology of the rank and file in the early 1930s." *Journal of Contemporary History* 17, no. 4 (October 1982): 651–70.

Fischer, Eugen. *Der Begriff des völkischen Staates, biologisch betrachtet*. Berlin: Preussische Druckerei- und Verlags-Aktiengesellschaft, 1933.

Fischer, Eugen. *Der völkische Staat, biologisch gesehen*. Berlin: Junker und Dünnhaupt Verlag, 1933.

Fischer, Eugen. *Rasse und Rassenentstehung beim Menschen*. Berlin: Verlag Ullstein, 1927.

Fischer, Max. "Adolf Hitler und die Rassenhygiene." *Psychiatrisch-neurologische Wochenschrift* 41, no. 15 (15 April 1939): 177–8.

Flanagan, John. "A study of psychological factors related to fertility." *Proceedings of the American Philosophical Society* 80, no. 4 (15 February 1939): 513–23.

Foucault, Michel. *The history of sexuality: An introduction*. Vol. 1. New York: Vintage Books, 1990.

Frei, Norbert, and Johannes Schmitz. *Journalismus im Dritten Reich*. Munich: Beck, 1989.

Friedlander, Henry. *The origins of Nazi genocide: From euthanasia to the Final Solution*. Chapel Hill: University of North Carolina Press, 1995.

Frischauer, Willi. *Himmler, the evil genius of the Third Reich*. London: Odhams Press, 1953.

Fritzsche, Peter. *Life and death in the Third Reich*. Cambridge, MA: Belknap Press, 2008.

Garver, Kenneth, and Bettylee Garver. "The Human Genome Project and eugenic concerns." *American Journal of Human Genetics* 54 (1994): 148–58.

Gasman, Daniel. *The scientific origins of National Socialism: Social Darwinism in Ernst Haeckel and the German Monist League*. New York: American Elsevier, 1971.

Gellately, Robert. "Situating the 'SS-State' in a social-historical context: Recent histories of the SS, the police, and the courts in the Third Reich." *The Journal of Modern History* 64, no. 2 (June 1992): 338–65.

Gellately, Robert. "Social outsiders and the consolidation of Hitler's dictatorship, 1933–1939." In *Nazism, war, and genocide: Essays in honour*

of Jeremy Noakes, edited by Neil Gregor, 56–74. Exeter, UK: University of
Exeter Press, 2005.

Gelwick, Robert. "Personnel policies and procedures of the Waffen-SS." PhD
diss., University of Nebraska–Lincoln, 1971.

Gerhard, Gesine. "Breeding pigs and people for the Third Reich: Richard
Walther Darré's agrarian ideology." In *How green were the Nazis?*
Nature, environment, and nation in the Third Reich, edited by Franz-Josef
Brüggemeier, Mark Cioc, and Thomas Zeller, 129–48. Athens: Ohio
University Press, 2005.

"German vital trends in War." *Population Index* 8, no. 4 (October 1942): 255–8.

Germany speaks, by 21 leading members of party and state. London: T.
Butterworth Limited, 1938.

Gerth, Hans. "The Nazi Party: Its leadership and composition." *The American
Journal of Sociology* 45, no. 4 (1940): 517–41.

Gerwarth, Robert. *Hitler's hangman: The life of Heydrich*. New Haven, CT: Yale
University Press, 2011.

Gilbert, K., and Heidi Danker. "Investigations on the changes of sex-ratio in
Germany from 1826 up to 1978." *Acta Anthropogenetica* 5, no. 2 (1981): 89–110.

Giles, Geoffrey. "The denial of homosexuality: Same-sex incidents in
Himmler's SS and police." *Journal of the History of Sexuality* 11, no. 1–2
(January/April 2002): 256–90.

Giles, Geoffrey. "The institutionalization of homosexual panic in the Third
Reich." In *Social outsiders in Nazi Germany*, edited by Robert Gellately and
Nathan Stoltzfus, 233–55. Princeton, NJ: Princeton University Press, 2001.

Giles, Geoffrey. "Straight talk for Nazi youth: The attempt to transmit
heterosexual norms." In *Education and cultural transmission: Historical studies
of continuity and change in families, schooling, and youth cultures*, edited by
Johan Sturm, 305–18. Ghent, BE: CSHP, 1996.

Gillette, Aaron. *Racial theories in Fascist Italy*. London: Routledge, 2002.

Gingerich, Mark Philip. "Toward a brotherhood of arms: Waffen-SS
recruitment of Germanic volunteers, 1940–1945." Ph.D. diss., University of
Wisconsin–Madison, 1991.

Glass, Bentley. "The current state of biological work in Germany." *American
Institute of Biological Sciences Bulletin* 2, no. 1 (January 1952): 11, 14–16.

Glass, Bentley. "A hidden chapter of German eugenics between the two world
wars." *Proceedings of the American Philosophical Society* 130, no. 1 (March
1986): 130–54.

Goebbels, Joseph. *Die Tagbücher von Joseph Goebbels*, edited by Elke Fröhlich.
Munich: K.G. Saur, 1998–2005.

Goebbels, Joseph. *The Goebbels diaries, 1939–1941*. Translated and edited by Fred Taylor. London: Hamish Hamilton, 1982.

Goeschel, Christian. *Suicide in Nazi Germany*. Oxford: Oxford University Press, 2009.

Goldin, Miltin. "Financing the SS." *History Today* 48, no. 6 (June 1998): 28–34.

Gould, Stephan Jay. *The mismeasure of man*. New York: W.W. Norton and Company, 1981.

Graber, G.S. *History of the SS*. New York: D. McKay, 1978.

Grabill, Wilson. "Effect of the war on the birth rate and postwar fertility prospects." *The American Journal of Sociology* 50, no. 2 (September 1944): 107–11.

Graham, Loren. "Science and values: The eugenics movement in Germany and Russia in the 1920s." *The American Historical Review* 82, no. 5 (December 1977): 1133–64.

Grant, Madison. *The passing of the great race or the racial basis of European history*. New York: Charles Scribner's Sons, 1921.

Grant, Thomas. *Stormtroopers and crisis in the Nazi movement: Activism, ideology and dissolution*. London: Routledge, 2004.

Greenblatt, Alan. "Asian, European nations fret over birthrate swoon." *NPR*, 2 November 2011. http://www.npr.org/2011/11/02/141901809/asian-european-nations-fret-over-birthrate-swoon.

Gregor, A. James. "Nordicism revisited." *Phylon* 22, no. 4 (1961): 351–60.

Grill, Johnpeter Horst. "The Nazi Party's rural propaganda before 1928." *Central European History* 15, no. 2 (June 1982): 149–85.

Groß, Walter. *Deine Ehre ist die Treue zum Blute deines Volkes*. Berlin: Elsnerdruck, 1943.

Groß, Walter. *Rassenpolitische Erziehung*. Berlin: Junker und Dünnhaupt Verlag, 1935.

Groß, Walter. "Wehrwesen und Rassenbiologie." *Praktische Gesundheitspflege in Schule und Haus: Zeitschrift für die Methodik der Gesundheitsziehung* 7, no. 5 (March/April 1939): 129–35.

Grothe, Ewald. "Model or myth? The Constitution of Westphalia of 1807 and early German constitutionalism." *German Studies Review* 28, no. 1 (February 2005): 1–19.

Grunberger, Richard. *Hitler's SS*. New York: Dorset Press, 1993.

Grunberger, Richard. "Lebensborn. Himmler's selective breeding establishment." *Wiener Library Bulletin* 16 (1992): 52–3.

Grunberger, Richard. *12 year Reich: A social history of the Third Reich*. London: Weidenfeld and Nicolson, 1971.

Gupta, Charu. "Politics of gender: Women in Nazi Germany." *Economic and Political Weekly* 26, no. 17 (27 April 1991): WS40–WS48.

Gutmann, Martin. "Debunking the myth of the volunteers: Transnational volunteering in the Nazi Waffen-SS officer corps during the Second World War." *Contemporary European History* 22, no. 4 (November 2013): 585–607.

Gutmann, Martin. "Fighting for the Nazi new order: Himmler's Swiss, Swedish, and Danish volunteers and the Germanic project of the SS." PhD diss., Syracuse University, 2011.

Gütt, Arthur. *Bevölkerungs- und Rassenpolitik.* Berlin: Industrieverlag Spaeth and Linde, 1938.

Gütt, Arthur. *Dienst an der Rasse als Aufgabe der Staatspolitik.* Berlin: Junker und Dünnhaupt, 1935.

Hachtmann, Rüdiger. *Wissenschaftsmanagement im "Dritten Reich": Geschichte der Generalverwaltung der Kaiser-Wilhelm-Gesellschaft.* 2 volumes. Göttingen: Wallstein Verlag, 2007.

Hagen, Louis. *Follow my leader.* London: A. Wingate, 1951.

Hale, Christopher. *Himmler's crusade: The Nazi expedition to find the origins of the Nazi race.* Hoboken, NJ: John Wiley and Sons, 2003.

Hale, Oron. "Adolf Hitler and the post-war German birthrate." *Journal of Central European Affairs* 17 (1977–78): 166–73.

Hale, Oron. *The captive press in the Third Reich.* Princeton, NJ: Princeton University Press, 1964.

Hamilton, Earl J., John U. Nef, Wesley C. Mitchell, A. B. Wolfe, and C. O. Hardy. "The Economic Effects of War." *The American Economic Review* 31, no. 1, part 2 (March 1942): 227–30.

Hancock, Eleanor. " 'Only the real, the true, the masculine held its value': Ernst Röhm, masculinity, and male homosexuality." *Journal of the History of Sexuality* 8, no. 4 (April 1998): 616–41.

Hankins, Frank. "German policies for increasing births." *The American Journal of Sociology* 42, no. 5 (March 1937): 630–52.

Hankins, Frank. "Is the differential fertility of the social classes selective?" *Social Forces* 12, no. 1 (October 1933): 33–9.

Harnack, Adolf von. *Handbuch der Kasier-Wilhelm-Gesellschaft zur Förderung der Wissenschaften.* Berlin: Verlag von Reimar Hobbing, 1928.

Hart, Stephen. "Indoctrinated Nazi teenage warriors: The fanaticism of the 12th SS Panzer Division *Hitlerjugend* in Normandy, 1944." In *Fanaticism and conflict in the modern age,* edited by Matthew Hughes and Gaynor Johnson, 81–100. New York: Routledge, 2005.

Hartmann, Max, ed. *25 Jahre Kaiser Wilhelm Gesellschaft zur Förderung der Wissenschaften.* Zwei Bände. Berlin: Verlag Julius Springer, 1936.

Harwood, Jonathan. "National styles in science: Genetics in Germany and the United States between the world wars." *Isis* 78, no. 3 (September 1987): 390–414.

Harwood, Jonathan. *Styles of scientific thought: The German genetics community, 1900–1933.* Chicago: University of Chicago Press, 1993.

Hatheway, Jay. *In perfect formation: SS ideology and the SS-Junkerschule.* Atglen, PA: Schiffer, 1999.

Hatheway, Joseph Gilbert. *The ideological origins of the pursuit of perfection within the Nazi SS.* PhD diss., University of Wisconsin–Madison, 1992.

Hauner, Milan L. "A German racial revolution?" *Journal of Contemporary History* 19, no. 4 (October 1984): 669–87.

Hausser, Paul. *Soldaten wie andere auch: Der Weg der Waffen-SS.* Osnabrück: Munin Verlag, 1966.

Hausser, Paul. *Waffen SS im Einsatz.* Göttingen: Plesse Verlag, 1953.

Häyry, Matti. "The historical idea of a better race." *Studies in Ethics, Law, and Technology* 2, no. 1 (2008): 1–26.

Heberle, Rudolf. "Social factors in birth control." *American Sociological Review* 6, no. 6 (December 1941): 794–805.

Heiber, Helmut. *Goebbels.* Translated by John K. Dickinson. New York: Da Capo Press, 1972.

Heiber, Helmut, ed. *Reichsführer! Briefe an und von Himmler.* Stuttgart: Deutsche Verlags-Anstalt, 1968.

Heiber, Helmut, and Hildegard von Kotze, eds. *Facsimilie Querschnitt durch Das Schwarze Korps.* Munich: Scherz Verlag, 1968.

Heidenreich, Gisela. *Das endlose Jahr: Die langsame Entdeckung der eigenen Biographie; ein Lebensbornschicksal.* Bern, CH: Scherz Verlag, 2002.

Heike, Wolf-Dietrich. *The Ukrainian Division "Galicia," 1943–45: A memoir.* Translated by Andriy Wynnyckyj. Toronto: The Schevchenko Scientific Society, 1988.

Heim, Susanne, Carola Sachse, and Mark Walker, eds. *The Kaiser Wilhelm Society under National Socialism.* Cambridge: Cambridge University Press, 2009.

Hein, Bastian. *Elite für Volk und Führer? Die Allgemeine SS und ihre Mitglieder 1925–1945.* Munich: Oldenbourg Verlag, 2012.

Heineman, Elizabeth. "Gender, sexuality, and coming to terms with the Nazi past." *Central European History* 38, no. 1 (2005): 41–74.

Heineman, Elizabeth. "Sexuality and Nazism: The doubly unspeakable?" *Journal of the History of Sexuality* 11, no. 1–2 (January/April 2002): 22–66.

Heinemann, Isabel. " 'Another type of perpetrator': The SS racial experts and forced population movements in the occupied regions." *Holocaust and Genocide Studies* 15, no. 3 (Winter 2001): 387–411.

Heinemann, Isabel. *Rasse, Siedlung, deutsches Blut: Das Rasse-und Siedlungshauptamt der SS und die rassenpolitische Neuordnung Europas.* Göttingen: Wallstein Verlag, 2003.

Hensen, Jeffrey Allen. "The role of *Das Schwarze Korps* in the SS's campaign against the Catholic Church." MA thesis, Mississippi State University, 1997.

Herbert, Ulrich. *Best: Biographische Studien über Radikalismus, Weltanschauung, und Vernunft, 1903–1989.* Bonn: J.H.W. Dietz, 2001.

Herzog, Dagmar. "Hubris and hypocrisy, incitement and disavowal: Sexuality and German fascism." *Journal of the History of Sexuality* 11, no. 1–2 (January/April 2002): 3–21.

Herzog, Dagmar. *Sex after fascism: Memory and morality in twentieth-century Germany.* Princeton, NJ: Princeton University Press, 2005.

Herzog, Dagmar, ed. *Sexuality and German fascism.* New York: Berghahn Books, 2005.

Herzog, Dagmar. *Sexuality in Europe: A twentieth-Century history.* Cambridge: Cambridge University Press, 2011.

Heydrich, Lina. *Leben mit einem Kriegsverbrecher.* Pfaffenhofen: Ludwig, 1976.

Heydrich, Peter Thomas. *Ich war der Kronprinz von Heydrich: Eine Kindheit im Schatten des Henkers von Prag.* Stuttgart: Kreuz, 2006.

Heydrich, Reinhard. *Meine Ehre heisst Treue.* Berlin: Reichssicherheitshauptamt, 1942.

Heydrich, Reinhard. *Wandlungen unseres Kampf.* Munich: Franz Eher, 1935.

Hilberg, Raul. *The destruction of the European Jews.* Vol. 2. New Haven, CT: Yale University Press, 2003.

Hillel, Marc, and Clarissa Henry. *Of pure blood.* Translated by Eric Mossbacher. New York: McGraw Hill, 1976.

Himmler, Heinrich. *Die Schutzstaffel als antibolschewistische Kampforganisation.* Munich: Zentralverlag der NSDAP, 1936.

Himmler, Heinrich. *Geheimreden 1933–1945 und andere Ansprachen.* Edited by Bradley Smith and Agnes Peterson. Frankfurt am Main: Propyläen Verlag, 1974.

Himmler, Heinrich. *Once in 2000 years.* New York: American Committee for Anti-Nazi Literature, 1938.

Himmler, Katrin. *The Himmler brothers: A German family history.* Translated by Michael Mitchell. London: Macmillan, 2007.

Hirsch, Kurt. *SS Gestern, Heute, und ...* Darmstadt: Progress Verlag, 1960.

Hitler, Adolf. *Hitler's second book: The unpublished sequel to* Mein Kampf. Edited by Gerhard Weinberg and translated by Krista Smith. New York: Enigma, 2003.

Hitler, Adolf. *Mein Kampf.* Translated by Ralph Manheim. Boston: Houghton Mifflin Company, 1999.

Hobsbawm, Eric. *Nations and nationalism since 1870: Programme, myth, reality.* Cambridge: Cambridge University Press, 1990.

Hobsbawm, Eric, and Terence Ranger, eds. *The invention of tradition.* Cambridge: Cambridge University Press, 2005.

Höhne, Heinz. *The order of the Death's Head: The story of Hitler's SS.* London: Secker and Warburg, 1969.

Hope, Keith. "Social mobility and fertility." *American Sociological Review* 36, no. 6 (December 1971): 1019–32.

Huber, Gabriele. *Die Porzellan-Manufaktur Allach-München GmbH: Eine "Wirtschaftsunternehmung" der SS zum Schutz der "deutschen Seele."* Marburg: Jonas Verlag, 1992.

Hüser, Karl. *Wewelsburg 1933 bis 1945: Kult- und Terrorstätte der SS.* Paderborn: Bonifatius, 1987.

Hutton, Christopher. *Race and the Third Reich: Linguistics, racial anthropology, and genetics in the dialectic of Volk.* Cambridge: Polity, 2005.

Huxley, Julian, and Alfred Haddon. *We Europeans: A survey of "racial" problems.* New York: Harper and Brother Publishers, 1936.

Infield, Glenn. *Secrets of the SS.* New York: Stein and Day, 1982.

Ipsen, Carl. *Dictating demography: The problem of population in Fascist Italy.* Cambridge: Cambridge University Press, 1996.

Ipsen, Carl. "The organization of demographic totalitarianism: Early population policy in Fascist Italy." *Social Science History* 17, no. 1 (Spring 1993): 71–108.

Ipsen, Carl. "Population policy in the age of Fascism: Observations on recent literature." *Population and Development Review* 24, no. 3 (September 1998): 579–92.

Jagemann, Normann. *"Der Studienführer": Zur Wissenschaftspolitik der SS.* Hamburg: Verlag Dr. Kovač, 2005.

Jahrbuch der Kaiser-Wilhelm-Gesellschaft zur Förderung der Wissenschaften. Leipzig: Haag-Drugulin, 1939–42.

James, William. "The categories of evidence relating to the hypothesis that mammalian sex ratios at birth are causally related to the hormone concentrations of both parents around the time of conception." *Journal of Biosocial Science* 43 (2011): 167–84.

Jeffords, Susan. "The 'remasculinzation' of Germany in the 1950s." *Signs* 24, no. 1 (Autumn 1998): 163–9.

Jerome, Roy, ed. *Conceptions of postwar German masculinity.* Albany: State University of New York Press, 2001.

Johst, Hanns. *Ruf des Reiches – Echo des Volkes! Eine Ostfahrt.* Munich: Franz Eher Verlag, 1940.

Johnson, Eric. *Nazi terror: The Gestapo, Jews, and ordinary Germans.* New York: Basic Books, 2000.

Kaienburg, Hermann. *Die Wirtschaft der SS*. Berlin: Metropol Verlag, 2003.

Kaiser, Jochen-Christoph, Kurt Nowak, and Michael Schwartz, eds. *Eugenik, Sterilisation, "Euthanasie": Politische Biologie in Deutschland 1895–1945; Eine Dokumentation*. Berlin: Buchverlag Union, 1992.

Kanter, John, and Robert Potter Jr. "Social and psychological factors affecting fertility. XXIV. The relationship of family size in two successive generations." *The Milbank Memorial Fund Quarterly* 32, no. 3 (July 1954): 294–311.

Kasarda, John, and John O.G. Billy. "Social mobility and fertility." *Annual Review of Sociology* 11 (1985): 305–28.

Kater, Michael. *Doctors under Hitler*. Chapel Hill: University of North Carolina Press, 1989.

Kater, Michael. "Dr. Leonardo Conti and his nemesis: The failure of centralized medicine in the Third Reich." *Central European History* 18, no. 3–4 (September–December 1985): 299–325.

Kater, Michael. *Hitler Youth*. Cambridge, MA: Harvard University Press, 2004.

Kater, Michael. *The Nazi Party: A social profile of members and leaders, 1919–1945*. Cambridge, MA: Harvard University Press, 1983.

Katz, Vern, Gretchen Lenz, Rogerio Lobo, and David Gershenson. *Comprehensive gynecology*. 5th ed. Philadelphia: Mosby Elsevier, 2007.

Kay, Carolyn. "How should we raise our son Benjamin? Advice literature for mothers in early twentieth-century Germany." In *Raising citizens in the "century of the child": The United States and German Central Europe in comparative perspective*, edited by Dirk Schumann, 105–21. New York: Berghahn Books, 2010.

Keegan, John. *The First World War*. New York: Alfred A. Knopf, 1999.

Keegan, John. *Waffen SS: The asphalt soldiers*. New York: Ballantine Books, 1970.

Kennedy, David, ed. *The Library of Congress World War II companion*. New York: Simon and Schuster, 2007.

Kershaw, Ian. *Hitler: Hubris, 1889–1936*. New York: W.W. Norton and Company, 1998.

Kershaw, Ian. *Hitler: Nemesis, 1936–1945*. New York: W.W. Norton and Company, 2001.

Kershaw, Ian. *The "Hitler myth": Image and reality in the Third Reich*. Oxford: Oxford University Press, 2001.

Kersten, Felix. *The Kersten memoirs, 1940–1945*. Translated by Constantine Fitzgibbon and James Oliver. New York: Macmillan, 1957.

Kessler, Leo. *SS Peiper: The life and death of SS Colonel Jochen Peiper*. London: Cooper, 1986.

Kevles, Daniel. *In the name of eugenics: Genetics and the uses of human heredity.* Cambridge, MA: Harvard University Press, 2004.

Kiernan, Ben. "Twentieth-century genocides: Underlying ideological themes from Armenia to East Timor." In *The specter of genocide: Mass murder in historical perspective,* edited by Robert Gellately and Ben Kiernan, 29–52. New York: Cambridge University Press, 2003.

Kirk, Dudley. "The relation of employment levels to births in Germany." *The Milbank Memorial Fund Quarterly* 20, no. 2 (April 1942): 126–38.

Kirkpatrick, Clifford. *Nazi Germany: Its women and family life.* Indianapolis, IN: The Bobbs-Merrill Company, 1938.

Kirkpatrick, Clifford. "Recent changes in the status of women and the family in Germany." *American Sociological Review* 2, no. 5 (October 1937): 650–8.

Kiser, Clyde. "Birth rates and socio-economic attributes in 1935." *The Milbank Memorial Fund Quarterly* 17, no. 2 (April 1939): 128–51.

Kiser, Clyde, and P.K. Whelpton. "Social and psychological factors affecting fertility. XI. The interrelation of fertility, fertility planning, and feeling of economic security." *The Milbank Memorial Fund Quarterly* 29, no. 1 (January 1951): 41–122.

Kline, Wendy. *Building a better race: Gender, sexuality, and eugenics from the turn of the century to the baby boom.* Berkley: University of California Press, 2001.

Knodel, John. *The decline of fertility in Germany, 1871–1939.* Princeton, NJ: Princeton University Press, 1974.

Knoebel, Edgar Erwin. "Racial illusion and military necessity: A study of SS political and manpower objectives in occupied Belgium." PhD diss., University of Colorado, 1965.

Koch, Ernst Walther. *Sichert die heutige Ehe noch den Bestand unseres Volkes?* Leipzig: Offizin Haag-Drugulin, 1940.

Koehl, Robert Lewis. *The black corps: The structure and power structure of the Nazi SS.* Madison: University of Wisconsin Press, 1983.

Koehl, Robert Lewis. "The character of the Nazi SS." *The Journal of Modern History* 34, no. 3 (September 1962): 275–83.

Koehl, Robert Lewis. *RKFDV: German population and resettlement policy, 1933–1945: A history of the Reich Commission for the Strengthening of Germandom.* Cambridge, MA: Harvard University Press, 1957.

Koehl, Robert Lewis. *The SS: A history, 1919–1945.* Stroud, UK: Tempus, 2000.

Koehl, Robert Lewis. "Toward an SS typology: Social engineers." *American Journal of Economics and Sociology* 18, no. 2 (January 1959): 113–26.

Koonz, Claudia. *Mothers in the fatherland: Women, the family and Nazi politics.* New York: St. Martin's Press, 1987.

Koop, Volker. *"Dem Führer ein Kind schenken": Die SS-Organisation Lebensborn e.V.* Cologne: Böhlau Verlag, 2007.

Korherr, Richard. *Geburtenrückgang: Mahnruf an das deutsche Volk.* Munich: Süddeutsche Monatshefte GmbH, 1935.

Krater, Wolfgang. "Feiern und Feste der Nationalsozialisten: Aneignung und Umgestaltung christlicher Kalender, Ritten, und Symbolie." PhD diss., Ludwigs Maximillians-Universität, 1998.

Kroll, Frank-Lothar. *Utopie als Ideologie: Geschichtsdenken und politisches Handeln im Dritten Reich.* Paderborn: Ferdinand Schöningh, 1998.

Kröner, Hans-Peter. " 'Rasse' und Vererbung: Otmar von Verschuer (1896–1969) und der 'wissenschaftliche Rassismus.' " In *Herausforderung Bevölkerung: Zu Entwicklung des modernen Denkens über die Bevölkerung vor, im, und nach dem "Dritten Reich,"* edited by Josef Ehmer, Ursula Ferdinand, and Jürgen Reulecke, 201–14. Wiesbaden: Verlag für Sozialwissenschaften, 2007.

Kröner, Hans-Peter. *Von der Rassenhygiene zu Humangenetik: Das Kaiser-Wilhelm-Institut für Anthropologie, menschliche Erblehre, und Eugenik nach dem Kriege.* Stuttgart: G. Fischer, 1998.

Kruger, Arnd. "Breeding, rearing, and preparing the Aryan body: Creating supermen the Nazi way." *International Journal of the History of Sport* 16, no. 2 (1999): 42–68.

Kuczynski, R.R. "The decrease of fertility." *Economica* 2, no. 6 (May 1935): 128–41.

Kühl, Stefan. *The Nazi connection: Eugenics, American racism, and German National Socialism.* New York: Oxford University Press, 1994.

Kühn, Alfred, Martin Staemmler, and Friedrich Burgdörfer. *Erbkunde, Rassenpflege, Bevölkerungspolitik: Schicksals Fragen des deutschen Volkes.* Leipzig: Quelle and Meyer, 1935.

Kundrus, Birthe. "Forbidden company: Romantic relationships between Germans and foreigners, 1939 to 1945." *Journal of the History of Sexuality* 11, no. 1–2 (January/April 2002): 201–22.

Lane, Barbara Miller. "Nazi ideology: Some unfinished business." *Central European History* 7, no. 1 (March 1974): 3–30.

Lane, Barbara Miller, and Leila Rupp, eds. *Nazi ideology before 1933: A documentation.* Austin: University of Texas Press, 1978.

Lang, Jochen von. *Top Nazi: SS General Karl Wolff, the man between Hitler and Himmler.* New York: Enigma, 2005.

Lange, Hans-Jürgen. *Weisthor: Karl Maria Wiligut; Himmlers Rasputin und seine Erben.* Engerda: Arun, 1998.

Lanzieri, Giampaolo. "Towards a 'baby recession' in Europe? Differential fertility trends during the economic crisis." *Eurostat: Statistics in Focus* 13 (2013). http://ec.europa.eu/eurostat/documents/3433488/5585916/KS-SF-13-013-EN.PDF/a812b080-7ede-41a4-97ef-589ee767c581.

Lauterbacher, Hartmann. *Erlebt und mitgestaltet: Kronzeuge einer Epoche 1923–1945; Zu neuen Ufern nach Kriegsende.* Preussisch Oldendorf: K.W. Schütz, 1984.

Layton, Roland V. "The 'Völkischer Beobachter,' 1920–1933: The Nazi Party newspaper in the Weimar era." *Central European History* 3, no. 4 (December 1970): 353–82.

Lebert, Stephan, and Norbert Lebert. *My father's keeper: Children of Nazi leaders – an intimate history of damage and denial.* Translated by Julian Evans. Boston: Little, Brown, and Company, 2000.

Lenz, Fritz. "Die Stellung des Nationalsozialismus zur Rassenhygiene." *Archiv für Rassen-und Gesellschaftsbiologie* 25 (1931): 300–8.

Lenz, Fritz. "Notizen: Ein Versuch rassenhygienischer Lenkung der Ehewahl." *Archiv für Rassen- und Gesellschaftsbiologie* 26 (1932): 460–2.

Lenz, Fritz. "Rassenhygiene (Eugenik)." *Handbuch der Vererbungswissenschaft.* Vol. 3, edited by Erwin Baur and Max Hartmann. Berlin: Verlag von Gebrüder Borntraeger, 1932.

Lepore, Jill. "Historians who love too much: Reflections on microhistory and biography." *The Journal of American History* 88, no. 1 (June 2001): 129–44.

Lepre, George. *Himmler's Bosnian division: The Waffen SS Handschar Division, 1943–1945.* Atglen, PA: Schiffer Military History, 1997.

Lerner, Daniel. *The Nazi elite.* Stanford, CA: Stanford University Press, 1951.

Lifton, Robert Jay. *The Nazi doctors: Medical killing and the psychology of genocide.* New York: Basic Books, 1986.

Lilienthal, Georg. "Ärtze und Rassenpolitik: Der 'Lebensborn e.V.' " In *Ärzte im Nationalsozialismus,* edited by Fridhof Kudlien, 153–66. Cologne: Kiepenheuer and Witsch, 1985.

Lilienthal, Georg. *Der "Lebensborn e.V.": Ein Instrument nationalsozialistischer Rassenpolitik.* Stuttgart: Gustav Fischer, 1985.

Lilienthal, Georg. "Rassenhygiene im Dritten Reich." *Medizinehistorisches Journal* 14 (1979): 114–37.

Littlejohn, David, and C.M. Dodkins. *Orders, decorations, medals, and badges of the Third Reich (including the Free City of Danzig).* Mountain View, CA: R. James Bender Publishing, 1973.

Littmann, Sol. *Pure soldiers or sinister legion: The Ukrainian 14th Waffen SS Division.* Montreal: Black Rose Books, 2003.

Livchen, René. "Net wages and real wages in Germany." *International Labour Review* 50 (July 1944): 65–72.

Livchen, René. "Wage trends in Germany from 1929 to 1942." *International Labour Review* 48 (December 1943): 714–32.

Longerich, Peter. *Heinrich Himmler.* Translated by Jeremy Noakes and Lesley Sharpe. Oxford: Oxford University Press, 2012.

Lösch, Niels. *Rasse als Konstrukt: Leben und Werk Eugen Fischers.* New York: Peter Lang, 1997.

Lovin, Clifford. "Blut und Boden: The ideological basis of the Nazi agricultural program." *Journal of the History of Ideas* 28, no. 2 (April–June 1967): 279–88.

Lukacs, John. *The last European war, September 1939–December 1941.* New Haven, CT: Yale University Press, 2001.

Lumans, Valdis. "The ethnic German minority of Slovakia and the Third Reich, 1938–1945." *Central European History* 15, no. 3 (September 1982): 266–96.

Lumans, Valdis. *Himmler's auxiliaries: The Volksdeutsche Mittelstelle and the German national minorities of Europe, 1933–1945.* Durham: University of North Carolina Press, 1993.

Lumsden, Robin. *Himmler's black order: A history of the SS, 1923–1945.* Stroud, UK: Sutton Publishing, 1997.

Mackensen, Rainer, ed. *Bevölkerungslehre und Bevölkerungspolitik im "Dritten Reich."* Opladen: Leske and Budrich, 2004.

Mackensen, Rainer, and Jürgen Reulecke, eds. *Das Konstruck "Bevölkerung" vor, um, und nach dem "Dritten Reich."* Wiesbaden: Verlag für Sozialwissenschaften, 2005.

MacMahon, Brian, and Thomas Pugh. "Sex ratio of white births in the United States during the Second World War." *American Journal of Human Genetics* 6, no. 2 (June 1954): 284–92.

Maibaum, Thomas. "Die Führerschule der deutschen Ärzteschaft Alt-Rehse." PhD diss., University of Hamburg, 2007.

Maiwald, Stefan, and Gerd Mischler. *Sexualität unter dem Hakenkreuz: Manipulation und Vernichtung der Intimsphäre im NS-staat.* Hamburg: Europa Verlag, 1999.

Mallet, Bernard. "Vital statistics as affected by the war." *Journal of the Royal Statistical Society* 81, no. 1 (January 1918): 1–36.

Manvell, Roger, and Heinrich Fraenkel. *Heinrich Himmler.* New York: Putnam, 1965.

Marcuse, Harold. "What is old German money worth?" *Historical dollar-to-marks currency conversion page,* http://www.history.ucsb.edu/faculty/marcuse/projects/currency.htm.

Marks, Jonathan. "Historiography of eugenics." *American Journal of Human Genetics* 52 (1993): 650–2.

Martin, Leo J. "Population policies under National Socialism." *The American Catholic Sociological Review* 6, no. 2 (June 1945): 67–82.

Marx, Anthony. *Faith in nation: Exclusionary origins of nationalism*. Oxford: Oxford University Press, 2003.

Mason, Tim. "Women in Germany, 1925–1940: Family welfare and work, part I." *History Workshop* (Spring 1976): 74–113.

Mason, Tim. "Women in Germany, 1925–1940: Family welfare and work, part II." *History Workshop* (Summer 1976): 5–32.

Massin, Benoît. "Anthropologie und Humangenetik im Nationalsozialismus oder: Wie schreiben deutschen Wissenschaftler ihre eigene Wissenschaftsgeschichte?" In *Wissenschaftlicher Rassismus: Analysen einer Kontinuität in den Human- und Naturwissenschaften*, edited by Heidrun Kaupen-Haas and Christian Saller, 12–64. Frankfurt: Campus Verlag, 1999.

Massin, Benoît. "From Virchow to Fischer: Physical anthropology and 'modern race theories' in Wilhelmine Germany." In *Volksgeist as method and ethic: Essays on Boasian ethnography and the German anthropological tradition*, edited by George Stocking Jr., 79–154. Madison: University of Wisconsin Press, 1996.

Massin, Benoît. "Rasse und Vererbung als Beruf: Die Hauptforschungsrichtungen am Kaiser-Wilhelm-Institut für Anthropologie, Menschliche Erblehre, und Eugenik im Nationalsozialismus. In *Rassenforschung an Kaiser Wilhelm Instituten vor und nach 1933*, edited by Hans-Walter Schmuhl, 190–244. Göttingen: Wallstein, 2003.

Mazower, Mark. *Hitler's empire: How the Nazis ruled Europe*. New York: Penguin, 2008.

McCleary, George Frederick. "Pre-war European population policies." *The Milbank Memorial Fund Quarterly* 19, no. 2 (April 1941): 105–20.

McMahan, C.A. "An empirical test of three hypotheses concerning the human sex ratio at birth in the United States." *The Milbank Memorial Fund Quarterly* 29, no. 3 (July 1951): 273–93.

McNab, Chris. *World War II data book: The SS, 1923–1945: The essential facts and figures for Himmler's stormtroopers*. London: Amber Books, 2009.

Meisler, Yoash. "Himmler's doctrine of the SS leadership." *Jahrbuch des Instituts für Deutsche Geschichte* 8 (1979): 389–432.

Messenger, Charles. *Hitler's gladiator: The life and times of Oberstgruppenführer and Panzergeneral-Oberst der Waffen SS, Sepp Dietrich*. London: Brassey's Defense Publishers, 1988.

Meusel, Alfred. "National Socialism and the family." *Sociological Review* 28, no. 2 (April 1936): 166–86.

Meusel, Alfred. "National Socialism and the family, part II." *Sociological Review* 28, no. 4 (October 1936): 389–411.

Meyer, Hubert. *The 12th SS: The history of the Hitler Youth Panzer Division.* Vol. 1. Mechanicsburg, PA: Stackpole Books, 2005.

Meyer, Kurt. *Grenadiers: The story of Waffen SS General Kurt "Panzer" Meyer.* Mechanicsburg, PA: Stackpole Books, 2005.

Miller, Marvin. *Terminating the "socially inadequate": The American eugenicists and the German race hygienists, California to Cold Spring Harbor, Long Island to Germany.* Commack, NY: Malamud-Ruse, 1996.

Mineau, André. *SS thinking and the Holocaust.* Amsterdam: Rodopi, 2012.

Mitchell, Otis. "Terror as a neo-Marxian revolutionary mechanism in the Nazi SA (1932)." *Wichita State University Bulletin* 63, no. 2 (May 1965): 3–10.

Mitscherlich, Alexander. *Society without the father: A contribution to social psychology.* New York: Harcourt, Brace, and World, 1967.

Moczarski, Kazimierz. *Conversations with an executioner.* Edited by Mariana Fitzpatrick. Engelwood Cliffs, NJ: Prentice Hall, 1981.

Moeller, Robert. " 'The last soldiers of the Great War' and tales from family reunion in the Federal Republic of Germany." *Signs* 24, no. 1 (Autumn 1998): 129–45.

Moeller, Robert. "The 'remasculinization' of Germany in the 1950s: Introduction." *Signs* 24, no. 1 (Autumn 1998): 101–6.

Moeller, Robert. *War stories: The search for a usable past in the Federal Republic of Germany.* Berkeley: University of California, 2001.

Moser, Tilmann. *Dabei war ich doch sein liebstes Kind: Eine Psychotherapie mit der Tochter eines SS-Mannes.* Munich: Kössel, 1997.

Mosse, George. *Nationalism and sexuality: Respectability and abnormal sexuality in modern Europe.* New York: Howard Fertig, 1985.

Mosse, George. *Nazi culture: Intellectual, cultural, and social life in the Third Reich.* Madison: University of Wisconsin Press, 1966.

Mouton, Michelle. *From nurturing the nation to purifying the Volk: Weimar and Nazi family policy, 1918–1945.* Washington, DC: German Historical Institute, 2007.

Mouton, Michelle. "Rescuing children and policing families: Adoption policy in Weimar and Nazi Germany." *Central European History* 38, no. 4 (2005): 545–71.

Moynihan, Michael, ed. *The secret king: Karl Maria Wiligut, Himmler's lord of the runes.* Translated by Stephen Flowers. Waterbury, VT: Dominion Press, 2001.

Muckermann, Hermann. *Eugenik*. Berlin: F. Dümmler, 1934.

Muckermann, Hermann. *Kind und Volk: Der biologische Wert der Treue zu den eugenischen Gesetzen beim Aufbau der Familie*. Freiburg: Herder, 1933.

Muckermann, Hermann. *Vererbung, biologische Grundlage der Eugenik*. Potsdam: Müller and I. Kipenheuer GMbH, 1932.

Muckermann, Hermann, and Otmar von Verschuer. *Eugenische Eheberatung*. Berlin: F. Dümmler, 1931.

Mühlberger, Detlef. *The social bases of Nazism, 1919–1933*. Cambridge: Cambridge University Press, 2003.

Mühlenberg, Jutta. *Das SS-Helferinnenkorps: Ausbildung, Einsatz, und Entnazifizierung der weiblichen Angehörigen der Waffen-SS, 1942–1949*. Hamburg: Hamburger Edition, 2011.

Mühlfeld, Claus. *Rezeption der nationalsozialistischen Familienpolitik: Eine Analyse über die Auseinandersetzung mit der NS-familienpolitik in ausgewählten Wissenschaften, 1933–1939*. Stuttgart: Ferdinand Enke, 1992.

Mühlfeld, Claus, and Friedrich Schönweiss. *Nationalsozialistische Familienpolitik: Familiensoziologische Analyse der nationalsozialistischen Familienpolitik*. Stuttgart: Ferdinand Enke Verlag, 1989.

Müller, Heinz. *Führerauslese in der Volksgemeinschaft*. Berlin: Industrieverlag Spaeth and Linde, 1937.

Müller, Klaus Jürgen. *Das Heer und Hitler: Armee und nationalsozialistisches Regime, 1933–1940*. Stuttgart: Deutsche Verlags-Anstalt, 1969.

Müller-Hill, Benno. *Murderous science: Elimination by scientific selection of Jews, Gypsies, and others, Germany 1933–1945*. Translated by George Fraser. Oxford: Oxford University Press, 1988.

Mundy, Paul. "Fertility variations with education." *The American Catholic Sociological Review* 7, no. 2 (June 1946): 107–17.

Nathan, Otto. "Consumption in Germany during the period of rearmament." *The Quarterly Journal of Economics* 56, no. 3 (May 1942): 349–84.

Nationalsozialistische Deutsche Arbeiter Partei. *Dich Ruft die SS*. Berlin-Grunewald: Verlag H. Hilger, 1942.

Neitzel, Sönke, and Harald Welzer. *Soldaten: On fighting, killing, and dying; the secret World War II transcripts of German POWs*. Translated by Jefferson Chase. New York: Alfred A. Knopf, 2012.

Neumann, Peter. *The black march: The personal story of an SS man*. Translated by Constantine Fitzgibbon. New York: Bantam Books, 1960.

"1940 population estimates for European countries." *Population Index* 8, no. 2 (April 1942): 78–82.

Noakes, Jeremy. *Nazism 1919–1945, vol. 4: The German home front in World War II, a documentary reader*. Exeter, UK: University of Exeter Press, 1998.

Notestein, Frank. "Class differences in fertility." *Annals of the American Academy of Political and Social Science* 188 (November 1936): 26–36.

Notestein, Frank, and Clyde Kiser. "Factors affecting variations in human fertility." *Social Forces* 14, no. 1 (October 1935): 32–41.

Nye, Robert. "The rise and fall of the eugenics empire: Recent perspectives on the impact of bio-medical though in modern society." *Historical Journal* 36, no. 3 (September 1993): 687–700.

Office of United States Chief of Counsel for Prosecution of Axis Criminality. *Nazi conspiracy and aggression.* Vol. 4. Washington, DC: US Government Printing Office, 1946.

Ogburn, William, and Dorothy Thomas. "The influence of the business cycle on certain social conditions." *Journal of the American Statistical Association* 18, no. 139 (September 1922): 324–40.

Ogburn, William, and Clark Tibbitts. "Birth rates and social classes." *Social Forces* 8, no. 1 (September 1929): 1–10.

Olsen, Kåre. "Under the care of Lebensborn: Norwegian war children and their mothers." In *Children of World War II: The hidden enemy legacy*, edited by Kjersti Ericsson and Eva Simonsen, 15–34. New York: Berg, 2005.

Olsen, Kåre. *Vater, Deutscher: Das Schicksal der norwegischen Lebensbornkinder und ihrer Mütter von 1940 bis heute.* Frankfurt am Main: Campus Verlag, 2002.

Oosterhuis, Harry. "Medicine, male bonding, and homosexuality in Nazi Germany." *Journal of Contemporary History* 32, no. 2 (April 1997): 187–205.

Opler, Morris Edward. "The bio-social basis of thought in the Third Reich." *American Sociological Review* 10, no. 6 (December 1945): 776–86.

Overmans, Rüdiger. *Deutsche militärische Verluste im Zweiten Weltkrieg.* Munich: R. Oldenbourg, 1999.

Overy, Richard. *Interrogations: The Nazi elite in Allied hands, 1945.* New York: Viking, 2001.

Padfield, Peter. *Himmler.* New York: MJF Books, 1990.

Panunzio, Constantine. "Are more males born in wartime?" *The Milbank Memorial Fund Quarterly* 21, no. 3 (July 1943): 281–91.

Patel, Karl. "The reign of the black order. The final phase of National Socialism: The SS counter-State." In *The Third Reich*, edited by Maurice Baumont, 633–77. New York: Praeger, 1955.

Paull, Hermann. *Deutsche Rassenhygiene. II Teil: Erbgesundheitspflege (Eugenik), Rassenpflege.* Görlitz: Verlag für Sippenforschung und Wappenkunde, 1934.

Pearl, Raymond. "Biological factors in fertility." *Annals of the American Academy of Political and Social Science* 188 (November 1936): 14–25.

Pendas, Devin. *The Frankfurt Auschwitz Trial, 1963–1965: Genocide, history, and the limits of the law.* Cambridge: Cambridge University Press, 2006.

Perry, Joe. "Nazifying Christmas: Political culture and popular celebration in the Third Reich." *Central European History* 38, no. 4 (2005): 572–605.

Pianigiani, Gaia. "Italy's 'Fertility Day' call to make babies arouses anger, not ardor." *New York Times*, 13 September 2016. http://www.nytimes.com/2016/09/14/world/europe/italy-births-fertility-europe.html?_r=0.

Pine, Lisa. *Hitler's national community: Society and culture in Nazi Germany.* London: Hodder Arnold, 2007.

Pine, Lisa. *Nazi family policy 1933–1945.* Oxford: Berg, 1997.

Ploetz, Alfred. "Rassenhygiene als Grundlage der Friedenspolitik." *Ahnen und Enkel: Beiträge zur Sippenforschung, Heimatkunde, und Erblehre* 3 (March 1936): 25–9.

Ploetz, Alfred. *Ziele und Aufgaben der Rassenhygiene: Referat erstattet auf der XXXV Tagung des Deutschen Vereins für öffentliche Gesundheitspflege zu Elberfeld.* Braunschweig: Friedrich Vieweg, 1911.

Pohl, Katharina. "Fatherhood in East and West Germany: Results of the German family and fertility survey." In *Fertility and the male life-cycle in the era of fertility decline*, edited by Caroline Bledsoe, Susana Lerner, and Jane Guyer, 257–74. Oxford: Oxford University Press, 2000.

Pollack, Martin. *The dead man in the bunker: Discovering my father.* Translated by Will Hobson. London: Faber, 2006.

Popkin, Jeremy. "Historians on the autobiographical frontier." *The American Historical Review* 104, no. 3 (June 1999): 725–48.

Posner, Gerald. *Hitler's children: Sons and daughters of the leaders of the Third Reich talk about their fathers and themselves.* New York: Random House, 1991.

Potter, Robert, and John Kanter. "Social and psychological factors affecting fertility. XXVIII. The influence of siblings and friends on fertility." *The Milbank Memorial Fund Quarterly* 33, no. 3 (July 1955): 246–67.

Powell, Irmgard. *Don't let them see you cry: Overcoming a Nazi childhood.* Wilmington, OH: Orange Frazer Press, 2008.

Preradovich, Nikolaus von. *Die Schutzstaffel der NSDAP: Eine Dokumentation.* Stegen/Ammersee: Druffel und Vowinckel Verlag, 2004.

Pringle, Heather. *The master plan: Himmler's scholars and the Holocaust.* New York: Hyperion Books, 2006.

Proctor, Robert. "From *Anthropologie* to *Rassenkunde* in the German anthropological tradition." In *Bones, bodies, behavior: Essays on biological anthropology*, edited by George Stocking Jr., 138–79. Madison: University of Wisconsin Press, 1990.

Proctor, Robert. "Nazi doctors, racial medicine, and human experimentation." In *The Nazi doctors and the Nuremberg Code: Human rights in human experimentation*, edited by George Annas and Michael Grodin, 17–31. Oxford: Oxford University Press, 1995.

Proctor, Robert. "Nazi medicine and the politics of knowledge." In *The "racial" economy of science: Toward a democratic future*, edited by Sandra Harding, 344–58. Bloomington: Indiana University Press, 1993.

Proctor, Robert. *The Nazi war on cancer*. Princeton, NJ: Princeton University Press, 1999.

Proctor, Robert. *Racial hygiene: Medicine under the Nazis*. Cambridge, MA: Harvard University Press, 1988.

Propping, Peter, and Heinz Schott, eds. *Wissenschaft auf Irrwegen: Biologismus – Rassenhygiene – Eugenik*. Bonn: Bouvier Verlag, 1992.

Quine, Maria Sophia. *Population politics in twentieth-century Europe: Fascist dictatorships and liberal democracies*. London: Routledge, 1996.

Rahden, Till van. "Demokratie und väterliche Autorität. Das Karlsruher 'Stichenscheid'-Urteil in der politischen Kultur der frühen Bundesrepublik." *Zeithistorische Forschungen* 2, no. 2 (2005): 160–79.

Rahden, Till van. " 'Germ cells': The private realm as a political project in the Bonn Republic: On some similarities between the fifties and the late sixties." Paper presented at "Gender and the Long Postwar: Reconsiderations of the United States and the Two Germanies, 1945–1989," German Historical Institute, Washington, DC, May 30–31, 2008.

Rahden, Till van. "Paternity, rechristianization, and the quest for democracy in postwar West Germany." *Forschungsberichte* (aus dem Duitsland Instituut Amsterdam) 4 (2008): 53–71.

Reagin, Nancy Ruth. *Sweeping the German nation: Domesticity and national identity in Germany, 1870–1945*. Cambridge: Cambridge University Press, 2007.

Reider, Frederic. *The order of the SS*. London: W. Foulsham and Co., 1981.

Reimann, Viktor. *Goebbels: The man who created Hitler*. Translated by Stephen Wendt. New York: Doubleday, 1976.

Reimer, Lydia. *Die Familie im neuen Deutschland*. Berlin: Deutscher Verlag, 1940.

Reitlinger, Gerald. *The SS, alibi of a nation*. New York: Viking Press, 1957.

Rempel, Gerhard. *Hitler's children: The Hitler Youth and the SS*. Chapel Hill: University of North Carolina Press, 1999.

Reynolds, Michael. *Men of steel: I SS Panzer Corps, the Ardennes, and the eastern front 1944–45*. Cambridge: Da Capo Press, 1999.

Rickmann, Anahid S. " 'Rassenpflege im völkischen Staat': Vom Verhältnis der Rassenhygiene zur nationalsozialistischen Politik." PhD diss., University of Bonn, 2002.

Riemer, Ruth, and P.K. Whelpton. "Social and psychological factors affecting fertility. XXVII. Attitudes toward restriction of personal freedom in relation to fertility planning and fertility." *The Milbank Memorial Fund Quarterly* 33, no. 1 (January 1955): 63–111.

Rissom, Renate. *Fritz Lenz und die Rassenhygiene*. Hasum: Matthiesen Verlag, 1983.

Rodnick, David. *Postwar Germans: An anthropologist's account*. New Haven, CT: Yale University Press, 1948.

Roos, Julia. "Backlash against prostitutes' rights: Origins and dynamics of Nazi prostitution policies." *Journal of the History of Sexuality* 11, no. 1–2 (January/April 2002): 67–94.

Rosenberg, Alfred. *The myth of the twentieth century: An evaluation of the spiritual-intellectual confrontations of our age*. Torrance, CA: Noontide Press, 1982.

Rosenberg, Alfred. *Race and race history, and other essays*. Edited by Robert Pois. New York: Harper and Row, 1970.

Rosenhaupt, Heinrich. "The male birth surplus." *Scientific Monthly* 48, no. 2 (February 1939): 163–9.

Rosenthal, Gabriele. *The Holocaust in three generations: Families of victims and perpetrators of the Nazi regime*. London: Cassell, 1998.

Rossiter, William. "Influence of the war upon the population." *North American Review* 203, no. 726 (May 1916): 700–10.

Rüdin, Ernst, ed. *Erblehre und Rassenhygiene im völkischen Staat*. Munich: J.F. Lehmanns Verlag, 1934.

Rupp, Leila. "Mother of the *Volk*: The image of women in Nazi ideology." *Signs* 3, no. 2 (Winter 1977): 362–79.

Rurup, Reinhard, ed. *The problem of revolution in Germany, 1789–1989*. Oxford: Berg, 2000.

Saetz, Stephen, Marian van Court, and Mark Henshaw. "Eugenics and the Third Reich." *Eugenics Bulletin* 3, no. 1 (1985): 1–31.

Saller, Karl. *Die Rassenlehre des Nationalsozialismus in Wissenschaft und Propaganda*. Darmstadt: Progress-Verlag, 1961.

Samuelson, Robert. "Behind the birth dearth." *Washington Post*, 24 May 2006. http://www.washingtonpost.com/wp-dyn/content/article/2006/05/23/AR2006052301529.html.

Saunders, Donald Jr. "Lessons from eugenics for the neoeugenic era." *The Journal of the South Carolina Medical Association* 94, no. 9 (September 1998): 383–8.

Schafer, Ingeburg, and Susanne Kockmann. *Mutter mochte Himmler nie: Die Geschichte einer SS-Familie*. Reinbeck: Rowohlt, 1999.

Schaffner, Bertram. *Father land: A study of authoritarianism in the German family*. New York: Columbia University Press, 1948.

Scharff Smith, Peter, Niels Bo Poulsen, and Claus Bundgård Christensen. "The Danish volunteers in the Waffen SS and German warfare at the eastern front." *Contemporary European History* 8, no. 1 (March 1999): 73–96.

Scharsach, Hans-Henning. *Die Ärtze der Nazis.* Vienna: Orac, 2000.

Scheinfeld, Amram. *You and heredity.* New York: Frederick A. Stokes Company, 1939.

Schellenberg, Walter. *Hitler's secret service.* Translated by Louis Hagen. New York: Pyramid Books, 1971.

Schelsky, Helmut. "The family in Germany." *Marriage and Family Living* 16, no. 4 (1954): 331–5.

Schlie, Ulrich. "Today's view of the Third Reich and the Second World War in German historiographical discourse." *The Historical Journal* 43, no. 2 (June 2000): 543–64.

Schmeling, Anke. *Josias Erbprinz zu Waldeck und Pyrmont: Der politische Weg eines hohen SS-Führers.* Kassel: Verlag Gesamthochschul-Bibliothek, 1993.

Schmidt, Fritz. *Presse in Fesseln: Eine Schilderung des NS-Pressetrusts.* Berlin: Verlag Archiv und Kartei, 1947.

Schmidt, Ulf. *Karl Brandt: The Nazi doctor, medicine, and power in the Third Reich.* London: Hambeldon Continuum, 2007.

Schmidt, Ulf. *Medical films, ethics, and euthanasia in Nazi Germany: The history of medical research and teaching films of the Reich Office for Educational Films – Reich Institute for Films in Science and Education, 1933–1945.* Hasum: Matthiesen, 2002.

Schmidt-Sarosi, Cecilia. "Infertility in the older woman." *Clinical Obstetrics and Gynecology* 41, no. 4 (December 1998): 940–50.

Schmitz-Köster, Dorothee. *Deutsche Mutter, bist du bereit: Alltag im Lebensborn.* Berlin: Aufbau-Verlag, 1997.

Schmitz-Köster, Dorothee. *Kind L 364: Eine Lebensborn-Familiengeschichte.* Berlin: Rowohlt Verlag, 2007.

Schmitz-Köster, Dorothee, and Tristan Vankann. *Lebenslang Lebensborn: Die Wunschkinder der SS und was aus ihnen wurde.* Munich: Piper Verlag, 2012.

Schmitz-Köster, Dorothee. "A topic for life: Children of German Lebensborn homes." In *Children of World War II: The hidden enemy legacy,* edited by Kjersti Ericsson and Eva Simonsen, 213–28. Oxford: Berg, 2005.

Schmuhl, Hans-Walter. *Crossing boundaries: The Kaiser Wilhelm Institute for Anthropology, Human Heredity, and Eugenics, 1927–1945.* London: Springer, 2008.

Schmuhl, Hans-Walter. *Rassenhygiene, Nationalsozialismus, Euthansie: Von der Verhütung zur Vernichtung "lebensunwerten Lebens," 1890–1945.* Göttingen: Vandenhoeck and Ruprecht, 1987.

Schnabel, Reimund. *Macht ohne Moral: Eine Dokumentation über die SS*. Frankfurt am Main: Röderberg Veralg, 1957.

Schneider, Michael, and Jamie Owen Daniel. "Fathers and son's retrospectively: The damaged relationship between two generations." *New German Critique* 31 (Winter 1984): 3–51.

Scholtz-Klink, Gertrud. *Die Frau im Dritten Reich: Eine Dokumentation*. Tübingen: Grabert Verlag, 1978.

Schoppmann, Claudia. *Nationalsozialistische Sexualpolitik und weibliche Homosexualität*. Pfaffenweiler: Centaurus, 1991.

Schulle, Diana. *Das Reichssippenamt: Eine Institution nationalsozialistischer Rassenpolitik*. Berlin: Logos Verlag, 2001.

Schulte, Jan Erik. *Zwangsarbeit und Vernichtung: Das Wirtschaftsimperium der SS. Oswald Pohl und das SS-Wirtschafts-Verwaltungshauptamt, 1933–1945*. Paderborn: Ferdinand Schöningh, 2001.

Schultz, Bruno K. "Rassenhyiene und Erbgesundheitslehre (Eugenik)." *Nationalsozialistische Monatshefte* 3 (March 1932): 97–9.

Schultze, Walter. *Die Rassenfrage und Erbgesundheitslehre und ihre Folgerungen für den nationalsozialistischen Staat*. Berlin: Beamtenpress, 1935.

Schulze-Kossens, Richard. *Die Junkerschulen: Militärischer Führernachwuches der Waffen-SS*. Osnabrück: Munin Verlag, 1982.

Schwan, Heribert. *Der SS-Mann: Josef Blösche; Leben und Sterben eines Mörders*. Munich: Droemer, 2003.

Schwarz, Gudrun. *Eine Frau an seiner Seite: Ehefrauen in der "SS-Sippengemeinschaft."* Hamburg: Hamburger Edition, 1997.

Seltzer, William. "Population statistics, the Holocaust, and the Nuremberg Trials." *Population and Development Review* 24, no. 3 (September 1998): 511–52.

Semmler, Helmut. *SS Flak: Memoir of SS-Sturmmann Helmut Semmler, SS-Flak-Abteilung 9, 9 SS-Panzer-Division Hohenstaufen, Ardennes, 1944–45*. Translated by Frank van der Bergh. Halifax, UK: Shelf Books, 1999.

Sereny, Gitta. "Children of the Reich." In *Living in Nazi Germany*, edited by Elaine Halleck, 72–84. San Diego, CA: Greenhaven Press, 2004.

Sereny, Gitta. *Into that darkness: An examination of conscience*. New York: Vintage Books, 1983.

Shalka, Robert John. "The General-SS in central Germany 1937–1939: A social and institutional study of SS Main Sector Fulda-Werra." Ph.D. diss., University of Wisconsin, 1972.

Shryock, Henry. "Trends in age-specific fertility rates." *The Milbank Memorial Fund Quarterly* 17, no. 3 (July 1939): 294–307.

Sichrovsky, Peter. *Born guilty: Children of Nazi families*. Translated by Jean Steinberg. New York: Basic Books, 1988.

Siemens, Hermann Werner. *Grundzüge der Vererbungslehre, der Rassenhygiene, und der Bevölkerungspolitik.* Munich: J.F. Lehmanns Verlag, 1917.

Siemens, Hermann Werner. *Vererbungslehre: Rassenhygiene und Bevölkerungspolitik für Gebildete aller Berufe.* Munich: J. F. Lehmanns Verlag, 1934.

Silverman, Kenneth. "Biography and pseudobiography." *Common-place* 3, no. 2 (January 2003). http://www.common-place-archives.org/vol-03/no-02/silverman/.

Sloan, Phillip. "Introduction: Eugenics and the social uses of science: Non-religious factors in the genesis of the Holocaust." In *Humanity at the limit: The impact of the Holocaust experience on Jews and Christians,* edited by Michael Alan Singer, 175–9. Bloomington: Indiana University Press, 2000.

Smelser, Ronald, and Rainer Zitelmann, eds. *The Nazi elite.* New York: New York University Press, 1993.

Smith, Bradley. *Heinrich Himmler: A Nazi in the making, 1900–1926.* Stanford, CA: Hoover Institute Press, 1971.

Smith, David Gordon. "Demographic worries: German birthrate rising – but for how long?" *Der Spiegel,* 18 February 2009. http://www.spiegel.de/international/germany/demographic-worries-german-birthrate-rising-but-for-how-long-a-608172.html.

Snydor, Charles. "The history of the SS *Totenkopfdivision* and the postwar mythology of the *Waffen* SS." *Central European History* 6, no. 4 (December 1973): 339–62.

Sofair, Andrè, and Lauris C. Kaldjian. "Eugenic sterilization and a qualified Nazi analogy: The United States and Germany, 1930–1945." *Annals of Internal Medicine* 132, no. 4 (15 February 2000): 312–19.

Sorkin, David. *The transformation of German Jewry, 1780–1840.* New York: Oxford University Press, 1987.

Speer, Albert. *Infiltration.* Translated by Joachim Neugroschel. New York: Macmillan Publishing Company, 1981.

Speer, Albert. *Inside the Third Reich.* Translated by Richard Winston and Clara Winston. New York: Macmillan, 1970.

Spektorowski, Alberto. "The eugenic temptation in socialism: Sweden, Germany, and the Soviet Union." *Comparative Studies in Society and History* 46, no. 1 (January 2004): 84–106.

SS-Oberabschnitt West. *Die Gestaltung der Feste im Jahres- und Lebenslauf in der SS Familie.* Wuppertal: Völkischer Verlag, 1937–8.

Staemmler, Martin. *Rassenpflege im völkischen Staat.* Munich: J.F. Lehmanns Verlag, 1934.

Staudinger, Roland. *Rassenrecht und Rassenstaat: Die nationsozialistische Vision eines "biologischen totalen Staates."* Hall in Tirol, AT: Berenkamp, 1999.

Steber, Martina, and Bernhard Goto, eds. *Visions of community in Nazi Germany: Social engineering and private lives.* Oxford: Oxford University Press, 2014.

Steigmann-Gall, Richard. *The holy Reich: Nazi conceptions of Christianity, 1919–1945.* Cambridge: Cambridge University Press, 2003.

Stein, George. *The Waffen SS: Hitler's elite guard at war, 1939–1945.* Ithaca, NY: Cornell University Press, 1966.

Steiner, John. *Power politics and social change in National Socialist Germany.* The Hague: Mouton and Company, 1975.

Steinmetz, George. "German exceptionalism and the origins of Nazism: The Career of a Concept." In *Stalinism and Nazism: Dictatorships in comparison,* edited by Ian Kershaw and Moshe Lewin, 251–84. Cambridge: Cambridge University Press, 1997.

Stenzel, Burkhard. "Buch und schwert: Die 'woche des deutschen buches' in Weimar (1934–1942). Anmerkungen zur NS-literaturpolitik." In *Hier, hier ist Deutschland: Von nationalen Kulturkonzepten zur nationalsozialistischen Kulturpolitik,* edited by Ursula Härtl, Burkhard Stenzel, and Justus Ulbricht, 83–122. Göttingen: Wallstein Verlag, 1997.

Stephenson, Jill. "Reichsbund der Kinderreichen': The League of Large Families in the population policy of Nazi Germany." *European Studies Review* 9, no. 3 (July 1979): 351–75.

Stephenson, Jill. *Women in Nazi society.* New York: Barnes and Nobles Books, 1975.

Stevenson, Alexander. "Some aspects of fertility and population growth in Vienna." *American Sociological Review* 7, no. 4 (August 1942): 479–88.

Stibbe, Matthew. *Women in the Third Reich.* London: Arnold, 2003.

Stix, Regine K. "Research in causes of variations in fertility: Medical aspects." *American Sociological Review* 2, no. 5 (October 1937): 668–77.

Stoltzfus, Nathan. "Tactical terror: Exceptions to Nazi reliance on terror for repressing dissidents and its social causes." In *Terror: From tyrannicide to terrorism,* edited by Brett Bowden and Michael Davis, 205–29. Brisbane, AU: University of Queensland Press, 2009.

Strauss, Frederick. "The food problem in the German war economy." *The Quarterly Journal of Economics* 55, no. 3 (May 1941): 364–412.

Stümke, Hans-Georg. "From the 'people's consciousness of right and wrong' to 'the healthy instincts of the nation': The persecution of homosexuals in Nazi Germany." In *Confronting the Nazi past: New debates on modern German history,* edited by Michael Burleigh, 154–66. New York: Palgrave Macmillan, 1996.

Supreme Headquarters Allied Expeditionary Force Evaluation and Dissemination Section G-2 (Counter Intelligence Subdivision). *Basic handbook: The Allgemeine SS (the General SS).* Wiltshire, UK: Antony Rowe, 1993.

Sydenstricker, Edgar, and Frank Notestein. "Differential fertility according to social class: A study of 69,620 native white married women under 45 years of age based upon the United States census returns of 1910." *Journal of the American Statistical Association* 25, no. 169 (March 1930): 9–32.

Sydenstricker, Edgar, and G. St. J. Perrott. "Sickness, unemployment, and differential fertility." *The Milbank Memorial Fund Quarterly* 12, no. 2 (April 1934): 126–33.

Sydnor, Charles. *Soldiers of destruction: The SS Death's Head Division, 1933–1945.* Princeton, NJ: Princeton University Press, 1990.

Taeuber, Conrad, and Irene Taeuber. "German fertility trends, 1933–39." *The American Journal of Sociology* 46, no. 2 (September 1940): 150–67.

Taeuber, Conrad, and Irene Taeuber. "Measures of changes in fertility in Germany." *Journal of the American Statistical Association* 33, no. 204 (December 1938): 709–12.

Tamagne, Florence. *A history of homosexuality in Europe: Berlin, London, Paris, 1919–1939.* Vols. 1 and 2. New York: Algora Publishing, 2004.

Tatlock, Lynne. "Our correspondent in Weimar: Gabriele Reuter and 'The New York Times, 1923–1939.' " *German Studies Review* 22, no. 3 (October 1999): 369–83.

"The demography of war: Germany." *Population Index* 14, no. 4 (October 1948): 291–308.

"The EU's baby blues." *BBC News*, 27 March 2006. http://news.bbc.co.uk/2/hi/europe/4768644.stm.

"The fertility of the professional classes." *The British Medical Journal* 2, no. 3122 (30 October 1920): 672–3.

Therborn, Göran. *Between sex and power: Family in the world, 1900–2000.* London: Routledge, 2004.

Theweleit, Klaus. *Male fantasies.* 2 vols. Translated by Steven Conway. Minneapolis: University of Minnesota Press, 1987.

Thompson, Larry. "*Lebensborn* and the eugenics policy of the *Reichsführer-SS*." *Central European History* 4, no. 1 (March 1971): 54–77.

Timm, Annette. *The politics of fertility in twentieth-century Berlin.* Cambridge: Cambridge University Press, 2010.

Timm, Annette. "Sex with a purpose: Prostitution, venereal disease, and militarized masculinity in the Third Reich." *Journal of the History of Sexuality* 11, no. 1–2 (January–April 2002): 223–55.

Tooze, Adam. *Statistics and the German state, 1900–1945.* Cambridge: Cambridge University Press, 2001.

Tooze, Adam. *The wages of destruction: The making and breaking of the Nazi economy.* New York: Penguin Books, 2007.

Trevor-Roper, Hugh, ed. *Hitler's table talk 1941–1944: His private conversations.* New York: Enigma, 2008.

Trial of the major war criminals before the International Military Tribunal, Nuremberg, 14 November 1945–1 October 1946. Nuremberg, n.p.: 1947–49.

Trials of war criminals before the Nuernberg Military Tribunals under Control Council Law No. 10. Vols. 1 and 2, Case 1: US v. Brandt. Washington, DC: US Government Printing Office, 1946–49.

Trials of war criminals before the Nuernberg Military Tribunals under Control Council Law No. 10. Vols. 4 and 5, Case 8: US v. Greifelt. Washington, DC: US Government Printing Office, 1946–49.

Tucker, William. *The science and politics of racial research.* Urbana: University of Illinois Press, 1994.

Tumpek-Kjellmark, Katharina. "From Hitler's widows to Adenauer's brides: Towards a construction of gender and memory in postwar Germany, 1938–1963." PhD diss., Cornell University, 1994.

The United States Strategic Bombing Survey: A collection of the 31 most important reports printed in 10 volumes. New York: Garland Publishing, 1976.

Vagts, Alfred. "The foreigner as soldier in the Second World War, II." *The Journal of Politics* 9, no. 3 (August 1947): 392–416.

Vedder-Shults, Nancy. "Motherhood for the fatherland: The portrayal of woman in Nazi propaganda." PhD diss., University of Wisconsin–Madison, 1982.

Verschuer, Otmar von. *Erbpathologie: Ein Lehrbuch für Ärzte und Medizinstudierende.* Dresden: Verlag von Theodor Steinkopff, 1934.

Verschuer, Otmar von. *Leitfaden der Rassenhygiene.* Leipzig: Georg Thieme Verlag, 1943.

Verschuer, Otmar von. "Rassenhygiene als Wissenschaft und Staatsaufgabe." *Der Erbarzt* 3, no. 2 (15 February 1936): 17–19.

Verschuer, Otmar von. "Vererbungslehre und Rassenhygiene." In *Das Studium der Medizin: Einführungsband,* edited by Ernst Bach, 43–6. Heidelberg: Carl Winter Universitätverlag, 1943.

Vieregge, Bianca. *Die Gerichtsbarkeit einer 'Elite': Nationalsozialistische Rechtsprechung am Beispiel der SS- und Polizei-Gerichtsbarkeit.* Baden: Nomos Verlagsgesellschaft, 2002.

Voss, Johann. *Black Edelweiss: A memoir of combat and conscience by a soldier of the Waffen-SS.* Bedford, PA: The Aberjona Press, 2002.

Wackerfuss, Andrew. "The stormtrooper family: How sexuality, spirituality, and community shaped the Hamburg SA." PhD diss., Georgetown University, 2008.

Waffen-SS im Bild. Göttingen: Plesse Verlag, 1957.

Waite, Robert. "Teenage sexuality in Nazi Germany." *Journal of the History of Sexuality* 8, no. 3 (January 1998): 434–76.

Wallace, Hamish, and Tom Kelsey. "Human ovarian reserve from conception to the menopause." *PLOS One* 5, no. 1 (January 2010): 1–9.

Wang, Yanguang. "A call for a new definition of eugenics." *Eubios Journal of Asian and International Bioethics* 9 (1999): 73–4.

Weale, Adrian. *The SS: A new history.* London: Little, Brown, 2010.

Weeks, Jeffrey. *Making sexual history.* Malden, UK: Polity Press, 2000.

Wegner, Bernd. "The 'aristocracy of National Socialism': The role of the SS in National Socialist Germany." In *Aspects of the Third Reich*, edited by H.W. Koch, 430–50. New York: St Martin's Press, 1985.

Wegner, Bernd. *The Waffen SS: Organization, ideology, function.* Oxford: Basil Blackwell, 1990.

Wehler, Hans-Ulrich. *The German Empire 1871–1918.* Translated by Kim Traynor. New York: Berg Publishers, 1985.

Weikart, Richard. *From Darwin to Hitler: Evolutionary ethics, eugenics, and racism in Germany.* New York: Palgrave Macmillan, 2004.

Weindling, Paul. *Health, race, and German politics between national unification and Nazism, 1870–1945.* Cambridge: Cambridge University Press, 1989.

Weindling, Paul. "The medical profession, social hygiene, and the birth rate in Germany, 1914–1918." In *The upheaval of war: Family, work, and welfare in Europe, 1914–1918*, edited by Richard Wall and Jay Winter, 417–38. Cambridge: Cambridge University Press, 1988.

Weindling, Paul. "Tales from Nuremberg": The Kaiser Wilhelm Institute for Anthropology and Allied medical war crimes policy." In *Die Geschichte der Kaiser-Wilhelm-Gesellschaft im Nationalsozialismus*, vol. 2, edited by Doris Kaufmann, 635–52. Göttingen: Wallstein Verlag, 2000.

Weindling, Paul. "Weimar eugenics: The Kaiser Wilhelm Institute for Anthropology, Human Heredity, and Eugenics in social context." *Annals of Science* 42, no. 3 (May 1985): 303–18.

Weingart, Peter. "Eugenics and race-hygiene in the German context. A legacy of science turned bad?" In *Humanity at the limit. The impact of the Holocaust experience on Jews and Christians*, edited by Michael Alan Singer, 202–23. Bloomington: Indiana University Press, 2000.

Weingart, Peter. "Eugenics: Medical or social science?" *Science in Context* 8, no. 1 (1995): 197–207.

Weingart, Peter. "Eugenic utopias: Blueprints for the rationalization of human evolution." In *Nineteen eighty-four: Science between utopia and dystopia*, edited by Everett Mendelsohn and Helga Nowotny, 173–88. Boston: Lancester, 1984: 173–87.

Weingart, Peter. "German eugenics between science and politics." *Osiris*, second series, vol. 5: Science in Germany: The intersection of institutional and intellectual issues (1989): 260–82.

Weingart, Peter. "Politics of heredity: Germany 1900–1940, a brief review." *Genome* 31, no. 2 (1989): 896–7.

Weingart, Peter. "Race-hygiene and human genetics – political and moral lessons." In *In science we trust? Moral and political issues of science in society*, edited by Aant Elzinga, 335–9. Lund, SE: Lund University Press, 1990.

Weingart, Peter. "The rationalization of sexual behavior: The institutionalization of eugenic thought in Germany." *Journal of the History of Biology* 20, no. 2 (1987): 159–93.

Weingart, Peter. "Science and political culture: Eugenics in comparative perspective." *Scandinavian Journal of History* 24, no. 2 (1999): 163–77.

Weingart, Peter, Jürgen Kroll, and Kurt Bayertz. *Rasse, Blut, und Gene: Geschichte der Eugenik und Rassenhygiene in Deutschland*. Frankfurt: Suhrkamp, 1988.

Weingartner, James. "Law and justice in the Nazi SS: The case of Konrad Morgan." *Central European History* 16, no. 3 (September 1983): 276–94.

Weingartner, James. "The Race and Settlement Main Office: Toward an order of blood and soil." *The Historian* 34, no. 1 (1971): 62–77.

Weingartner, James. "Sepp Dietrich, Heinrich Himmler, and the Leibstandarte Adolf Hitler 1933–1938." *Central European History* 1, no. 3 (September 1968): 264–84.

Weiss, Sheila Faith. "Essay review: Racial science at the Kaiser Wilhelm Society." *Journal of the History of Biology* 38, no. 2 (Summer 2005): 367–79.

Weiss, Sheila Faith. "Human genetics and politics as mutually beneficial resources: The case of the Kaiser Wilhelm Institute for Anthropology, Human Heredity, and Eugenics during the Third Reich." *Journal of the History of Biology* 39, no. 1 (March 2006): 41–88.

Weiss, Sheila Faith. *The Nazi symbiosis: Human genetics and politics in the Third Reich*. Chicago: University of Chicago Press, 2010.

Weiss, Sheila Faith. "Race and class in Fritz Lenz's eugenics." *Medizinhistorisches Journal* 27 (1992): 5–25.

Weiss, Sheila Faith. *Race hygiene and national efficiency: The eugenics of Wilhelm Schallmayer*. Berkley: University of California Press, 1987.

Weiss, Sheila Faith. "The race hygiene movement in Germany, 1904–1945." In *The wellborn science: Eugenics in Germany, France, Brazil, and Russia*, edited by Mark Adams, 8–68. Oxford: Oxford University Press, 1990.

Weiss, Sheila Faith. " 'The sword of our science' as a foreign policy weapon. The political function of German geneticists in the international arena during the Third Reich." *Die Präsidentenkommission "Geschichte der Kaiser-Wilhelm-Gesellschaft im Nationalsozialismus."* http://www.mpiwg-berlin.mpg.de/KWG/Ergebnisse/Ergebnisse22.pdf.

Weiss, Sheila Faith. "Wilhelm Schallmayer and the logic of German eugenics." *Isis* 77, no. 1 (March 1986): 33–46.

Welch, David. "Nazi propaganda and the Volksgemeinschaft: Creating a people's community." *Journal of Contemporary History* 39, no. 2 (April 2004): 213–38.

Westoff, Charles. "The changing focus of differential fertility research: The social mobility hypothesis." *The Milbank Memorial Fund Quarterly* 31, no. 1 (January 1953): 24–38.

Whelpton, P.K. "Why the large rise in the German birth rate?" *The American Journal of Sociology* 41, no. 3 (November 1935): 299–313.

Whelpton, P.K., and Clyde Kiser. "Trends, determinants, and control in human fertility." *Annals of the American Academy of Political and Social Science* 237 (January 1945): 112–22.

Whiting, Charles. *Heydrich, henchman of death.* Barnsley, UK: Leo Cooper, 1999.

Wildt, Michael. *An uncompromising generation: The Nazi leadership of the Reich Security Main Office.* Translated by Tom Lampert. Madison: University of Wisconsin Press, 2009.

Williamson, Gordon. *Loyalty is my honor.* Osceola, WI: Motorbooks International, 1995.

Williamson, Gordon. *The SS: Hitler's instrument of terror.* Osceola, WI: Motorbooks International, 1994.

Williamson, Gordon. *The Waffen SS: 11 to 23 divisions.* Oxford: Osprey Publishing, 2004.

Williamson, Samuel. "Seven ways to compute the relative value of a US dollar amount, 1774 to present." *Measuring Worth,* http://www.measuringworth.com/uscompare/.

Wilson, Perry. *Women in twentieth-century Italy.* New York: Palgrave Macmillan, 2010.

Wilson, William John. "Festivals and the Third Reich." PhD diss., McMaster University, 1994.

Winston, Sanford. "Birth control and sex ratio at birth." *The American Journal of Sociology* 38, no. 2 (September 1932): 225–31.

Winston, Sanford. "The influence of social factors upon the sex-ratio at birth." *The American Journal of Sociology* 37, no. 1 (July 1931): 1–21.

Winston, Sanford. "The relation of certain social factors to fertility." *The American Journal of Sociology* 35, no. 5 (March 1930): 753–64.

Wolfe, A.B. "Economic conditions and the birth-rate after the war." *The Journal of Political Economy* 25, no. 6 (June 1917): 521–41.

Wolfson, Manfred. "Constraint and choice in the SS leadership." *The Western Political Quarterly* 18, no. 3 (September 1965): 551–68.

Wolfson, Manfred. "The SS leadership." PhD diss., University of California Berkeley, 1965.

Yew, Lee Kuan. "Warning bell for developed countries: Declining birth rates." *Forbes*, 16 October 2012. http://www.forbes.com/sites/currentevents/2012/10/16/warning-bell-for-developed-countries-declining-birth-rates/.

Zeck, Mario. *Das Schwarze Korps: Geschichte und Gestalt des Organs der Reichsführung-SS*. Tübingen, DE: Maz Niemeyer Verlag, 2002.

Ziegler, Herbert. "Fight against the empty cradle: Nazi pronatal policies and the SS-Führerkorps." *Historical Social Research* no. 38 (April 1986): 25–40.

Ziegler, Herbert. *Nazi Germany's new aristocracy: The SS leadership, 1925–1939*. Princeton, NJ: Princeton University Press, 1989.

Zimmer, Oliver. *Nationalism in Europe, 1890–1940*. New York: Palgrave Macmillan, 2003.

Zipfel, Friedrich. *Kirchenkampf in Deutschland 1933–1945: Religionsverfolgung und Selbstbehauptung der Kirchen in der nationalsozialistischen Zeit*. Berlin: Walter de Gruyter and Company, 1965.

Index

GERMAN AND EUROPEAN STUDIES

General Editor: Jennifer J. Jenkins

www.ingramcontent.com/pod-product-compliance
Lightning Source LLC
Chambersburg PA
CBHW030237030426
42336CB00009B/137